OPEN HEART

BOOKS BY JAY NEUGEBOREN

FICTION

Big Man

Listen Ruben Fontanez

Corky's Brother

Sam's Legacy

An Orphan's Tale

The Stolen Jew

Before My Life Began

Poli: A Mexican Boy in Early Texas

Don't Worry About the Kids

NONFICTION

Parentheses: An Autobiographical Journey

The Story of Story Magazine (EDITOR)

Imagining Robert: My Brother, Madness, and Survival

Transforming Madness: New Lives for People
    Living with Mental Illness

The Hillside Diary and Other Writings (EDITOR)

Open Heart: A Patient's Story of Life-Saving Medicine
    and Life-Giving Friendship

OPEN
HEART

A Patient's Story

of Life-Saving Medicine

and Life-Giving Friendship

JAY NEUGEBOREN

HOUGHTON MIFFLIN COMPANY

BOSTON • NEW YORK   2003

For information about permission to reproduce selections from this book, write to Permissions, Houghton Mifflin Company, 215 Park Avenue South, New York, New York, 10003.

Visit our Web site: www.houghtonmifflinbooks.com.

Library of Congress Cataloging-in-Publication Data

Neugeboren, Jay.

Open heart : a patient's story of life-saving medicine and life-giving friendship / Jay Neugeboren.

p. cm.

Includes bibliographical references and index.

ISBN 0-618-11211-1

1. Neugeboren, Jay — Health. 2. Coronary artery bypass — Patients — United States — Biography. I. Title.

RD598.35.C67N484 2003

362.1'97412'0092 — dc21 [B] 2002191298

Printed in the United States of America

Book design by Robert Overholtzer

QUM 10 9 8 7 6 5 4 3 2 1

For Arthur, Jerry, Phil, and Rich

Two are better than one; because they have a good reward for their labor.

For if they fall, the one will lift up his fellow; but woe to him that is alone when he falleth; for he hath not another to help him up.

Again, if two lie together, then they have heat: but how can one be warm alone? And if one prevail against him, two shall withstand him; and a threefold cord is not quickly broken.

—ECCLESIASTES IV:9–12

Contents

OPEN HEART

1

How Little We Know

O N AN UNSEASONABLY MILD, sunny afternoon in early February 1999, I drive down from my home in Northampton, Massachusetts, to Guilford, Connecticut, 120 miles away, to spend an evening with my friend Jerry Friedland and his wife, Gail. Jerry is director of the AIDS programs at Yale–New Haven Hospital and the Yale School of Medicine, and he and I have known each other for nearly fifty years — since the fall of 1952, when we were both sophomores at Erasmus Hall High School in Brooklyn.

Early the next morning I leave my car at Jerry's house and we head in to Yale–New Haven Hospital together. As I have also been doing for the past dozen or so years with another high school friend, Phil Yarnell, a neurologist living in Denver, Colorado, I take a break once or twice a year from my own work — my writing and teaching — to spend a day with Jerry at his work.

This time, however, I am traveling with Jerry to New Haven not to spend a day with him at the hospital and in his AIDS clinic, but because he has helped arrange an appointment for me with Dr. Henry Cabin, chief of cardiology at the hospital, to see what's going on in my heart. Dr. Cabin, who will take an angiogram of my coronary arteries (injecting radio-opaque dye that makes blockages visible when x-ray pictures are taken), has told me that this is ordinarily an outpatient procedure. Even if he finds significant blockages and decides to perform angioplasty (threading balloons into one or more of my coronary arteries through a catheter to open the arteries), I should be able to drive back to Massachusetts following the procedure. Still, Jerry has insisted that I return home with him afterward and stay another night so I can rest up, and so we can have more time together.

Being with Jerry while he works with patients, staff, and medical students and talking with him about his work have given me great pleasure through the years — have inspired me, really. Jerry is one of my oldest and dearest friends; he is also a doctor whose work with AIDS patients and AIDS research has been literally life-changing and life-saving for thousands of people.

When we spend time together between my visits to Yale–New Haven, we continue the dialogues begun there — discussing patients I've met and how they're doing, talking about his AIDS research and his public health projects, and — as in my ongoing talks with Phil — moving from the particular to the abstract and back again while speculating on the causes, prevention, diagnosis, and treatment of disease in general — about where, in things medical, we've been, about where we are, and about where we might be going.

Also, a true joy, knowing each other as we do across most of our lives, our talks have meandered — inevitably, always — along more personal paths as, without needing to impress or dissemble, we've tried, in matters having to do with things more private — family and friends, above all — to understand just who *we've* been, who we are, and where we might, in the years ahead, be going. When we are together, the time between visits — whether days, months, or years — disappears. Our conversations, at sixty, are as warm and stimulating — as rich, delightful, and filled with laughter — as were our conversations nearly a half century ago when we were teenagers taking walks together along Flatbush Avenue in Brooklyn.

At the hospital, Jerry walks me through admissions, and, although he regularly puts in seventy-to-eighty-hour workweeks (Gail maintains this is a *very* low estimate), he seems to have nothing else to do but to be with me, and he stays with me until I am in the room where the angiography is to be performed. Later on he will recall how astonished he was to find that when I undressed to ready myself for the procedure, I had to roll up my clothes and place them on the floor in a corner of the room. If I hadn't been his friend, he said, he might not have noticed, and this was a reminder to him of how different things often seem, and are, from a patient's perspective.

When I wake from anesthesia a few hours later, I'm lying on a gurney, and Dr. Cabin is smiling down at me. Although Dr. Cabin is a decade or so younger than we are, he too grew up in Brooklyn, where both his parents were high school teachers, and this, along with his warm, direct manner, puts me at ease. He has straight dark brown hair, is about five-foot-nine — two inches taller than me — and is fit and athletic-looking. I look up at him, my head a bit woozy, and he looks familiar suddenly, like one of the guys I played schoolyard ball with in Brooklyn.

"Let me show you what we found," he says.

He points to a monitor hanging above me and explains that what I am seeing is film from the x-rays taken of my heart. The lines of colored fluid moving downward and outlining my coronary arteries — bourbon-colored squiggles, in my memory — come from the dye injected through a catheter he had inserted into the femoral artery in my groin.

On the screen I watch blood begin to flow into each of my three major coronary arteries, then stop. Dr. Cabin points to the spot where only a small amount of fluid continues to leak downward and says the angiogram tells us that only one of my three major coronary arteries is working and that no more than 10 percent of that artery is functional. Two of my three major coronary arteries (the right coronary artery and the circumflex artery) are 100 percent blocked, the third (the left anterior descending artery) 90 percent.

Dr. Cabin estimates my ejection fraction, which measures the heart's ability to pump blood and which is the best general indicator of the heart's overall functioning, at 30 to 35 percent; in a healthy heart, it would be between 50 and 70 percent.

"You've been going on nothing," Dr. Cabin says to me, and then: "We're going to try to get you into surgery tomorrow morning."

"Great," I say without missing a beat, and it is only later that Jerry makes me aware that my reaction — Hey, this is good news, so let's go for it and do whatever we have to — is not typical. At the same time, I am, if optimistically, in a daze. I hear everything Dr. Cabin says to me but still seem to believe that in an hour or so I'll walk out of the hospital with Jerry, get into his car, and drive back to Guilford. Instead of spending an evening with Jerry, however, I may instead — the possibility seems an ordinary piece of information — get to spend my last evening on earth alone in a hospital room in New Haven.

Dr. Cabin tells me that because the arterial occlusions are so massive, I am going to need a quadruple coronary bypass. (Like a bypass that reroutes cars and trucks around an avenue clogged with traffic, a coronary bypass graft, stitched in above and below an obstructed artery, reroutes blood through an unclogged artery and around the obstructed artery.) He tells me that he is putting me on several medications to minimize the possibility of a heart attack, that he has already conferred with Jerry about surgery, and that he has put a call in to Dr. Sabet Hashim, the man he and Jerry consider the best cardiovascular surgeon at Yale. If Dr. Hashim cannot arrange to operate the following morning, a Friday, I will stay in the hospital over the weekend so that Dr. Cabin and his staff can keep an eye on me. The slightest exertion — or no exertion at all — might cause some arterial plaque to flake off, or to rupture, and block the narrow portion of my one coronary artery that is still working.

Open-heart surgery (or, more accurately, open-*chest* surgery) is, I know, a major event, a procedure that seems as astonishingly primitive as it is technically remarkable: They will crack open my chest then slice open an arm and a leg to harvest a vein and an artery that, after they shut down my heart for several hours while recycling my blood through a heart-lung machine, they will stitch into my heart before reattaching major incoming and outgoing arteries, jumpstarting my heart with electricity, and stapling and sewing my chest closed. Even though I will be virtually dead for several hours — my body temperature lowered to 80 degrees (as with hibernating animals, cooling reduces the body's need for oxygen, thereby giving the surgeon extra time for suturing) while a team of doctors and technicians retrofit me with new interior plumbing made up of spare parts taken from within my own body — the procedure itself, for all the drama and miracle of the fact that one can perform it on living human beings, has become commonplace. Hundreds of thousands of bypasses are performed each year (more than a half million in the United States), and — given my state of health — the possibility of failure, error, or distressing side effects seems minimal.

Dr. Cabin talks with me about the surgery, and I ask if he was surprised to discover that my arteries are nearly 100 percent blocked.

"No. Little in my line of work surprises me," he says, and he adds — something he will repeat when I see him for a six-week checkup following surgery — "But you *are* totally anomalous."

True enough, I think, for despite the extent of the blockage, I have had few of the symptoms that usually accompany severe coronary disease: no chest pain or discomfort (no heaviness, pressure, tightness, or squeezing sensation), and no arm pain, dizziness, nausea, palpitations, faintness, or unusual fatigue. Luckier still, especially given the magnitude of the blockage, I do not seem, on the evidence of an echocardiogram, to have had a heart attack.

Nor do I seem to have had any of the classic risk factors for coronary disease. Until a week or so before surgery, I was swimming a mile a day, and at a good pace, as I had been doing for the previous twenty-five years, while also regularly playing tennis and half- and full-court basketball (sometimes with teenagers). I had never been a smoker, my cholesterol was normal, and so was my blood pressure. My resting pulse was fifty-eight. By all accounts I was in excellent physical shape and, at five-foot-seven and 150 pounds, I weighed perhaps 5 pounds more than I had forty-four years before when I was a senior in high school.

Genetics and family history? My mother was still alive at the age of eighty-seven, most of my thirteen aunts and uncles had lived well into their eighties, and some had survived into their nineties. My father, who died of emphysema at the age of seventy-two, had had a heart attack when he was fifty-nine, but he never exercised, had been overweight, and had smoked three packs of Chesterfields a day throughout his adult life.

About an hour after my talk with Dr. Cabin, when I've been moved to a hospital room and am lying in bed — the first time I've been hospitalized since I was operated on for Hodgkin's disease at the age of eighteen, forty-two years earlier — Jerry comes by to visit.

"Hey Neugie," he says, using the nickname all my old friends use. "How're you feeling?"

I tell him I'm feeling a little groggy, and very lucky — lucky they found what they found and that, as I've just learned, they *can* get me into surgery in the morning. (Later, Jerry and Gail tell me they felt lucky too, since Dr. Cabin had suggested that if Dr. Hashim was unable to perform the surgery on Friday they might take me home for the weekend. "Oh my God — what do I remember about CPR?" Gail, a registered nurse, asked Jerry when he told her of this possibility.)

Jerry tells me that after Dr. Cabin saw the results of the angiography, he had paged Jerry and they had discussed what to do next. Jerry says that *he* was surprised — very much so — at what the angiogram revealed, but that he is pleased to learn that Dr. Hashim will be performing the surgery in the morning. The sooner the better, he says, and he tells me that my swimming and being in such good shape have probably saved my life.

"It seems you've been living on your collaterals," Jerry says, and he explains that the collateral blood vessels I'd probably developed by swimming a mile a day for the past twenty-five years — hundreds of small steady-state blood vessels that lie between and connect the coronary arteries and that cannot expand and contract the way coronary arteries can — had been supplying the blood and oxygen to my heart and lungs that my coronary arteries were no longer providing.

Jerry then describes what he saw on the monitor. "A second or two after the blood stopped flowing into your heart, the entire bottom of the TV screen — the lower part of your heart — lit up, just blossomed with the glow of all those collateral blood vessels," he says. "It was an amazing sight."

We talk about telling my three children about the surgery, and this gives me pause — unsettles me for the first time since I arrived at the hospital. For a full half minute or more I cannot speak. Jerry smiles down at me. He is a strikingly handsome man, five-foot-eleven and about two hundred pounds, with a trim silver beard, a full and wavy shock of silver hair, and penetrating gray eyes that remind me of Jewish actors such as John Garfield and Paul Newman who have had the same captivating mix, in their looks, of toughness, intelligence, savvy, and tenderness. When, seeing my reaction, Jerry puts his hand on top of mine, I melt. Is this *it?* I wonder. Is the big basketball in the sky really about to fall on me?

Although Jerry's presence comforts, it is also sobering, since he does not hide the seriousness of his concern, and when he asks if I would like *him* to call my children, I shake my head sideways and see myself, a small boy again, sitting on the floor of my office at home, sorting through my baseball cards and glancing up now and then toward my desk, where the light is on but nobody is working.

For more than a dozen years, I have been a single parent to my three children. By this time, however, the last of my children having left home the previous spring, I am, for the first time in three decades, no longer an *on-site* single parent. All three have graduated from college and are living on their own: Miriam, at twenty-nine, in the Washington, D.C., area; Aaron, at twenty-six, in Northampton; and Eli, at twenty-four, in Brooklyn, not far from where I was born and from where Jerry and I grew up.

I had told each of my children about driving down to New Haven for the angiogram but, not wanting to alarm or burden them, had minimized its importance: everything seemed fine, I'd said, and I was still swimming a mile a day, but some anomalies had shown up on an electrocardiogram, and we thought it best to check things out further, so I'd decided to have an angiogram performed at Yale–New Haven. That way, I explained, I could also spend some time with Jerry.

When I find my voice, I tell Jerry that *I'll* telephone my children. Jerry says that he'll call them also and that they can stay at his house (into which he and Gail moved two weeks before) for as long as they want.

Jerry also tells me he's spoken with Rich Helfant and that Rich agrees about the need for emergency bypass surgery. Rich, too, is an old high school friend, and I've known him even longer than I've known Jerry, since, starting from a time when we were seven or eight years old, Rich and I went to the same Hebrew School (we later played together on our synagogue's basketball team). Rich is a cardiologist now living in California — most recently he served as chief of cardiology at Cedars–Sinai Medical Center in Los Angeles; before that he was director of the Philadelphia Heart Institute and chief of medicine and cardiology at Presbyterian-University of Pennsylvania Medical Center — and these past few weeks he and I have been talking nearly every day. In the week to ten days preceding the angiogram, a fact I found both welcome *and* disquieting, he had been calling me *several* times each day.

Later that afternoon Rich calls and says he is not at all surprised at what the angiogram revealed and that, based on his talks with Jerry, he has every confidence in Dr. Hashim and the people at Yale. He reminds me that he had been urging me into the hospital — gently, gently, so as not to scare me — for several weeks.

When my family practitioner, while not excluding the possibility of coronary disease, thought the symptoms that had made me call for an appointment — some occasional shortness of breath while swimming — were due to adult-onset or exercise-induced asthma, and when a local cardiologist, finding some anomalies in an electrocardiogram *and* an echocardiogram, while also not excluding coronary disease, thought the problem was probably viral, Rich had exploded. *"It's not viral, goddamnit!"* he had exclaimed, in the first burst of exasperation I'd heard from him since I'd begun talking with him about my concerns. "I want you in the hospital as soon as possible."

The local cardiologist had recommended that I have an angiogram done at Bay State Hospital in Springfield, but when I called his office to make an appointment, the colleague who performed the angiograms was booked for several weeks. I was persistent and secured a "brief office visit" a week later, not for the angiogram, but to confer about setting up an appointment *for* the angiogram. Then I had telephoned Rich, Jerry, and Phil.

"Listen," I'd said to Rich, as I had to Jerry the day after I'd received the results of the EKG and the echocardiogram, "why don't you guys all talk with one another and then just tell me what to do?"

On Sunday morning, Jerry phoned to say that he and Rich had decided I should come down to Yale and that Dr. Cabin would be calling me at home (as he did) to arrange for the angiogram.

Now, less than a week later, Rich says that, barring the unforeseen, he feels certain that the bypass surgery and the recovery from the surgery will go swiftly and smoothly. He asks about my children, and I tell him I've spoken with each of them and that they will all be arriving at the hospital before surgery the next morning.

Aaron is already on his way down from Northampton by bus; Eli is on his way from New York City by train; and Miriam and her fiancé Seth will be taking a three A.M. train from Washington, D.C., and will arrive early the next morning. I tell Rich I was surprised that they didn't hesitate, and will be with me — I note that I didn't *ask* any of them to come — and Rich tells me he is surprised that I was surprised. Why wouldn't my children want to be with me at a time like this?

After supper, Dr. Hashim stops by and talks with me for a while. Dr. Hashim is Lebanese and therefore, I expect, speaks French. I tell him I lived in France for two years some thirty years ago, before and after my first child, Miriam, was born, and Dr. Hashim and I proceed to talk with each other in both French and English. Although he describes the surgery and explains the possible risks attendant to it, such as stroke, retinal damage, cognitive losses, and infection, and says that, given the excellent state of my health, he sees no cause for concern, it is our conversation about things ordinary and familial that calms my fears and reassures.

When I comment on his name and its possible biblical origin, he tells me that yes, he believes he is a descendant of families that inhabited the ancient Hashemite kingdom. He asks about my name and I tell him my father's family came from Ryminov, a *shtetl* in the Carpathian Mountains — from a region now part of Ukraine — and that they had been in the butter-and-egg business there, as they were after they came to the United States. When, in the Austro-Hungarian Empire, civil servants assigned family names to Jews, probably at the end of the eighteenth century (so that we would no longer be Jacob-son-of-David, or Jacob-Mordecai-of-Ryminov), a state official, seeing thousands of baby chicks running around the family property, according to family lore, gave us the name *Neugeboren,* meaning, in German, "newly born."

Dr. Hashim says something about the appropriateness of my name, and then, to my surprise, reaches down, lifts the bedsheet, and takes my hand in his.

"Twenty or so years ago," he says, "I could not have done anything for you."

Phil Yarnell, with whom I've been talking regularly, and who has been offering me diagnoses by phone and conferring with Rich and Jerry about me, telephones from Denver. Phil started out as a neurosurgeon but switched to neurology early in his career. Before moving to Denver and becoming chief of neurology at Denver General Hospital and of the Neuroscience Division at St. Anthony's Hospital there, he taught at the University of California at Davis; since 1993, in addition to being in private practice, he has been clinical professor of neurology and neurosurgery at the University of Colorado School of Medicine.

Phil grew up on the same block in Brooklyn where I lived until I was two years old — across from Prospect Park — and though neither Phil nor I have clear memories of having done so, we like to imagine we played together back then: in front of our apartment houses, in the park, and in the sandbox and on the monkey bars in the playground that was directly across from my parents' building.

Phil moved to Denver in 1971, the same year I moved to Northampton, and has lived there ever since. He and his wife Barbara also own a 160-acre ranch in Kiowa ("That's one-quarter the size of Prospect Park," Phil says), a small town an hour east of Denver, where they keep cows, horses, and llamas. At a lean five-foot-ten-inches tall, with a full head of white hair and a broad white mustache, and wearing a bolo tie at home and at work, Phil could pass for sheriff of a Western frontier town. His accent and blunt, slangy way of talking about things, however, remain pure Brooklyn.

He tells me he was surprised to hear from Jerry that I *have* heart disease and that it is so far advanced, but he's glad I'm in Jerry's hospital, where Jerry can keep an eye on things. This, he says, is *very* important, agreeing with why Rich and Jerry have decided upon Yale instead of Massachusetts General, where Rich originally wanted to send me. Given the routine and often lethal miscommunications and other slip-ups that prevail in hospitals, Jerry wanted me at Yale, where he could monitor matters and where doctors and staff involved in my care would be accountable to him.

My friends had seen a lot of hospitals and doctors, and until you had, they said, you could not believe the difference there was between excellent care and care that was less than excellent. It was, more frequently than anyone dared acknowledge publicly, the difference between life and death. (And this was ten months before revelations appeared in front page articles around the country, based upon a report from the Institute of Medicine of the National Academy of Sciences, that as many as ninety-eight thousand Americans die every year in hospitals from preventable medical errors — a figure Rich thought grossly underestimated the reality. "That figure is just the tippity-tip of the iceberg," Rich said, "and includes only the most gross and undeniable errors.")

Early that evening my son Eli arrives (Aaron arrives an hour or so later), and while he is with me another old friend from Erasmus, Arthur Rudy, calls. I considered Arthur my closest friend in high school and have been talking with him regularly in recent weeks. Eli, who remains close with many of his high school friends, says something about how lucky I am to have remained friends with guys like Arthur — smart, successful, *menschy* guys who grew up rooting for the Dodgers and who have turned out to be delightfully quirky: Where's the downside? he asks.

Arthur was vice president of Erasmus when we were juniors and, when we were seniors, in a class of more than twelve hundred students, was voted Boy-Most-Likely-to-Succeed. (Jerry Friedland was elected our senior class president.) Arthur, too, is a doctor, though not an M.D. He is a psychologist, formerly chief of psychology at Roosevelt Hospital in New York City and now in private practice. He tells me that Jerry called him with the news. Jerry and Arthur, good friends at Erasmus, roomed together for a year in an Upper West Side apartment during our college years (the three of us went to Columbia together), and though both acknowledge they made lousy roommates, they have remained close friends ever since. (Arthur was best man at Jerry and Gail's wedding.) Arthur and I talk for a while, and — as with Phil, Jerry, and Rich — though I'm happy to have him calling to wish me well, what pleases more than anything we say is the knowledge that, before and after our talk, he, Rich, Jerry, and Phil will be talking with one another about me. *How's Neugie doing?* I hear them ask. And: *The Neug seemed in such great shape, and things seemed to be going so well for him . . .*

Given that, unlike my four friends, I have been living without a wife or companion for the past dozen years, the thought that while I am asleep in the operating room, my chest open and my heart disconnected, these four guys who have known me, and one another, for nearly a half century will be taking care of whatever needs to be taken care of, provides more than comfort. Largely because I cannot know but can only imagine what they will think, feel, and say, my sense of their concern and affection enables me, even before my heart is emptied of blood, to see myself in a life that will be mine *after* my heart is repaired. Among other pleasant fantasies, I picture myself at Miriam's wedding, scheduled eight months hence; and, too, I watch myself at my desk, alone in my third-floor office after my return home, going through notes and sketching out scenes for a new novel.

Now, and later on during my recovery, when I once again rely on these friends to get me through matters both medical and personal, I will find myself seeing us as boys, back again in Brooklyn and doing what we loved most of all: playing basketball. I see us in our favorite place — Holy Cross schoolyard on Church Avenue — and I imagine that we are a team: Phil and Jerry at the forwards, Rich (who is six-foot-two and played college basketball and baseball) at center, me and Arthur (who once scored 59 points in a league game when he was thirteen) in the backcourt. *Four Doctors and Neugie,* I think — five pretty good ballplayers ready to take on all comers: five guys who loved nothing more than to be away from our homes, sweating it out on a baseball field, or in a gym, or a fenced-in schoolyard — five guys who loved nothing more, win or lose, than to hang out together afterward, talking and laughing about shots made and missed, about passes threaded and passes gone wild, about girls we were going out with or dreamt of going out with — five guys who would have loved nothing more than to have gone on talking forever about those things — sports, girls, the Erasmus basketball team, and the Brooklyn Dodgers chief among them — that mattered most in the world to us in those days.

The next morning I telephone my brother Robert, who has been a patient in state mental hospitals for most of the last thirty-seven years and for whom I've been primary caretaker. I tell him (and the chief of psychology at Bronx Psychiatric Center, where Robert is this time) about the surgery. Robert is silent for a few seconds, then asks if my children will be at the hospital and who will be taking care of me at home after the operation. He says he will say a prayer for me.

Miriam and Seth arrive in the morning and, with Eli and Aaron, stay with me until I am taken to the operating suite. According to them, the last thing I say before I am wheeled away is that they should use my credit card when they go out for lunch.

The surgery lasts six and a half hours, and my heart is stopped, my blood processed through a heart-lung machine (during what physicians refer to as "pump-time") for one hour and fifty-five minutes. Dr. Hashim and his team perform a quintuple bypass (*five* grafts, one more than planned; when I tell this to Arthur, he laughs: "You were always an overachiever," he says), and there are no complications. When Rich calls after he has received faxes of Dr. Hashim's postoperative report, he is very pleased and tells me the surgeon was absolutely first-rate. But that's based on his own report, I say. How do you know how good he was? "Several things — but most of all, the pump-time," Rich replies, referring to the amount of time my heart was detached and my blood cycled through a heart-lung machine. "One hour and fifty-five minutes for five grafts is incredible. The man is terrific."

When I wake the next day, tubes and wires protruding from my chest, stomach, arms, neck, and mouth, my children and Seth are there, and I am able to get out of bed and take a walk with them along the hospital corridor. I feel very sleepy — and very happy. I fade in and out, and at noon I watch a nationally televised UMass basketball game. I have taught at the University of Massachusetts as writer-in-residence since 1971, and for most of those years my children and I have had season tickets to UMass games. We have also traveled to other cities — Albany, Worcester, Boston, Philadelphia, Washington, D.C. — to see games, and our home, where my friends and my children's friends would gather when the UMass team was on TV, was dubbed "Hoop Central" by the sports editor of the local newspaper.

"When I told you the game was on TV," Eli later tells me, "you got very intense and excited suddenly — as excited as anyone could be, given where you'd been less than twenty-four hours before. You'd fall asleep during commercials, but when the game came back on, your eyes would snap open."

It is only now, the operation over and successful and my children seeming so happy — and relieved — to be with me (none of us upset, as we ordinarily would have been, to see UMass lose a crucial end-of-season league game), that I realize just how frightened they had been, and — but why the need for such reassurance? — how much they do love me. The depth of their affection, like that of my friends, seems an unexpected revelation.

"We were pretty relieved your children were staying with us for the weekend — and that you *weren't*," Jerry says. "Your children were lovely, but they were walking into walls, they were so stunned. I remember that Gail made this great minestrone soup, with tons of fresh vegetables, and Miriam warned us that Seth had a very funny, quasi-religious thing about vegetables — he *never* ate them — but he just kept spooning the stuff in, one bowl after the other."

On the afternoon after the UMass game, walking back and forth by myself from one end of the cardiac care unit to the other while my children have gone off to eat lunch, and feeling a bit stronger, though still groggy from the anesthesia and pain medications, I think of how lucky — and happy! — I am to be alive, of how good it feels simply to be walking ("Listen, Neugie — keep breathing in and breathing out," Arthur advises. "It's the secret of staying alive"), and of how dear my children and friends are to me, and then of how strange, swift, and mysterious the entire experience has been: of how little we know about how and why I nearly died.

2

All the Time in the World

WHEN RICH CALLS ON Saturday evening, and after he tells me how great my surgeon was and how happy he is and that things went well, I talk with him about some of the notions my experience, before and after surgery, has set in motion.

If, I say, we know so little about the heart, which, in comparison to other organs — to the brain! — seems a relatively simple pump of flesh and blood, and which, in the context of the infinity of interactions not only within the brain or heart (consider, for starters, that the body replaces about a million cells per second and that there are more potential synaptic connections in any one brain than there are particles in the known universe), but also between the brain, the heart, the nervous system, and the immune system, how vast must be the realm of our ignorance. And yet, and yet . . . despite how little we know, how extraordinary and good it is that we know enough, sometimes, to be able to heal the body and the mind of disease and, as with me, to restore life when death has all but found a dwelling place.

"Oh yes," Rich says. "We know how to fix what was wrong with you — and thank God that we do — but about the rest we know very, very little. Despite all our researches, you see, we don't really understand the fundamental cause of your illness. We don't truly know how to prevent it. We don't know how to reverse it. We can't treat it very well short of invasive interventions such as stent angioplasty or bypass surgery, treatments we usually employ when the disease becomes life-threatening. And without catheterization we can't even diagnose it accurately, especially when we need to know the true severity of the problem and the magnitude of the threat."

Despite decades of intensive research, he says, atherosclerosis — the closing off of coronary arteries — remains the number one killer of both men and women in our time. And though theories abound, and though cardiology is generally considered to be the medical specialty wherein we have made the greatest progress in recent years, we really, he repeats, know very, very little.

"The first thing I tell my medical students," Rich says, "is that they should never be afraid to say 'I don't know.' It is far better to say 'I don't know' than to be comfortable thinking you understand something — or to think you're comforting your patient by *pretending* to know something — because then you're not open to possibility. Because if you think you already know something, you stop listening to the patient.

"In the end," Rich explains, something he will emphasize repeatedly in our talks, "— and the reason I became so alarmed and kept urging you into the hospital as quickly as possible — the surest way of diagnosing coronary disease now is exactly what it was when I started out as a doctor forty years ago: the patient's report of his symptoms over a period of time, and the pattern of those symptoms as reported by the patient. It was the progressive nature of your symptoms that worried me most."

We talk about the conversations we'd been having since the afternoon I first called him seven or eight weeks ago. In the course of talking about other things — mostly about a book Rich was writing (about the unexpected consequences, in his life and career, of saving the life of a Mafia Don) and that I was helping him with — I asked if he minded if I checked some stuff out with him about my own health. I also tell him that I had become aware that as time passed he was calling me with increasing frequency.

"I'll tell you this, pal," he says. "Despite all the progress and gains we've made — and I don't minimize them, for, especially in cardiology, I have seen miracles come to pass that now save hundreds of thousands of lives each year — medicine, even in cardiology, is still essentially an art, and one wherein the key element remains the relationship between the doctor and the patient. Most of what we know, and the basis for our decisions as to diagnosis and modes of treatment — despite all the advances in diagnostic testing — still comes from you: from what you tell us, and from our knowledge of how to judge new information when put into the context of our more general knowledge of who you are, and of your history."

Six days after surgery my son Aaron drives me home to Northampton and informs me that he is moving back in with me for a month. ("I'm not asking you if I can move back this time," he says. "I'm telling you.") The next day, Eli arrives for the weekend, and two days after this my cousin Madeleine drives down from Syracuse, New York, intending to help take care of me for a few days but discovering to her surprise that I am already making meals for myself and going up and down the stairs of my three-story house without difficulty. I am also back at work, writing a few hours a day in my third-floor office.

While Madeleine is with me, a team from the television program *Nightline* shows up to tape an interview with me. The interview, scheduled before the surgery, is for possible use in a special Ted Koppel will be doing about Moe Armstrong, one of the people I've written about in a book for which I'd corrected page proofs a few weeks before surgery and which is scheduled for publication in early May.

Whatever the book's virtues or deficiencies, or the response to it in the world, one undeniably good thing about it, I say to my cousin — the best thing, for sure — is that it is not going to be published posthumously.

A week after I arrive home — two weeks after surgery — Seth and Miriam fly up from Washington, D.C., for a few days, and we drive with friends to Amherst to watch UMass play Temple in the last home basketball game of the regular season. We park about three-quarters of a mile from the UMass arena and walk at a brisk pace, and in icy weather, to and from the game. (UMass wins 57–49.)

By the time Miriam and Seth leave, I am doing what I have been doing for most of my adult life — waking early, making myself breakfast, and then going up to my third-floor office, turning off my phone, and working at my writing. By the end of the following week, as I initially recall this period of my recovery, I am walking between five and ten miles each day, and a week after this — four weeks after surgery — I am back in the pool, once again swimming a mile a day.

My recovery is as swift and full as my crisis was sudden and surprising.

"You've had a true near-death experience," Phil says to me several times, but though I feel happy to be alive, and though I'm aware that friends and family also seem happy that I'm still here, what has happened, I tell Phil, hardly seems real. The moment when, two days after surgery, I was walking along the hospital corridor by myself, though, stays with me and seems *very* real — and the words that came to me then sing to me now, intermittently and insistently: *How little we know.*

But for some good fortune, good friends, and good doctors, I keep reminding myself, I could just as easily *not* be here, and I wonder if, for purposes of telling this story, I can do what I need to do for that moment to take root and — like collateral blood vessels? — begin to blossom.

Novels and stories have often come to me this way: moments, words, or voices, seemingly dissociated, attaching themselves to fragments of memory, or imagined scenes, or dimly lit and half-hidden faces, images, or remembered pieces of dreams — or to odd bits of diverse and arcane data, along with a curiosity concerning matters unknown and half-known that I long to know more about: of how certain things are or were or might be, and of how and why things work or happen the way they do. These seemingly random elements spin around in my mind, conspire in my imagination, and fire my desire *to know.* When the words, pictures, and dramas that take up residence within my consciousness become more real to me than the external world, I yield to them. Then, in and through the writing itself — the making of stories — I have sometimes been able to make sense out of what for me would otherwise remain senseless and confusing. It is largely through this process that I have, through

most of my adult life, been able to make peace with matters dispa-
rate, disturbing, and often terrifying.

I talk with my brother Robert several times. Although he is designated as mad by the world (the consensus of the staff at his present
hospital, as at his previous residence, South Beach Psychiatric Center on Staten Island, is that he will *never* be able to live outside the
locked ward of a hospital), in his conversations with me he seems
very realistic and very loving.

He says he is relieved and happy I have survived surgery and am
back home, and he asks about my new book — the one about to appear — and if I am going to stop writing about *him* and go back to
writing novels again. When will he be able to see me? I tell him that
I'm already back at work on a novel, and that the doctors want me to
wait four weeks before I drive again — not to protect my heart, but
to ensure that my chest, stapled, sewn, and wired back together,
won't experience undue strain. As soon as I'm given the green light,
I say, I'll come down to visit him.

When I do drive down to visit him six weeks after surgery, he is
allowed out on the hospital grounds with me. It is a clear, sunny,
early spring day, and we sit on the lawn in front of his building. In
the distance, a patient is feeding bread to some of the dozens of
Canada geese that regularly set down on this lawn, and I recall
times, a half century ago, when Robert and I, at summer camp — on
days the kitchen staff would get the afternoons off — would sit on
the grass by a lake and eat sandwiches together. Now, a few minutes
before I leave and Robert goes back to his locked ward in the hospital's main building — a tall, ill-kept, warehouse-like structure with
barred windows and prison-like security entrances and exits — he
says he'll understand if I say no, but would I be willing to do him
a favor? Of course, I say. "Would you show me your scar again?" he
asks.

Largely because of the intervention of Dr. Alvin Pam, chief of
psychology at the hospital, Robert is receiving the best care he has
had in years, and this has been a long time coming. After the publication of *Imagining Robert,* which chronicled Robert's history as a
patient in the New York city and state mental health systems, Dr.
Pam called and suggested Robert consider transferring to Bronx

State. "We think we can do better," Dr. Pam said. "No promises, of course — but if Robert's willing to give us a chance, we'd like the opportunity to work with him."

Now, at Bronx State, Robert is being treated with kindness, skill, and optimism — his medications carefully monitored and set at the lowest possible levels, his behavior, feelings, and concerns addressed regularly by staff and in regularly scheduled sessions with a therapist, and his expressed wishes to leave the hospital responded to respectfully and without, as in the past, skepticism or mockery. Rather the opposite. He is being treated as a human being, and not as a set of symptoms. This becomes clear early on, when Dr. Pam calls to tell me that everyone has been talking — and laughing — about something that happened that morning. Asked to give a urine sample, Robert had gone into the bathroom, filled the flask, brought it to the nurse, and then, just as she reached for it, taken it back. "I'd like a receipt, please," he said.

Being treated humanely — being in a place where the staff makes a genuine attempt to listen to him, to understand him, and to work with him, and where they appreciate his sense of humor — seems to enable Robert to act in increasingly humane and hopeful ways, and he talks with me now, a few weeks after my operation, about how much better he is feeling, about not wanting to be locked up for the rest of his life, and about getting out of the hospital.

Well, I say to him, then we are both in recovery, yes? He laughs, and when he does I am reminded of something that has impressed me in recent years with regard to those conditions we call mental illness: that all the warmth, good feeling, and good intentions in the world have been of little help to people like Robert if they have not been accompanied by knowledge and skills specific *to* mental illness. Compassion without skill, I've come to see, is as inadequate for people struggling with the complexities of severe mental, emotional, and neurological conditions as is skill without compassion.

But how different, I now begin to wonder, is this from what happens in other medical specialties, and in medicine in general? By way of reply, I hear again what Rich has been telling me with reference to cardiology, and what he, Jerry, Arthur, and Phil have been telling me through the years: that being a doctor is at least as much of an art as it is a science, that paying attention to and listening to the patient are crucial, that care is more important (and possible) than cure, that it begins in curiosity, attentiveness, and understanding, and that miraculous as many of the new biotechnological developments are, they are not at the heart of what matters most in the treatment of disease, and of what makes most of the difference for most people most of the time.

"There are no cures," each of them says to me. "There are only various conditions that, with skill and luck, we can manage to various degrees."

Put most simply: All the factual and scientific knowledge in the world does little good for people like my brother when those who own this knowledge do not care about the people they serve and are not committed, first and last, to trying to work with them and understand them in the context of their histories, of the ongoing nature of their conditions, and of the uniqueness of their individual selves.

And so with me. My experience has been dramatic enough, but what begins to seem more significant and intriguing — what, once my life has been saved and given back to me by the prompt and excellent medical care Rich and Jerry were able to provide, and by technologies and skills nonexistent a few decades ago (the heart-lung machine, the cardiac care unit, clot-busting drugs, stent angioplasty, bypass surgery), seems more essentially life-*giving* — is the friendship of four men I have known for most of my life.

And those life-giving qualities of friendship that enrich our lives and get us through hard times, I muse, don't they have a good deal in common with those elements of medicine, and of the doctor-patient relationship in particular, that often sustain us in ordinary times and restore us when we are ill? Sensing, too, especially when talking with my friends, that the science and the art of medicine have, in recent years, become increasingly and dangerously disconnected, I wonder what we might do to begin to repair this breach.

In my desire to understand what we do and don't know about disease, I ask my friends about the changes they have seen since they started out in medical school forty years ago, about what we know and don't know about their specialties, and about medicine in general. If they could draw up an agenda for medical care in the near and distant future, what would be on it, and in what order of priority, and what changes and reforms would they urge?

My friends talk with me at length, they offer suggestions for reading, for areas of investigation, and for people I should talk with; in talking with me freely about their lives, both personal and professional, they also offer further proof of how fortunate I am to count them as friends.

"You're not cured," Dr. Cabin says to me at the time of my four-week postsurgical checkup. "But you're as close as it gets. One of the reasons I went into cardiology, in fact, is that the outcomes, as in your case, are so often positive — so much more so than in other branches of medicine."

How bad was I when you first saw me? I ask, and he smiles and says that I was as bad as it gets, and that we have no real understanding of why my condition was what it was. And my life from now on?

"No restrictions," he says. "Absolutely no restrictions. You've been given a new lease on life."

A day or two after my visit with Dr. Cabin, I act on a decision I made a few days after surgery while I was still at Yale–New Haven Hospital: I decide to move back to New York City, where I have not lived for more than thirty years, and, my friends and my children cheering me on ("It's your time now, Dad," Miriam says), I start looking for an apartment in Manhattan.

As my health and strength return, they bring with them large desires and ambitions. I put myself on a writing schedule both new and exhilarating — working on one book (fiction) in the morning and on another (nonfiction) in the afternoons, and leaving myself open to the possibility that on some days I may not get to both, or — who knows? — I might wind up working on something else altogether. The main thing, I tell myself, is to be open to possibility.

When I talk with a friend in Northampton about moving to New York, about my new schedule, and about the vast wells of energy I've been discovering within me, she says something about my doubtless realizing, given what I've been through, just how short life is, and about my wanting to "grab in" all the pleasure, excitement, and living I can.

"Not at all," I reply. I've decided to move back to New York, I explain, not because life seems short, but for an opposite reason: because my sense of things now, given what I've been through, is that I have all the time in the world.

3

The Consolation of Diagnosis

THE STORY I TELL others in the weeks and months following surgery — and the story I first tell (and sell) to myself — is this: A sixty-year-old man in good spirits, excellent physical shape, and seeming good health, without apparent risk factors or symptoms, discovers that his major coronary arteries are nearly 100 percent blocked. Although two doctors miss the diagnosis, an old friend who is a cardiologist makes the correct diagnosis, and he does so by telephone from three thousand miles away. The sixty-year-old man is rushed into emergency surgery, his life is saved, and he emerges from the surgery, like his name, newly born — healthy, energized, and radiant with the gift of life.

When I tell the story, and friends ask about cholesterol levels, blood pressure, smoking, exercise, diet, stress, and the rest, and when I reply that I seem to have had none of the classic risk factors or symptoms, most people nod and say, "Oh — then it must be genetic."

When I respond by saying that I don't really have what doctors call "a positive family history of coronary disease," I sense that people feel not merely puzzled, but betrayed. If a man in excellent health, without risk factors or overt symptoms — a sixty-year-old man swimming a mile a day and able to play competitive tennis and basketball with twenty-year-olds — can be this close to death, and if doctors seem clueless as to why this is so, then in how much danger are most of us most of the time?

More than two dozen friends go on what they call "Jay Neugeboren–inspired diets" (two close friends lose more than fifty pounds each within six months) and/or to their doctors — for checkups, cholesterol screenings, electrocardiograms, stress tests. You were in the best shape of any of us, they say. If this could happen to *you* . . .

Although we may give lip service to the notion that our fates are never really in our own hands and that the forces that determine our destinies — when and how and why we die, or when and how and why we survive and live on — are beyond our control, when it comes to our own lives, most of us are reluctant to believe we are as ignorant and helpless as it often seems we are.

(On the day I begin writing this chapter, Arthur Rudy calls to tell me about a colleague — a fifty-three-year-old doctor in excellent health, who, while exercising on a treadmill, died this past week of a heart attack. The man was not a smoker, not overweight, had no apparent risk factors or symptoms. His case seemed so surprising — so anomalous — that the family requested an autopsy. The results from the autopsy? No help, Arthur says. Not the least clue as to the possible cause of the heart attack.)

Celebrating my first Thanksgiving after surgery, in November of 1999, thirty of us gathered at a cousin's home, one of my cousins looks at our children — a dozen of them, some with spouses and children of their own now, sitting around their own table as they have each Thanksgiving for the past twenty-five years — and says that she envies them and their generation the great medical progress they are going to benefit from during the first decades of the new century, including the miracle, not merely of innovations such as bypass surgery or gene therapy, but of "total body transplants."

When I suggest to my cousin, as to others, that, my own good fortune notwithstanding, things may not be quite as miraculous as the media would have us believe, what I usually hear back is that yes, there may be some glitches along the way, but if, say, current medications stop being effective, *they* — the mysterious, omnipotent, omniscient *they* — will doubtless come up with new medications, gene therapies, or as-yet-undreamt-of remedies to replace old and ineffective treatments.

For just as science has come up with vaccines and antibiotics for measles, diphtheria, smallpox, whooping cough, polio, pneumonia, typhoid, and tuberculosis, so, people tell me, it will come up with new cures for virtually all our remaining illnesses — for heart disease, cancer, multiple sclerosis, schizophrenia, clinical depression, AIDS, et cetera. When I mention new and reemerging diseases — *E. coli,* ebola, malaria, tuberculosis, hospital-acquired staph — people acknowledge their existence yet talk of them as if they are, in their danger to us as in their geography, distinctly remote. (Consider, though, that 70 percent of hospital-acquired infections now involve drug-resistant organisms, and that in metropolitan New York City alone, in 1995, 7,800 patients acquired drug-resistant staph infections during hospital stays, from which 1,400 died.)

For friends and family in the months following surgery, I seem to be living proof that science, in the guise of technology, will, like God, always provide. My initial reading and research, however, along with conversations with Rich, Jerry, Phil, and Arthur, begin to tell me another and quite different story.

The advent of the germ theory of disease in the late nineteenth century, along with early successes in the management of infectious diseases, encouraged a faith in medical science that was grounded not in clinical experience but in laboratory research, which research was grounded in the late-nineteenth- and early-twentieth-century assumption that disease was defined by some biological defect or anomaly taking place in an otherwise normal human being, and that for each such specific abnormality we have or will discover a specific medical treatment that will cure it.

In our time such beliefs — beliefs that, as one doctor writes, have downgraded "the importance of wisdom and experience in favor of spurious objectivity" and that have effectively devalued clinical judgment and the interaction between doctor and patient — are constantly encouraged in both the popular media and in direct-to-consumer marketing by drug companies.

This, for example, from a *Time* magazine preface to a Special Issue, *The Frontiers of Medicine* (Fall 1996): "Throughout history, bursts of knowledge — the Renaissance, the Age of Exploration, the Industrial Revolution — have created a succession of new plateaus for human achievement. Medicine is now experiencing just such a surge of enlightenment and advance, producing a parade of break-throughs so flabbergasting that they are routinely described as 'revolutionary' or even . . . by the decidedly unscientific encomium of 'miracle.'" Or this announcement, in large type on the front cover of *New York* magazine (February 7, 2000): "We are going to see a *global conquering of cancer* in five to ten years." Or this, in a full-page ad in the *New York Times* (October 3, 2000): "At Pfizer we're determined to find the cures of the future. A cure for your father's Alzheimer's, your sister's heart disease, your best friend's diabetes. A cure for the ailments that touch all our families. To help create this better world, we've decided to create an even better company . . ."

Or consider, too, that the success rate for cardiac resuscitations dramatized on television shows such as *ER* is 75 percent, while the figure in real hospitals is 15 percent.

Although people are moved when I tell the story of how several lifelong friends were instrumental in shepherding me through my crisis — what saved my life as much as the angiogram and surgery, I suggest, was the fact that Rich and Jerry *knew* me and *listened* to me — most conversations invariably return to the "miracle of bypass surgery."

And who can argue with this? Surely it is wonderful that this procedure exists, and yes, I wouldn't be alive if it didn't. What seems at least as significant as the fact that we could fix what was wrong with me, however, is the fact that we have little understanding of what went wrong, and why.

Although in telling my story I often quote Dr. Cabin saying that I was "totally anomalous," my initial research suggests that I was not, in fact, all that anomalous, and that what mattered most in my case, as in the majority of cases of heart disease, was not the existence of the disease or the surgery that fixed it, but the *judgment about the disease* that led to the decision concerning surgery, and the clinical experience from which that judgment derived.

According to the American Heart Association, for example, nearly two-thirds of all sudden deaths from heart attacks in women occur in women who have no history whatsoever of chest pain. And though nearly 40 percent of women will die from heart disease, only 4 percent fear it as their leading cause of death. (Compare this to the fact that, according to the National Center for Health Statistics, 40 percent of women fear dying from breast cancer, though only 4 percent actually will.)

When I talk about such findings with Rich, who has published a book on heart disease in women, he is hardly surprised. Despite our sophisticated testing and screening technologies, the diagnosis of heart disease, he insists, is tricky and problematic. And when I talk not only of having been anomalous, but of having been *asymptomatic,* he corrects me.

"You weren't asymptomatic," he says. "The problem was that the doctors didn't diagnose your symptoms, or their cause, accurately."

Later on, Rich will walk me through my experience again and explain how and why, from our phone conversations, he became convinced, despite my seeming good health, that my heart was severely diseased and my life in grave danger. Before he does this, however, my research reinforces much of what he has already told me: that except in rare and unusually straightforward cases (a patient presenting to a doctor while in the midst of a massive heart attack, for example), for both diagnosis *and* treatment, it is the judgment of the cardiologist that is critical.

My story, then, may *seem* anomalous, unlikely, and unpredictable, but what I learn is that *many* people, like me, have severe and progressive heart disease without having the risk factors and symptoms we so often hear about. (The high percentage of women who die from heart disease without having chest pain, for example, Rich suggests, is due largely to the fact that in many such instances a woman's heart disease is complicated by the coexistence of diabetes.) The American Heart Association reports that 50 percent of men and 63 percent of women who die suddenly of coronary heart disease have no previous symptoms of disease, and other studies, as Rich confirms, suggest that up to 50 percent of *all* people experiencing severe coronary disease and/or heart attacks have no traditional presenting symptoms or risk factors. Moreover, Rich believes that most so-called silent heart attacks are not really silent, but present with symptoms that are either missed or, more frequently, misdiagnosed by the patient's physician.

Until quite recently, most researchers believed that heart attacks were usually caused by the buildup of plaque (a combination of lipids, smooth muscle cells, inflammatory cells, and extracellular matrix) in the arterial walls. When this ruptures, it causes clots that create the blockages that lead to heart attacks. But we now learn that ruptured plaque is found in only two-thirds of people who have had heart attacks. What, then, causes the clots that cause the heart attacks in the other third?

And what about cholesterol, invariably the first subject that comes up when people talk with me about my experience? "More than a third of individuals who have heart attacks have normal cholesterol levels," Rich says. "This despite biannual meetings of the 'experts' who decide that 'normal' cholesterol is really lower than they said it was at their last meeting, and who say so with no credible data to back them up."

The number one and number three best-selling prescription drugs in the United States in 2001, Lipitor and Zocor, are anticholesterol medications that have been proven effective in lowering cholesterol levels, and doing so while lowering the "bad" (LDL) cholesterol and raising the "good" (HDL). Lowering cholesterol, studies indicate, reduces heart disease and seems especially helpful to those who have already experienced a heart attack or have had heart surgery. In addition, studies indicate that giving the cholesterol-lowering drugs known as statins (Lipitor, Zocor, Lescol, Mevacor, Pravachol) to heart attack patients in the hospital before and after surgery can substantially improve their chances of survival.

But the paradoxical finding, across *all* studies, is that lowering cholesterol does *not* prolong life. Among people whose cholesterol is reduced there is a consistent, mysterious, and unexplained increase in deaths from other causes. In addition, most studies indicate that the risk of death *increases* when blood cholesterol levels go below 180 mg/dl. And we don't understand why.

It turns out, moreover, that if *all* commonly known risk factors are combined — smoking, high-fat diets, high iron levels, high blood pressure, markers for inflammation, implicated genes, diabetes, *and* high cholesterol levels — they still account for no more than half the risk of acquiring atherosclerosis. Approximately 50 percent of people with atherosclerosis, that is, acquire it even though they do not have *any* elevated risk factors for the disease. Furthermore, these risk factors represent only statistical associations, not proven causes, and the exact mechanisms by which they may contribute to the development of atherosclerosis are unknown.

In addition, some researchers believe that heart disease is influenced most significantly not by the usual set of biological, genetic, and environmental factors, but by our fetal environments. The English epidemiologist David Barker has carried out surveys suggesting a relation between nutrition in fetal life and the likelihood of developing heart disease in middle age. In several large studies, he found that death rates from cardiovascular disease fell progressively with increasing weight, head circumference, and other measures of increased development at birth. Among individuals who weighed eighteen pounds or less at one year, death rates from coronary artery disease were almost three times higher than among those who weighed twenty-seven pounds or more. Barker and his colleagues hypothesize, further, that low growth rates up to the age of one year are associated with an increased prevalence both of several risk factors for heart disease and of death rates from heart disease.

And a recent Stanford University and Veterans Affairs Health Care study of more than six thousand men, more than half of whom had an abnormal exercise-test result or a history of cardiovascular disease, concluded that "in both healthy subjects and those with cardiovascular disease peak exercise capacity achieved was a stronger predictor of an increased risk of death than clinical variables or established risk factors such as hypertension, smoking, and diabetes, as well as other exercise-test variables."

It is not surprising, then, that despite my having coronary arteries that were almost totally blocked, two doctors, after examining me, after listening to my report of symptoms, and with data in hand — cholesterol screenings, family history, blood pressure, and echocardiogram and electrocardiogram results — while not excluding heart disease, did not diagnose it accurately.

If diagnosis is difficult, the choice of treatment for coronary disease is equally problematic, and here again, it is the judgment of the physician, and not the data from laboratory testing, that is crucial.

When diagnostic tests are competently administered and interpreted, they can, as in my case, identify the existence of coronary disease, its extent, and its physiological effects. But they are, as Rich says and others confirm, notoriously unreliable, or even useless, as guides when it comes to selecting the best form of treatment.

Emergencies and life-threatening situations aside, the better I *know* the person I am treating, my friends tell me, the more effective I can be as a doctor. This may sound unscientific, they allow, but then the practice of medicine is not quite as scientific as people like to think.

"Put a patient with even the simplest set of maladies in front of five doctors," Rich says, "and you might get five different diagnoses, five different prognoses, *and* five different recommendations for treatment." For that matter, he adds, give any five doctors the same set of lab tests and you will probably get a similar range of diagnoses, prognoses, and treatment plans.

"In fact," Rich advises when, a year or so after surgery, my cholesterol levels are slightly elevated and my doctors recommend that I take a cholesterol-lowering medication, "the first thing I would do would be to take the test again. If you send the same blood sample to two different labs, there's a strong likelihood that you'll get two different results." (In January 2001, Rich persuades his own physician to have his cholesterol test redone — to have the same lab run the same blood sample back through its machines. The result? A 17 percent rise in his score, from 152 to 176. "If I had had a 17 percent rise, from 200 to 234, say — 34 points above what's supposed to be 'normal' — and I'd been seeing all the ads about cholesterol and heart disease, I might have gone on a cholesterol medication for the rest of my life, and who knows what the side effects would be for me down the road, since we have no long-term studies of what these medications will do to us.")

P. W. Medawar, Nobel Prize–winning doctor for his contribution to organ transplantation, observes that when people speak about the "art and science" of medicine, they invariably get them the wrong way around, assuming that the art involves merely being sympathetic to and talking with a patient, while the science involves the more difficult task of interpreting the results of sophisticated tests, which interpretations will lead to the correct diagnosis. But Medawar contends that the reverse is true — that the real "science" in medicine is, in fact, that thorough understanding of the nature of a medical problem that comes from talking at length with a patient and performing a physical examination that elicits the relevant signs of disease. From such an old-fashioned way of practicing medicine, he says, it is possible to infer precisely what is wrong in 90 percent of cases.

By contrast, Medawar points out, technological tests and procedures can frequently be misleading, and he points to the paradox that the more tests a doctor performs, the less scientific — in the sense of generating reliable knowledge — medicine becomes.

Sherwin Nuland, a Yale physician, surgeon, and author (*How We Die* and *Doctors: A Biography of Medicine*), in considering the idea of medicine as "an imperfect science," says that he "would go further even than that. It is not a science at all. It remains what it has always been and will ever be — an art that uses science as well as it can, and too often incorrectly and inconsistently."

Thus, for example, even when a test does lead to effective treatment, as with Pap smears, the troubling finding is that when the test is performed more often, the result is both fewer missed cases of disease *and* more false-positive results. Reducing one kind of mistake, that is, increases others. Over the course of her lifetime, a woman's chance of having more false positives, in fact, becomes considerably higher than her chance of developing cervical cancer itself. (In addition, such false positives typically lead to more tests, often inaccurate, and to treatment, and these tests and treatments, while often conferring little or no benefit — compare the situation with prostate cancer — are themselves anxiety-producing, painful, and risky.)

"With respect to cardiology," Rich explains, "the problem goes something like this: the more likely the test is to be abnormal — treadmill ECT [electrocardiogram tracing] testing, nuclear cardiology, echocardiography, cardiac MRI, et cetera — and therefore suggest the presence of heart disease, the more likely it is that the result will be a 'false positive' — meaning that the test is abnormal, but the patient is normal. In addition, these tests and scans all miss a certain percentage — ballpark, 15 percent — of abnormal patients. In these cases the test is normal, but the patient is not."

Clinical trials and outcome studies that evaluate various ways of treating heart disease are, it turns out, remarkably inconclusive: whether a doctor recommends angioplasty, bypass surgery, drug therapy, or beating-heart surgery (bypass surgery performed without using a heart-lung machine, and sometimes without cracking open the chest), chances are patients will end up about the same. Even if one receives treatment considered optimal, there appears to be less than a 50 percent chance it will improve the likelihood that one will live longer than one would have lived *without* the treatment.

Such studies and statistics, moreover, are themselves highly misleading, for the truth, as with me, is that some treatments are better for some people than they are for others. Not only is each of us different and unique, but each person's *disease* is also unique, and this is what a skilled cardiologist takes into account when diagnosing a condition and when prescribing treatment. Then, too, statistics themselves represent, at best, an *approximation* of reality.

Stephen Klaidman, in *Saving the Heart: The Battle to Conquer Coronary Disease,* summarizes much of what I hear from my friends: "Clinical judgment is not an exact science, which is where the art comes in," he writes. Each person "is a distinct entity, anatomically, physiologically, and psychologically, and the clinician must take account of the differences. Each person's disease is also distinct, and that, too, must be taken into account. Furthermore, since randomized clinical-trial results as reported in the medical

journals provide only generalizations, there is no way of being absolutely sure, except in some relatively small number of clear-cut cases,
that for patient X angioplasty is a better choice than drugs or surgery."

"I have always been plagued by our ignorance when confronted
by an individual patient," Rich says, "and the problem we have in
cardiology is that while tests can reveal the status of the disease,
their prognostic accuracy is far worse than their diagnostic accuracy.

"Having atherosclerosis ain't so bad if you know you'll live happily with it for the next thirty years — as compared to the next thirty
hours. Lowering cholesterol levels, controlling blood pressure and
diet, quitting smoking, and the rest are surely important, but in
each *individual* case, sad to say, the situation is neither so clear nor
so rosy."

But why not?

The answer, as I begin to understand it, is that it takes more than
tests and screenings, scientifically true as they may seem, to deal
with the complexities of each disease as it makes its home in each
one of us. Klaidman makes the essential point: "The cardiologists
who diagnose with subtlety and accuracy, and who best understand
the idiosyncrasies of each individual patient and his or her disease
. . . may be the most valuable clinicians because they do better than
others in guiding their patients toward treatment choices that are
most appropriate for them. Their special gifts, which are becoming
rarer all the time, are clinical judgment and clinical skills — that is to
say, using the most basic methods to figure out what is wrong with a
patient and the best way to fix it."

"The great secret, known to internists . . . but still hidden from the
general public, is that most things get better by themselves," Lewis
Thomas writes. "Most things, in fact, are better by morning." And
one of the essential ingredients in the healing process is the belief
the patient has in the person doing the healing.

What happens, then, I wonder, if the thoughtful and well-trained
doctor we see one time may not be the doctor we see the next time
— and if, because of such experiences, trust and faith in the doctor,

or in any provider of health care, begins to erode? What happens when, under policies initiated by managed-care companies, people not only don't have access to doctors who know them, and whom they know and trust, but see a series of doctors whose clinical skills and judgment are compromised by guidelines (guidelines monitored, generally, by people who have no medical expertise themselves) as to how much time they can allow for seeing, talking with, and examining each patient?

The answer, according to my friends, and according to preliminary outcome studies such as those sponsored by the Robert Wood Johnson Foundation and the Rutgers University Institute for Health, Health Care Policy and Aging Research, is that we are courting disaster. These studies point out that patients' trust generally depends upon the perception that their doctors are free to act in their best interests. But how believe this when the utilization review boards and structural arrangements that govern managed care restrict choice, contradict medical decisions and control, and limit (and sometimes obstruct) doctors' communication with patients? These studies also show that policies such as "gatekeeping" (whereby primary care providers must *approve* the use of specialists), along with incentives to limit care, further erode our trust as well as the independence and ability of our doctors to act freely on our behalf.

John Kirklin, a cardiac surgeon at the Mayo Clinic in Rochester, Minnesota, asserts that "the perpetually increasing demands on surgeons, pediatric cardiologists and adult cardiologists, and their responses to these demands, have resulted in their being, as a group, less contemplative, less able to understand intimately the special circumstances of each of their patients, and perhaps less fit to help patients with heart disease make the many complex decisions required."

A 1997 study of 453 recent medical school graduates — residents in internal medicine and family practice — illustrates such concerns. In this study, the 453 doctors could not correctly identify the distinctive sounds of *common* heart abnormalities with a stethoscope 80 percent of the time. "While directors of internal medicine programs consider [cardiac auscultation] to be an essential skill for every practicing physician and would like more time to be devoted to its teaching, fewer than one third of all internal medicine programs offer any structured teaching of cardiac auscultation," the study notes, and points out that "an even worse situation exists for lung auscultation."

Although a human being using a stethoscope may not be the only or best way to detect heart or lung abnormalities, it remains a most reliable and accurate way of doing so. "We chose cardiac auscultation," the authors conclude, "because there is evidence that this skill, competently performed, is a sensitive, highly specific, and cost-effective method of detecting valvular heart disease in asymptomatic subjects. In a larger sense, however, we chose cardiac auscultation as a paradigm for all bedside diagnostic skills. Thus, deficiencies similar to those we found for cardiac auscultation might exist in other important areas and deserve further exploration."

The danger implicit in such a deterioration of clinical skills came home to me when my son Aaron went for a routine physical and our family practitioner, David Katz, listening to Aaron's heart with a stethoscope, heard something he thought abnormal. Dr. Katz sent Aaron to a cardiologist. The cardiologist heard the same sound, did an echocardiogram, and confirmed Dr. Katz's suspicion — that Aaron had a leaking aortic valve. Because blood normally flowing directly from the left ventricular chamber into the aorta was backwashing into the heart through the leaking valve (aortic insufficiency), the left ventricular chamber of Aaron's heart was slightly enlarged. In addition, because the aortic valve did not fully close, pathogens could adhere to the rough surface of the valve, thus making it prone to infection (endocarditis).

Had Dr. Katz not recognized the tell-tale sound, and had Aaron not, since that time, had regular exams and echocardiograms to monitor his condition (a condition that requires no restriction of activity), and taken medications (antibiotics for dental work or any so-called dirty surgery, and a blood pressure medication to reduce the pressure on the enlarged ventricle), the consequences for him might have been grave indeed.

(William Osler, the famed Johns Hopkins physician, according to his biographer Michael Bliss, would tell his students that "if they did not do their business properly, when they got to heaven they would be met by large numbers of little children, shaking their fingers and saying, 'You sent us here.'")

There are also, my friends report, tangible costs that arise from our infatuation with technology, including the tendency for doctors to perform needless and costly interventions (screenings, angioplasties, bypasses), as well as interventions at which they are less than competent. Rich is incensed, for example, by the numbers of useless and often failed bypasses and angioplasties he has witnessed, and by the conflicts of interest that too often determine the kind and quality of treatment patients receive. His indignation and his fears are confirmed by others. Dr. Stephen Oesterle, director of interventional cardiology at Massachusetts General Hospital, for example, believes that "50 percent of the angioplasty that goes on is unnecessary" — a figure that translates to more than one hundred thousand unnecessary procedures a year in the United States alone.

In addition, many cardiologists and cardiac surgeons have financial interests in the companies whose products — stents, medications, catheters, surgical instruments — they use; many are investigators in clinical trials in whose outcomes they have a financial stake; and many go on the road as paid speakers to medical conventions and hospitals, promoting new drugs or devices in whose sale and use they have financial interests. Generally, too, patients will be totally unaware of these interests and conflicts of interest, or of the degree to which these interests influence diagnosis and treatment.

Technology companies survive and grow by innovating, a by-product of which is the continuing obsolescence of their products as they are replaced by newer ones, and so they inundate practicing physicians with new technologies, many of which have not been adequately tested. Before a complicated new system for opening arteries is in place, for example, a new one may arrive on the market to replace it. And while this, as Stephen Klaidman explains, "might be fine for cutting-edge cardiologists and cardiac surgeons who thrive on such challenges . . . it is not the best thing for average practitioners with average skills operating in small, understaffed community hospitals, or for their patients."

But patients rarely know that their local cardiologist, who may do only a few dozen balloon angioplasties a year, should not be doing complicated stent placements without proper training. "All they know," Klaidman writes, "is that they've seen an (often hyped-up) version of the new device or procedure in the news media or maybe even on the Internet, they want it, and they tell the local cardiologist, in effect, 'If you can't or won't do it, I'll find somebody else who will.' This creates pressure to use the latest technology, whatever it is . . ."

In *The Lost Art of Healing*, Nobel Prize–winning physician Bernard Lown, no stranger to the benefits of technology — Lown is the inventor of the defibrillator and of cardioversion for cardiac resuscitation, and is also responsible for many elements of the modern cardiac care unit — emphasizes the priority of listening to the patient and of taking a careful history. "The time invested in obtaining a meticulous history is never ill spent," he asserts. "Careful history-taking actually saves time. The history provides the road map; without it the journey is merely a shopping around at numerous garages for technological fixes."

"I am convinced," he writes, "that listening beyond the chief complaint is the most effective, quickest, and least costly way to get to the bottom of most medical problems. A British study showed that 75 percent of the information leading to a correct diagnosis comes from a detailed history, 10 percent from the physical examination, 5 percent from simple routine tests, 5 percent from all the costly invasive tests; [while] in 5 percent, no answer is forthcoming."

It does not seem at all nostalgic, then, to hear my friends quote the familiar saying that the secret of the care of the patient is in caring for the patient. "The good physician knows his patients through and through," Dr. Francis Peabody wrote in 1927, "and his knowledge is bought deeply. Time, sympathy and understanding must be lavishly dispensed, but the reward is to be found in that personal bond which forms the greatest satisfaction of the practice of medicine. One of the essential qualities of the clinician is interest in humanity, for the secret of the care of the patient is in caring for the patient."

In the weeks and months following surgery, I reflect, also, on elements of my experience that *are* truly anomalous but that have little to do with biology or technology: if I had not had the kind of excellent health insurance I had (a kind that allows me to use any doctor or hospital anywhere) and the job that allowed me this health insurance; and if I had not been as well connected as I was with doctors who knew me and listened to me; and if I had not received the prompt and expert medical care I received in an excellent hospital because of my insurance and my friendships; and if I had not had the self-confidence to persist in trying to discover why I was experiencing seemingly unexceptional symptoms; and if I had not had the education and the will (are there genetic markers for will, self-confidence, or persistence — medications that can bring them into being or correct their absence?) that enabled me to be in otherwise good health; and if I had not had the good health that allowed me to survive coronary artery disease and surgery without harmful or permanent side effects, would I be here to tell my tale?

I think of the hours I have spent on the phone with insurance companies, for my children and myself — trying to get coverage for procedures, arguing about referrals and reimbursements, calling again and again (I once logged more than three dozen calls — plus letters — in an attempt to get our provider to provide basic psychotherapy services), and wondering, in the midst of my own rising frustrations, how people without my determination and persistence — and/or people for whom English is not their native tongue — even got through the telephone menus one has to navigate simply to talk with a live human being. After an afternoon rich in such frustration, a friend of mine — a self-confident, articulate professional woman who is director of a large division of a major publishing company — responded to my tale of futility with one of her own: of how the week before, having to deal for most of an afternoon with her health insurance company, she had been left depleted and defeated. "I couldn't believe it," she said. "I got off the phone finally, closed my door, and just wept."

Consider, too, what happens to those who are not, like my friend and I, white, well educated, well insured, or insured at all. In all significant categories of mortality and morbidity, for example, blacks in America, like the poor in general, lag significantly behind whites, and it has been well established that this is largely a result of their receiving inferior medical care. For when blacks have access to the *same* quality of medical care, the results are markedly different. One recent study, for example, involving 39,190 men admitted for illness at 147 Veterans Administration hospitals, found that black patients treated at these hospitals had *lower* mortality rates than white patients for six common diseases — pneumonia, angina, congestive heart failure, chronic obstructive pulmonary disease, diabetes, and chronic kidney failure. Death rates at thirty days after admissions were 4.5 percent for blacks and 5.8 percent for whites, and this pattern also held true at six months and for longer stays.

I wonder also about the degree to which my attitude before and after surgery — the optimism Jerry found so unusual — contributed to the success of the surgery and to my swift recovery, and to what degree the friendship and affection of friends and family contributed to this attitude.

What my friends tell me they have seen again and again — the role a patient's attitude plays in a patient's ability to get well and recover, and often from conditions that prove fatal to those with less hopeful or optimistic attitudes — is something doctors see every day in their practice, and something they have seen throughout recorded history. (In his *Precepts,* Hippocrates, in the fifth century B.C., noted that "some patients, though conscious that their condition is perilous, recover their health simply through their contentment with the goodness of the physician," and Plato is said to have remarked that "the mere belief in the efficiency of a remedy will indeed help in a cure.")

I seemed anomalous because little in my condition or history indicated the need for or probability of bypass surgery, but perhaps the fact of bypass surgery itself, with its often spectacular successes, is, in the larger scheme of things medical, also anomalous. Perhaps, too, our gratitude for the existence of this and other instances of what we have come to call heroic medicine (bypasses, transplants, neonatal technologies) often blinds us to more fundamental and urgent medical needs.

For the two million people living with AIDS in the developed world, for example, the introduction of highly active antiretroviral treatment (HAART) in recent years has cut the rate of disease development and death from AIDS by over 90 percent. But for the more than thirty million HIV-infected people who live in poorer countries (including at least a half-million children who become infected each year), these drugs, largely because of their high costs, are not available, and so these men, women, and children are condemned to premature death.

Nor is it merely the availability, or lack of availability, of medications that proves decisive. Despite the demonstrated success of new AIDS medications, studies of a kind Jerry has been conducting at Yale tell us that the key element in the course of treatment — in whether a person gets well and stays well — is not medication, but *adherence:* whether or not the infected person takes his or her medications as prescribed (no easy thing, given the quantities and daily regimen required for what, in virtually all instances, become lifetime medications with nasty, debilitating, and dangerous side effects). Fewer than 50 percent do, and if one does not, the results are grave.

And the key element in whether or not one takes the medications is *trust* — whether or not the patient believes and trusts the doctor who prescribes the medications.

"Some of what I've come to understand," Jerry explains, "is that when you look at every route of AIDS transmission — whether it is drugs, sexual behavior, bathhouses, needles, urbanization, migrations, or social disruption — you see that what explains the widespread transmission is that they all have something to do with *how we live as human beings* much more than they do with the biology of the organism."

Phil explains that for people suffering from disabling neurological conditions — stroke, spinal cord injury, or brain injury — the best predictor of recovery and of a good rehabilitation outcome is whether or not the person has a strong family support system in place.

What Phil worried about most in my case, he says, was not the coronary artery disease or the surgery, but the fact that I had no wife or companion.

"I thought what happened to you was very frightening mostly because you were all alone and had only your children," he says. "I mean, your kids were adults, but they didn't have established families — and I thought: here you are, still in the position of being the primary caretaker for your kids and your brother and your mother — and all of a sudden you're helpless and in the clutches of a life-threatening illness. I mean, you could have had a stroke on the table — not uncommon in heart surgery — and what would have happened then?"

Phil talks about a patient I met in Denver — a woman who had been totally disabled by a stroke. "You would have been like her, and wound up in a nursing home for sure, because if you were like her, your kids couldn't take care of you," he says. "Without a strong family system, who's going to help you get better? Who's going to manage your affairs? It's not like one of your kids is a forty-year-old lawyer. So that was very difficult, and it just goes to show that we all live just one step away from a potentially lethal event. It's why I usually advise my patients not to go too far away from their support system if they have anything major done. It's why I voted with Jerry for you to go to Yale, where he could look after things, and not to Mass General, where nobody knew you."

When I say that if I'd had a stroke or been otherwise debilitated, surely he would have come by regularly, flying in for visits, he laughs. "Sure," he says. "I would have wiped the dribble from your face, and when I left I would have said, 'Thank goodness it's not me.' That's what people do. It's human nature to empathize as best we can, and when we get home to say, 'Thank God this didn't happen to me.'"

What matters, then — whether we talk of AIDS and antiretroviral therapies, heart disease and bypass surgery, or brain injuries and rehabilitation therapies — is not only what we know or don't know about the disease or about how to ameliorate its effects, but our ability to make what we know available to those in need of our knowledge and expertise.

"It's a cruel world, you know, and before 1940, if you had a paralysis you often died because you would get a skin infection, or a urinary tract infection, and we had no way of treating these, so you died," Phil says. "It was as simple as that." What we can now do for infectious diseases, he adds, is "the true miracle of our age," and though our gains in neurology have not been miraculous, we *have* made genuine progress — most specifically, through the advent of evacuation teams that start treating injuries right at the scene, as well as through new ways for treating brain swelling and new and better rehabilitation therapies in the treatment of trauma.

Like Phil, my other friends extol the virtues of our new medical knowledge and technologies, and the ways these have eased the burden of disease in their specialties. Arthur talks about how the discipline of psychology, especially with regard to depression, has been revolutionized by antidepressant medications. Jerry talks about new AIDS medications and new ways of employing them, and he tells me that in 1999, for the first time since the early eighties, when he worked in the Bronx during the outbreak of the AIDS epidemic, not a single one of his AIDS patients died. And Rich talks about how the treatment of heart disease, and especially of heart attacks, has been revolutionized by the advent of the coronary care unit, the monitors that detect potentially lethal heart rhythm disturbances, and the stent angioplasty and clot-buster drugs that dissolve clots that might otherwise kill people.

But my friends all add a cautionary note: that our new technologies promise good only if used wisely and judiciously — if, that is, we maintain a clear-eyed and humane view of the ways medicine remains both a science *and* an art, and if we remember to remind ourselves of how little we truly know.

What happened to me, Phil reminds me, happened the way it did — diagnosis *and* treatment — precisely because we do *not* know what causes atherosclerosis. Because we don't, we had to crack open my chest *after* the disease was advanced and perform a procedure that involved a team of highly trained and high-priced professionals. (The cost, for my surgery and hospitalization, came to more than sixty thousand dollars.) In addition, bypasses, along with angioplasties, are often less than fully successful. According to the National Heart, Lung, and Blood Institute, 8 percent of individuals who had bypass surgery and 54 percent of those who had angioplasty needed another surgical procedure within five years. Nor, in two-thirds of all cases, does surgery or angioplasty provide any proven survival benefit over drugs. What benefit is provided —

mostly pain relief and exercise tolerance — comes at a price: a combined risk of death, nonfatal heart attack, stroke, and infection that adds up to 6 or 7 percent in the case of surgery and, in the case of angioplasties and angioplasties combined with stenting, a 20 to 40 percent probability of one or more repeat procedures (one of which may be surgery).

Moreover, a study published in the *New England Journal of Medicine* (February 2001) concludes that 42 percent of patients who have undergone bypass surgery show "a significant mental decline," due most probably to brain damage caused by the surgery. (In this study, subjects were considered to have declined mentally if test performances that could not be attributed to aging were at least 20 percent lower than their scores before surgery.) In addition, at least 5 percent of women and 3 percent of men die during bypass surgery.

When we understand what causes a disease, and the biological mechanism that enables it to do its damage, Phil explains, things become much simpler. Look at all the polio and TB wards and sanitariums that no longer exist, he says. And someday, if and when we know what causes atherosclerosis, he predicts, all these screenings, angioplasties, transplants, cardiac care units, and the rest will become things of the past. "Once we know these things —" Phil says, "— and this was the great triumph of the early part of the century, with respect to a host of infectious diseases — we have a much better shot at *managing* disease, and at doing so in much less complicated and less costly ways."

In the meantime, we make do with what Lewis Thomas has termed "halfway technologies" — patch-up procedures that ameliorate or fix symptoms but neither cure disease nor address the causes of disease. More than a quarter century ago, Thomas defined these technologies as "the kinds of things that must be done after the fact, in efforts to compensate for the incapacitating effects of certain diseases whose course one is unable to do very much about." The outstanding examples of these technologies "in recent years," he wrote, "are the transplantation of hearts, kidneys, livers, and other organs, and the equally spectacular inventions of artificial organs."

"In the public mind," Thomas explained, "this kind of technology has come to seem like the equivalent of high technologies of the physical sciences. The media tend to present each new procedure as though it represented a breakthrough and therapeutic triumph, instead of the makeshift that it really is." But, he continued, "this level of technology is, by its nature, at the same time highly sophisticated and profoundly primitive. It is the kind of thing that one must continue to do until there is a genuine understanding of the mechanisms involved in disease."

Thomas contrasted the complex and costly technologies for the management of both heart disease and cancer with the type of technology that is effective because "it comes as the result of a genuine understanding of disease mechanisms" — such as immunizations for childhood viral diseases and the use of antibiotics and chemotherapy for bacterial infections. And when such technologies become available, they are "relatively inexpensive, and relatively easy to deliver."

Sometimes, when I review our conversations and reflect on the world the five of us came from, I wonder how much of our resistance to seeing technological procedures displace human interactions between doctor and patient derives from values present in the lower-middle-class, Brooklyn Jewish world in which we grew up. Is our concern for the well-being of others, especially for those dispossessed of the essentials of life, merely a consequence of having been nurtured by a generation of Jewish immigrants and first-generation Jewish Americans, and by those habits and values specific to our parents' generation — by those socialist views and rabbinic teachings that formed and informed our parents' lives and our coming of age?

But to speculate about how our intense work ethic, or our love of books and learning, or our capacity for self-discipline, frustration tolerance, and perseverance were nurtured in the Brooklyn of our childhood (the schoolyard's Golden Rule: *"If you keep making the right moves, eventually the shots fall"*), or to consider how, where, and why we all seem to share, as if it were a genetic inheritance, an ambition and desire to leave the world a better place than we found it — all this need not diminish the value of what we may actually have done.

Rich often describes Jerry's devotion to AIDS patients as "saintly," and when I tell Phil this, he agrees. "When I think of Jerry I always think of the old Boston Blackie radio show," he says. "Remember how it went? *'Boston Blackie — friend to those who have no friends.'* That was Jerry. He made his modus operandi the bringing of quality care to people on the fringes of society, to drug addicts and the homeless and the poor — to the people medicine left behind. To be a Harvard doctor in the sixties and to go into Dorchester and Roxbury the way Jerry did was not the usual thing. Harvard academia didn't see the value of what they considered nonscientific medicine, or medicine that had a social basis and content. And when it came to AIDS, Jerry was a very brave man. He leapt right in with both feet, and made a real contribution."

Phil and I talk about some of the specific contributions Jerry made — discovering, at a time when people wanted to ostracize and quarantine everyone with AIDS, that one could not transmit AIDS through casual contact but only through blood and genital secretions; persuading the Centers for Disease Control and Prevention that AIDS was transmitted not only by homosexual men but also by heterosexuals — and Phil also reminds me that there were surgeons back then who refused to operate on people with AIDS for fear of contracting the disease themselves. "If this is what you did every day in your life as a doctor, would *you* risk dying?" Phil asks. "But Jerry just leapt in."

At the same time, while Phil sees Jerry as a true hero, he doesn't see him as being more noble than anyone else. "Jerry does what he does because he doesn't have a choice," Phil says. "He couldn't be a high-priced lawyer screwing people because that's not who he is. He's like Jane Goodall with the monkeys. She had to spend her life the way she did, and Jerry spends his life the way he does, as a doctor trying to help people other doctors don't usually care about. It's what he was made for so that's what he does."

Later, when I read Phil's comments about Jane Goodall back to him, he laughs. "Did I really say that?" he asks.

Phil's no-nonsense way of seeing things often serves as a useful corrective to my tendency not only to idealize others, but to make of my own life what I might want some other writer to make of it were I the hero in that writer's book. I am only mildly surprised, then, when I review my journal entries for the periods before and after surgery, to find that I've done it again — that the story I've been telling others is less than fully consistent with what actually happened at the time.

In the story I've been giving out to others, until Rich exploded and told me he wanted me in a hospital as soon as possible, *everything* in my life was just fine. The proof? I was swimming a mile a day until just a few days before surgery, I had no traditional symptoms or risk factors, and I was more free from stress than I had been in years (my children were well launched, my writing career was thriving, I had no financial problems for the first time in ages), yet everyone, including my doctors — two of whom "missed" the diagnosis — was surprised to discover how severely advanced my heart disease was. Phil confirms this version of my story. "I remember that it was a very unusual event," he says. "You were in great shape and you had no risk factors — so I couldn't understand why you would have coronary disease."

What Jerry recalls is my attitude before and after surgery. Since he too thought I had no significant risk factors or symptoms, Jerry was shocked when he discovered how advanced my coronary disease was. "How could this be real?" he remembers saying when Dr. Cabin showed him the results of the angiogram. "You were hanging by a thread," he tells me. "I mean — imagine! — you were walking through the valley of the shadow — and it turned out to be much much more serious than we thought it would be. But the amazing thing about you was your positive attitude — that you were immediately accepting and trusting of the intervention and said, 'Just do what you have to do.' Often in this kind of situation the first response is denial. People say, 'You must be talking about somebody else,' or 'Why did this happen to me?' But you immediately said, 'Aren't I lucky this was caught in time and something could be done about it, so go ahead.'"

Jerry talks about the relaxed evening we had in his home the night before the angiogram, and he reminds me that we had done the same thing just two weeks before that, when I'd come down to Yale to give a talk for the medical school faculty in their series "Medicine and the Humanities." He also remembers cautioning me about the fact that most people become depressed after surgery — especially heart surgery — something he had seen frequently following serious illnesses.

"But this didn't happen either," he says. "You never seemed depressed or anything but positive. At every point you kept on saying how grateful and fortunate you were, and I thought that was amazing."

The truth, though, is that I was scared shitless. Despite the face I showed to the world *and* to friends and family (no matter the troubles or disasters taking place at home, for those beyond our immediate families, we were all trained to put a sign in every window of our lives that said, "Business is Good"), and despite the seeming absence of symptoms and risk factors, I was, especially before the angiogram, worried, depressed, and frightened: worried that something was terribly the matter with me, frightened that I was going to die imminently, and depressed because I believed I was going to die alone.

4

It's Not Viral, Goddamnit!

LESS THAN TWO MONTHS before surgery — on December 21, 1998, the winter equinox — while swimming my usual mile at the Northampton YMCA, I become suddenly and alarmingly short of breath. Most days I swim seventy-two lengths of the twenty-five-yard pool in slightly under thirty-six minutes, but on this day I find myself gasping for air after swimming only eight lengths. I rest for a minute or so at the shallow end of the pool, resume swimming, and after another eight lengths the same thing happens: I am sucking air as if I've just run a grueling series of wind sprints.

I get out of the pool, shower, drive home, and call my family doctor, David Katz. I talk with his nurse, describe what happened, and she sees nothing to be especially concerned about. When I ask for an appointment, the nurse, looking at my chart, notes that I have not had a regular checkup in more than two and a half years. She schedules me for an office visit in four weeks time, on January 18, 1999.

My journal entry for this day — seven and a half weeks before surgery — begins as follows:

December 22, 1998
Strange experience. Swimming at 545 [PM], find myself breathless, unable to continue. I rest, after 8 laps, then try again, and go another 8, but dont push my luck. Seems to be anxiety. *Seems?* For sure. Had

been having increasing trouble of late, during first 24 lengths — would begin to feel that irritating pain between shoulder blades, after about 16 . . . but then, after doing 24, resting, would be fine for the next 24 or 36 or 48 . . . but decided not to be counterphobic. Sense: all the anxieties and sadnesses and fears (re death, being unloved, aging) somehow focusing between those shoulder blades, and in constriction of chest muscles.

What irritating pain, increasing trouble, and constriction of chest muscles? When, two years after surgery, during the week of February 12, 2001, I read through my journal entries for the days and months preceding December 22, 1998, I find no mention of pain between my shoulder blades, constriction of my chest muscles, or difficulties swimming. Given that my daily entries are lengthy and self-indulgent in the extreme — two to three pages, generally, of typed single-spaced prose filled with rambling enumerations of this kind of mundane detail — I am surprised.

What also surprises — memory, as ever, being the great editor — is that not only do I find no mention of these problems before December 22, but that even now I have no memory of having *had* these problems before December 21.

Going through my 1998 journal entries, the only items I find having anything to do with my health are occasional mentions of feeling slightly tired when swimming, which feeling I have been attributing to two things: the fact that I've been away from home and traveling a lot; and the fact that I have been upset — and unable, often, to sleep — because, over a period of several months, of the deterioration of a relationship with a woman, Ellen, which relationship I ended on December 1, 1998.

The December 22 journal entry continues: "hope it's not some incipient angina! (do realize-cf dan reeves, marvin newman [a friend who had a bypass operation] — that by my age, many men have had angioplastys, bypasses, etc. . . . but will see how i do today. try to relax, and see if there is a physical problem, or if this is anxiety. do find self a bit more breathless after long walks, stairs, etc . . ."

The day before, returning from New York City, where I have spent time with Eli, with Robert (helping him look for a place to live for the time when he is discharged from the state mental hospital), and with friends, I make no mention of my health.

On the morning of December 22, I list events of the previous day: lunch with a friend (who brings me a certified chunk of the Brooklyn Bridge her father, recently deceased, had given to her); a call from *Nightline* about interviewing me; a decision to return a pair of shoes that are uncomfortable; communication with Yale Medical School concerning my upcoming talk there; the purchase of a bottle of champagne for friends who are getting married; a talk with Robert about our time together; a talk with Miriam, who is heading to California with Seth, et cetera.

I also write about visiting a friend, Norman Kotker, who has just been moved into a local nursing home. Norman has had multiple sclerosis for more than a quarter century, and the prognosis is not good.

> Visit Norman [and] when i turn into driveway and see the place — Pine Manor Extended Care Facility — I become enraged, and just start shouting FUCK OH FUCK FUCK FUCK, NORMAN! . . . how terribly unjust life can be . . . damn and damn and damn

> norman v v weak . . . says: "people here are more decrepit than i am." he has a small shelf of his published books, has his word processor, but has no strength at all. sadness incarnate.

The next day I have only minor difficulty while swimming. ("Swim goes well — anxiety lessens. I do 18, then 18, then another 18. A bit of suck-chest after first 18, but by last 18, swimming smoothly and easily and could do more.") And on the following day, though I swim a mile and a quarter without difficulty, I tell myself that it's time to make an appointment with my psychotherapist, whom I have been seeing once or twice a year for the past half-dozen years.

On December 27, I write about becoming "tight in chest and a bit breathless around 14–18; but after that do another 26 and easier." The next day, this: "then nautilus and a swim. Have to stop at 17 lengths, rather than test self re loss of breath . . . but then go to 54 with no trouble. will check this out with dr katz at january physical."

I am looking forward to spending the first week of 1999 with

Miriam, Seth, and Eli in London (Aaron is unable come because of his work schedule), where I have rented a house for us in the Kensington Gardens area. Happy as I am about this reunion, however, as the time of departure and the end of the year approach, my anxieties about my health, and my life, intensify.

December 29: "Decent day, but v anxious, nervous, etc . . . hard getting used to being alone (tho to others, it would seem, i do it well, have an enviable life: last nite — Jerry Friedland hesitates, and then says what he is thinking, and hopes I dont take it wrong way: but that *his* ideal would be to have *my* life!)."

Immediately after this: "trouble swimming again: I go 18 laps, then 12, then 18 . . . shoot some hoops for first time in a while, and find some shortness of breath there too."

"It may just be 60 years old, neug," I write, "but but: why has it started — this shortness of breath, right after breakup with Ellen?" I continue: "clearly, a fear I can't make it — dont have the stamina, etc. . . . a panic at being alone (and recall that in childhood, early early, to ward off my mother, and maintain separateness, I held my breath till i was blue in the face) . . . well: can work some of this thru, but mostly it will work thru in the living. No need to test myself re swimming . . . we will pay attention."

But why, given all the ordinary reasons to have shrugged off or explained away the shortness of breath, *did* I pay attention? I was rarely sick, went years without having even a common cold, and just as rarely called or went to the doctor (witness the two-and-a-half-year hiatus between exams). In more than thirty years of teaching, I had never missed a day because of illness. I never took flu shots, and the last time I had had the flu was eight years before, at the start of Eli's senior year of high school. When I took myself to bed that fall, Eli had become frightened, he told me then, because he could not remember *ever* having seen me sick.

About the only worries concerning my health I find in journal entries through the years (this also proves true when I go through my medical records) have to do with muscles torn, pulled, or bruised while playing ball. Now, however, I am speculating daily on possible reasons for shortness of breath, fatigue, burning sensations and pain between my shoulder blades, and "incipient angina."

In the absence of any clear organic causes for distress, my usual tendency is to look for physical causes for physical problems — I'm out of breath because I'm out of shape and getting older; I'm tired because I'm not sleeping well — and for emotional and psychological explanations for emotional problems, and for those conditions, often physical, that I believe are being brought on, at least in part, by emotions: I am worrying about my heart, then, because I am beginning to believe that loneliness and loss have worn me down in some irreparable way, and because, having recently ended the relationship with Ellen, I fear my heart may finally, in some terribly literal way, be breaking.

On December 30, I set down my last entry for the year:

> oh so anxious re stuff: begin to think the swimming anxiety is focusing my fears of aging — have i blown it all? have i used up my chances with eligible women I could care for and who could care for me? Begin to notice that the problem is in my throat, which begins to shut down after about 14 lengths . . . this also when walking fast: and then it loosens up. But I decide not to push and test myself just to "prove" i can do it: for the proof wont allay the anxieties: we want to allay them from within, and in good, lasting ways. Also: being alone, without a woman = nonexistence emotionally: what my mother taught me in all kinds of ways. and when i am at the pool, about to do my mile, i am alone, vs the elements (cf the 100 Gormley men in the water in norway, looking out to sea). I do 18 pretty easily yesterday — sense i can go and do more: but want to get to garage in time to get new tires . . .

In this final entry for 1998, I look back over events of the past year, talk with myself about things I am looking forward to in 1999 — the publication of a new book (*Transforming Madness*), Miriam and Seth's wedding, getting started on a new book, Robert's discharge from the hospital — and I close by wishing myself a happy new year. "So, here's to a good and safe trip, and to a healthy, happy, surprising 1999 for all those I love," I write, and add: "and for me too."

On our third or fourth day in London, Miriam, Seth, Eli, and I climb to the top of St. Paul's Cathedral — 629 steps, the last section a long, narrow, spiral staircase — and I do so without having to stop at landings and without difficulties. The day after this, in chilly weather and at a brisk pace, we walk for five or six hours across the city — from our house in DeVere Gardens, across Kensington Gardens, Hyde Park, Green Park, St. James Park, all the way to the Tower of London and London Bridge, and then along the Thames and back home again — and I do so without experiencing any pain, fatigue, or shortness of breath.

I have arrived in London on the last day of 1998 (Seth, Miriam, and Eli fly in on New Year's Day), and I spend New Year's Eve with friends. In my first journal entry after returning to Northampton, this: "spend time with donna and bob [Donna and I grew up together; she babysat me and Robert when we were children], and that is deliteful. gorgeous dinner at stanley and annabel meadows for new years eve, and then a party afterwards, where a gorgeous young woman comes on to me . . ."

Months later, when we know that on New Year's Eve my coronary arteries were nearly 100 percent blocked, we will wonder what angel was looking after me when I made the choice I made that night. For at the New Year's Eve party I spend most of my time with an attractive young woman ("She looks just like that actress — Jennifer Jason Leigh," Donna whispers to me) who appears to be in her late twenties or early thirties. We talk, flirt, dance, touch, laugh, and drink lots of champagne. About an hour and a half into the New Year, Donna and Bob come to me while the woman and I are dancing, to wish me a Happy New Year again and to tell me they're leaving.

"I'll leave with you," I say.

Donna and Bob can't believe it. Nor, when I wish her a Happy New Year and say good night, can the young woman, who urges me to stay. The next day I will tell Donna that happy and ardent as I was feeling, it seemed a good idea at the time to follow a suggestion Miriam, now thirty years old, made some years before: that I never go out with women younger than her.

And after the surgery, we will recall that at our New Year's Eve dinner, Stanley Meadows had told a story about Joe E. Lewis and Benny Hill and how, one night when the three of them were performing together in a London music hall, and Benny Hill had finally prevailed upon a very beautiful and much younger woman to go out with him after the show, Joe E. Lewis had smiled and, waving goodby, said to Benny: "If you get lucky, she'll kill you."

"A brief welcome home entry, with more to come," I write on January 8, 1999, my first morning back in Northampton. I tell, in summary fashion, about the New Year's Eve party and the lovely times with my children, then add: "yet i am doleful, sad, in the extreme at times." A few lines later: "concerned re the breathlessness, and possible heart stuff. damn! fuck."

For the next ten days I keep scrupulous track of how many lengths of the pool I swim, how often I have to stop, how well or poorly I am sleeping, how much pain I am having between my shoulder blades, and, given my emotional state, now labile in the extreme, I spend more and more time, in longer and longer entries, indulging in and rationalizing away my fears:

To sleep near 1 AM, and wake just past 5. Feeling ok tho: best when working on book . . . but when i take a break, the loneliness settles in, bone deep. [January 9]

miserable snowstorms all around us . . . ice, then 8 inches of snow, then rain, then snow, then sleet . . . i take my time shoveling . . . v glad to be having physical monday. almost laugh re my anxieties: yes, i became breathless, etc, anxious (minor panic disorder?) . . . but jay: you did climb to top of st pauls . . . you did do 50 pushups . . . but want to get to bottom of the loss of breath, and, during walks, the burning sensation betw shoulder blades [January 15]

The sweetest, easiest most peaceful feeling mid day yesterday — and again before sleep: the book is done, and all is well. I swim an easy 48 lengths, without breathlessness — 24 + 24, and am less breathless at end than I have been when i stopped at 12 or 10 or 18. so, diagnosis: acute anxiety re being able to make it. [January 17]

"Annual physical today — first in 2½ years! — and eager to get david's diagnosis, if any, re shortness of breath," I write on the morning of January 18. The next morning I report the results.

January 19, 1999

Good news at physical exam. Blood pressure not a problem. Starts at 150/90 — but goes down, on next readings, to 130/84.

No other problems. Talk over the shortness of breath with David, and he recommends a stress test — to see if any coronary disease, incipient or there. But the more we talk, the more he tends toward interp of late-blooming mild asthma. Confirmed a bit when he gives me basic breath strength test — blow into a tube. I come out below average for age and size, whereas given my good condition, we would expect at least average or above average.

I give Dr. Katz a detailed description of my symptoms and also talk with him about the breakup with Ellen and my feelings of depression. Since I have never had a stress test, Dr. Katz suggests I schedule myself for one with a local cardiologist, Dr. Flynn, and if that proves negative, as he expects it will, we might see about a pulmonary function test. Noting that the quality of the air in our region of New England is especially bad (pollution from industries in the Midwest settling over the Connecticut Valley), and given my below-average score when I blow into a tube (he jokes about the cardboard tube, called a peak flow meter, being state-of-the-art technology), his best guess is that I am suffering from a mild case, not unusual in our area of Massachusetts, of adult-onset or exercise-induced asthma. He gives me a prescription for an inhaler and suggests, should the shortness of breath continue or increase, that I take one or two puffs from it before swimming.

In my journal, this: "go for a swim, and feel again the constriction start in throat and chest, high up — also: cold weather and asthma discomfort go together, as with me. but: schedule for stress test [the first appointment I can get is in three weeks time: for February 5] . . . and may or may not get breathalizer, to see if that helps."

Despite the fact that Dr. Katz, like his nurse four weeks before, sees little likelihood of coronary artery disease, and nothing urgent about my condition, my own sense of urgency — fueled by my loneliness — mounts.

"Busyness will only stave off loneliness for so long," I write, a day after the exam. "Nobody to talk to about the ordinary stuff of life on an ordinary day. Miss that dearly . . . MLKing jr day [and] i weep away, while listening to spirituals: Marian Anderson and others — 'Give me Jesus' 'Deep River' . . . i am washed away with feeling . . . just so so sad sometimes . . ." The entry ends with a two-word paragraph: "sadness reigns."

I continue to keep a record of my problems while swimming and exercising, and for a few days I try to believe — who wouldn't? — that Dr. Katz is right: what I have is asthma, and not heart disease.

Less than a week after the exam, the shortness of breath while swimming coming more often and at shorter intervals, I decide to try the inhaler. I telephone Dr. Katz to tell him about my concerns. In my medical record for this day, Dr. Katz's entry:

> January 24, 1999
> Phone call:
> He has been monitoring his breathing difficulties while swimming. On a normal day he will swim up to 24 lengths w/o stopping. At times when his chest gets tight he will stop after 8 lengths and recuperate and then swim more shorter intervals. He also gets some tightness when he walks out in the cold. One of his sons has similar sx [symptoms]. His father died at age 70 [72]of emphysema. I had given him a prescription for an inhaler which I recommended taking 1 or 2 puffs of prior to swimming. He does have an ETT [stress test] scheduled in about 1½ wks.

The inhaler, alas, doesn't help, and when it doesn't, I return to my sense that there is something terribly wrong with my heart, and with my life. "worried re my heart," I write, "tho david thinks it is asthma. but i take puffs of the stuff and it doesn't seem to make a diff. I do 14 lengths pretty easily, but then the pool goes from 6 lanes to 2, and I am not up to fighting and circling and the rest . . . a bit of panic, apprehension, anxiety here."

At the same time that my anxieties about my heart are increasing, I continue to record everyday occurrences that, in their happy abundance, would seem to belie anxiety. Among other events itemized on the day I first use the inhaler, for example: I talk with Miriam about wedding plans; I talk with a friend and former student, Bret Lott, whose novel has been chosen by Oprah Winfrey for her book club; I work on a course in Jewish American literature I'll be teaching in the spring at UMass; I make final revisions on my novel. I also write about looking forward to driving down to New Haven the next day, where I will give a talk at the medical school, spend time with Jerry and Gail, and attend the closing on their new house with them.

Despite what seems a full, rich, and good life — and despite my trying to convince myself that it *is* a full, rich, and good life — my loneliness continues bone deep, and for the first time I find I am asking the same question Phil will ask: "but i do feel so alone. and with the drug not making a diff (on the first day), the isolation leads to that other realization: *Who will take care of Jay?*"

Ellen telephones, and talks about how she wants to get back together, and to care for me. Given the burdens in her own life (a ten-year-old son with a disability that requires constant, exhausting attentions), this seems to me as impossible in the future as it has proven to be in the past. ("I didn't want to say anything before," Miriam says to me in London, "but after all the years of raising the three of us and taking care of your brother and of Grandma, what were you doing with a woman with a disabled son?" A busman's holiday? I reply. Miriam smiles, and repeats what she and her brothers have said before: "It's your time now, Dad.")

On January 26 I report on a conversation I have with Robert's social worker, who urges me to talk with Robert about how he will spend his days when he's back in the city.

> i call robert at about 9 [PM], and he yells at me for waking him ... and i feel so fucking lousy: same old, same old ... not to be able to say back: hey, go fuck yourself — where do you get off treating me like this???

> evening, after swim, sans progress [with inhaler], I am really worried that the pain between shoulder blades is some kind of blockage at the aorta ...

But if I'm in such good shape, and if I have little in my history that suggests the possibility of coronary artery disease, and if my doctor diagnoses asthma and sees no urgency about checking out heart disease, why, even while in part of me I was rationalizing away symptoms, did I, at the same time, feel more and more certain that something was gravely wrong? Why, that is, were my intimations of mortality at least as strong as my inclination to denial?

On January 27, before I drive down to New Haven, I telephone Rich.

we shmooze and i ask if he minds my checking in re problem, and i go thru it with him . . . he asks me to fax him results [of the stress test], and not to hesitate re talking. also says: everything else is in my favor — 200 cholesterol, low weight, no smoking, exercise, etc . . . it is rare for pain to be in mid back, but it does happen . . . what we want to do is to exclude things: so let us check this out . . . at our age, we need to pay attention to stuff. but even if we find something, there are lots of things we can do.

rich: sign of heart [disease] is that exercise makes the pain come, and then it goes away . . .

During our conversation, I also mention that once before — a year and a half ago — I had gone to see my doctor about pain between my shoulder blades. The pain had been there, on and off, for some time, and I had ignored it until, during a talk with my cousin Jerrold, who lives in Jerusalem, I had asked about his father's death. Had it been peaceful? Jerrold said it had — that his father (my father's younger brother, and the youngest of nine), eighty-two at the time, had been sitting at the table with them, eating and talking, when, after complaining of pain in his back, he had suddenly slumped over, and died.

I called for an appointment that day, and I saw Dr. Katz three weeks later. Dr. Katz did an EKG and, based on our conversation and my having noticed that the pain, which could last anywhere from one to ten minutes, sometimes occurred in the middle of the night, or when writing had drained me and I needed food, concluded (this from his notation in my medical record): "cardiac etiology of the pain is extremely unlikely. Thoracic [chest] aneurysm also unlikely. Most likely etiology may be gastrointestinal such as esophageal reflux or spasm."

Looking back, one wonders if this pain — persisting for at least four years — was related to what may then have been, or have been becoming, coronary artery disease. I recall, too, and describe for Dr. Katz — as I now do for Rich — a time when, flying to Europe two years before this on my way to teach for a semester at the University of Freiburg in Germany, I awoke in the middle of the night in a very dark, quiet, and mostly empty plane (I was stretched out across several seats), to find my heart pounding away. I was sweating profusely, and felt a pain so severe in the middle of my back — along with dizziness and faintness — that I recall thinking, as if it were the simplest fact: *I am dying.* And then, as if from a Henry James story: *So — is it here, at last, the great thing?* I remember being afraid to get up and walk to a flight attendant to ask for help (afraid I was so weak and dizzy I might not make it), or to buzz for one and thereby create a crisis, and I recall thinking too: *Well, Neugie, if this is it, this is it.*

I had had some champagne before the in-flight meal, a glass or two of red wine with the meal, and cognac after the meal, and at the time I attributed the pain, dizziness, and weakness, along with the booming of my heart and the distinct sensation that if I did not simply lie there and wait — if, instead, I rose and tried to do anything — I would keel over and die, to a variety of possibilities: to the mixture of champagne, wine, and cognac; to being apprehensive about being on my own for the first time in many years; to a touch of the stomach flu; to in-flight turbulence while I was asleep; to a nightmare — night terrors? — I'd had but could recall only vaguely; to being in transition from the known (my life as single parent in Northampton) to the unknown (life as a single guy in a city and nation foreign to me), and to who-knew-what-else.

So I lay there quietly, and after a while I sat up, put my head down between my legs, and waited. In about seven or eight minutes, the physical symptoms, and the fear, passed.

Like Dr. Katz, Rich doesn't see any connection between this experience and what I am experiencing now. But who knows? Rich says. Maybe the pain in my back two years before was a symptom of coronary disease, and maybe it wasn't. And yes, he says, given the manner of your uncle's death, your father's heart attack at fifty-nine (which he survived), your symptoms, and *your* age (fifty-nine), the doctor probably should have ordered a stress test for you back then. But hindsight is easy, and the main thing now is to pay attention to the symptoms, and for us to stay in close touch with each other.

And this — staying in close touch with Rich about my symptoms — is exactly what, in my memory, I believed I had been doing all along.

When, after surgery, I begin telling my story to others, I am certain I was talking with Rich nearly every day beginning with the day on which I first had an episode of shortness of breath. More than this: in my memory, not only had I called Rich as soon as I came home from the YMCA, but I had also immediately telephoned Arthur, Jerry, and Phil, and then had begun checking in with each of them regularly.

When I go through my journal, however, I discover that it was not until I had seen Dr. Katz — four weeks *after* the shortness of breath first occurred — that I began talking with Rich and my friends about my symptoms and anxieties. I discover, too, that once Dr. Katz told me that what I was describing didn't seem to indicate major heart problems, rather than being reassured, I became *more* convinced than ever that I *had* heart disease.

What was happening, I now believe, is that I was trusting what I was feeling more than what my doctor was telling me. Was I, as we commonly say, "listening to what my body was telling me"? Perhaps. But what I was experiencing in my body was in no way separate from what I was, in my mind, thinking — and what I was thinking seemed in no way separate from what I was feeling. More exactly: I found myself believing that my fears, anxieties, and premonitions, along with my bodily symptoms, were not unrelated to what I knew to be true; and what I knew to be true came to me in words that seemed quite plain: physically *and* spiritually, I was suffering from a sickness unto death.

On the day I first call Rich to talk with him about my concerns and about Dr. Katz's diagnosis, I also talk with my father, who died at the age of seventy-two in 1976.

Ever since his death, when I'm especially troubled or have had especially good news, and usually when driving, I will talk with him, and our conversations invariably help me through to seeing things as they are and to understanding and articulating what I'm feeling about them. Conjuring up his presence — "Hey, Dad, it's me again," I'll begin, aloud — I will look upward through the windshield and usually find him floating in the sky, Chagall-like, just above the car. In our talks I'll generally report, first, on what's going on with my children (his grandchildren), with Robert, and with my mother (his "Shugie" who, afflicted with Alzheimer's since 1992, has been living in a nursing home). Giving him basic family news, though, is merely prelude.

Although my father was a failure in worldly matters — he never earned a living from his own businesses, went bankrupt before he was fifty, and spent the rest of his life as a clerk in a stationery store — and ineffectual and submissive at home, his judgment always seemed to me sound, and he seemed never to complicate things more than was necessary. Given the grim and unhappy nature of so much of his life, it was a mystery and wonder that this was so.

"Shit or get off the pot," was his routine response if I expressed indecision. If I invited his opinion about a specific situation — should I do A, or should I do B? — he never turned the question back to me (as in: "Well, what do *you* think you should do?"); but instead would give a direct Yes or No answer — Do A, don't do B — and if I asked for reasons, he gave them without elaboration: C, D, E, F, G.

Though for most of his married life he was consumed by frustration and rage (he had a violent temper, and would often slap me and knock me around) — ashamed because he could not support our family and give our mother the life he wanted to provide for her, and humiliated regularly by my mother for his failure to do so — and though he and I, until the last few years of his life, were seldom able to have an easy, extended conversation, I had come to count on his direct, no-nonsense opinions and responses. More often, though, fearful of coming to him with a problem since doing so could make him attack and humiliate me, I relied on what I imagined he *might* have said to me had he been capable of being the man he wished he could be, and the man I wished he would be.

And so, when times are especially good, or particularly difficult, I conjure up his spirit, and we talk. At these times, though imagined, he is totally present; though kind and loving, he is brutally honest; though idealized, he is the most realistic and practical of men.

We talk most of the way down to Guilford to Jerry and Gail's new home and on the way back from New Haven the following day, and words, feelings, and tears flow easily and in abundance. As often happens during these conversations, his good judgment and his kindness — both having increased enormously with the passage of time — help me through.

After giving him news about his grandchildren, his wife, my forthcoming book, and Robert, I tell him that all is not well: that I am becoming more and more certain my heart is fatally diseased — broken, flawed, failing — and that I am frightened I am going to die soon.

I immediately apologize for complaining — of course I realize how blessed I am: in my work, my job, my home, my friends, my children — and I start talking about people I know who have *real* troubles and who don't have the wherewithal in life I have, and when I do, my father interrupts me. "Listen, sonny boy," he says, "it doesn't matter what troubles — what *tsuris* — others have. Your *tsuris* is still your *tsuris* and you shouldn't bury it."

Do I remember a radio play I was in, he asks, called "No Shoes" — about a man who complained because he had no shoes until he met a man who had no feet?

"Well, it's certainly not so hot to have no feet," my father says. "But if you have no shoes — like now, in the middle of winter — that's not so hotsy-totsy either."

"Not a lot of time to dwell on the sweetness of being with Jerry for two days, [or] my talk to Yale doctors," I write on my return, and then: "my ride there and back, alone. Weeping when i talk with my dad and tell him just how scared i am — that I might have heart problems and nobody to take care of me . . . this is what hurts more than the problems."

The day after this, I take myself to my psychotherapist's office for the first time in more than a year. "Going to session with D. v v helpful: a way of talking here that i cant quite do with friends," I write. "And we agree that i will go for 6–8 weeks, and get some work done on me — not my children, not Ellen, not etc . . . but me, and the elusiveness of what i have always desired so deeply: love and companionship."

The next day I travel down to New York City by train, where I meet with my editor and publicist and spend time with Eli. I also, this week, begin regularly telephoning Arthur, Jerry, and Phil.

Two days later, upon my return to Northampton:

V worried re my health. V clear in the city — walking any distance in v cold weather, and the pain starts — usually between shoulder blades, and often, too, in chest . . . shit!

I find myself having to go inside stores — or looking for pretexts to. Granted, it is bitter bitter cold, and etc . . .

the usual from all — helfant, et al — is: get it checked out, which i am doing. but i am so fearful that i am just going to keel over. also: sense of aging — failing of powers, etc.

I now write at greater and greater length in my journal, and do so not only first thing in the morning, but in the evening too. I keep itemizing all the things I have to be happy about, as if to convince myself there is no reason to be depressed, and I write about my talks with my friends ("all the buddies call back — sounds to [Phil] like exercise induced asthma. the stress test will show . . . also suggests chest xray [to check for dissection of aorta], and to call him after. sure you worry, he says. one day, you're fine, and suddenly . . .").

I telephone Dr. Katz, who suggests I get some nitroglycerine, and that I take it when the pain comes and see if it stops the pain. He is now more inclined, given my descriptions, to suspect coronary disease, and he advises me to go easy between now (Tuesday evening) and Friday morning, when I am scheduled for the stress test.

relieved, at first: to have somebody say — maybe it is your heart . . . and then, lying on floor and doing stretching exercises, i begin weeping. oh neugy, neugy, after all you have been thru, for this to happen, and now. I am sentimental, maudlin: imagine people saying — gee he was in such good shape, and what a good heart, and how he doted on his children . . . and and: i just break down, imagining bypass surgery, a long illness, recovery, and who to care for me?

During the three days between my call to Dr. Katz and the stress test, despite moving as fast as I can on long winter walks, I do not get anything resembling the kind of acute pain I'd been having, and when mild pain does come and I put a nitroglycerine pill under my tongue, it makes no discernible difference.

In Brooklyn the previous week, however, walking with Eli near Prospect Park, the burning sensation in my back becomes so severe that I find frequent pretexts to stop so as to give myself respite from the pain — I remark on the architecture of some building, or an item in a store window, or somebody passing by, or I share a memory with Eli of what Brooklyn was like when I was growing up here.

I read the sections on heart disease in Sherwin Nuland's *How We Die,* and these are "encouraging, longterm," I write. "It is natural for the system to begin to run down; and [what Rich has been telling me] does seem true: lots of things we can do for the heart to ameliorate problems, to prolong life, etc . . . a major area of progress, biomedical."

More sobering, though, is Nuland's description of the very ruse I have been using to disguise my condition. Writing about the common pattern by which severe coronary disease manifests itself, Nuland describes a patient of his, and says that while he observed him and listened to him, he was reminded of a practice commonly resorted to by so-called cardiac cripples in order to disguise the advanced state of their illness: A patient feeling the onset of an anginal attack while on his daily stroll finds it useful to stop and gaze with feigned interest into a shop window until the pain disappears. "The Berlin-born medical professor who first described this face- (and sometimes life-) saving procedure to me called it by its German name of *Schaufenster schauen,* or window-shopping. The *Schaufenster schauen* strategy was being used by Giddens to give him just enough respite to avoid serious trouble . . ."

When Rich calls — and he is calling once or twice a day now, to ask how I am doing, and — his pretext? — to talk with me about the book *he* is writing — I tell him about my time in New York, and about *Schaufenster schauen* and Nuland's description of the behavior of "cardiac cripples." To comfort myself, I try also to use some of what I have learned during the past few years from people I've met who have recovered from long-term mental illness, and apply it to heart disease — that is, how to live with a condition that is sometimes distinctly unpleasant and frequently terrifying, but, like any long-term condition that comes with being human and having a full and complicated life, manageable.

"Do sense mortality," I write. "These things happen — and if something in an artery, valve, whatever, suddenly stops fcning, then it does, and i need to take care of it, manage it. all the lessons of [*Transforming Madness*]: that finding out i may have what is called coronary disease is not a death sentence (except ultimately) — it simply means i will have a condition that needs care and management."

On the day before the stress test, I treat myself to a massage and come away "encouraged by fact that the massage gave me my best day in weeks!" I experience no pain in my back, no shortness of breath, no fatigue. I have dinner with a friend, Doug Whynott, who was Massachusetts state javelin champion in high school and who thinks my problem is muscular — he says he had similar problems a few years back: pain between his shoulder blades that came on slowly and cut into his breathing. I am both very frightened — convinced my condition is as advanced as, within a week, we will learn it is — and encouraged: what I have is merely a muscular problem (so-called swimmer's shoulder?) resulting from all the years of swimming and playing ball.

"V v scared," I write on Friday, February 5, 1999, the morning of the stress test, "tho less so the last day or two. I made it! no crises from time of check up to time of stress test — 3 weeks."

At 11:15 I walk to Dr. Flynn's office a block away, fill out some forms, and when I am called in to the examination room, talk with the doctor for a few minutes, after which the nurse hooks me up to an electrocardiograph machine to get a reading before I step onto a treadmill.

The heart is, as Rich has explained to me, partly an electrical organ, but even when there are severe blockages within the heart's arteries, the electrocardiogram may not reveal tell-tale abnormalities. By placing electrodes at and across various points on the heart and recording electrical activity, it becomes possible to get information concerning the location and extent of changes, or of damage. When there has been a heart attack (what physicians call myocardial infarction [MI]: the death of part of the heart muscle), the part of the heart that has died is replaced by scar tissue, and, since scar tissue does not conduct electricity, the EKG may reveal this development. But though the EKG can uncover problems, Rich explains, it is a crude, often inaccurate means of evaluating the heart: it will sometimes suggest abnormalities that, upon further investigation, prove nonexistent or of no consequence — and often it will not recognize problems, minor and serious, that require attention. In addition, whatever the EKG reveals must be read and understood, always, in the larger and more specific context of the individual patient.

Dr. Flynn's nurse performs the EKG and brings the results to Dr. Flynn. I am left alone for a while, sitting on the examining table, from where I watch Dr. Flynn talking on the phone. As the minutes go by and I continue to sit by myself, in my underpants, wondering what the delay is about, I feel strangely intimidated: if I walk into the reception area to ask if they've forgotten about me, I imagine them scolding me and ordering me back into the examining room — asking me why I am bothering them, and what I am doing in their office without any clothes on . . .

I am anxious, frightened, and worried, especially when I try to figure out what I might say to my children if the news is as bad as I fear it will be.

After about ten minutes, Dr. Flynn returns to the examining room and tells me that we are not going to go ahead with the stress test.

"I think you've already had a heart attack," he states.

"Oh shit," I say.

"Something happened," he says. He has called Dr. Katz's office to get a fax of my most recent EKG in order to compare it with the EKG his nurse just performed. There is no need for a stress test now, no matter what the previous EKG reveals, since the point of a stress test would be to determine if there were any coronary problems that needed attention. (In a stress test, a continuous EKG reading, along with blood pressure readings, is taken while the patient walks on a treadmill whose speed and incline are gradually increased so as to raise the heart rate and enable us to see what happens when the heart is subjected to "stress" — to a greater and greater need for blood and oxygen.)

Something happened, Dr. Flynn repeats, though it is not clear, from the EKG, exactly what — but he tells me that it *is* now clear why I have been having these episodes of shortness of breath and pain in my back. He asks if I can meet him, within fifteen or twenty minutes, at Cooley Dickinson Hospital — about a half mile away — so he can do an echocardiogram. He expects that the echocardiogram, a film of my beating heart (much like the sonograms a woman undergoes to monitor the developing fetus during pregnancy), will show us exactly where the heart attack occurred, and how extensive the damage is. What he will look for in the pictures of my heart are those portions of the muscle that, when the heart contracts, do not move.

I walk home in a daze, yet feel curiously relieved: at least I know what the problem is — *I have had a heart attack* — and then drive to Cooley Dickinson Hospital.

Dr. Flynn and I meet in a small room crowded with equipment. Dr. O'Brien, one of Dr. Flynn's colleagues in their cardiology practice, is in the room with us. He is the doctor Aaron has been seeing for his heart problem, and though the three of us, along with the technician who will perform the echocardiogram (anointing my chest with vaseline-like gook and tracing paths along my skin with a hand-held instrument that looks like a detachable shower-head from a bathtub), are shifting around in a very small space — the two doctors and the technician talk with one another and often refer to me by name — Dr. O'Brien never says hello or acknowledges my presence. This confirms the dreamlike sense I have that I am both very much there (*I've had a heart attack I've had a heart attack,* I keep repeating) and that I am not there at all — that what is happening is happening to somebody else who happens to look like me and is also named Jay Neugeboren.

Dr. Flynn studies the echocardiogram on the monitor while the technician performs it, and when it is completed he runs the film through again. He seems puzzled. To his surprise, he tells me he cannot find any damage — any portion of my heart muscle that is not moving. Instead, what he does discern is a general weakening of the heart muscle.

"Your heart is not contracting as strongly as it should," he tells me. I have already taken a beta-blocker he prescribed in his office (beta-blockers are medications that slow the heart rate and the force of contractions, and lower blood pressure by blocking the beta-adrenergic receptors of the autonomic nervous system — that part of our nervous system over which we have no conscious control), and he says that this fuzzes things up a bit. He looks at the film once more, and still cannot find any area of dead muscle.

In his letter to Dr. Katz, dictated after the EKG and before the echocardiogram (again: how memory transforms events! I thought I had gone straight from his office to the hospital, and have no memory of doing anything else — of the hours in between — yet the letter indicates I had the EKG in the morning and the echocardiogram in the afternoon), he begins, "Mr. Neugeboren came to the office today for an exercise test.

As you know, he is a 60 year old gentleman who has a history of elevated cholesterol [220 at most recent test, two months before] who noted a decrease in exercise tolerance beginning in December of last year. He swims regularly and over the past month noted a significant decrease in his exercise tolerance with easy fatigue and shortness of breath. He also has had intermittent pains in his mid back associated with exertion and cold weather. He denies any period of prolonged chest pain and has not had rest pain.

After noting that my blood pressure was 150/80, my heart rate 70 and regular, he states: "Cardiac exam was unremarkable." The EKG, however, is "suggestive of a possible recent anteroseptal infarction [MI in the septal portion of the left ventricle]," which he suspects occurred before the first episode of shortness of breath on December 21. "Other potential etiologies for these EKG changes include a cardiomyopathy [disease of the heart muscle] which is certainly less likely."

After the echocardiogram, however, Dr. Flynn comes to an opposite conclusion. "Findings cannot exclude coronary disease," he reports, "but seem most consistent with a cardiomyopathy." In the echocardiogram report, he also notes other findings: no evidence of aortic stenosis (a narrowing of the aortic valve), mild mitral regurgitation and borderline left atrial enlargement (of no consequence), and overall left ventricular ejection fraction "calculated at 40–45%." He now tells me that he does *not* think I've had a heart attack, but a cardiomyopathy, most probably from a virus that is slowing down and weakening the force at which my heart is pumping blood.

He recommends catheterization and tells me I should call his office when I get home and arrange for his partner, Dr. Beck, to perform an angiogram at Bay State Medical Center (a half-hour away, in Springfield, Massachusetts) sometime soon, so we can find out exactly what's going on. In the meantime he gives me prescriptions for Atelenol (a beta-blocker) and for Vasotec (a vasodilater, so called because it dilates blood vessels, thereby reducing pressure within the circulatory system), tells me to use nitroglycerine if I have discomfort, and — as I've been doing for several years — to continue taking one aspirin a day. (Blood clots in our arteries are formed by a complex interaction between clotting elements in the blood and small cells called platelets, which are designed to patch up tiny holes in our blood vessels. We have been using aspirin, a derivative of willow bark, as a medicine for at least two hundred years, yet it is only since 1971 that we have learned that a small amount of aspirin, by reducing the stickiness of blood platelets, makes them less capable of generating blood clots, and thus is of great help in reducing both heart disease and strokes. This property of aspirin was first noted in 1950 by Lawrence Craven, a family physician in Cleveland who, observing that giving aspirin to children following tonsil removal resulted in increased bleeding, suggested in a series of papers which, during his lifetime, went unnoticed that aspirin might also reduce the tendency of the blood to clot following coronary thrombosis.)

"I think it's viral," Dr. Flynn tells me again just before I leave.

Back home ten minutes later, I telephone Dr. Flynn's office and say that Dr. Flynn said I should set up an appointment with Dr. Beck for an angiogram. The secretary tells me that Dr. Beck is booked for several weeks. I can make the appointment now, or call back. Although I am wild with anxiety and rage, I remain outwardly calm. Talking on the phone with a stranger who works for a doctor I have never seen, and feeling mildly panicked — if I let the anger fueled by my helplessness show, will they simply tell me to go to another doctor? will I have to go through the whole routine again? — I am persistent and insistent: I want an appointment as soon as possible. When the secretary looks through the schedule for a third time, she tells me she can squeeze me in for a brief office visit with Dr. Beck in the middle of next week — not for the angiogram, but to confer about setting up an appointment *for* an angiogram.

I hang up and telephone Rich, who had called earlier and left a message asking me to call him as soon as I got home, and to have the doctor fax him the results of the exam right away. I go over what has happened, beginning with Dr. Flynn telling me, first thing, that I've already had a heart attack — and when I get to the end of the story and tell Rich that the last thing Dr. Flynn said to me was that he thinks the problem is viral, Rich explodes.

"*It's not viral, goddamnit* — I want you in the hospital as soon as possible!" he exclaims, and he now insists I go to Massachusetts General Hospital, and not Bay State, because Massachusetts General is "the best" and because he knows several excellent cardiologists there. He will call ahead and help with arrangements. Catheterization is no big deal, he says, but if they have to go beyond catheterization and do angioplasties or a bypass, he wants me where he knows the doctors and knows they are "the best of the best" — the most experienced surgeons, the best diagnosticians.

("My medical antennae were tingling with that sense I always get when I know something's terribly wrong," Rich will later tell me. "My initial goal was to keep you from total panic while getting you to Mass General, and as time went by, my anxiety deepened — thus the more frequent calls. But I knew how serious the situation was, and there I was, three thousand miles away, agitated as hell. I knew the clock was ticking, and I knew where you could get the best help — two hours down the road.")

We talk for a long time, and Rich goes over everything with me carefully, continuing to insist that I go to Massachusetts General Hospital. He is concerned about my ongoing discomfort, but — to reassure me? — says that the fact that I have been able to swim so strongly is a good sign.

"I want you to know I am here for you one hundred percent, Jay," he says, but, alas, "here" is southern California, and what is imperative now is "to get the very best and most expeditious help" for me he can, and as soon as possible.

He also talks about how fortuitous our reconnecting after many years apart has been, and about how much this has meant to him. (After having read *Imagining Robert*, Rich wrote me a long letter — not only about how moving he found the book, but also about how touched he was by our many affinities, and how close he felt — much like a brother — to me.)

In my memory, Rich — high scorer on our synagogue's basketball team, undefeated in singles through three years of varsity tennis at Erasmus, hard-hitting third baseman for the Tufts College baseball team, and a guy who helped put himself through college and medical school by winning substantial sums of money at poker — was a tough, fiery ballplayer, as competitive as any guy I knew. Though he had a most winning smile off the court, in the schoolyard he was all business — all elbows, hips, butt, and shoulders under the basket — a guy who would go through the proverbial brick wall after a loose ball — and, on the perimeter, a guy with a soft, deadly touch on his jump shot.

Now, however, as I've been learning from conversations and letters, and from manuscripts he's been sending me, though he still plays tennis regularly and competitively, he has mellowed in unforeseen ways. In his talks with me, and during our times together — in Massachusetts, Denver (where his two children live), and California — especially with his children, and when talking about his patients, he will be the most attentive and patient of listeners, the most thoughtful and gentle of men.

In his life away from the hospital and medical school, in his home in Redondo Beach, he now devotes significant portions of each day to Buddhist meditation, to practicing piano (Chopin, Beethoven,

Mozart, Schubert), and to that reading and writing by which he is attempting to understand what to him are the real, mysterious, and often mystical relationships of our minds to our bodies.

A brilliant researcher and clinician who has authored several textbooks on cardiology, along with several hundred medical journal articles, and who pioneered studies in angiography, electrophysiology, and nuclear cardiology, in recent years Rich has become especially interested in those forces, beyond scientific measurement, that he believes frequently prove crucial in matters of life and death. He is, in fact, well along in the writing of a book that describes how many of his patients have lived on against all ordinary rules of medical diagnosis and prognosis — and how others are able, in what are for them most uncharacteristic ways, to come to peaceful accommodations with illness and with death.

"Rich urges me to call anytime, just to talk," I write. "This is very important, he says. And explains to me why i am going to be okay — the really good news is that we have no localized damage to any part of the heart so far, it seems, and what we want to do most is to preverve as much of this muscle as possible."

Rich has become such a sweet new age type, for such a brilliant, formerly competitious Brooklyn boy: says he feels our reconnecting was meant to be . . . and this is why, etc . . . he has felt strange and definite sense of communion with me.

After I talk with Rich — he is going to call people he knows as soon as we hang up, and I am to call him back that evening, 9:30 West Coast time — I telephone Jerry, Arthur, and Phil.

Phil and Arthur say that they defer to Jerry and Rich, and Jerry suggests I come down to Yale–New Haven instead of Massachusetts General, where he can arrange things for me, and where I can stay over at his house before and after the angiogram. He says he will make calls to cardiologists he knows in both New Haven and Boston, and this is when I say to him — as I will to Rich when I call him back — that he and the other guys should just talk with one another and then tell me what to do.

Sharon, a woman I have known for several years — we'd been friends, but within the past several months our relationship has become romantic — is supposed to come by for dinner, and our times together, our telephone conversations (she lives in Boston), and the warm, eager way we look forward to being together are, I tell myself, proof either that I am correct in my conviction that things are definitely over between me and Ellen — or that I am more profoundly shallow than I care to know. Not for nothing, I remind myself, am I in these matters, as my friends keep telling me, perhaps the world's oldest living teenager.

Ellen calls, and during our conversation, I tell her about what happened at Dr. Flynn's office. When she asks if I would be willing to have lunch with her the next day, I say no — that I don't think it would be a good idea (for me); when she asks if there is anything she can do for me, I say no again, that there isn't.

Shortly after I hang up, Dr. Katz calls and tells me he has spoken with Dr. Flynn. "david katz v concerned," I write. "Says he is surprised and shocked, really. think he may feel he missed this some [by] not thinking coronary disease for a few weeks."

"Well," I comment. "He is human too," and add: "so are we all so are we all."

5

Coronary Artery Bypass Graft
Times Five

WHY IS IT, I wonder in the hours following the exams in Dr. Flynn's office and at Cooley Dickinson Hospital, that some people who smoke and drink at will, eat whatever they want and in great quantities, live under large and constant pressures, never exercise, and are obese, live to ripe old ages in good health and without loss of faculties, while others, who do all those things touted as leading to long and healthy lives, suddenly find themselves cut down in the prime of life?

The answer to the age-old question — "Why me?" — I remind myself as I walk from room to room in my house, wondering how and when I will give the news to my children, seems the same as it has always been: "Why *not* you?"

I think too of my father's prescription for longevity: If you drink a malted every day for ninety-nine years, he used to tell me, you'll live to be very old.

Sharon arrives late in the afternoon, and though we have planned to go out for dinner, we never leave my house. Sharon's mother, living alone in a small town near the Connecticut border an hour west, is quite ill, and Sharon tells me she will probably need to spend the night there.

We sit on the couch in my living room for a while, messing

around — kissing, talking, playing — and then I make supper. Several times I start to talk about what happened earlier in the day, but stop each time, afraid that if I give Sharon the news, it will frighten her away, and while we eat, I find myself recalling the time, less than two months before my nineteenth birthday, I was operated on for what I would learn, many years later, was Hodgkin's disease.

Near the end of my sophomore year at Columbia, I noticed that some swollen glands in my neck were not going away, and one Sunday afternoon while visiting my cousin Leatrice, a doctor then doing her residency in pediatrics, I asked her to feel them. She told me to get myself to the Columbia Health Services, located in St. Luke's Hospital, the next day. After classes the following afternoon, I walked across the street to the Health Services, where a young doctor felt my glands, and then called in an older doctor. The older doctor examined me, told me he wanted me in the hospital on Friday for a biopsy, and that I should plan on staying overnight.

At the time I didn't know what a biopsy was — I thought it was probably some kind of test to see why my glands remained swollen. When I arrived home, in Brooklyn, I told my mother I'd be going to St. Luke's on Friday for a biopsy, and that I might have to stay overnight. After my father arrived from work, my mother drew him into their bedroom, where, behind closed doors, they shouted, wept, and argued. Within a day, my mother, a registered nurse, had arranged for the biopsy to be performed, not at St. Luke's, but by a doctor she knew at a hospital in Brooklyn.

A week later, the doctor operated on me, took out all the glands he could reach — *stripped* them, in the words my mother used — and for several months after this I received cobalt radiation treatment at St. Luke's. At the time — this was 1957 — I was not informed of my diagnosis. My mother told me that the pathologists, including Sidney Farber, director of the Child Cancer Foundation in Boston, to whom the specimens were sent, reported that the tissue from the glands was benign.

Why then, I asked, was I being given radiation to both sides of my neck? That, my mother explained, was merely a "precaution" — to "burn out a few suspicious cells" the surgeon couldn't get to during surgery, "just to be on the safe side."

I received weekly checkups for a while, then monthly check-ups, and, during my last two years of college, checkups every three months, the exams administered by Dr. Carl Wise, director of Columbia's Student Health Services. All information about my condition was channeled through my mother. Those were years when, if somebody was diagnosed with cancer, the word, when used at all — or the initials (as in: "Aunt so-and-so has CA") — were whispered.

Some two dozen years later, driving home from UMass one afternoon, I heard a report on the radio stating that new studies showed that children and young people who had once been irradiated on the neck or throat area with dosages now deemed excessive (often following tonsilitis, or for acne) were at risk for throat or thyroid cancer and should have a thyroid scan. Shit, I thought, and recalled a joke about a man walking along the side of a road when a pickup truck zooms by and knocks him into a ditch. The truck brakes to a stop thirty yards down the road, and the driver sticks his head out the window and yells: "Look out!" "Why?" the man in the ditch asks. "Are you coming back?"

I called a radiologist I knew, who scheduled me for a thyroid scan and asked me to send for my records. I did, and received, among other documents, a copy of a letter Dr. Wise had written to the doctor I was seeing after my graduation from college. For the first time I saw the unequivocal findings, confirmed by several pathologists, of Hodgkin's disease ("giant follicular lymphoma"). I was, according to Dr. Wise's report, given 1,000 roentgens to each side of my neck, "with disappearance of the glands in question." (And, two decades later, without the radiation having caused any new cancers.) "Mr. Neugeboren has never been told the extent or diagnosis of his condition," Dr. Wise wrote in the last sentence of his letter, dated February 29, 1960, "but I believe he is aware of what is going on."

And so I was. Believing that cancer would do me in before my twentieth birthday, I did what I had, for some time, been wanting to do: during the next few months I wrote and completed my first novel — the first of what would be, until the publication of *Big Man* in 1966, when I was twenty-eight, eight unpublished books.

I also believed, as I do once again this Friday evening forty-two years later, that revealing to a woman that I am afflicted with a fatal disease will make me more interesting — exotic, desirable, tragic. (I think of the story Susan Sontag tells in *Illness as Metaphor,* about Lord Byron looking into the mirror and saying, "I look pale. I should like to die of a consumption." Why? asks his friend Tom Moore. "Because," Byron replies, "the ladies would all say, 'Look at that poor Byron, how interesting he looks in dying.'")

At the same time that I hope to excite a desire in Sharon equal to my own, I also tell myself that telling Sharon what Dr. Flynn has told me — revealing to her the fragile state of my heart — will give her reason to do what I lack the desire, or will, to do: to act sensibly so that I will be saved from myself — from that angel of death colluding happily with my sudden and supreme loss of judgment. (Old schoolyard joke: Why do men often give their dicks affectionate nicknames? Answer: Because they want to be on a first-name basis with that entity that makes all their major decisions for them.)

After supper, I talk about what has happened, and I am aware that everything I say, while nothing if not, given my condition, heartfelt, is also calculated to achieve the end I long for: that, moved by my tale, Sharon will be kind to me in ways that will finally *(finally?!)* bring peace and forgetfulness.

We kiss, and kiss again, and after a while I suggest we go upstairs to my bedroom. We lie together on my bed while I conjure up, in fully scripted scenes, mundane complications that may follow from what I hope we will soon be doing (phone calls to friends and family; the arrival of ambulances, police, and my rabbi; my brother decompensating extravagantly). I recall old schoolyard jokes about guys dying-in-the-saddle, visualize reunions in heaven where I trade stories with those celebrated men who have gone before me in the same way (Nelson Rockefeller, John Garfield), and I imagine how others — friends, family, students, colleagues — will react to news of my death.

We begin to remove our clothes, and the knowledge, both that I may be risking my life for a brief moment of pleasure, and that my fantasies about the aftermath of this moment are remarkably banal, does little to stop me from the longing I have to slip quietly and happily from this world — from one heaven to another? — and while so doing, to wonder: Will anybody care if and when I'm gone? Will anybody miss me?

Caught between feelings of passion and despondency, I tell myself that this is as good a way to go as any, while at the same time another voice — *not* my father's this time — talks to me: *"Are you out of your mind, Neugie?"* it says. "Are you out of your — apt adjective — *fucking* mind? Stop and get up. Come on. Just stop and get up and let this dear, kind woman go take care of her mother, and then do whatever you can to make the time pass until you call Rich and find out what's going to happen next."

An hour or two later, without having taken extraordinary risks, we dress and go back downstairs. Sharon telephones her mother, who, Sharon reports, is feeling lonely, weak, and frightened. "I can identify," I say. A short while later, Sharon leaves.

I telephone Rich after midnight — at 9:30 California time — and he says he and Jerry have spoken, that Arthur and Phil have talked with each of them too, and that so far the consensus is that I should go to Yale–New Haven for the angiogram and for any possible follow-up procedures. He and Jerry will talk again in the morning. He asks how I'm doing, and I tell him that I'm doing okay — some nervousness, but no pain or discomfort — and that as far as I can tell, the best news is that I'm still here.

In the morning I walk into town and get a haircut, and then find Aaron at La Fiorentina, an Italian pastry shop where he works part-time. He has arrived early, and is drinking coffee and reading the *New York Times.* I tell him what the doctor said, wording the news in a way I hope will minimize alarm: something has happened in or to my heart, but they're not sure what — obviously it's not fatal: I'm here, right? — but they want to run some more tests, probably later this week. Visibly upset, Aaron scoffs at the idea that *anything* can be wrong with me or my heart — "Just look at what great shape you're in!" he declares. "You're in better shape than most twenty-five- or thirty-year-olds!"

When I call and tell Miriam what's happened, she is silent for a long while, and despite my efforts to keep things as low-key and optimistic as possible, says little.

Eli responds warmly. An hour or two after our talk, he "leaves a lovely loving message on machine," I write, about "how he is thinking of me, etc., and how i have a good heart even if . . ."

"Yet when he calls back at midnite," I note, he is "upset somehow bec mom's mom and dad died of heart stuff, and your parents did (me: my mother's still alive), and aaron has his problem . . . as if: he has recd a genetic bad deal."

"I'm still here," I write. "A long day, and what to say? I am getting used to being a man who has a v imperfect heart living within him. Good talks with Jerry and Rich, and by tonite, they will have a plan for me. Like the notion that my old friends will be talking with one another about the Neug . . . oh my but I do bask in their affection and regard for me!"

Between errands, talking with my children, and talks with Rich and Jerry, I get other things done: I work on a review of a book about families coping with mental illness; I complete a report to a foundation that awards fellowships to fiction writers; I read a new novel by my old friend Jerry Charyn ("vintage Jerry"); I take a nap.

Yet all the while I am at home, working most of the time in my third-floor office, each time I hear a car approaching I find myself going to the window to see if the car is stopping in front of my house or turning into my driveway (I live on a quiet, dead-end street of private homes), and I realize, despite my having told her I didn't think it was a good idea for us to get together today, that I am hoping I will see Ellen get out of her car, smile, and wave up to me.

Early the next morning Jerry calls and says he and Rich have decided it is best for me to come down to Yale, where, in his words, he can be an *ombudsman* for me.

"Who do you know in Boston?" he asks. "You'll get lost in the system, but if the staff at Yale knows it is accountable to me, that will maximize your chances for getting the best possible care." He tells me I will be receiving a call from Dr. Henry Cabin, who is *his* cardiologist, and with whom he has already talked.

My friends Sam and Elaine Rofman drive in from Boston for the afternoon, and we go to a UMass basketball game together. UMass wins, and afterwards, walking across campus and up a steep hill toward the parking lot where I left my car, Sam — an M.D. several years younger than I am — is soon out of breath and cannot keep up with me; he laughs and assures me again, as he has been doing for the previous few weeks, that I have nothing to worry about.

Back home, there is a message on my answering machine from Dr. Cabin, saying he is looking forward to meeting me, telling me he will be doing the angiography, asking me to bring along the results of the EKG and the film of the echocardiogram, and alerting me to the fact that his secretary will call on Monday to set up our appointment.

The following morning, at exactly 9 A.M., Dr. Cabin's secretary calls and informs me she has scheduled me for the angiogram at Yale–New Haven on Thursday morning. She walks me through everything else: the blood work they need to do, where I am to go, what I should bring, and, should they find significant blockages, their plan to go ahead with angioplasty and stenting immediately following the angiogram.

Phil and Arthur call, and they each talk with me for a long time. I telephone a few other friends, including Doug Whynott. It wasn't a rotator cuff problem, I tell him. A half-hour or so after we talk, his wife Kathy calls. She and Doug offer to drive down to Northampton. They can stay over at my house, she says, or, if I prefer, I can drive up to Walpole (New Hampshire) to be with them. Doug also offers to drive me down to New Haven on Thursday. They are, Kathy tells me, stunned by the news.

Rich calls and tells me he is "thrilled" to see that there are no "Q waves" on my EKG (it took three calls and three days to get Dr. Flynn's office to fax it to him), which means that there is no evidence of any serious localized abnormality, of a previous heart attack, or of any significant damage to the heart muscle itself. This is very good news, he says.

When Eli calls again, he tells me that he and his sister have been talking frequently, and that Miriam cried for a long time the night before. When I give him the good news Rich has given me, he seems reassured; still, he wonders if maybe after this I will "slow down a bit," and he talks to me about how I don't realize how hard I work, how many responsibilities I have, how busy my life is.

*

I spend the next few days taking care of things at home and at the university. I talk frequently with Rich, Jerry, Phil, and Arthur. I write in my journal, work on my novel, imagine various scenarios ("my prediction: they will find some blockage that has been inducing the discomfort/cramping in back . . . will angioplast it, and within 2 weeks, i will be swimming"), and think more about living alone than I do about my heart and what might be wrong there. I think, too, about what I have learned while working on *Transforming Madness* — how for people who have been afflicted, long-term, with a serious mental illness, and for those family members and friends who care for them, the isolation in which they too often live becomes at least as deadly as the condition itself.

When I get a copy of the echocardiogram results, Rich interprets them for me. That my ejection fraction is within a normal range is an excellent sign, he says, for it means the heart is basically sound. "Also," I write in my journal, "he thinks the general weakening [cardiomyopathy] may be paradoxical good sign: the heart slowing down so as not to rupture — recognizes that oxygen and blood not flowing as they should, and so self-protects [by pumping with less force]."

"Wake feeling queasy, back cramping a bit: nerves for sure — along with side effects, i suspect, of the 2 new meds. dont like that stuff," I write on the morning of February 10, 1999. "wake feeling v slow — moving with measured pace, and with sad heart."

"Strange too: the emotions dont transform to words this morning," I tell myself. "but this is not bec there is a dearth of feeling. i am overwhelmed by feelings, by my mortality . . . washed away by both sadness and fear . . . and then, at times: by goodness — the kindness of others, the good luck despite the bad news: i have survived whatever happened, and this is an area of medicine that is wonderfully advanced, etc . . . and i should be able to move into a few more decades of good and rich life."

"Make calls here and there," I write at the close of this last entry before the drive down to Jerry's house. "love talking with my old buddies — what bright, sweet guys we were and are! me, phil, rich, jerry, arthur . . ."

I spend the day taking care of business: get the book review and the foundation report in the mail; teach my classes at UMass; talk with students; have a meal with a former student who is in transition between teaching and acting jobs; revise a chapter of my novel; and write out a note to my children about what to do and where things are and who will take care of what in case I don't return. I leave the note, in a sealed envelope, to one side of my desk.

"So: will tend to business re the book, re novel, re packing — leave here at 6 [P.M.], for CT," I write, "and the day will pass, and by this time tomorrow, my guess, i will be in hospital, recovering from an angioplasty that will give me many more good years. blessings, neug. we love you."

Only when I wake from the anesthesia and Dr. Cabin shows me the results of the angiogram and tells me he wants me in surgery as soon as possible, and only when I learn that I am at least as gravely ill as I'd been believing I was — only then: when I *know* — do my fears depart. Only when I am sitting on a table in the room where Dr. Cabin has performed the angiogram do I feel, for the first time in several months, not merely relieved, but eager to get on with things: with the surgery, with whatever follows from surgery — with *life!* I am not only, as Jerry will later say, positive and optimistic, but I am also feeling a new and wonderfully liberating sensation: at peace in a way I don't quite understand. All will be well, I think — not despite the surgery and what has made it necessary, but because of it — and I know this as surely as, for the previous few months, I have feared the opposite.

In that small aseptic room where my clothes lie in a neat pile on the floor, and in the hours that follow, when I move from one hospital room to another, I take stock of things, and think: I would love nothing more than to hold on to the life that is still mine and that, when all is said and done, I don't have a great desire to leave. I don't *want* to die, but if my time here is near its end, and — the thought occurs in an easy way, as if it is merely a fact like others: whether it will rain or snow, or whether UMass will or won't win its next basketball game — if I do not, tomorrow, wake from surgery, that seems all right too. I find myself without regrets, whether for things done, or not done.

And when, the next morning, I am readied for surgery, and when I am wheeled into a narrow hallway outside the operating room, I am acutely aware of being neither depressed, afraid, nor alone.

I recall feeling vaguely sleepy, somewhat nervous, and distinctly exhilarated — bypass surgery is simply high-tech plumbing, I tell myself: something doctors are experienced and proficient at, so let's do it as well and quickly as we can — and I recall, too, while I lie under a sheet, being fascinated by the way a member of the surgical team attends to my left arm and hand: securing the arm to the operating table, palm up, while taping my fingers down in what seems a weirdly intricate way — some fingers bent upright at curious angles, others fastened down as if to get them into position for forming a tricky chord on the neck of a guitar. (What the man is doing, I realize afterward, is preparing my arm for the removal of its radial artery, which will be stitched into my heart.)

I recall how drab and institutional the corridor we wait in is, how numerous, efficient, and busy are the people on the surgical team — nurses, aides, technicians, surgeons, anesthesiologists, all robed in lime-green sterile gowns — involved in the surgery itself, and with what incredible swiftness — like life itself? — time seems to move. Neugie, I remember saying to myself, this is *not* a first draft.

When I revisit this moment, though, what I see first of all and most of all is the way my daughter Miriam, closest to the gurney I am lying on, follows me with her eyes. Her brothers and her fiancé Seth beside her — Jerry, in hospital lab coat, standing slightly behind — Miriam stares at me with the steadiest, saddest, most loving of gazes, so that, as I am rolled away into the operating theater, my spirits, helped along, doubtless, by medications, soar, and the feeling of calm and readiness — the faith that all will be well — spreads through me. What can be amiss, I think, with having lived a life wherein one ends without regrets and with the unwavering affection of those one holds dearest?

In the weeks and months that follow surgery, when I consider how and why it was, without typical symptoms or risk factors, I nearly died — and when I explore these questions in conversations with my friends, and through the reading and researches our conversations lead to, I am, again, surprised by what I find.

My life has, blessedly, been saved by what is generally considered the most spectacular success of twentieth-century medicine: coronary bypass surgery — the ability doctors have to open my chest, shut off my heart, harvest veins and arteries from my own body, use them to bypass occluded arteries, start my heart going again, and return me to the world in better condition — and with, in all probability, many years of healthy, productive life ahead — than I was in before they put me to sleep.

The advent of what is often called heroic medicine — high-tech life-saving and life-prolonging biomedical interventions such as open-heart surgery, organ transplants, genetic engineering, and neonatal procedures — is surely, in many instances, as in mine, not only welcome, but so technologically dramatic as to seem miraculous. In the lives of those who are the beneficiaries of these successful interventions — adults who without transplants or bypasses would otherwise die or live out their lives as invalids; children who would otherwise perish or be permanently disabled — their effects are, day to day and year to year, quite real. (That this is so gives tangible proof to a favorite saying: "The rabbis tell us that a person who does not believe in miracles is not a realist.")

Yet what I begin to discover after surgery is that when it comes to life and death in matters medical, what has made and will probably continue to make the greatest difference for most of us remains distinctly *low*-tech.

This is a revelation to me, as it is to most people I talk with during and after my recovery. But it is not news to the four friends who attend to me through this period of my life.

6

The Ponce de León Thing

PRIOR TO 1940, PHIL explains, the primary function of medicine was the diagnosis of disease. Prior to 1940, in fact, we were helpless to ameliorate *most* conditions, especially the many lethal and debilitating childhood illnesses. Before 1940, what doctors refer to as their "therapeutic armamentarium" was hardly impressive. Except for a very few medications (digoxin, thyroxine, insulin), immunization for a handful of infectious diseases, and some surgical procedures, doctors had little understanding of the causes of most diseases, and little wherewithal to alleviate their effects. "Indeed," as Gerald Grob notes in the prologue to *The Deadly Truth: A History of Disease in America,* "some of the therapies deployed before 1940 were very likely harmful."

Sixty years later, however, there are few diseases for which something cannot be done to alleviate symptoms and to prolong life. Although we have made extraordinary advances in the treatment of diseases such as AIDS, of childhood illnesses, and, as in my case, some of what were formerly life-ending conditions, when it comes to those diseases that currently account for the greatest portion of our morbidity and mortality — heart disease, cancer, diabetes, the major mental illnesses (schizophrenia, depression, bipolar disorder), many infectious diseases, and the vast proportion of other long-duration illnesses — we continue to remain largely ignorant of their etiologies.

The essential point, my friends emphasize, is that while we have become wonderfully efficient at controlling the symptoms and progression of the diseases they commonly encounter in their clinical practice — heart disease, AIDS, stroke, depression — we have made much less progress in understanding the underlying *causes* of these diseases and, therefore, in being able to prevent or to cure them.

"The great problem with neurology, for example," Phil says, "is that we don't know how to help the brain heal itself. All the other organs and body parts can heal themselves, and we can, to varying degrees, aid these processes better than we used to. But not the brain. Our knowledge of the brain is way behind our knowledge of, say, the heart and the circulatory system."

My readings in the history of disease, and of medicine, confirm what my friends tell me. David Weatherall, professor of medicine at Oxford and a specialist in human genetics, puts matters this way: "While genuine progress has been made in our understanding of how to manage heart disease, stroke, rheumatism, the major psychiatric disorders, cancer, and so on, we have only reached the stage at which we can control our patients' symptoms or temporarily patch them up."

Reiterating what Lewis Thomas wrote about half way technologies more than a quarter century ago, Weatherall continues: "Our lack of success over the last fifty years, in getting to grips with the basic causes of these diseases, combined with our increasing understanding of the pathological consequences of diseased organs, has bred modern high-technology medicine. Much of it is very sophisticated and effective at prolonging life, but it neither prevents nor cures many diseases."

Like my friends, Weatherall is acutely aware of the many gains we *have* made. "Our ability to patch up patients and to prolong their lives seems to be almost limitless," he states. Still, like my friends, he also notes a curious anomaly — that the more we can do to enhance and prolong life for those suffering from diseases whose underlying causes we do not understand, the more this seems to lead to both a "dramatic increase in the cost of medical care" and "a dehumanizing effect on its practitioners and the hospitals in which they work."

This dehumanizing effect on doctors and the institutions in

which they work — the devaluation of those practices that enable a doctor to know and understand patients in their uniqueness, and, when treating their patients, to have the wherewithal and time to be thoughtful in their judgments — is not only lamentable for reasons we usually term personal or humanistic but, as my friends contend, profoundly inimical to the practice and efficacy of medicine itself.

"Insurance companies don't blink much when it comes to lab tests or procedures for my patients that cost hundreds of dollars," Jerry explains. "But they won't pay, or will pay only minimally, for me to sit with a patient for a half-hour or an hour and take a thorough history, or to sit with a patient and talk about the patient's problems — or the patient's *progress*. And if I don't know my patient well, and my patient doesn't trust that I know him and care about him, then I can't be the kind of doctor I want to be and should be."

Although taking a thorough history and listening attentively to a patient, like caring for people with chronic and disabling diseases, or providing public health measures that help prevent disease, may not seem as heroic or glamorous — as *sexy* — as a bypass, a transplant, an artificial heart, a reengineered gene, a new "miracle" drug, or some other biotechnological innovation, it is prevention and rehabilitation that, these past hundred years, have made and continue to make the greatest difference in terms of both morbidity (how sick we are) and mortality (how long we live).

Before the advent of the Salk vaccine in 1955, the word *polio* would spread in whispers through our world each summer: news would reach us that a child we knew — a cousin or distant relative, the son or daughter of a friend, a boy or girl with whom we went to school or to summer camp — had contracted the disease, and would most likely be crippled for life.

In my memory, the polio scare (as in my parents' phrasing: "There's a polio scare — let's just hope it doesn't lead to an epidemic!") came regularly each year after school was out in June, and when it did, beaches and swimming pools were closed, I was warned to stay out of crowds, to wash my hands frequently, to be careful about the water I drank, and never to swallow water from a lake or stream. This happened both in Brooklyn and in upstate New York, where my mother, brother, and I either went to sleepaway summer camps (my mother, in exchange for tuition for me and Robert, worked as camp nurse) or rented rooms in a large old farmhouse where there was a communal kitchen, and where my mother's brother and four sisters, with their children, also rented rooms.

I recall, too, an earlier time — I was perhaps nine or ten years old — when, in my elementary school, P.S. 246, we lined up in the auditorium, the boys in white shirts and red ties, the girls in white blouses and dark skirts, to be given vaccinations. Class by class, we filed down to the front of the auditorium, and one by one we rolled up our sleeves, stepped forward, and received our shots. This occurred a few years after World War II, and we were told that by receiving these injections without complaint or tears we were heroes too: young Americans mobilizing against treacherous enemies — disease, disability, and epidemic — in order to keep our nation healthy, strong, and free.

I remember watching my friend Ronald Granberg — a tall, broad-shouldered, red-headed boy chosen to lead the Color Guard and carry the American flag down the center aisle at the start of assembly each Friday morning — get his shot, take a drink from the water fountain to the right of the stage, and faint straightaway into the spigot, chipping a sizeable triangle from his right front tooth. Twenty years later, our teacher, Mrs. Demetri (who lived around the corner from me, and gave me oil painting lessons in her apartment at night), told me she met Ronald in the street one day when he was a grown man, and that they recognized each other immediately. "Open your mouth, Ronald —" Mrs. Demetri told me she commanded him first thing "— and show me your tooth!"

My friends and I grew up and came of age in a time when, as David Weatherall writes, "it appeared that medical science was capable of almost anything" — in a time when the diseases that throughout our parents' and grandparents' lifetimes had been the chief instruments of infant and childhood death, and of crippling lifelong disabilities, were disappearing.

In these pre-AIDS years, Jerry explains, citing the success, among other things, of the worldwide program to eliminate smallpox, the medical community seemed to believe that infectious disease was, by and large, a thing of the past.

"When I was doing my internship, I was one of the few young doctors choosing to go into infectious disease," he says. "I did it because I wanted to work in areas of our country and the Third World — poor areas — where there was still work to do that might make a real difference, and where these diseases were still taking an enormous toll. For the most part, however, I was anomalous in my choice of specialty. Back then, infectious disease was certainly not considered a promising specialty for medical students and young doctors, either clinically or in terms of research."

Optimism about the "conquest" of disease — not only the infectious diseases, but *all* diseases — was widespread. The surgeon general of the United States, William H. Stewart, was frequently quoted as having declared, in 1967, that "it was time to close the book on infectious disease," and the sentiment was, Jerry confirms, widely accepted as a truism (even though the surgeon general, it turns out, never said it!) and has continued, despite the AIDS pandemic and the emergence — and reemergence — of other infectious diseases, to prevail.

In a more recent example, we have Dr. William B. Schwartz, in *Life Without Disease: The Pursuit of Medical Utopia* (1998), asserting that if "developments in research maintain their current pace, it seems likely that a combination of improved attention to dietary and environmental factors along with advances in gene therapy and protein-targeted drugs *will have virtually eliminated most major classes of disease*" (italics added). More: a molecular understanding of the process of aging, he predicts, may lead to ways of controlling the process so that "by 2050, aging may in fact prove to be simply another disease to be treated."

"The virtual disappearance overnight of scourges like smallpox, diphtheria, poliomyelitis, and other infectious killers, at least from the more advanced countries," Weatherall writes about the post–World War II period, "led to the expectation that spectacular progress of this kind would continue."

"But this did not happen," he explains. "The diseases that took their place — heart attacks, strokes, cancer, rheumatism, and psychiatric disorders — turned out to be much more intractable."

The more we were able to eliminate many of the infectious diseases that led to premature death, that is, the more chronic and degenerative diseases such as cancer and heart disease replaced them as our leading causes of sickness and death. In the 1880 federal census, for example, neither cancer nor heart disease — our major killers a hundred years later — was listed among the ten leading causes of death.

Throughout the nineteenth century, gastrointestinal diseases, especially among infants and children (manifested largely as diarrheal diseases), were the leading causes of death. By the end of the nineteenth century, in large part because of public health and public works projects (clean water, sewage, sanitation), deaths from gastrointestinal diseases had declined, and tuberculosis and respiratory disorders (influenza, pneumonia) emerged as the major causes of death.

In 1900, neoplasms (cancer) accounted for less than 4 percent of all deaths and ranked sixth as a cause of mortality, while diseases of the heart accounted for slightly more than 6 percent and ranked fourth. Eleven years later, in 1911 — the year of my mother's birth (she was one of eight children, two of whom died in infancy) — when respiratory diseases and tuberculosis were still the primary causes of death, heart disease and cancer accounted for nearly 17 percent of total mortality.

From 1911 through 1935, mortality from tuberculosis declined steadily, and influenza and pneumonia became, and remained, the two leading causes of death, taking their highest toll among people forty-five years and older, while the figure for heart disease and cancer, combined, rose to 30.4 percent.

By 1998, however, cancer and heart disease had replaced pneumonia and influenza as our leading causes of death, diseases of the heart accounting for 31 percent and malignant neoplasms for 23.2 percent. Of the fifteen leading causes of death, only pneumonia and influenza (3.6 percent, combined) now fell directly into the infectious group, and they took their greatest toll largely from individuals afflicted with a variety of other health problems, many of them deriving from what epidemiologists call "insult accumulation" — the long-term effects of organ damage caused by the childhood illnesses these individuals had survived.

But we should note that diagnostic categories and criteria are, then as now — especially with respect to heart disease — ever changing. "We didn't even know what a heart attack *was* until some time in the early years of the twentieth century," Rich says. "It hadn't really been invented yet — not until James Herrick discovered and wrote about it, and it took a while for the medical community to believe *him*."

Until 1912, when Herrick published a five-and-a-half-page paper in the *Journal of the American Medical Association,* "Clinical Features of Sudden Obstruction of the Coronary Arteries," the conventional wisdom was that heart attacks were undiagnosable, fatal events that could only be identified on autopsy. Although Herrick did not claim he was discovering anything new, his conclusions represented a paradigm shift — a radically new way of thinking about old problems that called conventional beliefs into question.

By comparing symptoms of living patients to those who, after death, were found to have had blocked arteries, Herrick demonstrated that coronary artery disease was recognizable in *living* patients. At the same time, he offered evidence suggesting that a totally blocked major coronary artery, as in my case, need not cause death, or even a heart attack. He concluded that heart attacks were most likely caused by blood clots in the coronary arteries, and that some heart attacks were survivable.

"Unsurprisingly," Stephen Klaidman writes, "no one believed him. The old paradigm was not ready to topple. Herrick said that when he delivered the paper, 'It fell like a dud.'"

Six years later, in 1918, Herrick provided additional evidence to support his theory, including comparative animal and electrocardiograph tracings that identified the existence of blocked coronary arteries, and this time, Klaidman writes, "the livelier minds in the medical profession finally began to take notice."

Although Herrick's theory remained the conventional wisdom from 1920 to 1960, at which time it began to be questioned, it was not until 1980 that another American physician, Marcus DeWood, using a technique unavailable to Herrick — selective coronary angiography — proved that it was, in fact, blood clots within the coronary arteries, and not the slow accretion of atherosclerotic plaque, that caused most heart attacks. Thus was Herrick's theory, nearly seventy years after he first proposed it, fully confirmed.

Thus, too, Rich contends, do we see how slowly and indirectly it is that we often arrive, in medicine, at the knowledge that allows physicians to be useful to their patients.

"And the most important element in our ability to be useful," Rich says, "and to continue to test old and new hypotheses, and so discover those things that, as with Herrick, allow us to be *increasingly* useful, remains what it has been since I began as a medical student: *listening.*

"Listening to the patient has been, is, and will continue to be, I believe, the hallmark of medical diagnosis, the most fundamental element in the practice of good medicine. Wasn't it Osler who said, 'Listen to the patient — and the patient will give you the diagnosis'? Well, he was right. For it is the careful taking of a history — and the *active listening* and observing that accompanies this — that enables doctors such as Herrick to see what's really there and what others, alas, too often do not see.

"This," Rich says, "is what I continue to believe is and should be at the true heart of medicine — the time-honored *art* of medicine — and, alas, it is fast disappearing."

In the years before Rich and I were born, and before cancer and heart disease had become our major killers — in the years when infectious and respiratory diseases were still the primary causes of death, and when doctors often had few resources at their disposal other than listening and consoling — the deaths of infants and children were grimly commonplace, and rates of infant and child mortality substantially, grievously higher than they are now.

In 1900, of the fifteen leading causes of death, infectious diseases accounted for 56 percent of the total. When total mortality from *all* causes is taken into account, the three cardiovascular-renal conditions — heart disease, cerebral hemorrhage, and chronic nephritis — came to only 18.4 percent.

Between 1900 and 1904 — the year my father was born — death rates per thousand for white males and females under the age of one were 154.7 and 124.8. (Comparable rates during these years for non-white Americans — mostly blacks — were more than twice as high.) The mortality rates for white males and females between the ages of one and four during these same years were 17.2 and 15.9, and for nonwhites 40.3 and 30.6. However, by 1940 — two years after I was born — the infant mortality rate had fallen by nearly 75 percent, while in the one-to-four-year age group, the figures had fallen even more dramatically (to 3.1 per thousand for males and to 2.7 for females). Moreover, infectious disease had become a minor cause of mortality. Whereas mortality rates for measles, whooping cough, and scarlet fever, for example, were 13.3, 12.2, and 9.6 per hundred thousand in 1900, in 1940 they were, respectively, 0.5, 2.2, and 0.5.

During the first half of the twentieth century, average life expectancy for Americans rose nearly 50 percent, from 47.3 in 1900 to 68.2 in 1950 (comparable figures for blacks were 33.0 and 60.7). In the second half of the century, figures for average life expectancy continued to rise, and infant and child mortality rates continued to decline, but they did so to a much lesser extent. From 1950 to 1998, however, life expectancy rose by only slightly more than 10 percent — from 68.2 to 76.5 for the total population, and from 60.7 to 71.1 for blacks, while infant mortality declined from 29.2 in 1950 to 7.2 in 1998. And while, in 1900, more than 3 out of every 100 children died between their first and twentieth birthday, today fewer than 2 in 1,000 do. Moreover, the American Academy of Pediatrics reports, "nearly 85% of this decline took place before World War II, a period when few antibiotics or modern vaccines and medications were available." (Note, though, the unexpected finding that, based on 1998 figures, the United States had the slowest rate of improvement in life expectancy of any industrialized nation.)

Just as Rich catalogues the remarkable advances he has seen in the treatment of heart disease since 1959, when he began his medical studies — the advent of monitors that can detect potentially lethal heart arrhythmias, of the cardiac care unit, of medications that break up clots and prevent atherosclerosis, of pacemakers, ventricular assist devices, electronic defibrillators, and of various new surgical procedures (bypasses, transplants, angioplasties, stenting) — so my other friends list the new means they have at their disposal for treating disease and the symptoms of disease: drugs and regimens that control high blood pressure, effective analgesic medications for the management of rheumatic disorders, remarkable diagnostic aids such as MRIs and CAT-scans, powerful medications that can put diseases such as AIDS, depression, schizophrenia, Huntington's chorea, multiple sclerosis, and various cancers into short- and long-term remission.

Not only can we now prolong life in ways that were previously not possible, but we have, especially in the last quarter century, developed effective ways to enhance the day-to-day quality of the lives being prolonged. Twenty years ago, as Rich and Dr. Hashim acknowledge, little could have been done for me. I would most probably have died, or if not, might well have been seriously disabled for the rest of my life.

But the optimism bred a half century ago by the elimination of many childhood diseases, and by the gains we have made since then, has also, in the practice of medicine, become responsible for dangerous illusions, false hopes, and wasteful policies.

The belief, for example, that *all* conditions are amenable to "cure" — the various "wars" against diseases that attempt to persuade us that we can "battle" and "conquer" diseases the way we battle and conquer wartime enemies — by "mobilizing" resources, and "attacking" alien invaders (bacteria, viruses) — tends to distort our medical and human priorities, and to show little insight into how the biological world actually works, and how scientific advances come into being. It also elevates the seeming *science* of medicine above the *art* of medicine both by greatly exaggerating the power of technology (often mistaken for and confused with "science") to improve and save lives, and by falsely dichotomizing the science of medicine and the art of medicine.

One effect of this is that we often begin and end by treating patients not as people — individual human beings with unique histories and identities — but as interchangeable humanoid vessels in which various diseases, along with treatments and cures for diseases, will interact in predictable, uniform ways. Such beliefs are championed by drug companies, medical groups, and hospitals in public relations and advertising campaigns that continually deluge the public with claims made no less dubious and misleading by their familiarity and vagueness.

"Discover the *Only* Cholesterol Medicine Proven to Do All This," states a February 12, 2001, full-page ad in the *New York Times* for Pravachol. There follows a checklist contending that Pravachol will lower "bad" cholesterol, raise "good" cholesterol, "extend life by reducing the risk of a heart attack," and also reduce the risk of first and second heart attacks, strokes, atherosclerosis, bypass surgery, and angioplasty. At the top of the page, this suggestion: "Clip this ad and bring it to your doctor." (The United States remains the only industrialized nation that allows prescription drugs to be advertised directly to the public.)

In widely dispersed print and television ads for Zocor, Dan Reeves, an NFL football coach, confides that "suddenly, lowering my high cholesterol became even more important than football." After undergoing emergency bypass surgery, Reeves reports he "had a full recovery, and was even able to coach [his] team in the biggest game of the season four weeks later." Having learned to "take better care of [himself]" he advises the following: "When diet and exercise are not enough, ZOCOR can help people with high cholesterol and heart disease *live a longer life* by reducing the risk of a heart attack" (italics added).

Columbia Presbyterian and New York Weill Cornell Cancer Centers claim, in typically militaristic language, that they have been "at the forefront of the fight against cancer" and are now "working together to defeat this relentless disease." In "one of the boldest initiatives ever undertaken," they offer "new hope that the fight will be won" because at these cancer centers "experts" are helping to "uncover genes that cause cancer — essential to conquering the disease."

And America's Pharmaceutical Companies, the public relations firm that represents the drug industry ("leading the way in the search for cures"), proclaims that "pharmaceutical company researchers are working hard to discover breakthroughs that will help to make many illnesses and diseases a thing of the past and bring more patients new hope for a better tomorrow."

Phil is blunt concerning such seemingly unexceptional claims and the false hopes and illusions they inspire, as well as the fact that patients, with increasing frequency, are coming to their doctors and demanding the medications they have read and heard about: mostly what have become known as lifestyle medications (Viagra, Prozac, Paxil, Rogaine) and the statins (Lipitor, Mevacor, Pravachol, Zocor), whose ads repeatedly suggest, in addition to banalities about "new hope," "new cures," and "better tomorrows," what has *not* been proven: that these drugs will "extend life" and enable us to "live longer."

"I call it the Ponce de León thing," Phil says. "Everybody's selling you the fountain of youth — eat this and don't eat that and you'll live forever. Take this medication, or exercise so much and so much every day, or have your doctor test you for this and perform that procedure and prescribe this form of therapy or that regimen and you'll feel better than ever, get rid of all your bad feelings, and live forever. And if these things aren't enough for you, there's always cryogenics. It's insane."

"The belief that disease can be conquered," Gerald Grob comments, "reflects a fundamental conviction that all things are possible and that human beings have it within their power to control completely their own destiny."

"The faith that disease is unnatural and can be conquered," he continues, "rests on a fundamental misunderstanding of the biological world. If cancer is the enemy, then the enemy is ourselves. Malignant cells, after all, are hardly aliens who invade our bodies; they grow from our own normal cells."

"Inflated rhetorical claims to the contrary," he insists, "the etiology of most of the diseases of our age — notably cardiovascular disease, cancer, diabetes, mental illnesses — still remains a mystery."

Then too, as my friends explain, not only do *most* diseases — including those that, in terms of mortality, predominate in our time (cancer and heart disease) — appear to have multiple causes (very few diseases are genetic in origin, and of those that are, most are quite rare, and even fewer are caused by single genes), but they are intimately bound up with the simple fact of aging: that we are mortal, we grow old, and we die.

Writing in the *New England Journal of Medicine* about ways publicity for medical research often encourages us to deny the reality of death and aging, Daniel Callahan, senior fellow at the Harvard Medical School and director of International Programs at the Hastings Center, a research institute that addresses ethical issues in health, medicine, and the environment, quotes William Haseltine, chairman and chief executive officer of Human Genome Sciences. "Death," Haseltine has proclaimed, "is a series of preventable diseases."

"The tacit message of the research agenda, is that if death itself cannot be eliminated," Callahan comments, "then at least all the diseases that cause death can be done away with.

"From this perspective," he continues, "the researcher is like a sharpshooter who will pick off the enemy one by one: cancer, then heart disease, then diabetes, then AIDS, then Alzheimer's disease, and so on."

The "thrust of the research imperative against death is to turn death itself into a contingent, accidental event," Callahan submits, and one result of this way of thinking is that it "promotes the idea among the public and physicians that death represents a failure of medicine."

"Since we are a self-replacing entity," William Haseltine informs the *New York Times,* "and do so reasonably well for many decades, there is no reason we can't go on forever." He explains: "The fundamental property of DNA is its immortality. The problem is to connect that immortality with human immortality and, for the first time, we see how that may be possible."

When Phil and I discuss my mother, who has been diagnosed with Alzheimer's disease and has been in a nursing home since 1992 (by which time she no longer knew who I was; for the last four or five years — I am writing this in the summer of 2002, shortly before her ninety-first birthday — she has not recognized even her regular nurses), Phil shakes his head.

"Sometimes I don't understand why Alzheimer's is such a big

deal," he says. "As we get older, *lots* of our systems begin to wear down, and that seems natural to me. In the old days, see, when her memory got bad and she couldn't take care of herself, Aunt Edith would live with one of her children or a brother or sister, and when people got together she would usually sit quietly by herself, and if anybody asked about her, the family would say, 'Oh that's Tante Edith — she doesn't remember things so well anymore, but she still bakes great strudel.'

"I mean, why are all these young people jogging and working out on treadmills and in health clubs all the time? Why is everyone on these diets all the time? Why do old men take up with young things, and women get boob-lifts and face-lifts? It's the Ponce de León thing if you ask me — thinking we can cheat the angel of death and stay young forever.

"And the drug companies, with all their power, they take advantage. Sure. That's the Willie Sutton thing. When he was asked why he robbed banks, he answered, 'Because that's where the money is.' It's the same with medicine — it goes where the money is. And these days the money's in Prozac and Lipitor and Viagra. Did you know that nearly a third of all stents fail, and that new studies are telling us that all the chemotherapy we gave for cancer, with the enormous suffering it produced, probably didn't make any difference in how long people lived? And as for all those cholesterol meds — for basically healthy guys like us, it's a crock. What do we need to take that crap for, without any proof that it makes a difference, yet knowing for certain that somewhere down the road, as with most meds taken long-term, there are going to be unforeseen, nasty side effects? What's wrong with growing old and dying is the question I ask."

To which I reply: Believing what you do, and dealing on a daily basis with people who have migraines and headaches of unknown origin, who have suffered severe trauma and/or irreversible brain damage, have had strokes, and have been struck with fatal, debilitating diseases — why do you do it, and, as I've seen through the years when I've been with you, how do you maintain such an optimistic, hopeful attitude? What motivates you day after day?

"Okay," Phil says. "I see it this way. In my specialty I'm always dealing with people who are sick. They're not *cured*, because if they were, they wouldn't be in my office or at the hospital. That's the given. But the longer I do it, the more I know and the more I can be useful to people. Why be a doctor? Because you make a decent living, you satisfy yourself, and you do good in the world. That's the beauty of it. Hopefully, you're helping people — and we do help people much more than when I started out, when we didn't know that a lot of what we did was harmful. The things we can do now for people are truly marvelous — but we're often constrained, mostly by the insurance companies and medical groups that want us to spend less and less time with our patients, and to get them out of the hospital as quickly as possible.

"I want my patients to go home — if they have a home to go to — as soon as possible too, but I wind up spending more and more of my time fighting with insurance companies, especially for how much care my patients need *after* they leave. I mean, look at you: if you'd had a stroke during surgery and were incapacitated, who would have paid for people to be with you in ways essential to your day-to-day life — to your will to live?

"But you're always learning, and that's what I love — I wake up each morning knowing there are going to be new challenges, and new things to learn, and that I can be useful to other human beings." Phil shrugs, says again what he has said before: "For me, that's the beauty of it."

While my other friends also talk about the beauty of a life in which they are constantly learning new things, and while they talk about the struggles and rewards they experience in trying to be useful to others, they also, like Phil, lament the devaluation of the doctor-patient relationship. They do so, not because they are nostalgic for some idealized and illusory golden era when family doctors with warm bedside manners made house calls and had their offices in their homes (as most of the doctors I knew did when I was growing up in Brooklyn, their wives often serving as their nurses or receptionists), but for decidedly *practical* reasons: because it is only by carefully listening to and examining a patient, by putting a patient's symptoms and concerns into the larger context of the patient's individuality and history, and by considering the individual patient in the context of their *own* knowledge and clinical experience, that they believe they have a good shot at an accurate diagnosis and a beneficial treatment plan.

Because Rich listened carefully to me over a period of time — because he *knew* me — he was, even though three thousand miles away, better able to gauge the exact nature and true gravity of my condition, and thus to urge me into treatment at once (and then, along with Jerry, to persist in choosing and getting the best possible care for me), than were the doctors who actually saw me and examined me in Northampton.

"But they weren't seeing *you*," Rich says. "Instead of seeing you and listening to you — and hearing what you said: the nature of your pain, its precise location, its comings and goings, its progress over time — they ran more tests. And tests have an aura of scientific certainty — especially if they come out of a computer, right? Oh there's nothing 'subjective' there!

"But they weren't seeing *you*, my friend," he says again. "And the more our technologies evolve, and the more we rely on them — and they can be wonderfully useful, let me assure you — the more we're in danger of not paying attention to the human being in front of us. So that if we think the machine knows more than we do — or rather, if we begin to think we can never know as much as the machine does — if we stop trusting those instincts and that knowledge based upon a lifetime of study and of seeing patients — then we are in real trouble."

7

Listen to the Patient

ALTHOUGH MY FRIENDS CHERISH the new diagnostic tools, medications, and technologies that enable them to be more effective doctors — "Whatever relieves symptoms and promises alleviation of pain and suffering is fine by me," Phil says — they all continue to direct my attention to the fact that most of the biotechnological innovations we spend so much money on, and that the media glorify, are not what has made and will continue to make the greatest difference in the health and well-being of most human beings.

When I ask Jerry, for example, who has witnessed advances in the ability to treat patients with AIDS considered impossible a few years ago, what he would put at the top of his medical agenda were he in a position to set priorities, his answer is simple.

"Clean water," he says. And not only in the so-called undeveloped world, but in those regions of developed nations, and our own country, where clean water, along with other essential public health measures, is lacking; where medications are either not available or so expensive as to be beyond the means of those who need them; where pathogens are fast becoming resistant to available medications (antibiotics especially); where diseases such as malaria, cholera, and tuberculosis are returning; where adequate sewage and sanitation are wanting; and where infant and child mortality remains high because there are not enough doctors or other caregivers to tend to the people in need and to educate them in ways that might prevent diseases that are eminently preventable. (According to figures from the U.S. Department of Health and Human Services for 2000, the United States ranks twenty-sixth in the world in infant mortality, with an average of 7.3 infant deaths for every thousand live births.)

Jerry and I have talked often through the years about the presence in our immediate families of individuals who have suffered from mental illness, and of our sense — confirmed by the years — that what often matters most in this area of illness, as with AIDS, is care and not cure. Although the kind of care that often matters most in the lives of people afflicted with mental illness — the relationship they develop on a long-term basis with a professional; the ways they learn to live *with* their condition; the ways they learn to become alert to early warning signs of impending crises; and the ways they learn to manage crises when crises arrive — may often seem too low-tech to be "scientific," these ongoing human activities and interactions — talk, companionship, education — are what create trust, and thereby make *all* the difference.

"In my work," Arthur says, reiterating with respect to psychological problems what Jerry and I have been saying about the treatment of AIDS and mental illness, "the key ingredient *is* trust, and I have been most useful to people only when we have been able to meet and talk over extended periods of time without the threat of having our sessions cut off, or cut down."

Like my physician friends, Arthur specifies the ways in which he is of tangible help to his patients — whether with ostensibly somatic disorders such as depression and obsessive-compulsive disorder, or with those problems of life, marital, sexual, or vocational, that though not commonly designated as clinical entities, still, as with the majority of conditions people go to doctors for, affect a person's ability to function in this world, and surely affect a person's susceptibility to other debilitating conditions, and to disease.

"Essentially, I'm a databank, the same way an M.D. is," Arthur says. "There are certain predictable things that a person who has dealt with human beings knows just from seeing them many, many, many times. The medical equivalent, I guess, is a cold and a sore throat, and the doctor says it's a viral infection and it will go away. He knows it because he's seen it many, many times.

"I'm a databank on how things tend to work out based on seeing lots of similar stories. Because if a therapist can do anything, it's to help people see the world as it truly is. A woman gets married at seventeen and has a child at eighteen and was a promiscuous adolescent, and now she's thirty-one and she's interested in going to college. She's with a blue-collar guy who drinks too much, and their connection is lousy, and she says, 'Is this my life?' Now one of the things I know is 'Yes — for sure this is your life for the next five to ten years. However, if you begin here, and you find your way, by the time you're thirty-seven, say, to a college degree, and by thirty-eight or thirty-nine, to a way to earn money, you will then have a choice as to whether you want to keep your package intact. But the key is not to think you must do something or *can* do something by thirty-one-and-a-half. Because if you do, you'll drive yourself crazy.'

"I can tell you how that woman's marriage is going to go, and how that person will develop. That's like your mother made ten thousand chickens so she knows how long to keep a chicken in the oven. I mean, these are the things *Bubbie* — our grandmothers — would have told us before there were shrinks.

"A woman comes to me and her boyfriend can't make love to her because he can't get an erection. I know that the worst thing for him is for her to say, 'I'll do this to help you get an erection — I'll read this book, try this, try that,' and it will drive him crazy. What I'll say to this woman is, 'Let him pleasure *you* and forget about it and not think about himself.' Now that's empirical stuff that comes from just seeing a lot of guys who can't get erections, and in time this marriage may not be saddled with sexual problems.

"Psychiatry comes out of the medical model — it's a stepchild in medicine's house, right? — and the medical model comes down to: Neugie has a sore throat, gets a strep test, takes his medicine. But a monkey could give you an antibiotic. In my field it doesn't work that way because it depends on which monkey for which patient, and whether it's an antibiotic or whether it's a laying on of hands. Because there will always be a certain percentage of problems that cannot be handled by hard science or by medications — psychiatry is not, for example, generally efficient or effective with addictions: smoking, gambling, alcohol — and there will always be a place for the judgment, instinct, and creativity that make this an essentially *humanistic* enterprise. Because in the end, you see, despite all I know — all the data I've accumulated — I'm still not sure of much more than I'm sure of."

I say that our three physician friends have said the same thing — that despite their expertise, much of the effectiveness of their work is essentially humanistic, and is based on trust; that a lot of what we think of as "science" in medicine is hardly scientific; and that the practice of good medicine is based on the very elements that Arthur values in the practice of psychotherapy: judgment, instinct, listening, and clinical experience — diagnostic and therapeutic skills that are not always teachable.

I remind Arthur that, in my own case, two experienced doctors failed to get the diagnosis of heart disease right, and I remind him of what Rich keeps saying — that though we could fix what was wrong with me once we found it, and though we know a good deal about heart disease and have some viable theories on what causes it and can prevent it, the root causes of heart attacks — the accumulation of abnormalities in the walls of blood vessels, and the rupture of atherosclerotic plaque — still remain largely unknown to us.

A large proportion of the work our friends do in medicine, like the work Arthur does in psychotherapy, I suggest, has to do with long-term management and care of conditions (brain trauma, stroke, diabetes, AIDS, migraine) that depend at least as much on the interaction of doctor and patient — on biology *and* behavior — as they do on machines and medications.

Although medications have been of enormous help in enabling people afflicted with mental illness to get on with their lives — to reduce their sufferings and confusion and enable them to survive, recover, and move beyond recovery — medications, for all their efficacy, are only one element in what usually proves decisive. And while most of the several hundred individuals I have met who have recovered from years of madness and institutionalization are grateful for medications (especially new "atypical" antipsychotic medications), they all, in various ways, tell me the same thing: that though you can ameliorate symptoms with a pill — and thank God that you can — you cannot reconstruct a life with a pill.

For that, they explain, you need people working with people, since, for individuals living long-term with those conditions we designate as chronic — whether schizophrenia, multiple sclerosis, diabetes, AIDS, heart disease, or various forms of cancer — it is precisely the long-term nature of the condition that makes attention to long-term care imperative.

But why, Jerry asks, given the history of medicine, should we be surprised that this is so — and why should we deny its claim upon our priorities?

Jerry's primary medical training, along with the study of infectious disease, was in public health, and he points me toward studies that demonstrate how public health measures, and not specifically medical measures, are what have made the great and decisive difference.

Thus, in one recent instance of the difference preventive measures can make, a study involving more than eighty thousand women aged thirty to fifty-five concluded that "in this population of middle-aged women, those who did not smoke cigarettes, were not overweight, maintained [a healthful diet], exercised moderately or vigorously for half an hour a day, and consumed alcohol moderately had an *incidence of coronary events that was more than 80 percent lower than that in the rest of the population*" (italics added). During the course of the study, begun in 1980, and which included follow-up studies on each participant every two years for fourteen years, researchers documented 1,128 major coronary events — 296 deaths from coronary heart disease and 832 nonfatal heart attacks — and concluded that "eighty-two percent of coronary events in the study cohort could be attributed to lack of adherence to this low-risk pattern."

In another recent example of the difference preventive measures can make, this time for individuals suffering from type 2 diabetes, a large clinical study determined that "even modest lifestyle changes" — eating less fat, exercising (walking briskly) two and a half hours a week, and losing a moderate amount of weight — can cut the incidence of type 2 diabetes by more than 50 percent among those most at risk. Type 2 diabetes (known also as adult-onset diabetes) accounts for between 90 and 95 percent of all cases of diabetes, and currently affects approximately nineteen million Americans. It often leads to heart disease, as well as to kidney failure, blindness, and stroke.

In this study, sponsored by the National Institute of Diabetes and Digestive and Kidney Diseases, which followed more than three thousand individuals at twenty-seven medical centers for three years, on average, and included a large number of people from minority groups at particularly high risk for the disease, participants were randomly divided into three groups: those given a medication (metformin), those given placebos, and those who received no pills but instead received guidance and training to help them modify their eating habits and incorporate exercise into their schedules.

While all participants in the study were advised to restrict diet, to exercise, and to lose weight, it turned out that only those who attended diet and exercise classes, and received follow-up help, were *able* to turn the advice into practice. Among those who took placebos, 11 percent a year developed diabetes; among those who took metformin, 7.8 percent a year developed diabetes; and among those who changed their eating and exercise habits, only 4.8 percent a year developed diabetes, a reduction of more than 50 percent when compared to the control group.

So dramatic were the study's results — so clear the hope that the alarming rise in diabetes in the United States could be significantly reversed (type 2 diabetes has risen by a third since 1990) — that researchers decided to make the results public and end the study in August 2001, a year early, in order, according to the *New York Times*, to find ways to begin "translating the results of the study into an effective public health policy."

Most of us are living longer, healthier lives than our parents and grandparents did, and our *average* life expectancy has increased greatly — by more than 60 percent during the past century — and this is largely because more of us survive our childhoods. And the fact that we do derives mainly not from practices that are specifically medical, as we ordinarily understand that term, but from measures that come, more generally, under the heading of public health.

"Life span has always been and still is somewhere between eighty and ninety-five for most people," Steven Harrell, of the University of Washington Center for Studies in Demography, explains. "What has happened in the twentieth century is that infant and child deaths have been reduced drastically . . . [so that] the average length of life has begun to approach the life span." In other words, when you average in all those infants and children who died before the age of five with those who died after, say, sixty-five, the result is a much lower *average* life expectancy than you get when the vast majority of us no longer die before the age of five.

Consider the following: In Plymouth Colony three hundred years ago, a male surviving to age twenty-one could expect to live to around age sixty-nine, while the corresponding figure for a woman was around sixty-two (the disparity due in large part to risks that accompanied childbirth). By age fifty, life expectancy for both men and women was nearly seventy-four (exactly what the census reports it is for men in 1998). Other colonies fared as well. In Andover, Massachusetts, in the seventeenth century, the average age at death of first-generation males and females was over seventy, and more than half their children who survived to age twenty lived to seventy or more.

Unlike southern colonies in the Chesapeake area of Virginia and Maryland, where life expectancy was significantly lower (those who survived to age twenty rarely lived past age fifty), New England colonies were spared from epidemic childhood infectious diseases largely because they had a clean and safe water supply, a varied and sufficient food supply, and relative isolation from the kind of commercial intercourse that spread epidemic diseases such as malaria.

In the United States during the past century, due mainly to the decline of infant and child mortality, what we see when we look at federal census figures is a consistent pattern: in each succeeding decade deaths that previously occurred at younger ages are replaced by a larger proportion of deaths occurring in advanced ages. And according to the evolutionary biologist Paul Ewald, the patterns of life expectancy that prevailed in New England three hundred years ago have also prevailed in other regions of the world, as they do, for example, among the !Kung Bushmen of southwest Africa and the Ache Indians of northern Paraguay.

But what about the contribution to our lives of the many new medical technologies — drugs, vaccines, diagnostic capabilities, and treatments (surgical techniques, neonatal developments, dialysis, transplants, bypasses, and DNA cloning)? Haven't they been central to our increasing longevity and well-being? The answer, though hardly uncomplicated, confirms what my friends say: these have been helpful, have made a difference in many lives (mine!), but have not been central or decisive.

The introduction of antibiotic therapy, for example, as we have seen with respect to infant and child mortality (where nearly 90 percent of the decline in infectious disease mortality occurred before 1940), happened during and after World War II, when infectious diseases were no longer a significant cause of mortality.

In a series of seminal studies, John and Sonja McKinlay have demonstrated "that the introduction of specific medical measures and/or the expansion of medical services are generally not responsible for most of the modern decline in mortality"; nevertheless, "it is not uncommon today for biotechnological knowledge and specific medical interventions to be invoked as *the major reason* for most of the modern (twentieth-century) decline in mortality."

The vital statistics are as follows. From 1900 until 1950, the annual rate of decline in overall mortality was 0.22 per thousand, "after which," the McKinlays write, "it became an almost negligible decline of 0.04 annually." And "of the total fall in the standardized death rate between 1900 and 1973, 92.3 percent occurred prior to 1950." Moreover, the "major part" of the decline, they explain, can be attributed to the virtual disappearance of eleven infectious diseases: typhoid, smallpox, scarlet fever, measles, whooping cough, diphtheria, influenza, tuberculosis, pneumonia, diseases of the digestive system, and poliomyelitis.

Charting the years in which medical interventions for the major causes of mortality were introduced — sulphonamide for pneumonia, 1935; penicillin for scarlet fever, 1946; and vaccines for whooping cough (1930), influenza (1943), measles (1963), and smallpox (1798) — and correlating these interventions with mortality rates, the McKinlays conclude that "medical measures (both chemotherapuetic and prophylactic) appear to have contributed little to the overall decline in mortality in the United States since about 1900 — having in many instances been introduced several decades *after* a marked decline had already set in and having no detectable influence in most instances" (italics added). With reference to five conditions (influenza, pneumonia, diphtheria, whooping cough, and poliomyelitis) in which the decline in mortality appears substantial *after* the point of medical intervention, "and on the unlikely assumption that all of this decline is attributable to the intervention," they estimate that "at most 3.5 percent of the total decline in mortality since 1900 could be ascribed to medical measures introduced for [these diseases]."

The McKinlays also comment on an irony my friends have noted: that *"the beginning of the precipitate and still unrestrained rise in medical care expenditures began when nearly all (92 percent) of the modern decline in mortality this century had already occurred"* (italics in original).

Others, before and after, corroborate the McKinlays' thesis. Dr. Thomas McKeown, for example, has argued in numerous papers and several books that approximately 75 percent of the decline in mortality in the twentieth century (from 1900 to 1971) is associated with the control of infectious disease.

Gerald Grob, surveying the history of disease in America, concludes that the "epidemiological transition in which chronic degenerative disease replaced infectious disease as the major cause of mortality, a process that began sometime in the late nineteenth century . . . was largely completed by 1940." He writes, "Whatever the explanation of the causes of [this] epidemiologic transition, there is general agreement that strictly medical therapies played an insignificant role."

Reviewing the history, and decline, of each infectious disease in detail, Grob notes the many and varied elements — differing in each instance — that most probably contributed to the decline in mortality, while also warning that the decline in mortality "from infectious diseases associated with childhood admits of no simple explanation." Thus, in the cases of scarlet fever and rheumatic fever, for example, there is strong evidence that diminutions in the virulence of the pathogens themselves were crucial (the complex ways whereby pathogens interact with their human hosts continually give rise to variable virulence levels). And the decline of smallpox turns out to have been due less to vaccination than to isolation of those infected and, especially, to the appearance of a far less lethal strain of the disease in the United States after 1896.

Although the origins of the decline in mortality from some diseases, such as tuberculosis, remain controversial, there is general agreement among scholars that the overall decline in mortality and poor health — our increasing longevity and well-being — derives most often, as my friends maintain, from changes that have been *socially caused* and have *not* been brought into being either by medical interventions (whether biotechnological, prophylactic, or chemical) or medical design.

We live healthier, longer lives, that is, largely because of changes arising from public health policies and public health measures: the education of families concerning maternal and child health care, disease, disease prevention, and hygiene (such as an emphasis on hand washing); public education concerning diet, exercise, and smoking; improved sanitation, sewage, waste disposal, and disinfection interventions; the availability of clean water and clean air; the elimination of chronic malnutrition; the general rise in standards of living; the reduced consumption of toxic waste; improvements and decreased population density in housing; quarantines and other means of controlling epidemics; and — as with smallpox — a sometimes fortuitous mix of elements: vaccination, surveillance, isolation of active cases, and diminished virulence.

And there is this too — a fact I find as surprising as it is unsettling: despite the abundance of new, highly publicized chemical and surgical interventions for various specific cancers, and despite President Nixon's "war on cancer," launched in 1971, along with subsequent campaigns against various specific cancers, if one excepts lung cancer, where substantial gains in mortality have been made in recent years (especially since 1992) because people have learned to smoke less, the incidence and prevalence of all other cancers (increases in some, decreases in others) have, since 1900, remained more or less constant.

More surprising still: from 1950 until 1998, during which decades most of the new technologies have been introduced, both for screening (early detection) and treatment (chemotherapies), the mortality rates for cancer have remained relatively stable. Although there have been slight fluctuations during the past half century, the mortality rate in 1998 — 123.6 — is roughly identical to what it was in 1950: 125.2.

There have, happily, been significant advances in the treatment of various specific forms of cancer in the past fifty years — cancer of the bone, stomach, uterus, and cervix, along with cancer of the prostate for those under sixty-five, has declined. Mortality from all types of leukemia, and in all ages, has decreased, and deaths from colorectal cancer have also decreased. At the same time, pancreatic cancer along with cancers of the urinary organs, kidney, ovaries, and intestine have generally increased. Small increases have been recorded for malignant brain tumors and malignant melanomas, and mortality from lymphomas — despite reductions in mortality from the cancer I had, Hodgkin's disease — has also increased.

The reasons for increases and decreases are variable, controversial, and complex; still, what the data reveal is that progress, as we usually understand it — despite the multitude of new medications, therapies, screenings, and technologies — has been, at best, irregular. Surely, the original objective of the National Cancer Institute — that we reduce age-adjusted mortality from cancer 50 percent by the year 2000 — has come nowhere near to being achieved. And again, as with infectious diseases, it turns out in many cases that the major salutary changes from which we do benefit occurred *before* the introduction of new cancer therapies — and that they came about not because of specifically medical measures, but because of preventive measures.

In a study published in 1986 by the Department of Health Studies at the University of Chicago, researchers conclude that "some 35 years of intense effort focused largely on improving [cancer] treatment must be judged a qualified failure." Choosing as the "single best measure of progress against cancer," the mortality rate for all forms of cancer combined, age-adjusted to the U.S. 1980 standard (a measure also adopted by the National Cancer Institute), they find that "age-adjusted mortality rates have shown a slow and steady increase over several decades, and [that] there is no evidence of a recent downward trend." In 1997, the University of Chicago researchers reviewed their 1986 findings. They write that "with 12 more years of data and experience, we see little reason to change [our earlier] conclusion."

"Despite numerous past claims that success was just around the corner," they write (Dr. Vincent De Vita, of the National Cancer Institute, predicted in 1981 that "fifty percent of all cancers will be curable within ten years"), "hopes for a substantial reduction in mortality by the year 2000 were clearly misplaced."

Moreover, they are skeptical about "new therapeutic approaches rooted in molecular medicine" because "the arguments are similar in tone and rhetoric to those of decades past about chemotherapy, tumor virology, immunology, and other approaches." They continue: "In our view, prudence requires a skeptical view of the tacit assumption that marvelous new treatments for cancer are just waiting to be discovered." While they "earnestly hope that such discoveries can and will be made," they suggest a modest reordering of priorities: "The effect of primary prevention (e.g., reductions in the prevalence of smoking) and secondary prevention (e.g., the Papanicolaou smear) on mortality due to cancer indicates a pressing need for reevaluation of the dominant research strategies of the past 40 years, particularly the emphasis on improving treatments, and a redirection of effort toward prevention."

But won't our new understanding of the human genome, along with ongoing developments in genetic engineering, gene therapy, DNA cloning, et cetera, lead to discoveries that will enable us to treat cancers with increasing success?

"What the human genome project gives us seems to me to be beyond the clinical realm at the present time," Phil says. "Now someday I think we may all go around with medical cards that have our genetic IDs on them because the genome project will help us to devise treatments specific to your specific genetic make-up. So that, for example, we wouldn't give Lipitor to everyone with high cholesterol, but only to those whose genetic ID shows a particular disposition to atherosclerosis for which Lipitor will probably be helpful. There may be some rare genetic diseases where what we learn from the genome project can be helpful sooner, but for a long time to come it's not going to have anything to do with the everyday practice of medicine."

"The genome project has been a remarkable achievement, even though the hype about its potential value in the diagnosis and treatment of disease has been overblown and simplistic," Rich says. "Currently, we know little about the factors that determine how genes cause disease, and we need to know a lot more about issues like gene penetrance, what turns genes on and off, and the importance of gene interactions.

"In my view, the most common diseases, such as coronary disease and cancer, result from a complex interaction of genes, the environment, and what's been called 'the mind-body interaction,' but to date, what's been done is simply to catalogue the genes, much like naming cities on a map without knowing much about them. Still, I'm optimistic that over the next five to ten years, we will increasingly understand how genes function and interact, and what the causative genes and combinations of genes are for significant diseases.

"Eventually I think the genome project will prove useful to our understanding and treatment of disease, though it will not be the panacea its enthusiasts have made it out to be. Many of our most worthwhile discoveries in medicine have come about not when we were looking for a specific cure for a specific illness, but serendipitously — look at penicillin, at peptic ulcers, at the uses we've found for cortisone and aspirin. When you have enough good people working on something, as we do in genetic research, then the probability of serendipity — of discovery — increases. That's just basic statistics and probability. But to date, the unbridled zeal for the genome project seems excessive."

"What bothers me about the attention given to the human genome project," Jerry adds, "is that while we extol its virtues and invest large sums of money in research that will not, for a long while, be useful to any but a small number of human beings, tens of millions of human beings are languishing and dying for want of basic care and of known treatments that can, as with AIDS, relieve suffering and save lives now."

Dr. Richard Horton, editor of *Lancet,* reiterates Jerry's view when he writes that "the major issue in medicine is not one of maintaining the past pace of discovery, but of making sure there is equitable access, throughout the world, to the discoveries we have already made."

And the distorted priorities that often determine how we appropriate human and economic resources would seem to derive, at least in part, from a glorification and, at times, deification of biotechnology. Thus we have President Clinton declaring that by deciphering most of the human genome "we are learning the language in which God created life"; or Frances S. Collins, director of the National Human Genome Research Institute, saying that "we have caught the first glimpses of our instruction book, previously known only to God"; or *Time* magazine proclaiming that "armed with the genetic code, scientists can now start teasing out the secrets of human health and disease . . . that will lead at the very least to a revolution in diagnosing and treating everything from Alzheimer's to heart disease to cancer, and more."

The problem with such extravagant claims, as Horton points out, is that "research tends to support [the] view that genes are mostly a minor determinant of human disease" and that "it is very unlikely that a simple and directly causal link between genes and most common diseases will ever be found." As to the usefulness of the genome project with respect to cancer, he notes that progress "will be painfully slow," and, like my friends, though a quarter century younger, Horton doubts that "we will get far along this path during [his] lifetime."

In *One Renegade Cell: How Cancer Begins* (1999), Robert Weinberg, a biologist who pioneered studies in gene therapy for cancer, estimates that by the second decade of the twenty-first century scientists are going to know the elements of cellular wiring in such detail that they will have a catalogue of tumor-suppressive genes that will enable them to predict an individual's susceptibility to a wide spectrum of cancers. Weinberg believes, further, that "the prospects for the development of totally novel anticancer therapeutics are bright." Nonetheless, he too concludes that "the big decreases in cancer deaths will . . . come from preventing disease rather than discovering new cures," by which he means dealing not with the biology of cancer itself, but with its "ultimate causes" — those that "really begin far outside the individual cell, in our environment, in the food we ingest, and the smoke we inhale."

Other scientists and scholars, however, are not as certain that, when it comes to cancer, prevention will have such large and propitious effects. Gerald Grob, for example, writes that "the effort to link cancer to diet, carcinogens, and behavior — which have been central to the campaign to prevent and control the disease — have been rooted largely in belief and hope rather than fact."

"Smoking," he adds, "is the one notable exception." (Weinberg contends that virtually the entire increase in cancer from 1930 to 1990 was due to the use of tobacco, and that had lung cancer been omitted, the overall adjusted cancer death rate between 1950 and 1990 would have fallen by 14 percent.) Moreover, most other proven carcinogens, such as asbestos and high-level radiation, Grob points out, affect few people.

In addition, prevention places a high premium on individual responsibility for one's own health and well-being. Most of us, for example, are aware of the ways in which friends and relatives who contract, say, lethal forms of breast or prostate cancer often blame themselves for their fate — for not having been vigilant enough; for not having had regular and timely screenings; for not having paid attention to this symptom or that health advisory; or for not having stuck to diet A instead of having indulged in diet B, and so on — all of which, by lodging cause and culpability in one's individual negligence, ignorance, and/or irresponsibility, becomes a particularly deadly way of blaming oneself for one's own execution.

Nor is this way of experiencing and understanding one's health — especially one's ill health — new. In the Psalms and, particularly, in the Book of Job, for example, we are told again and again that the presence of a physical affliction or ailment is the outward sign — the

visible punishment — for (unseen) irresponsibility and wrongdo-
ing. (See Psalm 1 — "Blessed is the man that walketh not in the
counsel of the ungodly, nor standeth in the way of sinners, nor
sitteth in the seat of the scornful . . . For the Lord knoweth the way
of the righteous; but the way of the ungodly shall perish.") Consider
Job's friends, who, though they consider Job a pious and righteous
man and know of nothing he has *done* that in any way is immoral or
evil, nevertheless assume, given his afflictions, that he *must* have
done something terrible to be suffering such a dreadful fate. (Thus
Bildad the Shuhite: "If thou wert pure and upright; surely now He
would awake for thee, and make the habitation of thy righteous-
ness prosperous." And Elihu: "Therefore He knoweth their works,
and He overturneth them in the night, so that they are destroyed. He
striketh them as wicked men in the open sight of others." And
Eliphaz: "Is there any secret thing with thee?")

In 1996, the Harvard Center for Cancer Prevention published a report that attempted to summarize current knowledge regarding
cancer risk. Its conclusion: cancer is "a preventable illness." The center estimated the "percentage of total cancer deaths" attributable to
what it determined were the established causes of cancer (for example, tobacco, 30 percent; diet/obesity, 30 percent; sedentary lifestyles,
5 percent) and calculated that "family history of cancer" was responsible for 5 percent of total cancer — thereby implying that virtually
all cancer risk, with the possible exception of this 5 percent, was a result of potentially modifiable environmental risk factors.

The alternative to this view, Grob suggests — "that the etiology of
cancer [is] endogenous and not necessarily amenable to individual
volition — [is] hardly attractive." Still, "it is entirely plausible," he
writes, "that cancer is closely related to aging and genetic mutations,
which together impair the ability of the immune system to identify
and attack malignant cells and thus permit them to multiply. If
there is at present no way to arrest the aging process, then cancer
mortality may be inevitable. Moreover, some of the genetic mutations that eventually lead to cancer may occur randomly, and thus
cannot be prevented."

"There is also," he concludes, "little evidence that cancer mortality is appreciably reduced either by screening to detect the disease in its early stages or [by] a variety of medical therapies."

But how can this be, I wonder, even as I review the data that seem to prove it is so. Is it possible that all these cholesterol screenings, CAT-scans, mammograms, and PSA tests, along with the much-publicized surgical and chemical therapies commonly used to treat problems revealed by the screenings and tests, are, at best, of secondary value (and may sometimes do more harm than good)? Have we really, in these matters, achieved only minor progress?

I review my own experience, where neither blood tests, cholesterol screenings, an EKG, an echocardiogram, nor a complete physical were helpful in revealing the seriousness of my condition. Nor, for that matter, had other much-lauded habits and activities — a lifetime of being a nonsmoker, along with years of vigorous daily exercise, the maintenance of a low-fat diet, and the taking of cholesterol-lowering medications and an aspirin a day — prevented my arteries from becoming clogged.

The more I read, and the more I talk with my friends, the more I come away thinking, again: How little we know about things medical and biological — about why what's beneficial to one person proves useless for another; about how and why and when, that is, some of us live and some of us die.

At the same time, skepticism leavened by my sheer joy at being alive, it becomes clear that, unlike the situation with respect to many cancers, when it comes to heart disease, no matter the vast realms of our ignorance, we *have*, in recent years, made truly significant life-saving and life-enhancing gains. "One advantage we have in cardiology," Rich says, "is that the heart lends itself to plumbing and mechanics — to gross approaches. I mean, just look at you and Dick Cheney — at David Letterman." He laughs. "Better living through plumbing, right?" Right indeed, I think — because hundreds of thousands of men and women, like me, are alive and doing well because of the gains we've made — a half-million benefiting from bypass surgery alone each year. And even when one reads outcome studies indicating that some of us may not live longer with this surgery than without it, it seems indisputable that the *quality* of our lives, whatever the number of years each of us may have left, will, in most instances, be better than it otherwise would have been.

Age-adjusted mortality figures give us a basic measure of the genuine progress achieved: whereas, in 1950, there were 307.2 deaths from diseases of the heart for every 100,000 people, by 1998 the figure had fallen to 126.6. And when, in September of 1998, the *New England Journal of Medicine* noted in an editorial that "over the past 30 years, mortality from [coronary heart disease] has declined by more than 50 percent," it emphasized that such a decline was "best explained by the joint contributions of primary and secondary prevention."

Although the news may not be as good as the drug companies and media would have us believe, and although we may sometimes do ourselves a disservice by glorifying biotechnologies, or by idealizing a mythical doctor of years gone by — and though we may not now understand the ultimate causes of most diseases — we do, in fact, know some things.

And what we know, I begin to understand in the months following surgery — whether about heart disease, AIDS, brain trauma, cancer, or depression — happily, in our time, when utilized wisely, and when tempered by our knowledge of what we do *not* know, does give us the wherewithal to do a great deal of good: not merely to palliate the harsher symptoms of disease, but to enable us to survive diseases that previously did us in, and to do so in ways undreamt of in our parents' and grandparents' philosophies.

8 🐛

They Saved My Life But . . .

Wʜᴇɴ ᴇʟɪ ᴡᴀs ᴇɪɢʜᴛ or nine years old, and the UMass basketball team was ranked number 303 out of 309 Division I teams, we began celebrating the rare UMass victory by going out to breakfast together the next morning. Our favorite place was the Miss Flo Diner in Florence, Massachusetts, and by the time Eli was in high school and UMass was on its way to a number 1 national ranking, we were eating breakfast there several dozen times a year.

One morning when Eli was ten or eleven, we sat down in a booth across from the short-order cook, and the waitress, setting down cups of coffee in front of us, took out her pad, looked at Eli, and asked: "The usual?"

Eli nodded nonchalantly, but as soon as the waitress left, he beamed and spread his hands sideways, palms up in a gesture of triumph, as if to say: *Hallelujah — I've arrived!*

"So: many many thoughts and feelings," I write on March 9, 1999 — my first journal entry following surgery. "Mostly they come down to: I feel v lucky to be here, and to be alive. And v blessed in my children and friends. Miriam telling me again and again how much she loves me, how happy she is that i am alive, how scared she was that i might not live. And Seth is wonderful with her, and with me. Aaron not waiting to be asked, but simply telling me that he is moving back home and will be taking care of me, and making sure i dont do things at my usual pace. And Eli, here my first w/e home, reaching across table and taking my hand in his, at miss flo diner, and telling me, moist-eyed, how happy he is that i am alive."

I see friends, I attend synagogue, I sleep ten to twelve hours a night, I take naps, I go for longer and longer walks each day, I read (Myriam Annisimov's biography of Primo Levi, Ron Rosenbaum's *Explaining Hitler*), and I write (reworking a novel I had completed before surgery). Members of my synagogue in Northampton deliver meals each evening for six or seven weeks; students — past and present — call, send cards, and visit.

Four weeks after surgery, Aaron drives me down to Connecticut for checkups with Dr. Cabin and Dr. Hashim, and when both doctors say I can drive again, Aaron moves back into his own apartment.

Within another week or two, I am walking a few miles several times a day, doing stretching exercises and sit-ups, and putting in a regular workday at my desk. Whereas before surgery I averaged five to six hours of sleep a night, I am now — still — sleeping eight, ten, or sometimes twelve hours a night, and also taking afternoon naps.

What I find perplexing is that I am more tired in the early morning — more *physically* tired — than I am during the rest of the day, when my energy and stamina seem to be at higher levels than they were before surgery. I ask Rich if it's possible that while I'm asleep my body is taking advantage of my being away, as it were, to work as hard as it can to repair itself. Rich says it's possible — who knows? — but assures me there's nothing to worry about.

The first week in April, I take the train down to New York City, spend time with Eli, meet with my editor and publicist, and begin looking for an apartment. Two weeks later, in Northampton, walking past Smith College on my way into town, my chest itches, so I unbutton the top button of my shirt, reach in, and scratch. A second or two later, I realize, happily, that this is the first time in two months I have experienced *any* sensation in my chest.

I return to New York City the first week of May, this time for a reading and party to celebrate the publication of my new book, and while I'm there, I take a sublet for the coming academic year. (Arthur to me: "Listen, Neugie — I know you're a mature man and all that, but if you want me to take a look at the apartment with you — I might notice some things you might not see — just say the word.")

Then, on May 7, 1999, two days after my return to Northampton, for the first time in three months (and not four weeks after surgery, as I initially recalled after the event), I walk to the YMCA, change into my bathing suit, take a shower, and head into the pool area. I set down my towel, sit on the side of the pool, put on my goggles. My hands, I notice, are trembling. Am I really here? I feel a pressure-like pain in my chest — the first time this has ever happened — and tell myself to take deep, slow breaths, in and out, in and out. I run my forefinger along the scar on my chest, as if to remind myself that what happened really did happen, and then, nervous, eager, and mildly terrified, I slip into the pool.

"I swim for the first time! I swim, I swim again," I write. "Fearful before going in — as if worried i will have shortness of breath again. no problems tho. arms not sore. no stiffness or awkwardness. Easily do a half mile, and then stop. so thrilled, delighted, eager . . ."

Two days later: "i swim 44, easily, am about to go to nautilus, but hear sound of bouncing ball, and instead go into gym and shoot hoops for about 20 minutes. dont leave until i hit 3 long jump shots in a row . . . oh my it is good to be alive! home and watch some hoops, repair bathroom floor, mow lawn, etc . . ."

(Two years later, however, visiting friends who have a lakefront home, and swimming in choppy water, the water sloshing into my mouth, I will panic. Each time I swallow water, I gasp. I switch from the overhand crawl to the breaststroke so as to be able to keep my head above water, and, as my friends get farther and farther ahead of me — we intend to swim about a mile out before returning — I want to cry out, *Help me help me — it's happening again!*" Although, swimming alongside them in an olympic-size pool, as I have previously, I am usually ahead of them, this time I stay behind, and even while I continue to move arms and legs, I vow that if I survive, I will never *macho* it again — that at the *first* incidence of breathlessness, I will stop and get out of any body of water I'm in. I swim more slowly — regain some confidence — and a moment or two before I decide that yes, I am going to call out that I'm turning around and heading back to shore, my friends turn around, and we swim to shore together.)

Sometimes, washing in the morning, or getting ready for bed at night, when I look at my arm, chest, or leg, I am surprised: How did these long, fresh scars get here? And: Do they really belong to me? When I touch them, it occurs to me that it has been only the briefest of intervals since my body was cut open, my arteries and veins harvested and relocated. (When the bills for surgery arrive, I wonder, too, why it is, since the spare parts the surgeons used for the five grafts were taken from my own body, I have not been given a discount.)

At my first postoperation checkup, Dr. Hashim examines the scar on my forearm, where the radial artery was removed. "The plastic surgeon did that one," he says. Then he runs his finger down the scar on my chest — the so-called zipper all survivors of open-chest bypass surgery wear. "I did this one," he says, smiling. "It is much better work — much finer, don't you think?"

He tells me to continue taking Norvasc (a calcium channel blocker used to decrease blood pressure by dilating blood vessels). This is a precautionary measure, he says, calculated to protect the internal mammary arteries he used for two of the bypass grafts. "Mammary arteries are God's gift to cardiosurgeons," Dr. Hashim tells me. They have wide openings, do not collect plaque, and, like the appendix, seem no longer to have any biological function within our bodies. They are composed of smooth muscle tissue that can contract and relax involuntarily, however, and in the immediate postoperative period, having been surgically traumatized — cut, touched, drained, moved, manipulated, and stitched — they become notoriously susceptible to spasms. "By lowering your blood pressure slightly," Dr. Hashim explains, "we will keep them from spasming."

I tell Dr. Cabin and Rich that Dr. Hashim wants me on Norvasc for a full year. "*Surgeons!*" they each exclaim, shaking their heads; they both say they think Dr. Hashim is being overzealous in order to protect his "artistry," and that in their opinions I could stop taking the Norvasc now.

"If the arteries didn't spasm in the first four weeks, they probably won't spasm for the rest of your life," Rich says. Still, I continue taking the Norvasc. When I tell Rich of my decision, he laughs.

"It's amazing," he says. "Here you are, a bright independent-minded guy who actually has researched these things and knows a good deal, yet even you succumb to the infamous 'authority of the doctor.' Do you see what power we're invested with? Can you imagine how awful it is — and I see it every day — when this power is coupled with arrogance and, too often — though not in your case this time, thank God — in the least competent doctors?" He sighs, says something about surgeons being brilliant from the wrists down, and then: "Your reaction's a sobering reminder of just how vulnerable and defenseless patients are most of the time."

After the trip to New York, I go on an "author tour" (Boston, Washington, D.C., Chicago), do some local readings, and continue to work on new projects, to swim and to play tennis and basketball, to spend time with family and friends, and to help Miriam and Seth plan their wedding.

On May 30, I celebrate my sixty-first birthday ("Peaceful happy day for me. V quiet, and that seems right: transition between lives. And now and now — the rest of my life"). And the next day: "Hard to recapture this a m the easy, peaceful, deep reflective feel of my new life, new sense of life: love talking with my old buddies. they get me through."

And then this: "In absence of an on-site family, these guys *are* my family it would seem . . . suspect this is so for many of us these days: friends doing for us what extended families used to do."

Arthur agrees. "I've done a lot of thinking about friendship," he says. "Like you, I'm a man who has always enjoyed the company of women, and I have, generally, found women more interesting than men. But it's very hard to have a long-term relationship with a woman if you're married. This doesn't have to be the case, of course. If I were a different kind of man I might have had more women friends. And I did, and do, have women friends, but the friendships were not of the same order as they are with you and me, with Phil, with Jerry. I mean, think about this: how many women that you were friends with in high school have you kept in touch with? And why not?

"We maintain no women friends from high school, and lots of male friends, and I think part of why this is so comes out of what I think of as a general cultural experience, which is that men have a way of relating, for the most part, that is different from the way women relate. Women are much more likely to talk about their feelings *about* each other *with* each other. 'I was very disappointed that you didn't come to my party,' a woman will say. 'It hurts me. All the important parties that I have — somehow or other you don't come to.' Now, a man's response in the same situation is not to say anything, but, instead, to take a step back. Men titrate the distance rather than work through an issue directly, and for the most part this makes relationships easier.

"There seems to me a kind of unspoken agreement among men — and remember: this is in *my* experience, in *my* friendships — that we don't confront each other about the *mishegas* — the craziness — that goes on in our relationships day to day. Most of my friends, like you, are Brooklyn men, and we went to the same high school, the same college, have the same cultural background, the same value system pretty much — our politics, our way of looking at the world. And there is a kind of implicit assumption that life is hard for all of us — we get our balls busted at work, and in a variety of other ways, and our friendships are a place to be in a nonjudgmental, let's-take-what-we-can and enjoy-what-we-can-from-life attitude, whether it's talking about women, whether it's burping, whether it's recalling happy days.

"Because it's like a vacation from life, and it is not going to be intruded upon by confrontations that involve expressed verbalizations of negative feelings — 'You hurt my feelings, I never treated you this way, et cetera, et cetera.' And I think women are much more likely to try to talk through conflicts, and the more you try to do this — I'm talking primarily about men — the higher the tension level, and the less you do it, the less likely there will be discomfort, and the easier the relationship will be.

"Okay. So it's interesting to me in the ways this relates to being a psychologist, because many of the most constructive parts of a relationship in psychotherapy involve providing a caring, neutral presence where there is no judgment — where there is an acceptance of people for who they are and where they are, and where there are also high hopes. Now, our responsibility in the professional area is to help people achieve their goals. But the *really* interesting question to me, in a personal vein, is that I was very competitive in high school, and all the men who are now my adult friends were the guys I was competing with: to get good grades, to make the team, to get the girl, to get into Harvard or Columbia — and it should have worked against that, and it didn't, and I don't fully understand it."

I suggest that what we have in common as friends is not only the texture of the life we shared — coming out of what was essentially the same apartment, with the same mother and father — but the fact that we have all *survived* that life, and have done more than survive.

"I agree," Arthur says. "I think the relief we felt when we were together — relief from the intense, sometimes incestuous, conflict-ridden homes we came from, and to be talking about baseball and basketball and girls — this relief muted some of the competitiveness. You might be competing with a guy to get into Cornell, but he's also a guy you could talk to about the Dodgers, and he's not nagging and bugging you about a thousand little things the way we were bugged in our homes. And there's also this: that we could *choose* one another as friends, as opposed to family, where we were stuck.

"Safety was going outside the home, where your friends became your family — you didn't want the same *tsuris* outside your apartment that you had inside — so once I left my house early in the morning, I was home free!"

It was the same for me, I say, and friends I've known across a lifetime — Jerry, Phil, Rich, others — have been like brothers to me, but without the sibling rivalries and emotional gook that pervaded family life.

"Well, we've all had long lives," Arthur says. "We've survived, and we are also, all of us, people who never gave up." He laughs. "Listen: we're so old now, Neugie, that we *can't* die young."

"But we do have these things in common, and we've been through stuff together," he continues. "So when you have heart trouble, I have heart trouble. You have cancer, I have cancer. I'm fine today and I have a brain tumor tomorrow. We know that's how life works. We're under no illusions. We've stayed the course, we've deferred gratification, we got the job done despite the pain, et cetera. When we were fifteen or twenty, though, we didn't give a thought to this. We thought about where to go to college, how to survive our families, hitting a clutch basket, going two for four, whatever."

As the weeks and months pass, I continue to feel stronger and, after a while, less fatigued in the mornings. My stamina, when swimming and playing tennis, is better than it's been in years; my weight stays steady at about 150, my body fat constant at about 12 percent; my cholesterol scores are ideal, my blood pressure within normal parameters, and my heart, at rest, now pulses consistently at about fifty beats per minute. (For the first several months following surgery, however, it beats at a rate that is, for me, unusually high: between seventy-five and ninety beats per minute; Rich tells me higher pulse rates are a common postsurgical event, and are of no concern.) Nor have I suffered any of the side effects, memory and cognitive losses in particular, that many people who have been through bypass surgery experience.

Through these months, and the months to come, my four friends remain a constant presence in my life. At the end of May, Rich flies in from California, and stays with me in my Northampton home. When I go down to see Dr. Cabin and Dr. Hashim for checkups, I stay in Guilford with Jerry and Gail. Hardly a day goes by when one of my friends does not call, and on some days (the same is true at this writing, three and a half years later) I talk with all four of them. We talk less and less about my surgery and recovery, and more and more about the things we usually talk about: our children, our work, our plans — and always, too, about what's new (and old) in the world of sports, about times past, about people we know and what they're doing, and about who has seen which old friend recently.

Arthur and his wife Paulette attend the reading and party for my book in New York City, and I find that Arthur and I are once again talking regularly in the way we did nearly a half century ago when we were at Erasmus, so that on days when, alone in my house, and later in my two-room sublet in New York City, I feel waves of sadness that, despite the knowledge of my good fortune in being alive, still recur, few things in life cheer me as much as a familiar boyish and enthusiastic voice on the other end of the phone saying, "Neugie — it's The Rude," followed usually by, "Listen. I was thinking about you earlier today when . . ."

In early July, I fly out to Denver, rent a car, and Phil and I drive four hours north, to Columbine, Colorado, for his daughter Elizabeth's wedding (Phil's wife and three other children have driven there a day before). We trade jokes and stories, and talk easily — about my surgery, about the book, about Phil's work (patients I've met and how they're doing), about former girlfriends and ex-wives (Phil has been married three times and divorced twice; I've been married twice and divorced twice), and about our friends (Arthur intends to retire from his private practice within the year, and Phil is concerned about him — about what life for such an energetic, intellectually curious guy will be like without the regular work he's been doing most of his adult life).

I stop in Denver again at the end of July, on my way back from a two-week trip to Alaska, and I visit with Rich this time (Phil is out of town), who has arranged to be there to see me, and has coordinated his trip with a visit to his two children, Sharon and Steve, both of whom live and work in Denver.

On September 1, 1999, my brother Robert, after six consecutive years of living in state mental hospitals, much of this time in locked wards and on isolation, moves into a supervised residence on West 48th Street, in the Hell's Kitchen section of New York City. The next day I move into my sublet in the same section of the city, six blocks north, on West 54th Street. It is the first time in thirty-three years Robert and I are living in New York City at the same time, and one night during our first week back, we have dinner together in a Chinese restaurant on Ninth Avenue.

"He keeps smiling at me," I write the next morning, "and when i say something re nice to see him with a smile on, he beams and says, Its because im so happy to be here with you . . . and then: i was looking forward to this all day, Jay." At lunch a week or two later, I mention that one of our cousins' children is going to be married, and tell Robert there's going to be a family function. "But Jay," he says at once, "our family *doesn't* function."

"Another day, and some gains, but boy am i lonely and at sea," I write during my first week back. "The grayblack clouds hover. and surely i feel the isolation as punishment for some wrong i have done. bec if i have done no wrong, why am i being punished by being so isolated from others?"

Such moments, however, occur with decreasing frequency. More often I come upon sudden expressions of joy: "what a time in my life! the surgery and, the further i travel from it, the sense of great good fortune — the realization, barely articulate, that i nearly died, and that everything, here to the grave, is a gift," along with descriptions of the peace and pleasure particular moments now bring.

> Wonderful day, and v happy to be here — deeply, slowly, savoringly so. wake a bit past 5 AM, and cant fall asleep again: so eager for life — for the day to begin: to be out doing things, being with friends, talking with people, working and eating and all ordinary and extraordinary things . . .

Late one morning near the end of my third week in New York, I walk to the local post office two blocks away. I wait in line until a middle-aged black woman, opening her station, waves me over.

"How are you today?" she asks.

"Just fine," I say. "And you — ?"

"Oh, I'm having terrible cramps today," she says.

"Really," I reply, without missing a beat.

"Listen," she says to me. "In my next life I'm coming back as a man —"

"Interesting ambition," I say. "Only you should know that it's not *all* good for my gender." I put a manilla envelope on the scale, and mention that I've been doing some research on heart disease — thus the envelope I'm mailing off, to a friend who's written a book on women and heart disease — and offer the information that once the condition that causes cramps passes, women need to be *more* wary than men, since from this point on — postmenopause — heart disease will affect them at least as much as it affects men, but without as many traditional warning signs.

"Like I said, next time I'm coming back as a man," she says. I pay and, leaving, tell her I hope the rest of her day is less painful. She smiles, wishes me a good day. "And hey — a good *life* for you too," she adds.

I walk back out into the street, look up at the sky, blow a kiss to the heavens, and think: I'm home.

When Miriam was a child — before she began kindergarten — she would dress up in silk and chiffon scarves and spend hours by herself, dancing to music — Tchaikovsky, Mozart, Debussy, Gershwin — and I would peek into her room sometimes, or enter to change the record, and I would marvel at her self-possession and her grace. Now, on the evening of October 30, 1999, at her wedding, toasting her and Seth, I recall this moment, and make what seems the obvious remark: that from now on she will not have to dance alone. She and Seth dance, after which, our friends and family surrounding us, Miriam and I dance. A few weeks later, I receive a letter that begins, "Dear Dad: It's not possible to put into words how much I want to thank you, but I hope you know that without your endless generosity the day I dreamed about would never have been the reality it was — it was truly the most beautiful day of my life . . ."

A month later, on the day before Thanksgiving, I drive down to see Dr. Cabin at his office in Branford, Connecticut, and when the exam is over he tells me that the surgery is "a complete success" (blood pressure normal, ejection fraction estimated at 50–55 percent), and that I don't need to see him for a year. (From his letter to Dr. Katz: "[Jay] is doing quite well and seems to be fully recovered . . . I have suggested to him that he come see me on a once a year basis if he wishes just for routine follow-up.")

When I give Rich the results of the checkup, I say something about the swimming and playing ball having had a seemingly paradoxical effect: having masked the severity of my symptoms while at the same time keeping me alive — and about how I seemed, before surgery, to have been living on the collaterals I'd developed from regular exercise. Rich responds by saying that being in good shape, and having a positive attitude (something he never discounts, un-quantifiable as it is), probably helped save my life, and surely helped me through surgery and in my recovery from surgery, but that we really don't know if the swimming and exercise built up my col-laterals.

Rich published a study on collateral blood vessels in the *New Eng-land Journal of Medicine* many years ago that excited a lot of contro-versy, he tells me, and he explains that the collaterals seem to be genetically predisposed channels that open up, often, when the cor-onary arteries shut down. Whether or not it is exercise that induces them to do so, though, is not yet clear.

What is clear, he says, is that exercise conditions the *entire* cardiac muscle so that, in his words, "it can do more with less," and this, he believes, is a major reason I was able to survive the occlusions in my arteries, and why my recovery has been so swift and full.

He compares the heart muscle to the skeletal muscles — to the difference, for example, between two people who have to run a long distance to get to safety, one of whom is a regular jogger, and one of whom is not. The jogger will have a better chance of making it be-cause his muscles have been conditioned to do more with less. So it was with me, he believes, and though he was seriously concerned about my survival, what encouraged him all along was the fact that despite the nearly total blockage in my arteries, my ejection fraction — the figure that represents the force and efficiency at which the heart is pumping blood, and thus best tells us about the general con-dition of the heart muscle — remained within normal parameters.

I also tell Rich that Dr. Cabin's assistant, while doing the echo-cardiogram, noticed something nobody had remarked on before: evidence of some slight heart damage. "You suffered a minor hit on one wall, I think — a small part of the muscle that is hypokinetic," she tells me. "It might have been there before, and we didn't notice it, or it might have occurred during surgery." It is, she and Dr. Cabin — and Rich — assure me, "of no consequence."

Although I find, once I have had my four-week checkup with Dr. Cabin, and more so after this nine-month exam, that I rarely, in my journal, refer to my health again, I notice that what I am learning about disease and medicine seems at times, when joined to old habits, to have little effect on how I *act*.

When both my cardiologist and family doctor recommend that I continue to take Lipitor, and my doctor-friends disagree, for example (Rich says that he thinks bad — LDL — cholesterol should be lowered when several blood tests in a row show that it's significantly elevated, but since my numbers are low, he advises against), I am once again, as with Dr. Hashim and the Norvasc, in a quandary.

I've been reading the studies, and except in extreme cases (obese, sedentary individuals who were heavy smokers, have sky-high cholesterol scores, high blood pressure, strong family histories of heart disease, etc.), the cholesterol obsession — grown men and women worried about variations in their scores the way they used to worry about grade-point averages and SAT scores — seems a kind of media-induced madness.

When I run my situation by Phil, he agrees with Rich, and tells me the story of a doctor friend of his who had a CT screening — a cardiac scan — to see how much calcium he had in his coronary arteries. "It was a new kind of test, experimental, and the doctor offered it to him for free," Phil says, "and it turned out he was in the ninety-ninth percentile for calcium. So his doctor sent him to a cardiologist. The cardiologist asked him about his history and my friend remembered once, a year or so before, having had an episode of tightness in his chest. So the cardiologist did a catheterization and found one stenosis, and ballooned it and stented it.

"But the stent failed, and now, for the first time in his life, my friend starting having angina — frequent chest pains. So the cardiologist did another stent and this one failed too, and my friend began popping nitroglycerine under his tongue all the time for the angina. He became depressed and fearful — that he was a good candidate for what we call 'sudden death' — and developed atrial fibrillation. The cardiologist now recommended a third stent, open-heart surgery, or a stent that would also include, as I recollect it, the implantation of some kind of radioactive material.

"So now my friend asked, 'Am I doing this to save my life?' And the doctor said, 'Oh no — not at all. I see no life-threatening situation here.' My friend asked what his alternatives to surgery were, and the doctor said he could lose weight, do some regular conditioning, stuff like that — and he told him that the surgical procedures he had been performing, and was now recommending, were not to save my friend's life, but only to improve his *quality* of life.

"But look at what his quality of life had already become!" Phil says. "And remember that it all started, the whole *megillah*, because of a number that may in itself be meaningless.

"I mean, the big thing now is doing whole-body CTs — CAT-scans — just to see *if* there are any tumors anywhere. But then what? If you find any, you have to find out if the tumors are malignant or not, and if they are, you have to decide if treatment will or won't make a difference, and then you have to decide on the kind of treatment, but to do so you have to weigh risks when you may not have much sound information to base your decision on. And remember this too — the scan itself is only as good as the doctor who reads it."

(On August 26, 2001, during the same week that Bayer takes Baycol, a cholesterol-lowering statin, off the market after at least thirty-one patients using the drug have died, the *New York Times,* on the front page of its "Style" section, runs an article about "the growing number of physicians who have invested in the hottest nonsurgical voluntary procedure around: full-body electron beam tomography." One company, with six offices in the New York metropolitan area, offers, in regularly placed ads in the *Times,* a "Spring Special — 50% OFF BODY SCAN for a Loved One or Friend with Your Body Scan." In many screening centers, however, Dr. Robert Grossman, chief of radiology at New York University Medical Center, cautions, there is just one doctor, who may not be a radiologist. "Do you want a cardiologist reading your gastrointestinal scan?" he asks. In addition, Dr. Grossman points out, scans are virtually useless in diagnosing the beginnings of prostate and breast cancer. Like Phil, he too worries as much about false positives as false negatives, since, in addition to needless anxiety and depression, they can lead to unnecessary tests and procedures, including biopsies, that carry surgical and anesthesia risks. "Mostly scans like this just play on people's irrational fears," he says. When I send the article to Phil, he agrees. "I think one of the main things in being a doctor these days," he says, "is making sure the technology doesn't overrun your judgment.")

So that even while I continue to talk with my friends nearly every day — asking them questions, listening to their stories, sorting out my confusions, checking out my research against their knowledge and experience, and even while I collect more and more data that reinforce what they tell me about the problematic value of cholesterol scores and the dubious value of much screening — I find myself reluctant, as if physically inhibited, to go against my regular doctors' recommendations.

For one three-month period, however, I do stop taking the Lipitor while at the same time exercising more strenuously and paying greater attention to my diet. I have eaten scarcely any red meat or whole-milk products for years, but now I cut down even more on fat intake. Without the Lipitor, however, my scores slide upward slightly — total cholesterol remaining under 200, but with good cholesterol (HDL) slipping downward into the mid-30s — and Dr. Katz, who previously suggested I might cut down to four pills a week, now tells me I should go back, on a daily basis, on the Lipitor. He gives me a new prescription.

I protest mildly, telling him that what I've been reading seems to indicate that cholesterol scores don't appear to matter much in terms of mortality. He shrugs, and tells me that what I say may well be so. "But in these studies there are subgroups and subgroups," he says. "Given your history of heart disease, you should go back on the Lipitor."

Although I am, at first, too embarrassed to tell Rich I've done so (when I do tell him, he laughs and asks if the doctor telling me to take Lipitor isn't the same guy who told me I had asthma), I find myself incapable of going against my doctor's advice. It is not so much that I make a medical Pascal's Wager (figuring I have more to lose — my life! — if I don't do what my doctor advises than if I do), but that I simply can't summon up what it would take to say to him, at this visit — or, more intimidating prospect, when I return for the next one — that I appreciate his advice, but that I decided to follow my judgment and not his.

I am bemused by this inhibition, and think again: how little we know, not only about the biological causes of disease and the relation of any particular disease to any particular person, but, more simply, about who we are, and about the often mysterious relation of what we know to what we *do* about what we know — about how and why it is, especially as we grow older, that we become so set in our ways: about how and why it seems to become more and more difficult for us to truly change, even when we should, as we ordinarily put it, know better.

Yet I also think: how curious — how wonderful! — it is that in this, as in so many things — in an infinity of instances — what we consciously know, and therefore believe to be a correct, proven, rational basis for choice and action, often proves no match for our habits of being.

Despite what I know, then — what I *think* I know — though I listen to my friends, I obey my doctor: I fill the prescription and start taking the Lipitor again, one 10-milligram tablet a day.

A few months later, in early March 2000, thirteen months after surgery and two weeks after I have returned from a ten-day trip to Israel with Eli, I notice several small, unfamiliar nodules under the skin of my penis — little bits of soft scarlike flesh along the shaft — and notice, too, that when my penis becomes erect, it now bends southwest at a slight angle. The nodules feel, to my touch, much the way I remember nodules in my neck feeling forty-three years ago, in March of 1957 — nodules that were surgically excised, diagnosed as malignant, and irradiated.

I am concerned and puzzled, while at the same time, and even before I talk with anyone, I find myself laughing. Just when you think all is well, right, Neugie? Just when you think you have all the time in the world . . .

When I was operated on in 1957, the surgeon removed lumps from the right side of my neck but did not remove several nodules from the left side, though following surgery both sides of my neck were irradiated. Nor was the surgeon able to get to a lump high up on the right side of my neck, situated close to my ear, one I have called through the years "my friendly gland."

I examine the nodules in my neck and in my penis — their fibrous texture is remarkably similar — and recall a joke I first heard when I was about thirteen: A cop shines his flashlight into the window of a car, onto a guy and girl who are parked somewhere near Coney Island. "What are you doing?" he asks. "Necking," the guy says. "Well, stick your neck back in your pants and get the hell out of here," the cop says.

But what *are* these lumps and how did they get here — and is it possible they've been here for a while, and that I've somehow not noticed them? Can there be a lymphoma of the penis? I wonder. Do I have some rare kind of sexually transmitted disease, or is the slight curvature along the shaft of my penis merely a natural occurrence that sometimes comes with age?

I recall a visit I made to my father, in 1976, a month or so before his death, when he was especially frail. "Oh I'm doing fine, son — in fact, I'm stronger than ever," he said. Then he glanced down at his lap. "Now I can bend it."

I telephone my friends. Rich says that what I describe has no relation to heart disease. Jerry says this is a new one for him, but after consulting with a colleague, he calls back to tell me that what I have turns out to be fairly common — it's what President Clinton is supposed to have — and usually is not progressive. He can't remember the exact name of the condition — sounds like some kind of French delicacy, he says — and suggests I see a urologist.

I talk with Phil, and he calls back a few hours later to tell me he spoke with a urologist in his building who has given him the name of a urologist in New York. The next morning, on his way to work, Phil calls again.

"Listen," he says. "I've been thinking, and I figured out what's wrong with you — what's causing the problem."

"What?" I ask.

"Atrophy," he says.

"Atrophy?"

"Yes, atrophy," he replies. "You're not using it enough."

Arthur says that through the years a few of his patients have mentioned a condition similar to the one I describe, and that as far as he recalls it did not inhibit their lives sexually. He gives me the name of a urologist whose office is a few blocks from me. "Not a great bedside manner, from what I hear," Arthur says, "but competent."

"The way I see things is this," he adds. "As long as something is not life-threatening, then everything's okay. And let me tell you this too, Neugie — and I say this based on having seen many, many men and women over the years, and in my office they've talked very freely about sex, much more so, you might be surprised to learn, than about money, for example — and I can assure you that there are lots of ways of pleasing a woman, and lots of ways a woman can please you."

I recall another friend — a musician now living in Turin, Italy — telling me, some years back, that he had contracted a rare condition called "bent-dick syndrome." I look through a few medical books I have at home, but find nothing under "bent," "curved," or "crooked" penis. I call my friend in Italy, and he tells me what he knows — in his case, he had become dysfunctional, but Viagra seems to have resolved the problem (though it only works, he says, when activated by desire) — and, laughing, tells me there is no such thing, medically, as "bent-dick syndrome." The name for the condition he has is Peyronie's disease.

I do some homework, and discover that my symptoms fit the descriptions I find — "Peyronie's disease: A fibrous inflammation of the shaft of the penis resulting in a deformity (a bend) of the organ." Though nobody understands what causes Peyronie's, except when it is the result of a known trauma (invasive procedure, blunt instrument, injury during sex) or when it is associated with another condition of unknown origin, Dupuytren's contracture (a thickening of the fibrous tissue beneath the skin of the palm, often accompanied by tell-tale spots on the palm), and though there are no known treatments thought to be generally effective (in some men the scarring process can progress to calcification and bone formation), what I read is vaguely reassuring: the condition is not fatal, it often responds well to one or another form of treatment, it does not spread to other organs, and it sometimes goes away on its own.

I make an appointment with Dr. Malcolm Haight, the urologist whose name Arthur has given me. Dr. Haight is associate director of the Department of Urology at a large New York City hospital. The waiting room of his office, which he shares with three other urologists, is small and cluttered. Among a stack of magazines, I find a loose-leaf binder thick with reprints of articles by Dr. Haight, including several about Peyronie's disease.

After a twenty-minute wait, I am summoned into Dr. Haight's office. I look at the clock, before and after, and note that the entire consultation, start to finish, in three different rooms, takes nine minutes, during which time I give a urine sample, have blood taken, and get a rectal exam, an examination of my penis and testicles, and a prescription. Dr. Haight never introduces himself, never says hello or goodby, never responds to any of my attempts at conversation.

To examine my penis, he has me lower my pants and lie on a table. Hands surgically gloved, he lifts my penis by its tip, as if, I think, holding a dead mouse by its tail, and to my query — "Is it Peyronie's?" — he replies, "Oh yes, it's definitely Peyronie's."

"Aha," he says a few seconds later, while examining my right testicle. "A cyst!"

Have I had a PSA test? he asks. I had a full physical within the last year, I respond, so I may have, but I'm not sure. "Well, let's do one," he says, and when I sit up, he draws some blood from my arm, after which he has me stand and bend over so he can, through my rear end, examine my prostate.

In his office, I continue to attempt conversation — remarking on photos of his children, on his publications — but get nothing in return.

He writes out a prescription for PABA (potassium para-aminobenzoate), and hands it to me. I am to take two dozen 500-milligram capsules a day. I should also take 400 units of vitamin E a day. I tell him that on the advice of a friend diagnosed with Peyronie's, I have begun taking 1,200 units of vitamin E a day, and Dr. Haight says this is far too much: 400 units a day is more than sufficient.

He stands, indicating that the exam and consultation are over, and tells me I should make an appointment to see him in three months. I ask about the cyst he found. Nothing to worry about, he tells me. What is the PABA for and are there any side effects? I ask. Will it reverse the condition? At best, it might cure it, he says. At

worst, it will stabilize it. As to side effects, they are well tolerated, but
I should read the manufacturer's flyer. I ask him about sex — is there
anything I should know? What about the future — am I going to be
okay?

"Oh you have a mild case," he says. "I've seen much worse. You
have no pain, and you can maintain an erection, so you'll be able to
penetrate."

Saying this, he turns and leaves his office. And that's it.

Although the news he has given me is encouraging — I have a
mild case of a condition that does not render me dysfunctional and
that will probably improve — I leave his office feeling incredibly
shaky: fearful, anxious, spent. The bill, which includes a forty-five-
dollar charge for "surgery" (the rectal exam? the lifting of the penis?), comes to over five hundred dollars.

From my journal, the next morning:

> Not a personal note in the entire exam. he never shakes my hand,
> never explains why he is doing anything he does, never responds to
> any attempts on my part to make the rel individual or personal . . .
> Dealing with my cock, but not a word re what peroni's is, what might
> cause it, what prognosis might be, doesnt ask if i have any questions
> . . . gives me a prescription without telling me what it is, and why i
> should take it: bam bam bam . . . i could be a stone he is testing and
> prescribing for . . . i am just a body to be measured and analyzed, di-
> vorced from a man who might have some anxieties, fears, questions
> about having his penis bend downward . . .

"I come away *more* fearful and anxious," I write, "and I come away
thinking: I need another opinion."

So I call the doctor Phil's friend in Denver recommended, and
a week later meet with Dr. Arnold Melman, chief of urology at
Montefiore Hospital in the Bronx.

Dr. Melman's nurse has me give a urine sample, after which I wait
in Dr. Melman's consulting office, which is large and handsomely
appointed: drawings, maps, African sculptures. Dr. Melman comes
in, shakes my hand, talks with me for a while, takes a history. Then
we go into another room, where he asks me to drop my pants. He

sits on a stool, examines me while I stand, and seems surprised by what he finds.

"Hmm," he says. "You have quite a lot of disease in there."

What he finds curious, he adds at once, is that the scarring in Peyronie's disease is usually near the outside of the penis, but the scarring in mine is near the center, next to the urethra. Back in his office, he draws a picture of my penis, and of the scarring, asks more questions about my medical history and, especially, about events of the last year or two. He is puzzled, asks more questions, looks at his notes, and then nods.

"Of course," he says. "The bypass surgery! The scarring is probably due to trauma from the catheter they inserted during your surgery. It makes sense. That would explain why the scarring runs along the urethra."

I tell him that Dr. Haight told me I had a *mild* case of Peyronie's, and that on Dr. Haight's recommendation I've been taking two dozen tablets of PABA a day. Dr. Melman declares that there is absolutely no evidence that PABA has any effect on Peyronie's — that this theory was disproven years ago. I tell him I am taking 400 units of vitamin E a day. He tells me to take five times as much — 2,000 units a day — and he says he is going to prescribe something else: colchicine.

Colchicine, he explains, is a medication that breaks up scarring by dissipating the molecules in the collagen — the fibrous deposits we hypothesize are causing the problem. Since blood has trouble getting around these deposits, the penis, when blood surges into it and causes it to become erect, only stays erect to the point where the collagen deposits lie; the absence of blood stimulating the erectile tissue at these points is what causes the penis to bend, sometimes to a ninety-degree angle.

Frequently, the condition causes considerable pain and makes sexual intercourse difficult or impossible. In some cases, when collagen deposits encircle the penis so that blood cannot rise to the shaft's full length, the penis will balloon out to the point of the scarring, and will remain limp for the remaining portion. In such cases, the only remedies are surgery — removing the collagen and transplanting in its place tissue from other parts of the body (a procedure that is rarely successful) — or the use of prostheses.

Colchicine is often used for gout, Dr. Melman informs me, and it has few side effects. If I start to have diarrhea, though, I am to stop taking the medication at once and to call him.

He asks if I have experienced any pain (I say no), or if my penis has become smaller (I say no again — not as far as I can tell), and he tells me he doesn't think things will get worse. He hopes they will reverse, but if they should get worse, there is an injection he can give me, or a simple surgical procedure he can perform, though he would do either of these things with great reluctance, and is inclined to wait and see if the colchicine does the job.

When, in his office, he asks me about myself — why I am in New York, why I moved down from Massachusetts, and I say that I'm a writer, he tells me about a book he has written (a woman's guide to men's urological problems) and how he is having trouble finding a publisher. He asks me to come back in six weeks but to call immediately if I notice any significant changes.

The bill for his services is one hundred and fifty dollars. When I take out my wallet, to give his secretary my five-dollar insurance copayment, she waves it off and tells me to forget it.

Six weeks later, when I return and Dr. Melman examines me, he is pleased to find that the scarring seems to have diminished. How can you tell? I ask, and he points to the drawing he made last time, after which he makes a new drawing.

"You're a very lucky man," he says, and then: "But don't *you* think it's improved?" he asks.

I say I do, but that he's the doctor. He shakes his head sideways, tells me that I am the best judge of whether or not the scarring has diminished.

"Look," he says. "Colchicine is a nonspecific medication. You might have improved without any medication — if we'd done nothing at all. We really don't know. Still, it's probably a good idea to continue with the colchicine."

He asks if I have experienced any difficulties during sex, and I tell him I haven't *had* sex with anyone since the last time I saw him, but that I have hopes. We talk about books and publishers, and he asks how my writing is coming along. I say that it seems to be progressing, inch by inch and page by page.

"I'll probably include something in the new book about Peyronie's," I say.

"Could prove interesting," Dr. Melman says. "It's what President Clinton has, you know — the famous distinguishing characteristic Paula Jones alluded to."

"I haven't written this part of the book yet," I say, "but if I use chapter titles, I think I know what I'll call this one."

He smiles. "Yes —?" he asks.

I smile too, and give him the title: "'They Saved My Life But Bent My Dick.'"

9

One Year Later

How curious, i think when I leave Dr. Melman's office the first time: I've now seen two urologists, both in positions of responsibility at large New York City hospitals, both with significant achievements in research and with extensive clinical experience, and yet, confronted with a problem familiar to urologists, one tells me I have "a mild case," the other tells me I have "quite a lot of disease"; one tells me I should take no more than 400 units of vitamin E a day, the other tells me to take 2,000 units a day; one prescribes 12,000 milligrams of PABA a day, the other says that PABA is useless and, instead, prescribes a medicine usually used for gout; one runs extensive blood tests, the other runs none; one wants to see me in three months, the other in six weeks . . .

More curious still: even though Dr. Melman has told me I have quite a lot of disease, and though he talks with me about dysfunction, impotence, and pain; injections, surgery, and prostheses — possibilities Dr. Haight never hints at — when I leave Dr. Melman's office, I feel relieved and reassured.

Ten days earlier, however, when Dr. Haight tells me I have a mild case of Peyronie's that PABA and vitamin E will probably cure, and that I should have no problems sexually now or in the future, I leave his office feeling more anxious than I was when I entered it.

On the six-block walk home from his office to my apartment, I talk with my father, and — this is New York City, so nobody seems to notice — I do so out loud. I am awash in insecurity and self-pity, and though there is no rational basis for being as upset as I am, something about the visit has unmoored me.

Will I ever be able to love again? I ask. Will any woman on this planet *ever* love me again — ever want to love me?

The doctor said you'll be able to make love — to fuck again, right? my father replies. Isn't that what you're really worried about? I mean, I know you, sonny boy. Let's talk *tachlis*. Didn't he say that the problem you came to him for — this little bend — will probably go away?

Yes, I say. Sure. But if he told me I'm okay, why do I feel so shaken? So *abandoned!* I mean, look at me — I'm actually trembling.

My father's voice softens. I can see that, he says. But you're a smart boy, Jay. So you tell me: What do *you* think is going on?

I don't know, I say. But — okay — I was wondering: maybe what's happening in me is just a delayed reaction to the bypass surgery — some postponed postpartum displacement of the fear and depression I didn't acknowledge a year ago. Everybody tells me I was so positive and optimistic before and after surgery, but maybe I was just overcompensating and covering up.

My father shakes his head sideways and puts a finger to his lips, to shush me.

If you want my opinion, he says, you analyze things too much. The doctor said you're okay and that you have a mild case, right? Then take his word for it. And listen: I'm glad your heart is working well, and that your recovery has been so smooth, and it's nice to hear from you again. You haven't spoken with me for a long time, you know.

That's true, I say. But things have been going well.

So? he says. You only talk with me when things are bad — when you need something from me?

But I'm scared, I say. I glance downward. I mean, this organ is nearly as precious to me as my heart. We've been through a lot together.

My father laughs, tells me to go home, to pour myself a stiff drink, to call some of my friends, and to talk with him again soon. Don't be a stranger, he says.

When I arrive home from Dr. Melman's office, the first time, I throw out the quart-size container of PABA tablets. Then I call Dr. Haight's office and cancel my three-month appointment. The next day I start taking colchicine (one 0.6-milligram tablet twice a day), along with 2,000 units of vitamin E a day.

By the time I return to Dr. Melman's office six weeks later, my anxieties have all but disappeared. I tell him that since my last visit, my hopes have, in fact, been realized, and that I have experienced no sexual dysfunction. And six weeks after my visit with Dr. Melman, and more than three months after my visit to Dr. Haight (and two months after Eli and I have returned from a ten-day trip to Israel — a trip we begin during the week of the first anniversary of my surgery), I write and ask for the results of my lab tests. When they arrive, I call Rich and read off the list of more than two dozen things Dr. Haight tested me for (cholesterol, triglycerides, albumin, calcium, chloride, iron, GGT, AST, glucose, alkaline phosphatase, et cetera), and ask why he tested for them if I only came in for Peyronie's. Is the guy running a factory?

Rich says he thinks I just answered my own question. I tell him that my PSA score is fine (0.87) — scores above 4.0 are those generally considered to be of concern (PSA stands for "prostate-specific antigen" and is a measure of an enzyme made by the prostate, an elevated level of which can signal cancer) — but that I remember being upset with myself at the time of the exam for having let Dr. Haight draw my blood and perform the test.

"Then why did you let him do it?" Rich asks.

"Because he was the doctor, and he told me to roll up my sleeve, and said we should do it," I answer. "I mean, in the moment, lying on the table with my pants down, I was mostly worried about my dick — and if I was ever going to have any sexual life again. And it all happened so fast."

"You've got it, pal," Rich says.

"But I also think I was a bit cowed — intimidated, hustled along

— and I felt I had no choice *but* to do what he told me to do. I mean, he was *The Doctor*. On another day, I might have protested, but —"

"Look," Rich says. "This is what goes on all the time. You knew why he was doing it, and you sensed there was no good reason to do it, and yet you succumbed."

"But I'm still not sure why he was doing it," I say.

"Why was he doing it?" Rich asks, and then answers his own question: "Because it's his bread and butter. If he gets results that are out of the normal range on anything he tested you for, he can have you back for more tests and more treatment, even though you didn't come in for anything he was testing you for."

Rich talks again about how vulnerable and defenseless most patients feel in the presence of a doctor, even when, as in my case, the patient is well informed and *knows* that what the doctor is doing or recommending is of dubious necessity; he also talks about how scandalous he believes this kind of medical practice is, and how doctors who work this way not only drive up costs unconscionably for all of us, but give other doctors — *good* doctors — a bad name.

Afterward, it occurs to me that the reason I came away from my first visit with Dr. Melman feeling reassured was this: at the same time that he was providing excellent medical care, he was also providing a human response to a human problem.

Most times no doctor knows what causes Peyronie's disease, or what treatments will ameliorate its symptoms. Dr. Haight's prescriptions might have dissolved the collagen — or the scarring might have diminished and disappeared if, as Dr. Melman suggested, I had done nothing at all. (Most medical books agree that Peyronie's disease resolves itself spontaneously about 50 percent of the time.)

I felt reassured after my visit with Dr. Melman not because he had done anything like promising a cure, but because he had dealt with me openly and thoughtfully, and by so doing, had engendered trust: he explained what Peyronie's disease was and told me that its causes were unknown; he examined me attentively and noted the way my particular symptoms varied from the symptoms he usually saw; he told me I had quite a lot of disease and he tried to figure out why this was so; he asked questions and listened to me; and he reviewed what we knew and came up with an explanation for the cause of my condition that made sense.

Although knowing what had probably been the source of my condition did not dissipate the collagen, it did dissipate the fear and anxiety I had been living with since I had seen Dr. Haight.

For all that Dr. Haight noticed there was a human being attached to the penis he was examining, I recall thinking, I could have mailed my penis in.

The crucial difference between these doctors, then, lay not in their disagreements concerning diagnosis and treatment, but in the way they each practiced medicine — one doctor relying almost exclusively (and impersonally) on the "science" of medicine — on tests, scores, and procedures — the other doctor, by listening and observing, and by placing the presenting symptoms in the context both of his clinical knowledge and of my history (as I presented it to him) — joining the science of medicine to what, for want of a less grandiose phrase, we have come to call the art of medicine.

In recent years, people with those conditions we call mental illnesses (schizophrenia, manic-depression, clinical depression), along with their caregivers and advocates, have been working to change not only the way we treat individuals with such conditions, but the way we talk about them and write about them.

It matters, we believe, that people like my brother Robert not be collectively grouped under labels such as "the mentally ill," and that we do not call *any* human being "a schizophrenic," "a psychotic," or "a manic-depressive" — much less a psycho, a nut, or a loon.

We urge, instead, that we talk about people suffering from these conditions in the same way we talk about anyone suffering from a debilitating condition — as someone who *has* an illness, or has been diagnosed *with* a disease, as in: John has the flu; Jane was diagnosed with breast cancer.

Robert is no more "a psychotic" than I am "a Peyronic." He is a complex, fascinating, fifty-nine-year-old man with feelings, talents, memories, hopes, desires — a man with a full, rich, and most unenviable life. To define a human being by the disease or condition from which he or she may suffer, in the short or long term, reduces that individual to the disease, and once we reduce an individual to a single element in that individual's life, especially something generally considered undesirable, dangerous, or alien — how easy it becomes to regard this person as less than us, and as less than human.

Because I have been witness to the inept and cruel ways people designated by the world as mad are frequently treated — the ways the media stereotype and denigrate them, the ways family and friends abandon them, the ways the institutions of our society neglect them, abuse them, and deprive them of necessities and rights most of us take for granted — I am sensitive in ways I might not otherwise be to situations wherein an individual, because of his or her *difference,* is treated in inhumane and harmful ways.

Yet at least as insidious as the ways human beings are treated for conditions they cannot change — whether disease or skin color, disability or ethnicity — are the ways they frequently internalize attitudes others have toward them. Thus, those suffering from diseases such as schizophrenia, and called "nut-cases" or "psychos" (or those called "lepers," "retards," "cripples"), may come to believe what others believe of them: that they are defective beings unworthy of the care and respect of others, and believing this, they become helpless and willing victims of a kind of medical Calvinism ("By their diseases shall they be known") that is pernicious in the extreme.

And what happens in situations for individuals who, disabled by their conditions, live in isolation from the larger society, happens in ordinary if less lethal ways in doctors' offices, clinics, and hospitals every day. It happens whenever doctors, in their practice of medicine, see and treat only the disease — or what they perceive to be the disease — and not the patient who has the disease.

I felt depressed and helpless when I left Dr. Haight's office — impotent — not because I thought I would become physically impotent (the doctor assured me I would not), but because, coming to him with a problem decidedly not a life-and-death matter, though one that made me apprehensive, he separated me — *my self* — from my problem, and made me feel I had been reduced to my symptoms. In his office, *I* did not exist.

Conversely, a year earlier, when told that my coronary arteries were occluded and that I would have to have open-heart surgery as soon as possible, I felt fortunate to know the nature of my problem, blessed in my friends and family, confident in my doctors, and optimistic about what was going to be done for me.

In the aftermath of my visits to Dr. Haight and Dr. Melman, what my friends had been explaining about the practice of medicine came home to me once more: I was reminded of how unscientific the science of medicine can be, and of how mysterious the processes both of disease and of the amelioration of disease often are. I was reminded, too, that just as healing is, at its root, a natural process, so too is disease a natural part of our ongoing lives, and that when this is denied and our ailments are treated as if they existed apart from us or, worse still, as defects we ourselves bear responsibility for bringing into being, then something of our essential humanity is taken from us.

For whether we are in a doctor's office, at our jobs, or with friends and family, the desire to be known: to be recognized as a particular and unique human being, and not another — like the desire to know, and the comfort that comes from knowing — would seem to be innate.

Consider what happens during the transplantation of organs, where the initial response of the recipient's immune system is to reject what it does not recognize as being itself. Only when medications that suppress immunological responses are knowledgeably employed do our bodies accept the physical gifts — parts taken from other human beings: lungs, livers, kidneys, hearts — that allow us to survive, to function, and to live on.

During the past few years I have met hundreds of individuals who have suffered from a history and condition similar to my brother's but who, unlike my brother, have recovered into full and independent lives. Without exception, though they often praise medications as being central to their recovery, each of them tells me that the most important element in his or her recovery has been a relationship. They explain that what has made the difference in their lives is the fact that someone, usually a professional, but sometimes a friend, family member, or member of the clergy, entered their lives at a particular moment, one they invariably describe as "the turning point," and said, in effect, "I believe in your ability to recover — to have a better life than the life you have now — and I am going to stick with you and by you, through whatever ups and downs may lie ahead."

The belief others had in them, they say, has allowed them to believe in themselves.

They do not underestimate the beneficial effects of medications. Nevertheless, just as Viagra cannot ameliorate erectile dysfunction in the absence of desire, so antipsychotic medications often cannot ameliorate emotional and social dysfunction in the absence of a caring relationship.

And just as surely, the *loss* of a caring relationship can attenuate the positive effects of medication. A few years ago, for example, Robert was put on clozapine, a newer medication that has proven uniquely effective for many individuals who suffer from long-term mental illness. Within a short while, he had improved so greatly — "miraculously," his doctors said — that he was, after four consecutive years of hospitalization, being prepared for discharge.

At this point, his social worker, whom he had known for many years, both at his present hospital and at a hospital where he lived previously, was, without warning, transferred to another location. Within a day, Robert, who had become increasingly lucid, realistic, and happy, became angry, confused, and volatile. He deteriorated rapidly into a wild state of rage, confusion, and irritability in which he once again, alas, became a danger to himself and others.

The salient question here — why did the medications that worked so well one day cease to be effective the next day? — would seem to be rhetorical.

For how different, in this, is Robert from the rest of us? What happens to any of us, especially in crisis, when those we believe we can depend upon suddenly disappear from our lives? For most of us, the presence — or absence — of such connections, as in my brother's life, has tangible issue. We know, from numerous studies, that, following heart attacks, people who are isolated, living alone, or unmarried and lacking a confidant are at significantly increased risk for death. We also know, to cite a familiar instance, that widows and widowers have higher mortality rates than married persons — that their death rates, when living without companions, are higher than would otherwise be expected on the basis of age.

We would seem, then, especially in difficult times, to need connections to others as dearly as we need food, air, sleep, and water. Writing this chapter during the last week of September 2001, I think of those men and women, trapped in the World Trade Center, who hold hands while they jump to their deaths. The act of joining hand in hand with another human being so as not to die alone would seem a sad instance of this human need.

"Our free will has no product more properly its own than affection and friendship," Montaigne writes in his essay "Of Friendship."

"It is not in the power of all the arguments in the world to dislodge me from the certainty I have of the intentions and judgments of my friend," he states, and continues, a few lines later: "I should certainly have trusted myself to him more readily than to myself."

At the heart of such a friendship — friendship of a kind Montaigne distinguishes from other, lesser forms of friendship that family bonds, laws, customs, erotic love, and various social and civil obligations impose upon us — is trust.

So: just as sorely as my brother's trust was taken from him by the transfer of that person upon whom he depended more readily than to himself, so was my trust strengthened when I was fortunate enough to have doctors recommended by my friends, and in whom I could trust — for specific needs, at a critical time — in the way I have trusted in my friends, "more readily than to myself," for many matters, large and small, through the years.

"When I give talks on clinical care for treating HIV/AIDS," Jerry says, "I call trust 'The Big T' — that hard-to-define but very special and most precious two-way commodity that makes it all work."

And when, thinking of my friends, I try to understand why and how each of these friendships has become what it is, I answer, with Montaigne, that "I feel this cannot be expressed except by answering: Because it was he, because it was I." On the nature of this "more equitable and more equable kind of friendship," Montaigne quotes Cicero: "Only those are to be judged friendships in which the characters have been strengthened and matured by age."

What we want, and require, in the practice of medicine, then, has much in common with what we want, and value, in friendship: knowledge of who we are, both in our similarities to others and in our differences; constancy and loyalty over the course of time; and accessibility and reliability in times of need. When we are ill or diseased, or when we are suffering or in need, we want our doctors to be those in whom we can trust more readily than we do ourselves.

When, two weeks after the World Trade Center tragedy, Arthur suggests to a friend that he speak with me about a book he has written, Arthur's friend, a man in his mid-thirties, says that Arthur spoke of me warmly. "He said the two of you are like brothers," the young man tells me.

From ancient times (as in David and Jonathan) to the present (as in the film about World War II, *Band of Brothers),* when we want to express the strength and importance of a friendship, we often speak of friends as being like brothers.

We expect from such friends, that is, not only the loyalty that results from obligation, but a depth of feeling — of *passion* — we ordinarily associate with family life. In part because friendships are created and sustained freely, we may elevate them above familial relationships and come to feel, with Montaigne, that some friends, like some brothers, are very nearly interchangeable with us. "In the friendship I speak of," Montaigne writes, "our souls mingle and blend with each other so completely that they efface the seam that joined them, and cannot find it again. If you press me to tell why I loved [my friend], I feel that this cannot be expressed except by answering: Because it was he, because it was I."

While what we want from our friends and from our doctors has much in common, there is this difference: we would have our doctors bring to our lives medical skills and knowledge of a kind we ourselves do *not* possess, and that they can utilize *dis*-passionately. We want, that is, to be able to rely upon them, as with friends, for their constancy and their caring, but also for their competence and their judgment. And it is the joining of such qualities in them — constancy, caring, competence, and judgment — that engenders trust in us.

Again and again my friends emphasize the importance of trust in their relationships with their patients. It is trust in Jerry that enables patients to adhere to the difficult regimens of antiretroviral therapies; it is trust in Arthur that allows his patients to talk about feelings, thoughts, and experiences that lie at the root of their difficulties, dysfunction, and pain; it is trust that allows Rich's and Phil's patients to talk with them in ways that elicit symptoms, events, and underlying conditions that maximize chances for helpful diagnoses and treatments.

"Most of the people with AIDS whom I've seen have been intravenous drug users," Jerry says, "and they have a reputation for being difficult, frustrating patients. They're engaged in illegal stuff, they're secretive, and they rarely have an established, ongoing relationship with a health-care provider, so they tend to elicit disapproval, and worse, from health-care workers. In turn, they become distrustful and expect judgmental treatment.

"But I've found that when you treat them with attention to their medical needs in a straightforward, clinical manner, most intravenous drug users can be disarmingly open about their lifestyle, and no more or less difficult than other patients. The essential point, as I see it, is that each person, intravenous drug user or otherwise, is unique, and does not comfortably conform to any stereotype."

Moreover, trust itself — Jerry's "Big T" — allows many conditions, physical *and* emotional, to resolve themselves more readily than they otherwise would for the very real reason that a doctor's knowledge of who each of us is in our particularity enables the doctor to judge more exactly the ways specific diseases and conditions may be acting in any one of us — and because, as the history of the placebo effect, and of healing, reveals, such trust in the physician frequently aids and hastens healing processes.

We know that mental and emotional states brought on by trauma can affect us physically — witness the paralyses and muscular contractures of arms, legs, hands, and feet; loss of sight, speech, and hearing; palsies and tics, choreas, amnesia, catatonias, and obsessive behaviors that resulted from shell shock in World War I.

We also know that patients who adhere to treatment, even when the treatment is a placebo — and adherence to treatment, as Jerry's studies, and others, have shown, is preeminently a function of trust in the doctor — have better outcomes than patients who adhere poorly. We know, too, that placebos are effective in reducing pain and depression. When medications known to be effective against pain are paired with a variety of neutral environmental stimuli, the environmental stimuli (a pill's shape and color, for example) acquire analgesic potency equal to, or surpassing, that of the medications. In one survey of (sham) surgery for lumbar disc disease, for example, although no disc herniation was present in 346 patients ("negative surgical exploration"), complete relief of sciatica occurred in 37 percent of patients, and complete relief from back pain in 43 percent.

In the relief of depression, placebo effectiveness, in a large number of studies, ranges from 30 to 50 percent, and, when compared with effective drugs, placebos are 59 percent as effective as tricyclic depressants, 62 percent as effective as lithium, 58 percent as effective as nonpharmacologic treatment of insomnia, and 54 to 56 percent as effective as injected morphine and common analgesics.

In a 1999 study ("Listening to Prozac but Hearing Placebo: A Meta-Analysis of Antidepressant Medications"), researchers conclude that "75% of the response to the medications examined in these studies may have been a placebo response, and, at most, 25% might be a true drug effect." The authors explain: "This does not mean that only 25% of patients are likely to respond to the pharmacological properties of the drug. Rather, it means that for a typical patient, 75% of the benefit obtained from the active drug would also have been obtained from an inactive placebo."

And with regard to heart attacks, studies show that emotional conditions affect survival at least as strongly as more purely medical factors — that, for example, "the presence of major depression after acute myocardial infarction increases six-month mortality more than and independent of such clinical factors as heart failure and extent of coronary disease." In another study, in which patients took drugs to lower their lipid levels after heart attacks, while only 15 percent of patients who took most of their prescribed medications died during the next five years, 25 percent of those who adhered less well died during the same period, and it made no difference whether the patients took active drugs or placebos.

And just as the loss of a loved one, or the end of a relationship with someone we have loved, can bring about depression and other distressing conditions of mind and body, so falling in love and being in love can enhance our well-being. Not only do we *feel* better because we are happier — appreciated, known, loved — but this state of being can help relieve preexisting conditions of mind and body (depression, impotence, headaches, gastrointestinal disorders), and, appearances *not* being deceiving at such times, may often lead friends to tell us we *look* better too.

On the cover of the January 9, 2000, issue of the *New York Times Magazine*, above a headline in large, bold type (**"Astonishing Medical Fact: Placebos Work!"**), are four pictures, each labeled — a pill ("Antidepressant"), the top of a man's head ("Fetal-Cell Implantation"), a knee ("Arthroscopy"), and a black-capped bottle ("Cold Remedy") — and across each picture, stamped in red ink: **FAKE.** In the accompanying article, the author, Margaret Talbot, concludes "that the placebo effect is huge — anywhere between 35 and 75 percent of patients benefit from taking a dummy pill in studies of new drugs."

Talbot surveys a substantial body of research that demonstrates the effectiveness of placebos used in place of medications and surgery (dummy pills for depression, make-believe surgery for knees, and so on). She also reports on studies that "show actual physiological change as a result of sham treatments." In eleven different trials, for example, not only did 52 percent of patients suffering from colitis (inflammation of the large bowel), when treated with placebos, report feeling better, but "50 percent of the inflamed intestines actually looked better when assessed with a sigmoidoscope."

Placebo effects have been explained in many ways — they may work because of conditioning (as in Pavlov's experiments); or because of the release of endorphins that stimulate the brain's own analgesics; or because of the diminution of stress. But what all explanations have in common, Talbot writes, "is the element of expectation, the promise of help on the way that can only be imparted by another human being."

What is clear, too, is that without the doctor who prescribes it, the placebo is powerless.

"It may seem strange to say this of a profession regularly accused of vanity and self-importance," Dr. Leston Havens, professor of psychiatry at Harvard Medical School, writes, but the fact is "that many professional people allow themselves to come and go among patients as if their knowledge and skills were all that counted, their persons not at all. One sees this most vividly with medical students, who cannot believe in their importance to the people they take care of. Yet we are the great placebos of our pharmacopoeia, and the power of the placebo can be measured by the results of its withdrawal."

In talking with my friends about placebos, they make a helpful distinction between illness and disease. For most doctors, they explain, *disease* is what the doctor sees and finds, whereas *illness* is what the patient feels and suffers. Given that what most doctors see most of the time is illness, the distinction is not insignificant. Although the two terms are, in general, used synonymously, disease can occur in the absence of illness (as in a person with hypertension — or heart disease! — who is asymptomatic), and illness can occur in the absence of disease (all those debilitating conditions of mind and body — stomach disorders, headaches, back pain, hives — that have no discernible physiological causes).

Because we have, since the end of the nineteenth century, been able to successfully treat many previously intractable diseases, we sometimes lose sight of the fact that, as Arthur Shapiro puts it, "the history of medical treatment until relatively recently is essentially the history of the placebo effect."

Some researchers contend that the placebo effect is a myth, and many, like Shapiro, are keenly aware of "faddish exaggerations about the extent of placebo power." Still others, like Dr. Howard Spiro, professor of medicine at Yale, while finding "no evidence that placebos helped disease or that they changed the objective, visible, measurable aspects that we doctors regard as important," believe that placebos do "help patients with the pain and suffering that the disease brings."

Yet clinicians, Spiro writes, "have a hard time accepting the idea that mental events may affect physical events, that faith can 'heal.' That is why placebos embarrass modern doctors, for they call attention to the persistent dualism of medicine and our so recent climb out of the prescientific swamp."

Although Spiro accepts the existence of the placebo phenomenon, he insists on the "difference between treating cancer with placebos and treating the pain that comes from cancer with them." Nonetheless, he cautions physicians to "be humble before our ignorance of how one person can relieve the suffering of another," and "to remember that the placebo is only a symbol of all that we do that we cannot measure."

How measure, then, the degree to which my own attitudes and responses, before and after surgery (my persistence in pursuing the cause of symptoms, my skepticism about preliminary diagnoses, my swift recovery, the absence of common complications such as infection, memory loss, and depression), were made possible and enhanced because of the trust I placed in my friends, and in the doctors they trusted?

10

In Friends We Trust

I N REVIEWING THE HISTORY of healing practices that have been used from ancient times to our own — in China, Babylon, Egypt, and India, and in the Western world for more than two millennia — Arthur Shapiro reports that "the astonishing total of these remedies is about 4785 drugs and 16,842 prescriptions. Even more startling is that with only a few possible but unlikely speculative exceptions, all were placebos."

He quotes Galen — a Greek philosopher of the second century A.D. and physician to the Roman emperor Marcus Aurelius — whose pharmacopoeia dominated treatment in the Western world for 1,500 years, and disappeared fully only near the end of the nineteenth century, as saying that "he cures most successfully in whom the people have the most confidence." (This from a physician not lacking in self-esteem: "Never as yet have I gone astray," Galen proclaimed, "whether in treatment or in prognosis, as have so many other physicians of great reputation.")

In *Care of the Psyche,* a history of healing practices through the centuries, Stanley Jackson describes measures that people in ancient Greece and Rome developed to aid them when they found themselves helpless in the face of disease and illness — in particular, their reliance upon magicians, sorcerers, priests, and physicians. "The healer's experience and reputation," he writes, "his status in the particular culture, his knowledge of the proper ritual, his use of the proper words with the proper tone and in the proper manner, and his belief in the efficacy of his words and actions all came together to calm and reassure sufferers, to soothe and comfort them, and to mitigate any sense of helplessness or hopelessness. Sufferers in need, and their willingness to believe and cooperate, completed the potentially healing situation."

While delineating the ways a healer was urged to be considerate and compassionate so as to maintain the patient's morale and thereby increase the patient's confidence in the physician and his treatments, Jackson, professor emeritus of psychiatry and the history of medicine at Yale, also remarks on something that reminds me of the place my friends hold in my life: "these issues were apparently addressed as aspects of being a good person and an effective physician rather than as an aspect of psychological therapeutics."

Philia, or friendship, was to the Greeks, in fact, the very basis of the doctor-patient relationship. For the doctor, friendship with the patient consisted of a correct combination of *philanthropia* (love of man) and *philotechnia* (love of the art of healing); the Hippocratic *Precepts* (c. 400 B.C.), in discussing the physician's approach to the patient, state that "where there is love of man, there is also love of the art of healing."

But what about trust in doctors who, like my friends, have a good deal more than placebos to offer? The Roper Center for Public Opinion Research, having conducted polls on this issue since 1945, reports that confidence in "the leaders of medicine has declined from 73 percent in 1966 to 44 percent in 2000." (The lowest public confidence rate, 22 percent, occurred in 1993, during the debate over national health-care reform.) In a series of recent essays on trust in medical care, David Mechanic, René Dubos professor of behavioral sciences, and director of the Institute for Health, Health Care Policy, and Aging Research at Rutgers University, suggests that patients have become increasingly distrustful mainly because they cannot freely choose their own physicians, or depend upon continuity of care from their health-care providers. In addition, aware that their physicians do not control some decisions concerning their care, they become less certain they will receive the care they need.

For their part, doctors, too, are disenchanted with recent changes in health-care policies; witness the following, from an editorial in the *New England Journal of Medicine:*

> Frustrations in their attempts to deliver ideal care, restrictions on their personal time, financial incentives that strain their professional principles, and loss of control over their clinical decisions are a few of the major issues. Physicians' time is increasingly consumed by paperwork that they view as intrusive and valueless, by meetings devoted to expanding clinical-reporting requirements, by the need to seek permission to use resources, by telephone calls to patients as formularies change, and by the complex business activities forced on them by the fragmented health care system. To maintain their incomes, many not only work longer hours, but also fit many more patients into their already crowded schedules. These activities often leave little time for their families, for the maintenance of physical fitness, for personal reflection, or for keeping up with the medical literature.

"The public has a low opinion of insurance companies, and an even lower opinion of managed care," Mechanic writes, and he lists some of the causes for this general dissatisfaction: negative media coverage, repeated atrocity-type anecdotes, the seemingly arbitrary power of large organizations in managing one's illness, opposition from physicians and other professionals, the shifting of patients among managed-care organizations and the resulting discontinuities in care, and so on.

"But a more fundamental reason for the public perception," he states, "is that most Americans are discomforted by the idea of having their care rationed and, at some level, they understand that managed care is a mechanism for doing so." Despite this public perception, a perception not always in accord with reality (Mechanic points out, for example, that medical care was rationed, if in different ways, before managed care; that patient office visits are *not* getting shorter; that managed-care companies rarely deny hospital admission), "most patients still view their medical care in terms of their relationships with a limited number of physicians," and "physicians continue to enjoy considerable public respect and credibility."

"There's lots of good information now, from smoking and weight reduction programs, that a doctor's participation in trying to get people to change behaviors actually *works*," Jerry says. "Patients still listen to their doctors. They might not trust the medical *profession* — but they trust their doctors."

Why is it, though, I wonder, that the more effective medicine has become — the more doctors can actually *do* for virtually every patient and every condition — the more we are dissatisfied with the medical profession, and the more often we cultivate a nostalgia for a medically primitive past?

One answer, Leon Eisenberg, professor emeritus of social medicine at Harvard, suggests, lies in an understanding of the role doctors, and healers, have always played. "It is not merely that patients 'get better' after they consult healers — they would have anyway, most of the time, because the common illnesses usually cure themselves (although that has never kept the doctor from assuming the credit nor the patient from granting it)," Eisenberg writes, and he offers reasons for the doctor's effectiveness, to the degree that this effectiveness exists apart from the efficacy of any medication the doctor may prescribe.

"The arrival of a physician and the expectation that relief will be forthcoming may diminish the severity of the attack even before the medication has had time to reach an effective blood concentration," he explains. "In a sense, the mere presence of the doctor is the medicine. When relief is produced, faith in the doctor is enhanced, and the power of the medical presence is even greater than before. What is true for respiration is true for any bodily function that is regulated by the brain through neural and hormonal pathways and therefore responds to psychosocial influences."

"For the most part, when people come to the office, you have to make a lot of judgments that don't come from machines," Phil says. "You have to listen to the patient and see if the pattern sounds familiar and if it could be a neurological illness. Where in the nervous system is the patient being affected? What tests should I do to look for it — and then, if I find any answers, what's the best way to treat it?

"Now, the major categories of the diseases we see are malignant tumors, and when it comes to them, the outlook remains bleak. We try to treat them with chemotherapy, radiation, and surgery, but until we understand the biology of these tumors, mostly we watch and see what it does to the patient and try to stop or reverse the growth — and we try to stay alert to the course of the illness so that if it changes, we can alter our thinking.

"In cases of stroke or brain injury, for example, I have to try to prevent things from deteriorating, or monitor the brain's swelling, or deal with the side effects of a person not being able to swallow. I try to prescribe therapies that will increase their chances of returning to maximum functioning.

"But no one has a good way to make the brain heal, and right now most of what we do, day to day, is to try to prevent complications of brain trauma and disease. A large proportion of the illnesses we see are chronic, debilitating conditions, you know — I mean, look at Christopher Reeve, at Michael J. Fox — so that what we want to do above all is to make sure things don't get worse, and to attend to the quality of life these people can still have. It's the old Hippocratic Rule — the first thing is to do no harm.

"I'll give you a more prosaic example. A mother comes to me with her son. He's a twitchy kid, she says. He twitches all the time, and she wants me to put him on medications. So I examine her son, and run some tests to make sure there are no neurological problems. There are not, so I ask the mother a few questions: Is your son doing okay in school? Is he getting along with his friends? Yes, yes, she says to both questions. But he twitches a lot, she says.

"'Well, then that's who he is,' I say.

"I mean, I'll keep monitoring the situation, and we'll see if the twitching gets worse, or goes away, or interferes with the kid's life, but my general philosophy is to leave things as they are — don't change anything unless you absolutely have to.

"These days, though, the premium is on doing more tests, and giving out more meds. I mean, I think it's always been like this, with the pendulum swinging back and forth between thinking the ma-

chines and technologies are where it's at, and thinking it's the doctor's judgment and listening that matters most. Right now, the technology's in the ascendancy, so you have to try not to let it swamp
your judgment, and to remember that no two people are alike, and
to do your work case by case, person by person."

What Phil describes, Stanley Jackson puts into perspective.
Through the centuries, he writes, beliefs and practices have "swung
back and forth between the significance of technological advances
and the need to retain humane influences in the practice of medicine." In our own time, he adds, the training of our young doctors
"is overwhelmingly skewed toward our technological advances and
seriously deficient with regard to these humane influences."

But the high priority that providers (doctors, hospital adminis-
trators, insurance companies, managed-care plans) place on technology would also seem to have an equal and opposite reaction: the
low priority given to the doctor-patient relationship, and the conse-
quent depreciation of skills, habits, and practices essential to this relationship. Thus, just as we often feel ill-equipped — vulnerable and
defenseless — when we find ourselves in a doctor's office, so the doctor may feel — and be! — equally ill-equipped, by temperament and
training, to deal with us as individuals.

End-of-life care, for example, is poorly taught, when taught at all,
in our medical schools, and virtually nothing is included about end-
of-life care in standard medical textbooks recommended to students
before or after graduation, this despite the fact that between 27 and
31 percent of Medicare expenditures (covering direct medical expenses for 80 percent of those over sixty-five years old) are for the
last year of life, and 52 percent for the last sixty days of life.

Nor, according to my friends, do medical students receive much
training in either the prevention of disease and public health or the
history of medicine, and they talk with me about how medical education influences the way a doctor practices medicine, and about
changes they would recommend in the training of doctors. Rich says
that when it comes to the medical school curriculum, for example,
"the very first course [he] would introduce — the first course a medical student would take — is one dealing with the doctor-patient relationship.

"At Irvine, I became involved in developing a course on the doctor-patient relationship. On the very first day we would have either a mock patient or a real patient sitting in front of the students, and start them off interacting with each other. That's day one, after which we use videotapes, and sit around in small groups of six or eight students, and critique the sessions.

"It was great fun, and there were no grades, or anything like that. What students noticed most — what was most important — was their embarrassment. They saw how they fidgeted, and how they wouldn't know what to do, or how to do it, since they felt they were essentially imposters who were pretending to be doctors, but without really knowing anything.

"And that carries over, you see. Because in order to shut down their fear and insecurity, students would assume what they thought of as *a more professional manner.* And if you ask me, that's the beginning of the end as far as the doctor-patient relationship is concerned. The trick is to break down that false, authoritarian facade by introducing students to medicine the right way from the get-go."

Such a course, and the intent that governs it, is not an anomaly. There are now many such courses being taught in medical schools around the country, but more often than not, David Mechanic reports, "these innovations are neither known nor recognized by other divisions of the parent institution or by the health services field." This is a shame, he writes, since effective communication "is essential to the cultivation of patients' trust in their doctors and their health institutions." Yet more and more, Mechanic tells us, "as their education increasingly centers on biomedical science, and as they more commonly are guided by randomized, controlled studies, most young physicians are trained to view their [own] interventions with skepticism. Instructed to practice evidence-based medicine, they are probably more detached and less committed to the effectiveness of their treatment strategies."

"In the Bronx — at Montefiore, when I ran training programs in medicine there, and at Yale since then — I've seen medical students come in idealistic, bright-eyed, and enthusiastic," Jerry says, "and I've seen them go out, at the end of their training, worn down, hardened, somewhat brutalized, in debt, and having endured an enormous struggle to maintain their humanity.

"Many of them reconstitute themselves, but many don't. I've always felt there's something wrong with the way we train doctors, and I think there are a number of things we can do — changes we can make — that will have real, effective ripples.

"The first thing is to work toward integrating public health — let's call it prevention — and clinical care. We've been suffering in this country, I think, because of a historical split between the two — there are schools of public health, and schools of medicine, and I would work toward integrating them so that we can make the disciplines of prevention that we know of from public health inform the skills and expertise we have in clinical care, and vice versa.

"Most doctors who work in clinical medicine are not trained, expert, or comfortable in prevention, even within the clinical context. Most doctors don't know how to take a sexual history. They don't know much about substance abuse. And these are treatable diseases. The same can be said for mental health, and I would work toward integrating these at a clinical level, and not concentrate so heavily, the way we do now, on the acutely ill in the inpatient hospital setting. The fact is, most doctors are not going to spend their careers working in the kind of technology-intensive environments our hospitals have become.

"I would also work toward changing the structure of how medicine is financed, so that it becomes oriented more toward prevention, and rewards doctors for preventing disease rather than for treating it once it occurs. I'm an infectious disease doctor, and infectious disease doctors don't have many procedures. We don't pass tubes into cardiac vessels or down the throat or up the tush. Mostly we look at your eyes, and your throat, and listen to your heart and lungs, and talk with you, and think about your case. Based on our expertise — our clinical experience — we make recommendations.

"But to think about *not* doing something because it was not indicated — the system doesn't support or reward that because it's a system that's technology-driven. If I stick a tube in you, I get four times as much money — or the system sucks four times as much out of whoever's paying for it — and that's a little ass-backwards. I mean, look at what's happening in Africa. The basic work we need to do there, for the millions who have AIDS, is *low* tech: it's educating people about transmission of AIDS; it's getting people to adhere to their medications; it's providing support for the families that care for their loved ones who are afflicted; it's learning to comfort people in their deaths and their dying; it's providing support for health-care workers who live with fear, and who burn out.

"In the clinical scheme of things, there *and* here, it's the patient and his or her family and loved ones, and not the disease itself, that should be the central focus and unit of care. Through the course of their illness, high technology plays a relatively minor role. I can't say it often enough: We should treat patients, not diseases."

Jerry pauses, continues: "Another way of making significant changes in the system is in the financing of medical education," he says. "In Europe, medical education is free. In Latin America, most of medical education is free. You get into a medical school and society pays to make you into a doctor. In exchange for that you spend a year or two performing national service — and you do that in a rural clinic or in a place that is under-doctored. We have something like that here, the National Health Service Corps. But it only subsidizes a very small percentage, and it's highly selective.

"Doing this would prolong medical education, of course, but it would also free these young people from the extraordinary debt burdens they wind up with that often influence their choice of medical career. Some of them owe 250,000 dollars when they start out in medicine, and they have a family, and they have this and they have that. So how will you make ends meet? You can't be a pediatrician in a rural clinic or you'll never dig yourself out.

"But I'm saying all this based on what I believe, which is that medicine is a fundamental social good that should be part of the social fabric of our society, and that our society should be providing doctors and universal health care."

It's late at night, in August of 2000, and Jerry and I are sitting in his home in Guilford after we've spent a day together at the hospital and his clinic, and only three weeks after he has come back from an international AIDS conference in Durban, South Africa — a city to which he will return in a year, during a sabbatical from Yale, in order to collaborate with health-care workers there in setting up AIDS prevention and treatment programs.

"But everything I'm saying, you know," he says, "is based on what I've come to see as the central medical issue of our time, whether in our country, or in Africa: the cruel disparities in access to prevention and treatment."

What had once been a traditional emphasis on the individual patient and individual practitioner did not decline only since my friends began their medical training in the late 1950s and early 1960s, or with the coming of managed care in more recent years, but began to be modified in the early nineteenth century, at a time when the hospital was assuming new and increasing importance.

With the emergence of hospital medicine, the attention of doctors started to shift from the diagnosis and treatment of complexes of symptoms in individual sufferers to the diagnosis and classification of "cases." The focus then shifted further, from the "'sick-man' as a small world unto himself" to the patient "as a collection of synchronized organs, each with a specialized function."

Stanley Jackson's summary of subsequent developments helps place current beliefs and practices in perspective. After laboratory medicine "began to take shape in German universities in the latter half of the nineteenth century," he writes, "the theories and techniques of the physical sciences were introduced into the study of living organisms, and experimental physiology flourished. Cell theory entered the scene. The microscope and staining techniques brought to histology a new importance. Bacteriological investigations brought new perspectives on disease and led to new modes of therapeutic investigation. And clinical diagnosis was gradually reorganized around various 'chemical tests of body substances designed to identify morbid physiological processes.' Attention gradually shifted away from the sick person to the case and then to the cell. Gradually the 'distance' between the sick person and the physician increased, and even when they were face to face. Or perhaps more accurately, the patient was gradually depersonalized in the doctor-patient relationship, and, all too often, the physician related to him or her more as an object than a sufferer."

Such changes, by the beginning of the twentieth century, came to be associated with the notion of "scientific medicine," wherein the "scientific" and "objective" treatment of patients — treatment based on data gathered in exams, from machines, and from laboratory tests, and, later on, from randomized controlled studies and evidence-based medicine — became the respected and prevalent mode for the practicing physician.

"As the scientific mode of gathering information, reaching a diagnosis, and planning a treatment increasingly took center stage in the clinical world," Jackson writes, "a humanistic mode of knowing patients, relating to them personally, and working with them as suffering persons often became less valued."

American medical schools, in fact, still seem dominated by reforms recommended nearly one hundred years ago by Abraham Flexner in the report of 1910 that bears his name. After reviewing ways doctors were educated in European universities, Flexner recommended that education in American medical schools start with a strong foundation in basic sciences, followed by the study of clinical medicine in a hospital environment that encouraged critical thinking, and, especially, research.

The appearance, rise, and hegemony of clinical academic departments between the two world wars that came about in large part because of the Flexner Report — that began in the late nineteenth century, and that accelerated after World War II — resulted in the emergence of what we know as "clinical science," wherein experimentation on patients or laboratory animals derived directly from the problems doctors encountered at the patient's bedside.

"In effect," David Weatherall comments, this "set the scene for the appearance of modern high-technology medical practice."

"Those who criticize modern methods of teaching doctors —" he continues, "— in particular, [a] Cartesian approach to the study of human biology and disease — believe that the organization of clinical departments along Flexner's lines may have done much to concentrate their minds on diseases rather than on those who suffer from them."

In *Time to Heal,* the second in his two-volume history of American medical education, Kenneth Ludmerer notes how the ascendancy of molecular biology in the 1970s and 1980s transformed biomedical research, especially in the fields of molecular biology and molecular disease, cell biology, immunobiology, and neuroscience, and created "a new theoretical underpinning of medical knowledge" wherein "the gaze of investigators focused on ever smaller particles, such as genes, proteins, viruses, antibodies, and membrane receptors." Although the results were often "gratifying in terms of medical discovery," Ludmerer writes, "for the first time a conspicuous separation of functions occurred between clinical research on one hand and patient care and clinical education on the other."

Many clinical departments established discrete faculty tracks: an academic track, pursued by "physician-scientists" (formerly called "clinical investigators"), and a "clinician-teacher," or "clinical-scholar" track, pursued by those whose interests lay primarily in teaching and patient care. The result, according to Ludmerer: "the growing estrangement between medical science and medical practice."

In addition, he submits, the premium put on speed and high productivity in academic hospitals (called "throughput") — a direct result of fiscal measures derived from managed-care policies, "carried negative implications" for the education of medical students. "Habits of thoroughness, attentiveness to detail, questioning, listening, thinking, and caring were difficult if not impossible to instill when both patient care and teaching were conducted in an eight- or ten-minute office visit," Ludmerer explains. Few medical students "were likely to conclude that these sacrosanct qualities were important when they failed to observe them in their teachers and role models."

In addition, Ludmerer shows, medical education began "to revert to the corporate form it had occupied before the Flexnerian revolution" and "a money standard [started] to replace a university standard." The greatest difficulties medical schools experienced in the 1990s were in receiving payment for time, yet "time remained the most fundamental ingredient of the rich educational environment that academic health centers had always been expected to provide,"

Ludmerer explains. "Without time, instructors could not properly teach, students and residents could not effectively learn, and investigators could not study problems."

"Medicine is still a guild really," Jerry says, "and it possesses many aspects of a guild. Mentoring and the passing down of traditions and expertise from one generation to the next are central because it's the way you become socialized into the profession. Unfortunately, we don't have enough strong role models these days to exemplify the best traditions in medicine, and this is due in large part, it seems to me, to the fact that so much of medical education is now dominated by basic science and new technologies."

Like Rich and Phil, Jerry believes that many of the deficiencies in the practice of medicine today derive from the kind of education common to most medical schools — two or three years of basic sciences, followed by pathology, and a further few years in which students acquire clinical skills by working on the wards of large teaching hospitals.

"In the early stages of medical education, you learn the bricks and mortar of physiology, anatomy, biochemistry, and microbiology," Jerry says, "and all that is very, very important. Given the paths most of our careers will take, however, we probably learn much more than we need to know — and to the neglect of other essential elements of our profession."

"Is this the best way to train a doctor?" Weatherall asks in his study of medical education, and he focuses on the questions my friends ask: "Do two years spent in the company of cadavers provide the best introduction to a professional lifetime spent communicating with sick people and their families? Does a long course of pathology, with its emphasis on diseased organs, and exposure to the esoteric diseases that fill the wards of many of our teaching hospitals, prepare students for the very different spectrum of illness they will encounter in the real world? And is the protracted study of the 'harder' basic biological sciences, to the detriment of topics like psychology and sociology, the best way to introduce a future doctor to human aspects of clinical practice?"

"Because most of us were trained since World War II in an era of antibiotics and other interventions," Jerry explains, "most doctors have come to believe they can cure most diseases. Certainly we were taught to believe that about my own specialty, infectious disease, where we saw that the administration of an appropriately chosen antibiotic could remarkably reverse the course of a virulent illness.

"But it turns out that most serious illness now is the result of chronic and not acute disease, and therefore *not* amenable to technical interventions."

Numerous studies validate Jerry's statement. Most of the conditions that afflict us as we age — heart disease, cancer, diabetes, depression, arthritis, stroke, Alzheimer's, and so on — are chronic conditions that require long-term, often lifetime management. But though we now live in an era of chronic disease, our system of medical education, as well as our system of health-care financing and delivery, continues to be based upon an *acute* disease model, and this fact, I begin to understand, is at the core of many of our health-care problems.

"The contemporary disarray in health affairs in the United States," Daniel Fox, president of the Milbank Memorial Fund, a foundation that engages in analysis, study, and research on issues in health policy, argues, "is a result of history. It is the cumulative result of inattention to chronic disabling illness.

"Contrary to what most people — even most experts — believe," he continues, "deaths from chronic disease began to exceed deaths from acute infections [more than] three-quarters of a century ago. But U.S. policy, and therefore the institutions of the health sector, failed to respond adequately to that increasing burden."

Fox explains: "Leaders in government, business, and health affairs remain committed to policy priorities that have long been obsolete. Many of our most vexing problems in health care — soaring hospital and medical costs; limited insurance coverage, or no coverage at all, for managing chronic conditions; and the scarcity of primary care relative to specialized medical services — are the result of this failure to confront unpleasant facts."

According to a report issued by the Robert Wood Johnson Foundation (*Chronic Care in America: A 21st Century Challenge*), approximately 105 million Americans now suffer from chronic conditions, and by the year 2030, largely because of the aging of our population, this number will rise to nearly 150 million, 42 million of whom will be limited in their ability to go to school, to work, or to live independently.

The report also notes that the question of how to provide adequately for people with chronic conditions has significant implications not just for our general well-being, but for national health-care expenditures. We currently spend $470 billion (calculated in 1990 dollars) on the direct costs of medical services for people with chronic conditions; by 2030 it is estimated we will be spending $798 billion. (In 2001, the Institute of Medicine reported that 46 percent of the U.S. population had one or more chronic illnesses, and that 75 percent of direct medical expenses went for the care of patients with chronic illnesses.)

These figures, however, represent only *medical* services, whereas treatment and care for people with chronic conditions require a multitude of *non*-medical services, from installing bathtub railings and finding supportive housing, to helping with basic activities such as shopping, cleaning, and cooking. In addition, the report emphasizes, "the best ways to provide these services often are not by medical specialists or in medical institutions. In fact, the services that keep people independent for as long as possible are frequently those that emphasize assistance and caring, not curing."

For the millions of people who require help with everyday activities, the assistance of family and friends is indispensable. In 1990, for example, 83 percent of persons under age sixty-five with chronic disabilities, and 73 percent of disabled persons over sixty-five, relied exclusively on these informal caregivers. Yet even as the number of people with chronic conditions is rising, the number of caregivers is falling. Whereas in 1970 there were twenty-one "potential caregivers" (defined as people age fifty to sixty-four) for each very elderly person (age eighty-five or older) and in 1990 eleven potential caregivers for each very elderly person, by 2030 there will be only six such potential caregivers for each very elderly person.

Moreover, most doctors work in community settings, not in hospitals or clinics, and in helping their patients manage chronic conditions they rely on the knowledge and experience they acquired in medical school. Yet their medical school experience has taken place almost entirely in hospitals, and has consisted largely of work with patients who suffer from *acute* conditions.

Add to this the fact that prevention — crucial to lessening the burden of chronic disease — is barely taught in medical schools and underfunded in both the private and public sector, and we see more clearly the magnitude of the problem, and the reasons for its tenacity and persistence.

"The resistance to prevention among decision makers in the private and public sectors has a long history," Daniel Fox writes. Since the end of the nineteenth century, "experts and advocates in health affairs promised that increasing the supply of facilities, professionals, and research would lead first to more successful and available technology for diagnosis and treatment and then to better health for Americans. Preventive services that could be delivered by injections or in tablet form fulfilled this promise. Prevention that required people to change their behavior was, however, outside the conditions of the promise. The promise of better health through procedures administered by professionals was central to policy to support medical education, to define health insurance benefits, and to establish priorities for research."

Despite the alarming situation that exists with respect to chronic conditions, "we still seem to believe," Jerry comments, "that the goal should be to cure, the way it was with infectious diseases — so that anything less becomes a failure.

"But AIDS, a disease of long duration and considerable cost — a chronic infectious disease — assaults this belief," he explains, "because it is all around us, and will be with us for the rest of human history, and because it creates an uncomfortable feeling of inadequacy and failure in physicians.

"AIDS forces us, especially if we're physicians, to confront our own vulnerability and inability to substantially alter the power and force of natural events. So that even though the goal of curing remains paramount, the parallel ethic of preventing disease, prolonging life, improving the quality of life, and alleviating suffering is more realistic, *and* more appropriate.

"Central to this ethic, of course, is compassion, and compassion for the sick doesn't just mean *feeling* for them — it means providing *competent medical care,* and I'm talking about the most comprehensive and technically superior care that's available.

"Personal compassion toward AIDS patients, especially by individual health-care workers, can only exist and be maintained within a framework of competence that exists within a system that provides both the necessary resources and an appropriate environment for such care. In this kind of setting, individual acts of compassion can flourish." Jerry stops, shrugs. "So the question's always with us, you see: What does the world do in a time of plague?"

Sometimes, it seems, we are so beguiled by our new technologies, and by all the hype from drug companies and the popular media about them, that we come to believe about our technologies what we used to believe about infectious diseases — that every human ailment has a singular, specific cause and is therefore susceptible to a single and specific remedy. If a laboratory test shows we have disease A, condition B, or illness C, then a doctor — or computer — will, with such knowledge, automatically prescribe medication C or treatment D or procedure E, and all will be well.

But diseases themselves are biologically variable, and make their homes in each of us in variable ways. "It is the sheer interactive complexity and unpredictability of the behavior of living organisms that sets the limits of the medical sciences," David Weatherall explains, "regardless of whether they involve highly sophisticated molecular technology or the simplest observational studies."

Although our new technologies can be marvelously helpful, like heart scans and brain scans, they are only as good as the doctor who makes use of them. The more diagnostic testing mechanisms we have, and the more sophisticated they become, the more the judgment and diagnostic skills of the doctor are needed. As Sherwin Nuland notes, "it is not information that leads to the best medical care, but judgment."

Under most recent managed-care guidelines, however (and managed care, now the dominant form of medical care in the United States, is itself variable — a generic term for a variety of approaches to financing and delivering medical care), not only are doctors encouraged to limit the amount of time they spend with individual patients, but patients often see one doctor on one visit, another doctor on the next visit, and so on. More: in an increasingly mobile society, each time one of us changes jobs, or moves (according to the Census Bureau, nearly 45 million Americans move in any one year, and approximately 40 percent of these moves are to different counties and states), we usually change health plans and doctors.

Thus, my friends lament, we frequently become strangers to our doctors and they become strangers to us, a condition profoundly inimical to the practice of medicine. The more this is so — the more we transfer from health plan to health plan (if we're insured and *have* a health plan; at this writing, approximately 41 million Americans lack health insurance, and the United States remains virtually the only industrialized nation without universal health care), and the more we transfer individual responsibility and accountability to machines — the less often and the less well can doctors make informed judgments that inspire trust, and that are worthy of trust. And without trust, the quality of medical care, and of our well-being, is dangerously compromised.

As my recovery proceeds, so that I do not even think of myself as being *in* recovery, I realize more and more just how lucky I have been, not only to have survived the blockages in my arteries, but to have had full access to friends whose thoughtfulness, knowledge, and judgment both saved me and sustained me. My talks with them, and the reading this stimulates, continue to persuade me of the validity of the old truism: that the secret of the care of the patient is in caring for the patient.

"Clinical research never produces definitive conclusions," Richard Horton explains, "for the simple reason that it depends on human beings, maddeningly variable and contrary subjects. Although medical science is reported as a series of discontinuous events — a new gene for this, a fresh cure for that — in truth it is nothing more than a continuous many-sided conversation whose progress is marked not by the discovery of a single correct answer but by the refinement of precision around a tendency, a trend, a probability."

Horton articulates what Rich said to me within a day or two of my surgery: "Advances in diagnosis and treatment depend on averaging the results from many thousands of people who take part in clinical trials. The paradoxical difficulty is that these averages, although valid statistically, tell us very little about what is likely to take place in a single person. Reading the findings of medical research and combining their deceptively exact numbers with the complexities of a patient's circumstances is more of an interpretative than an evidence-based process. The aim is to shave off sharp corners of uncertainty, not to search for a perfect sphere of indisputable truth that does not and never could exist."

And there is this too: even if my friends and doctors had been unable to do anything to save my life, as would have been true a generation ago — or if I had been among the small percentage of those who do not survive bypass surgery, or the larger number who emerge from surgery with various disabilities — how do we calculate all those things my friends did — those things that we *cannot* measure? How do we calculate what they did, and continue to do — by their kindness, their caring, their love — to enhance the quality of my life while I am still living it?

In ordinary times we go to our doctors for complaints that usually resolve themselves without medical intervention. Sometimes we go to them for what we think are minor problems — a swollen gland following a cold; some intermittent shortness of breath — and discover the problems are not minor at all. Sometimes we go to them in emergencies, or for matters grave in the extreme. And when we go to them, as I did — or are taken to them — we put ourselves in their hands, literally *and* figuratively, hoping they will understand our problems, and have the knowledge and skill to ameliorate them.

But whenever we go to our doctors, we bring our selves — who we are, with all our vulnerabilities, strengths, and mysteries — and to the degree that our doctors pay attention primarily to the numbers our bodies generate, it seems, to that degree do we lose not merely a portion of our humanity, but the benefit of those skills, essential to diagnosis and treatment, that continue to lie at the heart of good and effective medical practice.

11 🐛

So Why Did I Become a Doctor?

THREE DAYS AFTER MY sixty-second birthday, I fly to Stavanger, Norway, to attend an international psychiatric conference, after which I travel with my hosts, Dr. Gerd-Ragna Bloch Thorsen — organizer of the conference and director of the local psychiatric hospital — and her husband Olav, a general practitioner, into regions of Norway that can be reached only by foot.

For several days, along with two other couples, friends of Gerd-Ragna and Olav, we make our way into the Ryfylke mountains, north of the Lysefjord, into a part of the world that is, I write in my journal, "outrageously beautiful — the most extraordinary landscape I have ever seen: every few meters, a new vista, new and remarkable beauty. Fog and sun — mystery and radiance —!" Although it is now the second week of June, the weather is cool, and we hike through mist and drizzle much of the time, up and down hills of rain-slick, moss-covered rock, through muddy streambeds, across open fields, along forest trails bordered by shrubs and trees of astonishing diversity, and through narrow gorges and valleys that open suddenly onto sunlit, golden meadows, or give rise to steep, cave-pocked mountains. By the time we stop for lunch on the first day, take off our backpacks, and eat — we sit on boulders that form a half-moon around a waterfall — I am, through four layers of clothing, drenched through with sweat.

We take shelter for the night in an unelectrified cabin, fish in a nearby lake, watch wandering sheep graze in the distance, talk, read, and play cards by candlelight. Although we bring artifacts of civilization with us — cameras, watches, books, matches, canned food — the workaday world seems far away, and it feels wonderful to be bone-weary from the day's journey, to have sweat dry and cool on my body, to sit by candlelight, eating and sipping wine, laughing and exchanging stories.

I had visited with Gerd-Ragna and Olav two summers before, in June of 1998, when I was a guest speaker during Stavanger's annual psychiatric conference (called, refreshingly, banners heralding the event strung across the city's central square, "Schizophrenia Days"), at a time, eight months before surgery, when I had had no intimation that my heart's arteries were closing down. Gerd-Ragna now teases me about my "condition" — she claims we have gone at an uncharacteristically sluggish pace all day in deference to it — and when my companions inquire, I find myself telling them the story of what happened, then listening to them talk about illnesses and accidents they've survived.

We also trade stories about places we've traveled to in other years, and when I talk about my time in Alaska, what I recall first of all is the *openness* of the landscape — the absence of people and habitations in a place where slightly more than six hundred thousand people, most of whom dwell in and around the city of Anchorage, live in a territory more than double the size of Texas.

I describe flying in a single-engine plane north of the Arctic Circle, of circling in dense cloud for nearly an hour, then emerging to see a gorgeous expanse of land and water appear below: wide horizons and endless vistas — ocean, forests, inlets, streams, and fields that seem, in their sudden stillness and beauty, preternaturally pure and serene.

How, I recall wondering at the time, could a world that appears so lovely and peaceful contain *any* menace, *any* danger? And how, having had my life returned to me, could I ever be unhappy again — how ever again take even the meanest detail of life for granted? In that moment — I touch my chest with the palm of my hand, feel my heartbeat, feel heat rise through my clothing — the landscape below seemed to correspond to a landscape within: to a sense that within me vast expanses of wondrous territory were being born.

In the semidarkness of a cabin far from home, remembering and talking about this moment, ordinary things — eating, talking, laughing; a spoon, the reflection of candlelight on a window, the palm of my hand — seem extraordinary. I see myself in Alaska — in Kotzebue, at midnight — leaving my hotel and walking along the beach. The sky is a pale, clear blue, nearly white at the distant horizon, and I cannot tell where water ends and sky begins. The sun is out as if at midday, and on the Arctic Ocean young people are swimming and water-skiing. Saved from darkness for a while, a month past the summer solstice, the world lies all before me, suffused in mystery and wonder, alive with possibility.

I sit and look out to sea, and think about how, only five months before, I was deep in anesthetic sleep, my heart — this three-quarter pound oblong of flesh — disconnected, drained, and worked on by human beings who mended it and then returned it to me. It is the fact that people actually held my heart in their hands — that it was physically *touched,* and that, in a prolonged moment, tenderness and technology joined to save my life — that now astonishes, and humbles.

Imagining my heart, like the tiniest of infants, being cupped in skilled hands, and wondering about the unknown ways this literal laying on of hands has wrought changes in me, I find myself feeling grateful for having survived — of course — but more grateful for having been ill: for having *had* heart disease, for having had my chest opened, for having been operated on. This, I think, is my true and great good fortune, for had my arteries not been severely occluded, and had my heart not been repaired, I might never have known how dear I was to my children and friends, and how lucky I was, in a life as precious as it is fragile, to know them.

When I return and talk with Jerry about what I've been thinking and feeling, he responds by telling me about his travels, and about how they proved crucial in his career.

"Going to Nigeria, and living there for two years," Jerry says, "was the defining event of my life. I was one year past medical school, early on in my internship, and I was sort of groping around, actually thinking for a while of going into psychiatry.

"This was 1964, and I knew I didn't want to go to Vietnam. So I enlisted in the Public Health Service as a Peace Corps doctor. It was an option that closed down a few years later, but at that time it enabled you to do your national service without being in the military. And I was very lucky, you see, because what happened was that I experienced a series of revelations about what another culture and society are, and that led to a new understanding of disease."

Jerry and I are sitting in my living room on the West Side of Manhattan, an hour or so after he has given a lecture at Roosevelt–St. Luke's Hospital on the importance of adherence in the treatment of AIDS. The concept of "pharmacological forgiveness" (normally, if a patient takes 80 percent of a prescribed medication, there are few problems) does not apply to AIDS, Jerry explains. When it comes to AIDS, if you have 80 percent adherence you only get, at best, 50 percent suppression of viral replication. (This happens because in the presence of partially suppressive therapy, viral replication will select for viral variants with resistant mutations.) To have a good outcome, one needs at least 95 percent adherence — perfect or near-perfect adherence for the duration of the patient's life, and in this AIDS is unique, Jerry says, since no other infectious disease requires lifelong therapy.

He talks about the importance to adherence — and, thus, to survival — of the doctor-patient alliance. He cites studies, including several of his own, that document the most significant variable in the initiation of therapy, and the single, most important element in the doctor-patient alliance: trust in the doctor. He reviews ways of overcoming patient resistance and mistrust, and goes over protocols and design interventions that encourage adherence. The key is simplification — reducing pills and doses as much as possible. "It is naive and unrealistic," he says, "to expect that most patients can adhere to complex antiretroviral regimens, perhaps for life, without thoughtful, practical, and continuing support."

Most clinicians, alas, receive little training in assessment and support of adherence, but studies make clear that they, and their patients, benefit when they do, and when responsibility is shared. "The wonderful biomedical advances that have become available for the treatment of AIDS must be accompanied by parallel behavioral practices," Jerry tells his audience. "This is why the patient-provider relationship is very precious, and why we should be proud of it, and honor it, and not neglect it."

"Most of the time when we live in another place, we're tourists," Jerry says. "We're there for a little while, and then we move on, and we don't get to really understand much of the culture. By the end of my first year in Nigeria, though, I began to appreciate enough about both the culture and the society for things that had not made sense to me to begin to make sense."

My sublet is on the first floor, street-side, of a building on West 54th Street. Jerry sits in an easy chair in front of the window, and while he talks I watch men and women, policemen and policewomen, moving about in front of the station house across the street — the 18th precinct — coming and going to and from the precinct and the nineteenth-century courthouse — in former times, Men's Night Court — next to it.

"What am I doing here? I asked myself," Jerry says, "and the answer was, I'm here as an agent for change. But then I thought: Who am I to be here to change this culture? There's a certain arrogance in thinking that way — part of an old colonial mindset.

"Well, I said to myself, I brought Western medicine, and we could argue that perhaps medicine, of all things, is an intervention that, though it changes the culture, still provides a definable good." Jerry stops. "But okay — let me give you an example of what happened there — of how and why things changed for me.

"I wondered why it was that the Nigerian children had a higher infant mortality rate than we do, and part of the reason, I saw, was that they were exposed to multiple diseases at the same time during their first year of life, whereas our kids are protected by being separated from one another. We raise them in our own little nuclear environments, and only at a later point do they go on to nursery school and kindergarten. Then they start getting diseases, but one at a time — and they're already much stronger and able to handle them.

"But in Nigeria, the children would be together from six months of age on — as soon as weaning ended, the older siblings would take care of the younger kids and you would see these bands of kids who'd range in age from one year to about six or seven, and they'd all be together. And Nigerian kids have little in the way of toys or dolls or playthings. They have a stick or a hoop and they play with each other, not with objects.

"So a lot of kids would be sick with a lot of different things at the same time. In order to change the impact of multiple infectious diseases that result in higher mortality, then — and forget about vaccinations for a second — you have to change the tribal practices and separate the kids, but if you separate the kids, you change the way they learn to relate to one another, which is part of the genius of the culture.

"And I said 'Oh my God, look at that — we don't know how to organize our lives like this. It's different, and it has an effect on childhood diseases, and if you want to improve childhood mortality, in a sense you have to change childhood development, and do I really want to do this?'

"I mean, sure — kids shouldn't die. But on the other hand, there are certain things about this culture that are vibrant and beautiful and have to do with interpersonal and interfamilial kinds of things that we don't have, and that I think we suffer from not having. Now, on any scale of things it's better to prevent childhood mortality — of course — but on the other hand you have to appreciate that some of the technique for doing this is going to change the society at a fundamental child-rearing level. So this is what began to dawn on me near the end of my first year there.

"I'll give you another example," Jerry says, and he proceeds to tell me the story of the first medical article he wrote, about a disease called schistosomiasis.

"Many of the Peace Corps volunteers were high school biology teachers, and we organized a program and taught them to recognize schisto in the urine. The host for schistosomiasis — it's also called bilharziasis — is a snail called bulinus that comes from East Africa and is endemic to the Nile.

"But they didn't consider it a disease. The Yoruba word for it is *itosi aja*, which means 'dog's gonorrhea,' and they saw it as a kind of coming-of-age — the equivalent of menarche in girls. And this raises a very interesting question: If a pathologic entity occurs in a hundred percent of people, is it a disease?

"Now the natural history of schisto is that it goes away in time because your body creates an immune response to it. You'd see the rates rising in schoolboys up to the age of about twelve to fourteen, and then they'd go down. And the rates in girls were close to zero, and I said, How could this be? What's going on?

"So I sat on the banks of the rivers there and watched how the rivers were used, and this is what I learned. In the morning, before the sun would be fully out, the river was used by the mothers and their infants. The mothers would wash the clothes, and the babies would splash around in the water.

"At noon, when the sun was at its highest, the kids on their lunch break from school would play in the river. It would be the boys mostly, and not the girls, because they were a little modest and didn't have bathing suits and wouldn't go naked into the river. But the boys went in their underpants. And in the evening, the older men would come back from the fields and use the river, and wash themselves and then go home.

"Now the biology of schistosomiasis is that it has a complicated life cycle whereby the snails are the intermediate host. You pee or drop a load and it gets into the snail and then it grows in the snail and emerges into infection of the person — it's spread by contact with skin in infected water, and God, or nature, seems to have provided for the snail to come out according to the availability of sunlight, so the middle of the day was when the cycle for transmission was best set up: the sun was out, the snails were out, the boys were out peeing and swimming in the water, and bingo!

"So that explained why the rates were higher in boys of that age and it was kind of a revelation — like '*Boing!* Now look at that — it has to do with how the stream is used, and is a combination of biology *and* behavior,' and this made me appreciate that disease is not just about biology, but a combination of many forces that combine to result in disease etiology."

Jerry talks about having become enamoured of the richness of the spiritual world that was part of life in Nigeria, and about the complexity of their religious beliefs and practices.

"Yoruba have about four hundred deities," he says, "and they exist for every kind of life experience, and are involved in different forms of worship — different costumes, different music, different sculptures, different in everything that relates to each particular deity.

"So there was this enormous array and richness of religious practice that, although it contained within it a vague concept of a supreme deity called Oduduwa, was essentially animistic. And this meant that everything you touched was alive, and had a spiritual life, and was connected.

"So they had that, but they didn't have penicillin. And we have penicillin but we've lost *that* to some degree, and what I thought was that in an ideal world you'd want both. There are always tradeoffs. In order to have penicillin, I reasoned, we in some ways gave up some of our spiritual heritage. Now I'm a penicillin doctor and I'm surely not abandoning that. But what happened during my time there was that being in another culture took from me the belief in perfectability and progress I'd been schooled in as a twentieth-century American because it made it clear that progress always comes with a price.

"Then, my two years up, I returned to the States, and looking back, what politicized me when I got back here, I think, was living in the midst of the material wealth of our society after having lived in an environment poor in material resources but rich in other ways, and observing — feeling! — the maldistribution of wealth in our own country more so than at any other time of my life.

"Now my parents were socialists, and I used to go to these socialist summer camps, but nothing prepared me for the way things struck me on my return, and how, within our own society — and forget the disparities between rich and poor *nations* — but how there was such an enormous maldistribution right here at home, in access to health care especially, and what I decided was that if I were to be poor, it would be better to be a poor Nigerian than a poor American. Because in their culture if you were poor, although you'd rather be rich, you weren't *devalued* for being poor. Whereas in our society, if you're poor you're a nonperson.

"I had been a very honored man in Nigeria, and when I came back I lived on the Lower East Side, in an apartment as big as this rug" — he points to a ten-by-twelve-foot Persian rug on the floor — "for thirty-five dollars a month, and I went back to the grind of being a resident — to being on every other night — where I was low man on the totem pole.

"But I was determined to finish my training, and my intention was to prepare myself to go back to the developing world. I wanted to train in infectious diseases and public health, but at the time there was no opportunity to do this in New York, where there was only one school of public health, at Columbia, but it was separate from the medical school, and I had begun to have this vision of merging the two.

"I made inquiries, and I found out that there was a new program in Boston where you could train in infectious diseases while also getting a master's in public pealth at Harvard. So I went to Boston."

Jerry sighs. "I never really made it back to the developing world — though I still have hopes of doing so — because this was a period when we were at the beginning of community medicine, and after I arrived in Boston, I started getting involved with neighborhood health centers and clinics. I worked in Roxbury, with poor blacks and their families, and also with the Black Panthers. Did you know that?"

I say that he told me this before, but that he hadn't given me a lot of details. He closes his eyes as if to see again the world he knew three decades ago, and when he does, I see the young man I knew nearly fifty years ago.

How can it be, I wonder, that this guy I used to go to parties and basketball games with (Jerry was official timekeeper for our high school games), whom I hung out with on Flatbush Avenue, rode the trolley car and subway with, went to classes with, and played ball with all through high school and college — with whom I've spent hundreds of hours talking about sports and politics, about girl-friends and wives, about our friends, our children, our work, our hopes and dreams and hard times — has become this remarkable doctor: a man who fairly breathes optimism into the air around him, and a man who, during the epidemic outbreak of AIDS in the mid-eighties, was attending the funerals of dozens of patients every month in a time when not one of the hundreds of patients he treated recovered.

In 1982, early in the AIDS epidemic, Jerry alerted the Centers for Disease Control to the fact that AIDS could be transmitted hetero-sexually — that the sexual partners of heterosexuals with AIDS were in danger of contracting it.

"We had a few male patients who had female partners," he recalls. "The female partners were not drug users, so if they were at risk it was through sexual transmission, and I had one of the partners in clinic, and I started to examine her. I put my hands on her neck, and I felt these huge lymph nodes and I thought to myself, 'Oh shit, she's got it — it's the end of the world.' That was the way it came to me. I mean, there are a limited number of gay men in the world, I rea-soned, but many many more heterosexuals.

"Did you ever see *Wild Strawberries?*" Jerry asks. "Well, there's a scene in the movie where the old doctor's walking in a town, and there's a clock that doesn't have any hands on it — typical Bergman — and there's a hearse that drives off and a coffin falls from it. It was very disturbing — and I had a dream that was similar. I was walking on Jerome Avenue in the Bronx, near Montefiore, and this train is going by overhead, and the green grocer stalls are all out, and there are lots of cars and trucks — but there are no people. They've all died from AIDS."

Jerry was also the doctor whose research team, at Montefiore, made the discovery that HIV was not transmitted by casual and close interpersonal contact, and that therefore health-care workers tending AIDS patients were at little or no risk, not even from the ac-cidental needle pricks that had been causing terror on the wards. "The transmission of HIV," he concluded in the second of two arti-cles he published in the *New England Journal of Medicine* in 1986 and 1987, "occurs only through blood, sexual activity, and perinatal events." Moreover, "the available data indicate that HIV transmis-sion is not highly efficient in a single or few exposures," so that "the widespread dissemination of HIV is more likely the result of multiple, repeated exposures over time by routes of transmission that are strongly related to personal and cultural patterns of behavior — particularly, sexual activity and drugs."

What pleased Jerry most about these discoveries was their potential to reduce the epidemic of fear that had followed upon the epidemic itself. In this instance, as in others, his boundless optimism was matched by his clear-eyed realism. The fear of catching AIDS from someone at home, at school, in an office, swimming pool, or any other public place turned out to be unfounded; those who had contracted AIDS, therefore, did not have to be ostracized or quarantined.

"Although we are confronted by a public health problem of potentially catastrophic dimensions," he wrote at the time, "it is essential to appreciate that unwarranted fears of HIV transmission have compounded the suffering of young men, women, and children infected with HIV and have blunted an appropriate societal response aimed at reduction of transmission."

Just as, for Jerry, the patient is always more than his or her illness, so each medical student he works with is always more than the sum of his or her clinical experience and expertise.

After a patient with AIDS died one day, I was with Jerry when he took the young resident who had been the patient's doctor aside, and reviewed the case with her. "You worked very hard for her," he said, simply and quietly. "Thank you."

Later that day, he invited a young Chinese medical student, Karen Xiaoda, to talk with him privately. She was a brilliant student, he told me, and he had noticed that she was somewhat distracted and tired. When they met in a room used for AIDS patients to visit with their guests, and Jerry asked her how she was doing — he was concerned, he said, because she seemed unusually exhausted — she told him that yes, she was somewhat overwhelmed: her father had died during the past year, and now her mother, who was fifty years old, had breast cancer, and was in the Intensive Care Unit at a New York City hospital. As she talked with Jerry, she began crying, and Jerry put his hand on her arm (even before his discovery about the finite ways in which AIDS could be transmitted, Jerry had always been hands-on with patients and colleagues), and said, "You should be with your mother."

Karen protested, citing her studies, her work in the hospital. Jerry listened, then asked a simple question: "Where would you like to be now?"

"With my mother in the ICU," Karen said.

"Then go there," Jerry said, and told her she could make up the work some other time, that she should think only about being with her mother and shouldn't worry about anything else.

On the drive back to Guilford that evening, Jerry told me that Karen's situation reminded him of what happened when he was in his fourth year of medical school and his father was on a respirator, alone and dying.

"I received the news of his death a half-hour before my final med school exam," Jerry said, "and I bombed it. But I didn't tell anybody about my father." He laughs. "What — *me* have feelings? *Me* talk about my emotions with somebody? *Me* not show up on time — *me* not be responsible?

"The dean asked me to come in and talk with him. It was my only poor showing in four years, he said. What happened? So I told him about my father, and he said I should have told him about it — should have let him know I was under so much pressure."

When Jerry walks into a hospital room to visit a patient, or when a patient enters his examining room at the clinic, I am struck each time by the slight, subtle shift in his demeanor — by how, starting with the patient's hair, forehead, and eyes, his gaze moves slowly and carefully over the patient, as if, invisibly, to *touch* the patient with his eyes and, I assume, to take in all kinds of things — changes, symptoms, curious or troubling details, warning signs — even while he is engaging the patient, warmly and attentively, in conversation.

I sometimes think of him, and I tell this to the other guys, as being a kind of Brooklyn-born Jewish American Albert Schweitzer. He is a scrupulous and innovative researcher, a fine writer, a patient administrator (the part of his work he likes least), a gifted clinician and diagnostician, and a charismatic teacher who never pulls rank, and whose authority derives from his gentle, unaffected presence, and from his expertise.

He has dedicated his adult life to those in need of his medical knowledge and skills — men and women who often have been stigmatized and abandoned by others — and he does so without sentimentality. ("You are going to see the bottom of the bottom of the human barrel," he said to me on our way to his clinic the first time I spent an afternoon with him there.) But unlike Schweitzer (or, in our time, a man like Paul Farmer), he has done so without going into exile from the world in which he had grown up, come of age, and had been living.

Jerry is also my friend of many years, and in knowing him, and writing about him, as of my other friends, I remind myself not to try to separate who he is as a doctor from who he is as Jerry, for if I do, I sense, I will err in the same way a doctor errs when he or she separates the disease a patient has from the person in whom the disease has made its home.

Jerry lived in Boston from 1968 to 1981, where, at Harvard, he completed his training in internal medicine, after which he did a year of infectious disease training while also taking courses at the Harvard School of Public Health. He worked in Roxbury as a primary-care doctor, developed several community programs and neighborhood health centers, and was involved with the Medical Committee for Human Rights there, which was, Jerry says, "a kind of radical progressive health organization." He did this while retaining his affiliation with Beth Israel (Harvard Medical School), where he continued to teach in infectious diseases.

"The Black Panther Party wanted to develop a health center and asked me and another doctor — an African American opthalmologist — if we would help them," Jerry says. "We did, and I never felt any sense of discomfort in working with them. They were wonderful young people, and we developed a program with them, rented a trailer, and the Panthers put the trailer next to a housing project on land that had been cleared for I-95. It was their political statement: that this was how land should be used — for health care, and not for highways to take people to the suburbs.

"So we set up this clinic on abandoned land, and we'd sit there in the evening and a bunch of the young Panthers would come and take a cable out and plug it into one of the lampposts, and that was how we got our electricity. Every evening we'd see twenty or so patients from the neighboring projects, and we developed a program for blood pressure screening, tuberculosis screening, and sickle cell screening.

"I taught the Panthers how to take blood pressure and do the skin testing for TB, and they would go out into the community and knock on doors and do the work. It was wonderful, and I loved it. They lived in a house donated to them by a Jewish doctor who had practiced in Roxbury and retired to Florida, and we'd go into the house, and it was sandbagged, and the windows were blocked off, and there were weapons around, and it was pretty scary." Jerry shakes his head in disbelief. "But I did it! Sometimes when one of the Panthers was arrested, they'd call me and I'd go to the police station to make sure the person wasn't beaten up. I'd be introduced as 'Dr. Friedland from Harvard Medical School,' and the cops would look at me like — 'What are you — *nuts?!*'

"Gail was in terror too, and sure, I knew I was being used, yet I never felt in danger from the Panthers or the police. The police were smart, you see, and they'd drive past the clinic at night, but leave it alone. Still, it was strange, going back and forth — all you had to do was cross Columbus Avenue and you were in a different world. I mean, here you had what was probably the premier biomedical research institution in the world sitting right next to truly abject poverty."

It is late afternoon in the second week of August 2000 — nearly two months after my return from Norway — and Jerry and I are in his administrative office at Yale. The office is long and narrow, filled to overflowing with books, articles, journals, and photos. His desk is piled high with folders, as are several tables. There are framed photos of Gail and their children and, on the walls, posters from international AIDS conferences. I remark on a new, large framed picture facing his desk: a poster of the U.S. postage stamp honoring Jackie Robinson — Jackie sliding into home plate — and Jerry says, "He remains one of my only heroes." There is a framed *New Yorker* cover that depicts a paradisal New York — turbaned taxi drivers waving happily to each other, "WELCOME BACK DODGERS" on a banner strung across the middle of the street — and near to Jerry's desk, a framed hand-lettered passage from Albert Camus' *The Plague:*

> . . . so that he should not be one of those who hold their peace but should bear witness in favor of those plague-stricken people; so that some memorial of the injustice and outrage done there might endure; and to state quite simply what we learn in time of pestilence: that there are more things to admire in men than to despise.
>
> Nonetheless, he knew that the tale he had to tell could not be one of a final victory. It could be only the record of what had had to be done, and what assuredly would have to be done again in the never ending fight against terror and its relentless onslaughts, despite their personal afflictions, by all who, while unable to be saints but refusing to bow down to pestilences, strive their utmost to be healers.

Jerry, who has returned a few weeks before from an international AIDS conference in Durban, South Africa, talks with me about how inspiring the conference was, especially the moment when Nelson Mandela appeared, and thousands of people burst into cheers, South Africans dancing and singing, "Nelson Mandela! *Ga go no yo a swana na ye . . .*" ("There is no one like him . . . He brought us our freedom.")

Jerry has written an account of the conference for *AIDS Clinical Care*, and has titled his essay "Breaking the Silence." He shows me the manuscript, which he has prefaced with an African proverb: "The best time to plant a tree is twenty years ago. The second best time is now."

The great significance of the conference, and the international attention it received, we agree, is that the world can never again claim to be unaware of the horrific extent of the AIDS epidemic in the developing world. "We know how to prevent HIV transmission, yet the pandemic continues to grow unchecked in most of the world," Jerry writes. "Surely, lack of information can no longer be blamed for the worldwide shroud of silence regarding the pandemic's magnitude."

Attending the conference, he tells me, has also confirmed his decision to return to South Africa during his sabbatical a year hence.

In 1975, Jerry took a leave of absence from Harvard. "I liked being both in the Harvard medical school environment and in the black community," Jerry says, "and I felt fortunate, and was able to lead this life for a while, but it took its toll, and I burned out. So in 1975, I took a leave of absence, and Gail and I wound up going to Israel."

Jerry found out about a man from the Harvard School of Public Health, Asher Siegel, who was helping to develop a new medical school in Beer Sheva that would attempt to integrate public health, clinical medicine, and basic science. Jerry and Gail left for Israel with a single suitcase — they had never been there before — and they lived in Beer Sheva, where Jerry was visiting professor at Ben Gurion University of the Negev, and where he taught infectious disease, which was not a recognized specialty in Israel at the time. It was a wonderful place, Jerry says (one of the wonderful things about Jerry is how frequently he uses the word *wonderful*) — innovative, chaotic, and with a pioneering spirit. He developed a curriculum for the treatment of tuberculosis that integrated clinical care and public health, and he found the experience enormously gratifying.

After his return to the States, he continued teaching and doing clinical work at Harvard and in Roxbury, becoming, among other things, coordinator of clinical training for infectious disease at Beth Israel, Children's Hospital, the Sidney Farber Cancer Institute, and Harvard Medical School. The Black Panther Party gradually disintegrated, and in 1981, when a new chief of medicine came to Harvard and brought his own infectious disease people with him, Jerry decided to leave.

"Life is not a controlled experiment," Jerry says. "There's no way of *proving* whether you went in the right or wrong direction. It was a very hard move — traumatic for us personally. We'd been in Boston for thirteen years, and had close friends there, and we were integrated into both the medical and political community. We also had three children by then — our first two, as you know, Elisabeth and David, were adopted from Colombia, and then we had Sarah — and they were one, two, and three years old. But we decided to start all over again in New York.

"It seemed like an appropriate job for me, at Montefiore, and at Einstein — being involved with infectious disease and the training of doctors — and the first month I attended there, there were three patients who had this rare new thing called *pneumocystis carinii pneumonia* that I had never seen before. Now, I'd been in Africa and the Middle East — there were *lots* of infectious diseases in Israel — and at Bellevue, and here and there and everywhere. And somehow I knew from the very beginning that this was something new and different and bad, and that it was going to be very big."

Jerry talks about how, sad to say, he was the right person in the right place at the right time: everything in his life, personally and professionally, had prepared him for the work that would consume him from this point on — he was an infectious disease doctor, he had trained in public health, he had been overseas, he had worked with poor people, he had thought for many years about ways in which biology was bound up with behavior and social forces.

"I like to use the analogy of the seed and the wind," he says, "with the seed being HIV, and the wind being what's changed in terms of social, economic, and personal conditions that have resulted in the conversion of what was probably a local pathogen into a worldwide pandemic. Because if you look at all the routes of transmission of HIV that we understand — blood-borne, sexual, and birth — the thing that has changed and has resulted in the enormous spread of HIV are largely events of the last twenty five to forty years of human history.

"The most obvious one is the acceleration of international travel and the ability of people, and hence pathogens — like seeds — to travel from one place to another. Did you know, for example, that HIV was introduced in Japan through American-made Factor VIII, which is used for hemophiliacs? Even precious body fluids like blood and blood products travel all over the world now, whereas in the old days it was very local. If you had an uncle in the hospital who needed a transfusion, you called the family, and everybody came in and donated blood.

"And then there was what I can only call a diabolical alignment of forces that occurred just before HIV entered into the population of people who were injecting drugs."

Jerry describes how a series of public health measures designed to reduce heroin use by making needles and syringes less readily available — paraphernalia laws that resulted in imprisonment if one was caught with needles and syringes — led to the sharing of needles, and to the development of "shooting galleries," where you paid a dollar or two for a needle and syringe, injected the drug, and returned the paraphernalia, which was used by the next person, and then the next person.

But such sequential anonymous needle sharing was only one of the elements that led to the explosive spread of HIV, and Jerry lists others, among them the bathhouses used by gay men, the rise in anonymous sex that accompanied sexual liberation, and the detribalization and urbanization in developing nations following World War II that broke down traditional structures, and that resulted in social disruption — large populations of men, separate from women, migrating, becoming concentrated in urban areas, and contracting and transmitting disease.

Jerry says again what he has said before: "You can look at every route of transmission and you will see that what explains the transmission of each route has something to do with how we live as human beings more than it does with the biology of the organism."

It is this understanding of disease that informs the way Jerry has approached his work as an AIDS doctor for the past two decades. Like my other friends, however, he did not start out intending to become a doctor. At Columbia, he had been an undergraduate history and sociology major, and when he graduated in 1959, he entered Columbia's graduate program in sociology.

"Somehow or other, I thought of sociology as being social *activism* — as something that would *change* society, which is what I wanted to do," he says. "I spent some time at the Institute for Social Research, with Paul Lazarsfeld and others, and I quickly learned what sociology was, at least the way it was practiced there, and it was mostly statistical — market research and opinion polls and stuff like that, and I knew pretty soon that this wasn't what I wanted.

"In truth, I was quite a confused and unhappy young man then. But I kept asking myself, 'What can I do personally?' So I spoke with some people and came to believe that I could be the kind of sociologist I'd wanted to be, on a one-to-one basis, if I were to become a doctor. And I guess that in some sense this is what my career in medicine has been — that medicine has allowed me to be the person I am. So I chose to go to medical school both as a personal decision, but also as a choice that meant being involved in social activism. I'm not the kind of person who would lead a political movement, especially one that was without a personal basis, so that from the first there was never any question but that I would care for people, and in so doing exercise my politics through medicine."

Jerry talks with passion about the global politics of AIDS. He is outraged by the greed of drug companies, and by the restrictive policies of our own government and other Western nations regarding the dissemination of drugs, and he has his own ideas about what might be done, on an international level, to address the enormous needs of those suffering from AIDS in the developing world. He has begun writing and speaking about this, believing that while he is doing the work on an individual and personal basis, he should also be trying to figure out ways of affecting the larger forces that affect health care.

"So I guess I'm trying to figure out ways of influencing the larger systems — where power resides. I mean, think of it this way: what does a Jewish doctor who is white and whose parents lived through the Holocaust feel is our ethical responsibility to forty million people dying in Africa? And how do we begin to address that, politically, in the midst of our affluence? Now, I'll let the politicians figure out the strategies, but I can give them some medical advice, and this is what I've begun to try to do."

After Jerry dropped out of the graduate sociology program at Columbia, he enrolled in Columbia's School of General Studies, and, while living at home in Brooklyn with his parents, took the pre-med courses he had never taken as an undergraduate. He was accepted into the New York University School of Medicine (Bellevue) and began his studies in the fall of 1960, at the same time that Phil and

Rich, who had begun medical school there the year before, were starting on their second year.

Jerry shakes his head, as if bewildered to be looking back so many years. "Oh I was a very confused young man!" he says again, laughing. "So why did I become a doctor?" he asks. "It's a good question, and I really don't know the answer. But okay, we had this doctor in our family, Sidney Feldman, and he was our family doctor. He was a wonderful man, and he was a role model in our family of a gentle, caring person. He loved music — classical music . . .

"Yes." Jerry pauses. "Yes," he says again, to himself, and then: "I remember that he once told me that on his way to the hospital every day he used to drive down a certain street in Brooklyn because there was a beautiful maple tree on that street that was spectacular, and that it gave him great pleasure to drive down that street and look at it. So this man was not just a doctor, but he had a sense of beauty, and I was very taken by that. He was a special person in our family.

"Our family started out on the Lower East Side. My father was very smart, and went to Cooper Union for a year, but he dropped out, and the story we heard was that he dropped out because he had to support the family. But in retrospect, I wonder. Because I know my father was severely depressed, and was hospitalized at Hillside Hospital — but not in Queens where it was when your brother Robert was first hospitalized.

"The original Hillside is in Hastings, at the top of a place called Hillside Park, and my father was hospitalized there for a year, a ten-minute walk from where Gail and I wound up living, in fact, when I was at Montefiore. It was a family secret we don't know much about. Then, after he came out of the hospital, he became a window cleaner, and he worked as a window cleaner for the rest of his life. So he was limited not by his intellect, you see, but by his depression. And he used to say, 'Every window is a pane to me,' and he was a very gentle, loving man. But my mother was afraid of him, and she used to say, 'Don't say anything that will upset your father,' because I think she lived in fear of upsetting him in a way that might bring back the depression.

"My mother worked as a bookkeeper until she married my father. They were both socialists, and I went to a school run by a labor Zionist organization where I learned Yiddish. We were involved with the Henry Street Settlement House on the Lower East Side — I took piano lessons there — and we went to summer camps, Kindervelt and Kindering, and I worked in both places as a waiter. All the waiters and busboys were children of parents who belonged to this socialist organization, and there were Puerto Rican kids and Polish kids and black kids in the summer camps. We were all in it together, and I loved it, I really loved it, and I guess I was introduced early on to socialist ideals — to tolerance, and to racial tolerance especially.

"My father had a friend named Smitty, a black man who was the janitor for an Ebinger's bakery on my father's route, and when my father was on vacation, Smitty would wash the windows for him, and my father would reciprocate and do favors for Smitty. Smitty was the only person I ever remember, outside of family, who came to our home for dinner, and he came with his wife. This was in the 1940s. He was a lovely man, and he was my father's best friend, and he lived in a black neighborhood in St. Albans."

Jerry and I reminisce about our childhoods ("Sometimes," he says at one point, "I think a lot of what I do and the way I react in certain situations comes down to the fact that I'm still just trying to please my unpleasable mother and get my depressed father's attention"; I smile, tell him about Robert reminding me, recently, of the time our mother said, "Am I the only *man* around here?") — about teachers and friends from Erasmus, about the Dodgers, about the street games we played as kids: punchball, stickball, boxball, box baseball, kickball, Chinese handball, Ringalevio, Johnny-on-the-pony, hit-the-penny, heels.

He talks, with enthusiasm, about some of the new programs he has recently initiated at Yale, through which he is trying to find effective ways to teach clinicians not just to provide care, but to prevent disease and the spread of disease. We don't know how to do this in the clinical setting, he explains, and he has set up several pilot programs that work with primary-care physicians, teaching them how to integrate HIV prevention into clinical practice. It is hard to believe, he says, that this has not been done in an organized way before.

I attend one of these training sessions with Jerry — fifteen doctors sitting around and talking about how, step by step, to talk with patients so as to encourage adherence. Afterward, driving back to Jerry's home, we talk more about his new programs, and about health-care policy in general — about his belief in the absolute need to invest more resources in prevention and public health measures than in biotechnology, in basic medicine rather than in heroic medicine, and in care rather than cure — and though I agree with him, I say something about being grateful, too, for the existence of biotechnology and heroic medicine, which, after all, saved my life. Though I know, I add at once, that most people do not get the kind of care I did.

"Right," Jerry says. "You got the best, and the system didn't screw up for you. And you had access to very good care, and not everybody does. You can't expect everyone to have equal care all the time, of course, but people should have access."

I don't say anything for a while.

"Sure," he says. He takes his eyes off the road for a second, smiles, then reaches across and puts his hand on my shoulder. "Sure, Neugie. Everyone's entitled to the kind of care you received."

12 🐝

A Safe Place

ALTHOUGH ARTHUR COMPLAINS CONSTANTLY about living in New York City ("Mountains and streams mean more to me than bridges and buildings," he says), he is the only one of my four friends who is still there. Arthur often seems to me, in fact — as in his grumbling *about* New York — a quintessential New Yorker: eccentric, outspoken, and, with strangers as with friends, exceptionally direct, gregarious, and generous. He kibbitzes with virtually everyone he meets — the doormen and elevator operators in his building, waiters and delivery people; and when we go for walks — with his trim salt-and-pepper beard, a black beret aslant on his head, bright red sweatpants, and earphones clamped tight to the sides of his head — he looks like a wandering poet recently escaped from a Woody Allen movie. He says exactly what he thinks most of the time, mixing outrageously blunt comments, Brooklyn slang, and Yiddish expressions with sophisticated and learned speculations — and despite his leave-me-alone demeanor, he does not hesitate to act decisively in crises, large and small.

When, on one of our walks, a car skids to a stop in the middle of Eighth Avenue, near Columbus Circle, bringing five lanes of traffic to a horn-blaring halt, Arthur, without hesitating, walks straight into traffic, talks to the two women in the stalled car, its hazard lights now blinking, and begins to help. When a truck, coming around the corner, bears down on us — I've followed Arthur into

the street — Arthur turns and, like a traffic cop, puts up a hand to
stop the truck. To me, in a smiling aside, even as he turns back to the
two women: "I don't want anyone killing my friend Neugie before
he finishes his book."

Arthur and his wife Paulette, senior partner in a New York City
law firm, live in a two-bedroom apartment on Fifth Avenue, directly
across from Central Park. The apartment is handsomely furnished
— uncluttered, open, and airy, with bright light pouring in through
high windows, and Arthur and I are sitting in his book-lined study,
and talking about friendship. Arthur still maintains friendships with
at least a half-dozen guys he has known since about the third grade
of elementary school, and, like me, he remains close with many others with whom we went to Erasmus and Columbia.

"Maybe it's because I need these friendships," he says, "but who
knows why I do? I'll tell you this, though — it gives me *great* pleasure. The pleasure you get from reading books, I get from watching
you, seeing how you evolved, seeing who you've become, seeing
what you're hoping to be. I get the same pleasure from Phil and
from Jerry, and from all the guys I know. Because I love people — I
love being with them and I always have. I'm *fascinated* by people,
and getting to know people always satisfied a tremendous curiosity
and craving. Even in high school, when I didn't know I was honing
any professional career, I enjoyed playing with and marrying myself
to the different kinds of involvements I had with different people.

"So when I went into private practice and was doing fifty to sixty
hours a week of individual therapy, I was a very happy guy. I'd be
seeing, on any day, six or seven different types of people — maybe
there were two or three overlaps, maybe three Jewish lawyers — and
I was different with each person. I was talking about different things.
I was learning about the ways different minds work, and I was engaged in trying to help people deal. I'd go in at eight, I'd leave at
seven or seven-thirty at night, and it went like lightning. It was a gift,
a no-brainer — like Willie Mays playing center field. I did what I
loved, and I made a living doing what I would have done for pleasure."

Sitting in his study — he has shown me, earlier, his shelves of
books about Buddhism, and by and about the Dalai Lama ("These

belief systems contain a much healthier approach to life, for me, than the systems I was raised in, and I resonate to them.") — Arthur is less the outspoken, kibbitzing New Yorker, and more the relaxed, easygoing guy I've known for nearly half a century — more the man I imagine he is when he is working one-on-one with his patients, the guy I loved to take long walks with when we were teenagers, and to talk with about whatever came to mind: our friends and our family, our doubts and our dreams and our insecurities and our hopes.

He is, as ever, brilliant and canny (he graduated *cum laude* and Phi Beta Kappa from Columbia; was voted Most Likely to Succeed when we graduated, nearly thirteen hundred of us, from Erasmus), yet he is also thoughtful, direct, warm, and down-to-earth in his observations. When I ask a question, he rarely answers immediately, but will close his eyes, lean backward, and then, once he starts talking, pause frequently before he chooses words or phrases.

On this afternoon, however, he is the one who asks the questions.

"Okay," he says. "So tell me something, Neugie. Where does medicine come in? Where does friendship fit in with medicine in this book of yours, and what do they have to do with our growing up in Brooklyn — with what we've been talking about?"

Although I have not begun the actual writing of the book, I say (it is early summer of 2000, a week after my return from Norway), what I have begun to see — to speculate about and believe, if provisionally — seems fairly basic, and it's this: that the things people want from their doctors, and that they are, in recent years, getting less of, have much in common with what they want from friendship.

"Ah, you are a smart fellow, Neugie," he says. Then: "Why are you smart?" he asks. "Because I agree with you!"

We laugh, after which Arthur talks about his work as a psychologist, and although I am hearing his words, my mind is floating free, and I am thinking that this — being here with him and talking in the way we do — is one of the great and unexpected dividends from my surgery. The comfort and sheer pleasure these conversations bring, and the ways the five of us have become closer with one another — this has been an unexpected and precious gift.

Rich and Phil went to elementary school, high school, and medical school together, but lost touch through the years. Now, though, when Rich visits his children and their families in Denver, he spends time with Phil; and Phil is planning a trip to New York in September, when he, Jerry, Arthur, and I will hang out together. I say something about this — about how much more we've all been in touch with one another since my surgery, and about how much I've been enjoying our talks.

"It's our thing," Arthur says quickly. "Sure. I call it psychological *davaning*. It's what we do, but this kind of Talmudic self-absorbed, self-reflective, looking-at-yourself-as-an-object, commenting-on-yourself stuff — this wasn't, for example, Ronald Reagan's thing. I was just reading a biography of this man — president twice, governor of California, head of a lot of organizations, well respected, yet I don't think he did as much of this in a lifetime as we do in a day. And you know what? There are lots of very smart people who don't *davan* the way we do, and his way of living is a reasonable way to live, and there's only a certain percentage of us who will do what we do and get something from it and grow from it. I talk about what's inside me. You talk about what's inside you. These are my ideas. These are yours. This kind of self-revelation and self-reflection is different from going fishing together, but I'll tell you this — it's much more fun for me to do this than to go fishing, or even to a Knicks game.

"Now remember — I come at most things from the point of view of trust, and the way we get on with one another, and the work I do when it's effective is a function of trust, and I think trust is something very, very, very hard to come by," Arthur says. "I mean, how can you have it in today's medicine? It's my belief that it usually takes years of reliability, consistency, authenticity, maturity, and empathically resonant dialogue for patients to begin to trust therapists so that they will take some risks they wouldn't otherwise take.

"Look. At my best — in my snappiest suit and with my smartest verbiage, I could never engender trust, *real* trust, *fundamental* trust, in ten sessions. The idea that people can do that in a managed-care setting is just not comprehensible to me.

"There are times — when I was in the army, for instance — you see people six or ten times, and you do what you can do. But having seen many people for between one year and five or six years, I know the difference. When I work with somebody over a long period of time, I get to know that person so well I can feel that person's pain — and I do, and, like that person, I find myself up late at night sometimes, trying to think and feel my way through the pain. And it's the same in medicine, though I didn't used to think so. I've seen studies saying that across the board somewhere between sixty to seventy percent of what a doctor bases his treatment on is the report from the patient. But if there's no trust, how good is the report?

"Let's say I have some funny pains in my chest and go to the physician who's been treating me for twenty years. Now he knows I've never said this before, so he'll take it more seriously than a guy who's seeing me for the first or second time, doesn't know if I'm a whiner, or if I'm just having some gas — and that's where trust comes in. You trusted the cardiologist and the surgeon because they were an extension of Jerry, and you trusted Jerry.

"But trust is also a function of time, and of age." Arthur goes to his bookcase, and comes back with a book. "I think part of growing older," he says, "is that we've given up illusions of control — of what we can and can't control. And that makes life easy — with our children, with everything. As certain responsibilities — raising our kids chief among them — start to slip away, we begin to use time and to think about it differently, and there is something peculiar and wonderful, I think, when time becomes our ally. But read this — it's from a speech Adlai Stevenson gave to a class of college graduates."

I read:

> What a man knows at fifty that he did not know at twenty is, for the most part, incommunicable. The laws, the aphorisms, the generalizations, the universal truths, the parables and the old saws — all of the observations about life which can be communicated handily in ready, verbal packages — are as well known to a man at twenty who has been attentive as to a man at fifty. He has been told them all, he has read them all, and he has probably repeated them all before he graduates from college; but he has not lived them all.

> What he knows at fifty that he did not know at twenty boils down to something like this: The knowledge he has acquired with age is not the knowledge of formulas, or forms of words, but of people, places, ac-

tions — a knowledge not gained by words but by touch, sight, sound, victories, failures, sleeplessness, devotion, love — the human experiences and emotions of this earth and of oneself and other men; and perhaps, too, a little faith, and a little reverence for the things you cannot see.

Arthur and I talk about how time, age, and experience, whether in psychology, psychiatry, or medicine, relate to clinical judgment. "Let's take depression," he says. "Somebody comes to me depressed, and what I can do is make a judgment, probably within a couple of sessions, as to whether that person is a candidate for a psychopharmacological agent that, maybe within three to six weeks, will be helpful. Secondly, I can assure him, based on my clinical experience, that virtually everyone who has been placed on antidepressants, over time — and when he gets the mixture right — will feel better. I can assure him of that because it has been my clinical experience. Third, I can tell him that if he takes the medicine, it will make it easier for him, without the pain and depression, to talk about some of the things that have led to the depressed feelings.

"So now, with that out of the way, I can begin a relationship with him where I learn about how he became the person he is — how the kind of family he grew up in, and the way he chose to deal with his childhood home, led him to feel *less* about himself — to have thoughts he's ashamed of — and I can help point out how that was happening, and is still happening, and he can begin to look at himself somewhat differently. And maybe three or four years from now he'll have a thirty to sixty percent better feeling about himself that will make the rest of his life better."

In a World Health Organization study that covers the period from 1990 to 2020 (actual data plus projections), unipolar depression (also called major, or clinical, depression) is second, behind ischemic heart disease, in the rank order of the global burden of disease (a measure of health status that quantifies not merely the number of deaths but also the impact of premature death and disability on a population). In addition, of the ten leading causes of disability worldwide, five are psychiatric conditions (depression, alcoholism, bipolar disorder, schizophrenia, and obsessive-compulsive disorder). Moreover, I say to Arthur, his field — psychology and psychiatry — has proven at least as effective in diagnosing and treating these conditions, and in enabling recovery from them, as medical disciplines have been in the diagnosis and treatment of, for example, neurological, infectious, and heart diseases.

Arthur says that even though he knows this is so, he cannot shake the belief that psychotherapy is more of an art than a science, and less of a science than medicine is. And this belief, we agree, derives, at least in part, from the reverence with which, when we were growing up, we were taught to regard physicians.

"My first experience with a physician was, literally, with the man next door to us, who was an old-timer even then, probably in his seventies," Arthur says. "And he would always cure me! Not hard to do given that I was getting sore throats and minor stuff. But he would also take time to affirm things — like how well I could tell time at whatever age I could tell time.

"So there he was — a safe, concerned, benign person who I thought was omniscient. And in my case he was omnipotent too — he could do things that made me *better* — and so I came into my adulthood assuming that doctors possessed all kinds of secrets, and knew everything, and this intimidated me. I think I was afraid to go into medicine, in fact, because then I'd have to see if *I* could know everything.

"But his presence also drew me, which is partly why I ended up in psychology, which is a healing field. And you know, when I was in Florida during my mother's final illness a few years ago, and I was getting into the elevator in the hospital and there was this promo poster for the head of the cardiac surgery unit, with all his credentials — he was bar mitzvahed in 1952, he played quarterback for Tulane, he did his residency at Harvard, he's done six thousand angioplasties — I said '*Whoa!*' because this was so at odds with the model I'd had in my head, which was the *doctor-as-teacher* — a wise, caring, rabbinical practitioner, and not somebody in Nike sneakers who's on the front page of the Yearbook. All this advertising in subways and newspapers — these are not the doctors I knew.

"But if not an M.D., why a psychologist, right? — and this had to do with my wanting to understand *myself* better. I started out in Yale Law School, you know, and made a decision after three days there to get out — that being in an adversary profession was not for me. Probably because it would have put me in touch with my anger, which I was afraid of, though I didn't realize it then. Law school — and being a lawyer — that seemed like a life where I'd be fighting under the boards for rebounds again and again, and I didn't want to do that.

"Now in my home I never heard, 'You should make a lot of money — go out and become rich.' And I never heard it in my friends' homes. Once, when somebody asked me what I was going to do when I grew up, thinking I was very clever, I said I was going to make a lot of money. And my mother got upset, and my father spoke to me and said this wasn't the way one should move toward a vocation. So it was my assumption always that I would do something that would be of service, would save me from mediocrity — that enormous fear of being *'average'* — and make me into a professional: a teacher, doctor, lawyer, engineer — and that the money would follow, and it would be enough for me to be able to live a good and decent life.

"But from a psychoanalytic point of view, since as a young person I was very competitive and ambitious, I think I was also ashamed of the competitiveness, and when I got into Yale and realized I was entering into a profession where I would be making a living from the competitiveness, I said 'Stop!' — and then I thought about how much I loved being involved with people, and recalled that in my second year of college I took a psychology course I loved, and that I had decided then to go into psychology, and it was like 'Whoa — I can play basketball and get paid for it!' and so, at twenty-one, I left Yale — I measure my time there in hours and not days — went back to Columbia, and to CCNY, and took the necessary undergrad courses.

"After that, I went to Clark University, in Worcester — the place where Freud gave his lectures when he was in America — but I didn't like the way they looked at psychology there, so I came back and went to Columbia for my doctorate, and I never looked back or second-guessed myself again. If I had to make a decision today for a new life, I can't imagine doing anything else.

"And this was always connected to the idea of being a *professional* — and my idea of a professional was a guy who was a .320 batter year after year, a regular sixteen-to-nineteen game winner, a man who routinely pulled down fifteen rebounds a game. One of the things I took enormous pride in during my years as a shrink was that I almost never did *not* get to my office and do my day's work. It's like Ripkin and Lou Gehrig being out there, game after game — something about consistency, the doing of the work and not letting minor colds or sore throats interfere.

"Now I was blessed with good health, I didn't have horrific accidents — though I once did a whole day of therapy with cotton swabs sticking out of my nose after it was cauterized for a nosebleed — nothing that compromised me in terms of getting to the office. Because the notion of consistency and reliability is something I associate with the idea of a professional, and this is bound up with a certain measured, thoughtful way of going about one's life — of a consistent availability to the people one serves. When people are exploring and risking themselves, consistency is very, very important."

I say that Phil says Arthur is really just doing the same thing in his sixties that he was doing when we were teenagers — being on call to his friends, listening to our problems, talking with us, giving advice, getting us through.

When, for example, after my move to New York, I am upset about the deterioration of a relationship, Arthur assures me I have given the relationship every chance, that I have been generous and open — a *mensch* — and that there are no issues I am blind to in the situation, or in myself. It is his judgment — both personal *and* professional — that I should get out. He also speculates, briefly, about what he thinks may be going on in the woman, in terms of what psychologists call "projective identification." "But look," he says then. "Let me put it another way: if we were walking along Flatbush Avenue and you told the guys what you were going through, they would say to you, 'Neugie, she's busting your balls.'"

When I remind Arthur about how helpful he's been to me, he

shrugs off my gratitude, says he is a lot less sure of things — of what he truly *knows* — than I might think, and he talks about his clinical experience and its relation to the education of therapists.

"My most energizing experience — my highest level of gratification — comes from my involvement with people," he says. "Now, in my field there are three variables in the treatment process. There's a patient, there's a therapist, and there's a treatment modality. If one of the three isn't appropriate — wrong patient for the right modality and the right therapist, right patient for the wrong therapist, et cetera, psychotherapy will not be a success. And in my field we have done far too little scientific investigation of the match — of the integration of proper therapist — by age, life experience, psychotherapeutic skills — with patient. And the failures in my field — what you and Robert have experienced in spades — or a high percentage of them certainly, are a function of our inability to put together the three variables in a way that's synergistic.

"My sense of things is that it's different in medicine — for Rich, let's say — and that in your prototypical heart arrhythmia situation you're pretty sure you're as good as the next guy in town. But I don't know if people in psychology or psychiatry can feel the same way. Or maybe this is just my fantasy about doctors — that here is somebody who's sure of things, and that there *are* answers, and that if only I studied harder, had been smarter, I would have gotten it." Arthur smiles. "It's like believing WASPs don't sweat."

Like our physician friends, Arthur laments the premium that has been put on speed. "At least since the mid-eighties," he says, "more and more people were saying to me, 'Look, I really don't want to spend four years here, Doc. Listen less, tell me what to do, and help me make things okay.' And on top of the pressure coming from the patient, managed-care people are saying, 'You get six sessions for a buck-and-a-half and then you gotta pay the guy's regular fee,' so they want it even faster. Maybe in a medical situation there's a quick resolution, but not always in my work.

"Because the work I do is very private, and depends upon confidentiality — a place where people can talk about their most private thoughts, feelings, fears, experiences — and it seems to me that in a cultural way, unfortunately, there are almost no sacred private areas anymore. Everything — like those ads for doctors and hospitals — is for public consumption, and I don't really know what that means. It is what it is, I guess, but it certainly is not good for the doctor-patient relationship."

Vietnam was for Arthur what Nigeria was for Jerry. "It changed my life forever," he says. "And it changed it forever even before I got there. Because I was a young man who did everything the way his mother and father wanted him to: I wore a white shirt to school, I went to the right college, I was a doctor, I married a Jewish girl, I had a piano and a nice house, I had a lovely daughter, things were all working out terrifically, and all of a sudden I was one of two people chosen in the entire U.S.A. in my specialty to be sent to Vietnam.

"So this was the first time I fully understood that life was neither good nor fair — that you can do everything right and the way you're supposed to, and still get fucked. Now that's a big thing to take in at any point in your life, and I should have been weaned from it earlier, but I was twenty-eight years old and it hit me like a ton. I mean, if being a good boy was not going to pay off, why should I marry a Jewish girl? Why should I be polite to my Aunt Sophie?

"I did my clinical internship at Walter Reed General Hospital — this was just before I was chief of psychology at Fort Monmouth — and the head of psychology at Walter Reed became the head psychologist in the army. Now, for reasons I absolutely to this day cannot fathom, he said to himself, 'This guy Rudy, out of the two hundred fifty or three hundred psychologists in the army, will be somebody who I think will do a good job in Vietnam.'

"And I know this, because I said to him, 'Why'd you pick me? You have a lot of psychologists who want to go there and get medals and ribbons so they can build up a career in the army.' And he said, 'Because I believe in this war and I believe in you.' So I became one of only two people who did my work in Vietnam, and it was truly transformative — and traumatic.

"I was with a Mobile Army Surgical Hospital — the 98th Medical Detachment, 8th Field Hospital — and I was chief of the Psychology Section, and even on the boat going over there I knew that I was alone in a way I had never understood aloneness before. I couldn't be bailed out by people who loved me. I was an interchangeable number, replaceable by some guy who was at that moment sitting down to dinner with his wife in Topeka or Des Moines.

"The other thing I realized was how provincial my vision of America had been. I'd grown up in an insulated parochial convent of middle-class Jewish kids, and most Americans viewed the world differently from the way I did. From that point on — in Vietnam, and for the next six or seven years — I began to realize that no matter how much you are loved or cared for, and no matter how much people want for you, you are ultimately alone — whether in your dying, in a serious illness, in childbirth, in the pain that comes from failure with your child.

"I saw the kinds of things I never wanted to see — ghastly stuff: people burned up, people being carried out of helicopters with pieces of metal sticking out of them, and it's one thing to see that in an ER, but another thing when you know the metal was put there on purpose. You go down to the psychiatric unit and on one side there are American boys who've lost limbs and on the other side there are Vietnamese prisoners who've lost limbs. And they look at each other across the unit, and it's okay. Now that they've been mutilated for the rest of their lives, no one's killing anyone.

"Not only did I experience feelings about the potential for my *own* mutilation, but my feeling of insecurity — of being separated from everything that made me feel safe — was very intense because I also knew that the doctor *I* saw was as scared as I was, and was running from his own diarrhea, and that we could all be dead in the next millisecond. And I don't know if I have ever felt secure since. But maybe security was an illusion. Maybe it was *always* an illusion.

"Vietnam is the one year of my life I can remember in complete detail because it was *alien,* and in an infinite number of ways, and I think the core of my experience there would ultimately translate into some of what I've been talking about — that life isn't fair, that you can die in the next minute even if you'd done everything right, and that you've got to live in the present and not postpone or defer gratification the way we were trained to do.

"When I came back home after a year, I found myself having symptoms of the sort I was seeing in patients. They were coming out of nowhere, and they were frightening to me, and they were confusing. They made me feel that I really had to get my own stuff cleared up if I was ever going to be of use to anyone else, and this led to my analysis.

"I found myself intensely concerned about my health, and I had never thought about my health before. And when you begin thinking about your health, you find parts of your body you never knew existed. It's like when you go through a terrible experience and you do fine, but then afterward you tremble and shake, you know?"

Arthur talks very quickly now — when he talks about his experiences in Vietnam, I have noticed, his words come faster than at any other time in our conversations — and says that the nature of his defensive structures was such — compartmentalized — that he had no clue for a year or two as to what was going on, or that the symptoms he was suffering from — with his health, with bodily obsessions, with driving a car — came under the heading of what we now know as post–traumatic stress disorder.

"I just thought I was probably screwed up and that I never realized just how neurotic I was, but that maybe I should speak with someone about it. Now we all have the same body parts, but the configurations make each of us different, and I began to see that there were few things that came to my doorstep as a therapist that I hadn't experienced in my own way. Because I have felt sexual longing, fear, despair, helplessness, anger — because there were things I was frightened of and ashamed of, I could tap into that fear, anxiety, and depression for the people I worked with.

"So that the changes I worked through in myself came to help me in my work with others. No one was going to come to my office, especially if they came with issues relating to shame, embarrassment, vulnerability, or self-esteem, tell me something, and not have my internal reflexes not work for them. I understood. 'Poor baby,' I'd think, though I wouldn't say that to them, of course. I'd maybe look poker-faced, but I believe that what I understood from my own life was informing the process with my patients *all* the time. At some level they knew they were not being judged — because I had been there, and worse, and in my chosen profession that was a gift to me.

"And there's this too: that the reason I made a living was because the former custodians of these things — of healing — were representatives of the ministry. And ministry is informed by 'oughts' and 'shoulds' and the Ten Commandments, and my Bible is different from their Bible and I didn't judge, and I really tried to understand, and to give compassion, and with empathy, and with the best I could intelligently give to people to help them cope with the parts of themselves they were ashamed of, and had difficulty with — because I had been there too."

"No quality of human nature is more remarkable, both in itself and in its consequences," David Hume wrote nearly three hundred years ago, "than that propensity we have to sympathize with others, and to receive by communication their inclinations and sentiments, however different from, or even contrary to our own."

When I think of us as young men, it occurs to me that the quality of human sympathy that Arthur has always given to his friends — a quality enhanced by his Vietnam experience, which made him indelibly sensitive to the vulnerability of others — he has also, for nearly forty years, been giving to his patients.

"This principle of sympathy is so powerful and insinuating a nature, that it enters into most of our sentiments and passions," Hume explains, "and often takes place under the appearance of its contrary . . . The sentiments of others can never affect us, but by becoming, in some measure, our own; in which case they operate upon us, by opposing and encreasing our passions, in the very same manner, as if they had been originally deriv'd from our own temper and disposition."

In a world where so much remains mysterious, even — especially! — in medicine and science (If we know so much about the genome, for example, why is it that 90 percent of DNA has no seeming purpose?), the quality of human sympathy — like the quality of mercy? — is one that, in joyous times or troubled times, and whether between friends or between doctor and patient, seems as rare as it is precious.

In the mid-sixties, in New York and California, I was active in the antiwar movement, organizing marches and protests, giving speeches, and writing articles in which, among other things, I encouraged those of us above draft age to commit civil disobedience in support of those of draft age who were refusing to serve. During these same years, Arthur was in the army, first at Walter Reed Hospital, and then at Fort Monmouth and in Vietnam. We corresponded regularly, talking about the usual — our families and friends, books and sports — and in our letters we also debated American policies and actions.

This, then, in one of Arthur's letters — from Nha Trang, Vietnam, dated Monday, June 20, 1966, and written at a time when Arthur was living in a place where, he wrote, the temperature was "easily 110–130 consistently," where he was separated from his wife and daughter, and where he was constantly fearful for his own life:

> Little question in my own mind that Noog of all people should not be required to serve in Viet Nam theater — your efforts on behalf of a more sensible solution to this whole mess speak well for the legitimacy of your contentions in this regard — G-d knows, I've written Marcia [Arthur's first wife] about this just yesterday — I empathize with the tremendous bind you're in (may not be too clear above — I wrote that I particularly felt for you, Jay, because if you're called upon to serve it would not only be a bitter separation experience, a frustrating personal experience, but perhaps most significantly, an activity in polar contrast to beliefs you've been committed to for several years now). Of course, this is all the Rude and if he were in the Pentagon he would have absolutely no compunction about crossing Noog off the list, if he were on the list . . .

After giving me detailed advice on what I should do to establish Conscientious Objector status *before* I was called to serve — the extreme fears he lived with in Vietnam seeming only to intensify his ability to empathize with and be helpful to others — and advising me not to "irrationally get hung up on hopes" but instead "to get to work," this: "I'm scared shit so often — to a great degree quite unreasonably for thank G-d I'm safe as a human being in VN can be — that the anxiety just rolls off me."

A few weeks later, shortly after the publication of my first novel, *Big Man,* a story set against the background of the basketball fixes of the early fifties, Arthur comes across a review in *Time* magazine and writes to tell me "how *very very* thrilling it was to see you — my buddy Noog — among the premier new novelists. I'm sorry that it had to be a *Time* publication but these are the burdens of the more public posture you have assumed. In any event, you must know how very exciting it was for me — in the wilderness — to see my boy Noogie looking at me." He writes that he has not received his copy of the book yet, but hears from another Erasmus friend that "Yudi Rudy is among the cast of characters — mucho thanks — I'm sure, with due respect to the models, that this guy goes well to his left & is an outstanding court figure!!!

"Life is routine here — work challenging with much sadness always," he continues, "— but I can help — I see that now — I am useful and at least feel that way (my use being relevance to my patients, rather than the organization I work for) — and this provides some meaning for me in the midst of the madness I see around."

Two months later I write him a letter in which I set forth what I see as reasonable arguments about why and how we should get out of Vietnam (a letter in which I also suggest, "Why not play the VC a game of stickball — the winner gets the country. Is this any less sensible than what's going on?").

On October 25, when his tour of duty is about half over, he writes back: "My response to your political letter — you're right!" Then, after disagreeing with me, point by point, about several political issues I've raised, this: "But overall I agree that the whole thing makes no sense with the rights and wrongs so unclear."

"By the way," he adds, before signing off, "Phil was remarried last week."

13 🐚

It's Not the Disease

I'M JUST A PATCHER-UPPER," Phil says about his work as a neurologist. "I mean, I'm like the shop mechanic. You come in and there's something wrong with your car and you want me to fix it. I may tell you I don't find anything very wrong with it, or I may tell you that it needs a minor overhaul, or I may tell you that there's a serious problem, and we have to investigate further, and that I have to keep the car in the shop — or you in the hospital — longer. These are the things that I do."

Although Phil is one of the smartest guys I've ever known — when we graduated from Erasmus, he received full scholarship offers from both Princeton and Cornell — and though the list of his honors, achievements, and publications is long and impressive (he was chief resident in Neurology at Bellevue, chief of Neurology at Denver General Hospital, chief of the Neuroscience Division at St. Anthony Hospital in Denver, et cetera), he remains so modest, blunt, and direct — so boyishly unsophisticated and unpretentious — that one can be fooled by his plain speech and unassuming manner into not recognizing just how brilliant and insightful he is.

What I did with Phil on my first visit in 1988 — going on rounds with him at hospitals, and spending the rest of the day with him in his office — I have done the other half-dozen times I've spent with him in Denver. He introduces me to patients, family members, and staff, as a friend from high school who is a writer, and he always asks — Jerry does the same when I spend days with him — if it's all right for me to be present during their talk and/or examination. We usually start the day on the intensive care unit at the Trauma Center, where most of the dozens of patients I have seen are unconscious, suffering from major head injuries, and, usually, from severe damage to various limbs and organs. The majority of the patients are young, often in their teens, and the majority of these young people are in the hospital because they have been in car accidents. Several times, after he has examined a patient and reviewed test results, when the patient asks what he or she thinks is the problem, or its cause ("If it's not carpal tunnel, Doctor Yarnell, what could it be?" a woman has asked earlier on this day), I have been surprised at the easy way he simply shrugs, and, without missing a beat, says, "I don't know."

Or — this to another patient during afternoon office hours — "There are some abnormalities in your hand, thumb, and finger, but I can't make a diagnosis." He will, then, as with this woman, discuss what *might* be going on, and when, at the end of the visit, he records his notes into a tape recorder, he invites the patient's collaboration. "Now listen to me, Shirley," he says. "I'm going to talk about you and I want you to correct me. I'm going to talk about your illness."

"I could confirm — yes —" he tells me afterward, "— but I was no help to the lady."

"Because neurology, you see, is where cardiology was maybe forty years ago," he explains. "When I was in medical school we didn't have intensive care units. There was no treatment for a severely damaged heart other than digitalis. Bypass was just in its infancy. The heart-lung machine had a very high mortality rate, and there was no transplantation.

"So all these things are what we're trying to find for the brain. But we're in our infancy. In cardiology, if you have an abnormal rhythm, Rich may put in a pacemaker. If you have an abnormal brain rhythm, we give you some medicines to try to stabilize it, but we don't have a pacemaker for the brain.

"No one really has a good way to make the brain heal — it's the great mystery. We don't have the antibiotic that cured pneumonia.

We don't have an aid like portable oxygen — I mean, you see people carrying portable oxygen because their lungs don't work. You don't see people carrying around anything if they have Alzheimer's — maybe a note pad, and they make notes. But you need a certain amount of cognition to do that.

"That's why right now all our efforts are to prevent complications of the injury, to prevent too much pressure on the brain, to prevent inadequate oxygenation of the body. If someone bruises your arm, it may heal, but if you injure the brain in certain places, it can make you paralyzed, and nothing will change that. We don't have a treatment for coma, no way of making that better, so all our efforts are to make the milieu the best for adequate healing.

"We don't have a splint for the brain, or a nutrition for the brain. You can't say, 'Take this diet and you won't get brain problems.' You could say, 'Control your blood pressure and you're less likely to get a hemorrhage, and you probably won't get a stroke,' but once you get a stroke all we can do is try to teach you to maximize your life with what you have left. If you're a paraplegic, my job is to try to teach you how to live the best life you can in a wheelchair, and if anything gets better than that, it's extra."

It is late at night, and I am sitting in Phil's office with him in his home in Greenwood Village, Colorado, just outside Denver. I often think of Phil's office, a large room he and his wife Barbara added on to the house on the far side of the garage — fifteen feet wide and twenty-five feet long — as being the Brooklyn/Southwest annex of the Victoria and Albert Museum. It is filled to overflowing with an extraordinary assortment of things, including sculptures (bronze, wood, clay), paintings and prints (the American West), family photographs (some life-size), baseball and sports memorabilia (especially about the Brooklyn Dodgers), Judaica (menorahs, the Tablets of the Law), geometric forms (bright yellow plastic cubes, rhomboids, cones, pyramids), encyclopedias, medical books, magazines, skeletons, skulls, spinal cords, geodes, rocks, exercise machines, bicycles, skis, sculptures-in-progress, four-pound plastic jars of chocolate-covered raisins (Phil never eats lunch, but snacks on these all day), and lots of cartons filled with who-knows-what.

His desk abounds with a similar variety of items, along with medical papers, articles-in-progress, partly completed clay sculptures, several dozen model cars and trucks (Matchbox reproductions of racing cars, pickups, forklifts, et cetera), and lots of rocks. Phil has had a long, sustained interest in geology and archaeology (on my first visit with him in Denver, in 1988, he took me out of town to a highway cut on Interstate 70 in order to explain the geology of the region to me), and a passion for sculpture. He has made most of the several dozen bronze sculptures that are in his office and around his home, as well as those in his Denver medical office — abstract creations, along with sculptures of heads, skulls, torsos, hands, spinal columns, brains, children (*Sibling Trio*), baseball players and objects (*Broken Bat*), athletes (*Women Volleyball Players*), and scientific subjects (*Showing the Moebius*).

(After I reported on my visits with Dr. Haight and Dr. Melman, he sent me a one-and-a-half-inch-tall African sculpture of a man making love to a woman. "Note the straight organ — may it ever be so!" he wrote in an accompanying note; when I called to thank him, he told me he hoped to be able to send a life-size version of the sculpture soon.)

There are also, around the room, more than a dozen different sculptures Phil has made of Phineas P. Gage, foreman of a railroad construction crew in Vermont, who, in 1848, survived an explosion that propelled a three-and-a-half-foot-long crowbar through his head — it entered below the cheekbone and left eye, and exited through the top of his skull. Although, after the accident, a doctor could make his fingers meet if he put one finger through Gage's cheek and another through the top of the skull, Gage lived for another twelve years without suffering any paralysis or physical disability (other than the loss of sight in one eye). Phil has written about Gage and the personality changes the trauma induced: in effect, Gage suffered the inadvertent effects of a frontal lobotomy, and his case became seminal in the history of neurology for it allowed doctors to begin filling in data on functional brain localization by revealing relationships between physical damage and personality and character change.

Since my arrival a week before, Phil has done his best to avoid having me tape a conversation with him — he keeps saying that he's not articulate or good at this kind of thing, that he won't have much to say that's interesting — and I recall that at the time of his daughter Elizabeth's wedding the previous summer I was able to record a conversation with him only by turning on a tape player while the two of us were on our way to and from a local shopping center to pick up pizzas.

Now, however, when I tell Phil about some of my talks with Arthur, he responds easily.

"For a period of ten years, you know, Arthur and I didn't speak to each other," he tells me.

I say that I did not know this — they had been good friends in high school and during the years when Phil was at Bellevue and Arthur was getting his doctorate at Columbia, so I assumed they had remained close ever since.

"I was very hurt about what happened," Phil says. "After he and Marcia got divorced and I was friendly with both of them, he married Paulette, and he heard me once say, or I think he thought I said, or I *may* have said, that I liked his first wife very much and that I didn't really know Paulette.

"And also he felt that I didn't understand his illness, which I didn't at the time. I didn't understand that he had had a major post-traumatic syndrome, and that this had led to the divorce."

I say that Arthur has talked with me about how his experience in Vietnam and its aftermath, along with his analysis, led to profound changes in the way he looked at the world, and that for the first time he came to think of divorce — unthinkable before Vietnam — as an alternative he could seriously consider, even though he knew he was married to an absolutely lovely person.

"Yeah," Phil says. "So after ten years I just called him up. It was on Yom Kippur, and he and Paulette were living in New York then, and I called to tell him that if in any way I did anything to offend him that I beg his forgiveness, because it was the Day of Atonement, and this is what you do."

"You *did?*" I say.

Although, like Phil, I was taught that this was what one was *supposed* to do on the Day of Atonement — that God could forgive us for sins committed against God, but that only other people could forgive us for wrongs we had done to them — I cannot remember knowing anyone who had acted so literally on this rabbinic law.

"Yeah, I did," Phil says. "So then he said, 'Oh let's get together!' and when we got back together he told me about what had happened to him after he came home from Vietnam, that it was almost like a psychiatric break, and we became friends again, and it was like we never missed a beat.

"So I feel like I'm in the same relationship with Rich and Jerry now that I was in high school, and I think it's because we have an underlying understanding of what we are — there's a common cauldron and experience we share — and each of us has succeeded in some way, and none of us has regrets.

"None of us had fathers who said, 'Look, you take over the garment business after me.' We all knew we had to make it on our own. None of us were trust fund babies, and that was reassuring even though I resented it then. Because I look at us now, and I see how we made our way based on who we were then. Everyone did as best he could with what he had, and I don't think any of us would have changed anything."

"Nothing at all?" I ask.

"Well, I would have liked to have had less tumultuous marriages maybe — to have been smarter at that, at relationships — marital relationships."

We talk about patients I've seen with Phil earlier in the day and, especially, about Beth Granger. I had last seen Beth in 1988, when she was lying in a bed at St. Anthony Hospital, in a coma. She was seventeen years old (a year younger than my daughter Miriam at the time), a junior in high school — an exceptionally pretty young woman, with long silky blond hair, large blue eyes (closed except when Phil opened them) — and while Phil examined her, tapped on her chest, talked to her and shouted at her, he told me he did not know whether or not she was ever going to wake up.

Phil referred to her as "Sleeping Beauty," and in the weeks and months following this visit, he would call me, usually on his way to or from work — the way he still does, several times a week — to report on Beth's condition. ("Remember that girl we saw at St. Anthony — the pretty blond girl in a coma — Sleeping Beauty? Well, this morning . . .") What I found especially chilling at the time was the contrast between Beth's outer condition — her exceptionally serene appearance (the accident had spared her face) — and her inner condition, potentially fatal, about which we knew so little.

More than 50 percent of all traumatic brain injuries in America result from car accidents, Phil tells me, and more than 50 percent of these cases are alcohol-related. In some instances, the patient is the only survivor; some teenagers who are in comas when I visit them do not recover — they either die or are condemned to marginal lives, mentally and/or physically, forever after.

"I could never own a liquor store," Phil said to me the first time I went on rounds with him in 1998. I saw five or six of Phil's patients that day — some of them grotesquely injured and disfigured: suffering from missing and maimed limbs and body parts, from horrendous damage to their skulls and faces, and with tubes and wires going in and out of all parts of them — before the floor began to rise, darkly, toward my face. I excused myself, walked into the hallway, found a chair, sat, and put my head between my legs.

"I forget that you're not used to this," Phil said to me a few minutes later, his arm around my shoulder. (On subsequent visits, I have done somewhat better, and have usually been able to make a complete set of ICU rounds before becoming faint.)

Going on rounds with Phil — after we visit the Trauma Center we go to Craig Rehabilitation Center, to visit with people who are in various stages of recovery from trauma — I never cease to be amazed by the fact that he does what he does virtually every day of his life, and that, as with my other friends, the disease and misfortune he has to deal with rarely seem to dim his spirits or his optimism.

On any given day, however, the sadness of what he sees can get to him. Thus, his call to me late one afternoon on his way home from work when, without preface — not even his usual "Hey Neugie — it's Phil!" — he just started in talking.

"Oh, I had a very hard day today, Jay," he said. "Very hard. Yesterday I was talking with this young woman — she's twenty-two years old, and she came in with a brain injury — she fell while horseback riding — and today she's dead.

"Yesterday she was confused and disoriented, somewhat agitated, but she was talking, and moving all her parts, and following commands. So we did a CAT-scan and saw that she had some bifrontal brain bruises. We observed her — restrained her for her safety: she was drowsy and tried to go to the bathroom on her own — and then she had a seizure-like activity, and her pupils were dilated. An hour later she had another seizure and we did another CT-scan, and there were no marked changes from the initial CT.

"I mean, she was stable all day yesterday, then today she went into sudden and irreversible brain swelling, which is a known but rare complication of brain bruises in young people."

Phil was silent for a few seconds. Then: "I'm very experienced, you know, and for a young person to die like this, it's just devastating. I didn't expect it, and I wouldn't have done anything different. We did what we could to reverse the brain swelling — medications — but nothing helped."

That night, after Phil arrived home, we talked again, and we did so frequently during the next few weeks, and it was as if this young woman was the first patient he had ever lost. He was inconsolable.

"The problem we have is with anything that causes swelling of the brain," he explained during one of our talks, "because when the brain swells, it pushes on the brain stem and that's why all our treatments are to prevent an increase in swelling.

"The brain looks like a cauliflower, you see, and when we're young it's made up mostly of coral-like indentations — sulci — and small empty spaces. As we get older, the brain shrinks, and there are more empty, fluid spaces — less tissue — so you have more slack, and if there's a bruise, say, the swelling has room to expand, and you're usually okay. The skull's a closed box, with three elements — the brain, spinal fluid, and blood — and with a young person, it's very tight in there, and we watch out for anything that makes it tighter. When the swelling becomes too great, the pressure affects the brain stem, and when the brain pressure gets too high it impairs the ability of the heart to perfuse the brain — to get blood and oxygen into it — and we get no flow. When the pressure in the brain's greater than the heart's ability to get blood into the brain — greater than the blood pressure — you're deprived of blood and oxygen, and this is why some young people die from just what starts out as *moderate* brain injuries."

When Phil was explaining things to me, he sounded like the guy I usually talk with. But when he talked about the young woman who died — "This is terrible," he said again. "It's tragic. I mean, what do I say to her parents?" — he sounded like a very young person himself — distraught, helpless, bewildered.

Beth Granger, the young woman who, a dozen years before, had been in a coma, suspended between life and death for nearly three months, has come to Phil's Denver office with her husband Tom and their daughter Samantha. Phil's consulting office, though considerably smaller than his Greenwood Village study — about seven feet by nine feet — is as un-self-consciously disorganized as his home office. A large LeRoy Neiman print of Willie Mays, a black-and-white photo tucked into the corner of the frame, takes up most of one wall, surrounded by prints, diplomas, neurological charts, and assorted photos (some of Phil's ranch and llamas). When patients sit across from Phil, I notice them stare at the clutter on his desk in a mixture of perplexity, amusement, and awe. How can this brilliant, busy doctor maintain such a diverse range of interests — sports, Judaica, the American West, archaeology, geology, lightning (Phil belongs to the Lightning Data Center, an organization, founded by a neurologist and two meteorologists, that meets on the second Friday of each month) — and, equally puzzling, how can he cram so much stuff into such a small space?

Phil had been at Beth's high school graduation, and at her wedding — she is now pregnant with her second child — and I talk with Beth about having seen her when she was in a coma. I'm surprised, I say, that she doesn't remember me.

Beth laughs and tells me she doesn't remember the accident at all, but knows that the car she was in rolled over, that she was thrown from it, that her best friend, in the car with her, was killed, and that she was in a coma for nearly three months. Her short-term memory and her hearing have been permanently impaired, but, she says, gesturing to her husband and daughter, she feels very blessed to be here, and to have the life she has.

Me too, I say, and Phil tells her, briefly, about my surgery. Then he leaves, and Beth and I talk about surviving, and about feeling that *we* are the lucky ones — "Because I came so close to death," Beth says, "I appreciate life that much more."

After her recovery, Beth attended college and hoped to become a social worker. "But I learned that society is not set up for people with head injuries," she says, "and the most difficult thing for me, during my recovery, was being isolated from people my own age.

"My parents were wonderful — they were there for me every day, and for everything I needed — and when I was well enough to leave home, they took me to live in this Transition Living Center." She shivers, closes her eyes. "But when I saw it, I said I'll kill myself or run away before I'll ever live in a place like this."

Tom tells the story of how they met — he had been in a car accident too, and one day while he was at home recovering from his injuries he saw Beth on television. "She was talking about her illness and her rehab, and I fell in love with her right then," he says. "There she was, this beautiful woman and she had a head injury like I did, and I thought, 'Hey — maybe we can get together.' So I called the TV station, and —"

"— and then came the famous one-thing-led-to-another," Beth says. She and Tom show me pictures from Beth's high school graduation, and from their wedding, and they tell me about the house they are in the process of buying.

Tom works twenty hours a week in his family's floral business, and Beth works for an organization that helps people who are in recovery from brain trauma. "What's best," she says, "is what Dr. Yarnell taught me — whatever is most normalizing. Isolation is as bad as — no, it's worse — much worse than the deficits you may have from the trauma."

When she says this, her daughter Samantha climbs onto her lap. "My life seems too good to be true sometimes — though I don't feel this way *every* day," Beth says. "That wouldn't be real. But when I first came to, you know, after the accident, I couldn't walk, or talk, or hear — I was *completely* deaf for a long while, and what I thought was happening was that I had already died and was watching it all — my family, the hospital room, *me* — from up above — from heaven."

When I tell Phil about my conversation with Beth, he responds by saying the kind of thing he often says about his work: "You see, I'm merely a caretaker. I try to help patients make the most of what they have, but sometimes they say it's too hard, and that they're completely dependent on someone to turn them over in bed or prop them up, and they can't answer the phone, or if there's a fire, they can't move unless someone moves them. Some patients get depressed and don't want to be here, and just say it's not worth it, the heck with it.

"And it's frustrating to work very hard and get a result where the person's totally disabled — or in a vegetative state — for the rest of their lives. Their eyes may blink, but they don't seem to understand their environment, or they can type a little with one hand on a small computer to say, 'I'm okay. Hello,' and they need twenty-four-hour care, and you wonder. I mean, you wonder if they would have wanted to be saved if they knew what was coming — or if you knew, maybe you wouldn't have worked so hard to save them.

"But no one knows, you see. So you give everyone the best shot you can, and hope for the best. And you saw the people today — some of them were grossly debilitated. And then there's Beth and her husband — but if they didn't have parents who had a business that Tom could go into, they wouldn't be talking about buying a house with a yard."

Phil repeats what he has said to me several times: that a family support system is the most important element in the rehabilitation of neurological illnesses — and that his biggest worry wasn't about my heart, or the surgery, but about the fact that I didn't have a wife or companion, so that if I came out of surgery with a major disability, who was going to be there to help me, and to manage my affairs?

"I mean, if you have to live with a debilitating illness and you're not rich or don't have the world's best insurance, where's your means of support? They don't kill you, but they put you in a run-down nursing home where there's barely enough help, and let's hope your constitution is strong enough to make it. And the help there turns over quickly, and you might meet an aide you strike up a friendship with who's good-natured and helps you. I mean, you remember that young woman who was living with the man who was a quadriplegic? As soon as she left him, he died. So that's the real world.

"But I had two thrills today," Phil says then, and his face brightens. "Two patients spoke to me who never had conversations with me during the entire month I've been taking care of them. I had three conversations with that boy you met who was paralyzed from the night he had a car wreck. And with that boy who was sitting and playing cards — the one who fell off a cliff while mountain climbing. I never had a conversation with either of them before today — and, as with Beth, that's a thrill for me — the highlight of my week.

"And I sent one lady home! That's the really good part of my life. I get to send them home. So I feel lucky, because I get to do a kind of work that's meaningful every day, and there's always new things happening and something to learn."

I listen to Phil talk about his work, and why it remains ever fascinating to him, and I think of the fact that his attitude — his love of his vocation — is, alas, becoming less and less common. In a 1999 study of young California physicians (those under forty-five), for example, the authors report that in 1996 "only 61 percent of primary care physicians said that they would go to medical school again," this figure "down from 79 percent in 1991." Among specialists during these same five years the proportion fell from 68 percent to 63 percent.

Other surveys report similar findings — that young physicians' "perceptions of a career in medicine may be both more critical than those of other professionals and worsening over time." High medical school tuition, huge educational debts, long hours, high malpractice premiums, growing corporate influence, and, especially, the loss of autonomy are the major reasons young physicians give for their dissatisfaction, and for saying that, given a choice, they would *not* choose to become doctors again.

And many of the autonomy issues relate directly to a doctor's freedom to make decisions about, and to care for, patients. For example, the report on young California physicians notes, only 67 percent of these doctors believed they had the freedom to care for patients who could not pay, and only 64 percent indicated they had the freedom to care for patients who required heavy time and resource commitment — these levels down from 83 percent in 1991. "The psychic toll of declining satisfaction with practices and careers," the authors comment, "may reduce even the most dedicated physicians' ability to function at their best."

Like my other friends, Phil — his nickname is "Yago," from Yagolnitzer, his family name until his father changed it when Phil was in the seventh grade ("I had mixed feelings — I felt like I lost part of my identity, but I also was happy not to have kids make fun of me on the first day of classes every year when the teacher called my name") — did not start out intending to become a doctor. He entered Cornell, in the fall of 1955, as an engineering student.

"I always had an interest in learning how the human body works, and I didn't like mysteries," he says, "so I thought that if I would understand it, it wouldn't be a mystery to me. But I didn't like the idea of the pre-medical route, which seemed too conventional. Engineering seemed more scientific.

"So I was in the department of engineering physics at Cornell, but I saw that the profession was mainly either the business of running manufacturing outlets or you could be a pure scientist, only I didn't think I was good enough to be an independent pure scientist. So medicine seemed a combination of technical knowledge, and also being able to make a contribution to helping people."

I say that Arthur wonders sometimes if this desire we all have — to be of service to others, to make a contribution, to leave the world a better place than we found it — is as purely altruistic as people think, or whether, instead, it simply comes from our compulsive need to be productive — from our Brooklyn brand of Jewish Calvinism.

Phil shrugs. "I don't know about that," he says. "Maybe. But I know that by the third year of engineering school, I decided to look into going to medical school, and I took a few extra courses, and then I applied to medical school and got a scholarship, so instead of finishing the engineering degree — it was a five-year program — after four years, I went to medical school."

"You never got a college degree?"

"No. I never got a college degree." He laughs. "My mother was upset, because she said what would happen if I didn't like medicine, and all I'd have was a high school diploma. I couldn't even be a high school teacher, which she thought was a very noble profession.

"But mostly I just wanted to be educated — and I wanted to get out of Brooklyn. I think it's like being a good ballplayer. If you're a good ballplayer, you don't care where you play, and you can play at any level. So that's how I felt about learning and, later on, about becoming a doctor.

"My father pressed clothes in a dress factory — it was called 'piecework' because he was paid by the number of dresses he pressed — by the piece — and it was seasonal work, so he was unemployed a lot of the year, and he sat around and my mom yelled at him, and it was very disheartening because he was trapped, and he was a passive man who couldn't figure out how to get out of the trap.

"We always ate separately. The kitchen was too small so my mother prepared three meals — one for her two sons, one for my father, and one for herself. My brother Allen and I ate on TV stands. We never ate together unless there was a special event, and then we ate in the living room.

"The bathroom was small too — it was so narrow that when you sat on the pot, the only way you could be comfortable was to keep your right leg over the side of the bathtub. Allen used to go upstairs to our aunt's apartment to go to the bathroom. There was no air conditioning, one tiny bathroom for four people, waiting in line, no privacy.

"So I still have a recurring nightmare — like an anxiety attack in which I actually *shvitz* — where I sweat like crazy. I'm in my last year of medical school, and I miss an exam, or I fail it, and I have to go back and repeat the year again, and in order to do this I have to move back into my Brooklyn apartment. That's the nightmare I still have all the time.

"Which is what I did — I was married for my last year of med school, but I lived at home for my second and third years, in the same room I used to share with Allen, and carrying my microscope on the BMT, hugging it like a baby.

"In high school, you see, I figured out that there were only two tickets out of Brooklyn. One was to be a great athlete, which was my dream until I got to high school and saw that there were guys ten times bigger and fifteen times faster than me."

I remind Phil of the time, during our sophomore year at Erasmus, when we were on the junior varsity baseball team together and we got to play against the varsity. "Yeah," Phil says. "And then, after my freshman year, when I gave up on being a pro ballplayer and saw I could get good grades by doing the things I did naturally, I said, 'Well, if I do it a little more I'll get *very* good grades.' So I did a little more.

"And I knew that would give me power, and would be a way out. Everything I did was so I could get out of Brooklyn and escape my apartment. I mean, I felt it was all on me, even when I was away at college, because if my parents got sick I'd have to drop out and help them, and I resented that. Only, I was fortunate, and it never happened."

I ask Phil about what has and has not changed since he started out in medical school.

"Well, the smartest doctors will still tell you that if you listen to the patient, the patient will tell you what's wrong with him," he says. "Because it's not the disease, you see, but it's how the particular disease affects the individual patient. I mean, a lot of us went into medicine because it's first of all a science — you have to look at the illness, at the state of tissues, at organ systems, and try to understand what's going on, and what you can do or have to do. Like, if a person has pneumonia, and you give antibiotics, you check the x-ray to see that the pneumonia's gone. But you also have to look at the individual patient who has the disease, and see how the *story* of the illness takes place in this particular person — so that a doctor is somehow at the juncture of what's both objective and subjective.

"Now, neurology started out by studying diseases of the brain, spinal cord, and nerves — how they express themselves — and we looked at the patient's complaints, and examined the patient through the years, and then the patient would die, and we would examine the tissues at death. That's how we started out. And we knew things grossly — like if there was a gunshot wound to the right side of the head, the left side of the body might be paralyzed, and if someone died and we saw a lesion on the right side of the brain it showed why the left side had been paralyzed.

"So neurologists took care of people who had something wrong with the ability of the nervous system to work, or it was hyperactive — like epilepsy, where there were seizures — or it was underactive, so a lesion was causing paralysis, weakness, loss of vision on one side, loss of speech, clumsiness. And once you localized it to where in the nervous system the problem was, you could make a presumptive diagnosis of disease and tell the patient he had something wrong with the right side of the brain, or the spinal cord at this or that level, or with the nerves coming out of the spinal cord. Then, if they decided it was amenable for surgery, you talked with the neurosurgeon, and maybe you'd have an operation.

"But that all changed when neurologists had a way of looking inside the black box of the nervous system. It started with x-rays, in the beginning of the century, which let you tell if there was an abnormal collection of calcium inside the brain, or if it was pushed to one side or the other, or if you had a broken head — if you fell down and got a fracture and there was air inside your head, or a bullet fragment, or a calcified tumor. After x-rays, then angiography came, or probably pneumoencephalography first, where you injected air inside the nervous system, and it filled the fluid structures and you could see if they were distorted in any way. Then the next thing was the injection of contrast material — metallic dyes into the arteries — and then you take an x-ray, and you can outline the arteries of the brain and see if they're blocked, or if there's an abnormal bulging of an artery, and so you could make inferences as to the disease that was causing the patient's symptoms.

"At the same time, or about the same time, people also injected dye into the spinal canal, and studied the spinal cord, and all of those we called interventional techniques, and they all had risks associated with them. It involved the patients being punctured, and foreign materials being put into them.

"Then along came the CAT-scan, and that came after I finished my residency, in 1973, and you could put yourself inside a tube, and by mathematical analysis of x-ray absorption, you could get a look at the structure of the brain, which before that had only been visible at autopsy. And that revolutionized the field of neurology because you no longer had to make a guess based on the examination of the patient and the patient's complaints. You now had a way of verifying things without risk to the patient.

"When it first came here, the governor of Colorado said Denver should have only one CAT-scan for the whole city. Now most *hospitals* have two, and we keep them running around the clock, and you can't work without them.

"Then, in 1986, I think, came magnetic resonance imaging — MRIs, and PET-scans — and they gave you further anatomical clarity for the problems you were dealing with so you can fairly well localize a great deal of lesions. Some you can't, and they still remain a diagnostic problem, but for those you can, the characteristics, on CAT-scanning and MRIs, may even tell you what the tissue type is."

I remind Phil of how excited he was a dozen years before, to show me the first MRI machine at his hospital, a huge metallic cylinder that looked like a space capsule, and of how I watched with him while one of his patients was inside the machine. The patient was frightened, and Phil kept calling to him — "Just enjoy it, Sidney — make believe you're in the love canal!" — and afterward Phil showed me how the dozens of images the machine produced were able to give him a three-dimensional picture of Sidney's brain.

"The tubes are more comfortable, and some people have open MRIs now," Phil says, "and we can tell the difference between a stroke and a tumor — we don't have to guess — so our diagnosis rate is much better. The detail is just miraculous. In the old days, the very best neurologists — our teachers — maybe had a fifty percent accurate diagnosis rate, but now we're up to eighty or ninety percent. We can localize much better, so the neurosurgeon knows exactly where he's going to operate. He can cut down right on top of the tumor, or put a needle through the skull that will go right into the tumor instead of just searching around."

Phil talks about the gains that have come about because of emergency response teams and evacuation teams that begin treatment at the site of the accident; about medications, antibiotics especially, that cure infections and prevent complications; about medications that are effective for high blood pressure; and about various ways we're better equipped to deal with trauma and to enhance rehabilitation.

In the regular course of his work, he explains, people come to him with headaches, migraines, backaches, troubles with memory, dizzy spells, strokes, and the aftereffects of head and spinal injuries. He also deals with long-term management problems relating to degenerative diseases such as multiple sclerosis, Parkinson's, amyotrophic lateral sclerosis (Lou Gehrig's disease), and Alzheimer's.

"So I see anybody who has these things," he says. "My interest is in what happens when people get hurt. You know, what the doctor did when we were kids was he sort of held your hand and watched the natural course of the disease. A neurologist still does a lot of that.

"But he tries to see if he can alter it for the good, and manage it, and make sure nothing makes it worse. That's why if you're excluded from the patient's pathway of care, or made ancillary — especially with chronic, long-term conditions — your expertise is not taken advantage of, and the patient suffers. A patient needs continuity of care and consistency. If you have a chronic illness and you switch doctors, it means the patient and doctor have to start all over again trying to understand things. The heart of medicine is the doctor-patient relationship, and if the patient does not feel he's hired a specific doctor to work for him to maximize his health, then the patient loses trust in the system.

"With managed care, there's a great emphasis on general practitioners, because with the insurance companies and the HMOs it's much cheaper for them to have a generalist or a nurse practitioner do everything, and only ask advice from the specialist, rather than have the specialist manage the illness. This is backwards. You wouldn't ask a high school physics teacher to work on the atom bomb or solar energy, although he might understand the concepts. You wouldn't say, 'Why don't we just get the nuclear physicist to come and spend a day with you, tell you what's wrong, and then you take over the experiment.'

"I mean, the patient may have only two visits with you when the illness is something that needs to be managed consistently. Or an MS patient may have several symptoms that a well-trained neurologist would understand in order to prevent further flareups. But if the patient is not encouraged to see the neurologist and just calls the doctor's office and gets the nurse on the phone, she may or may not realize the significance of the symptoms. I mean, look at what happened when you first called and got the nurse! And if you hadn't thought to call Rich after that, we wouldn't be talking now.

"How you manage the illness, what advice you give to the patient, who you pick to do an operation, or what you advise about chemotherapy or radiation — that's still the art of medicine. A test can't give a diagnosis.

"Now, not long ago I advised two people against having radiation for malignant brain tumors — and for malignant brain tumors we're still pretty much where we were forty years ago, unfortunately — and they both went ahead and had it, and they both sort of ruined their lives, whatever lives they had left.

"I recommended against radiation because I said it will debilitate the remainder of your life. But the radiation therapist recommended it, and the standard of care was that they should have it. So everyone wants to grasp onto something — that maybe this thing will stop it. Everyone would like to live to a biblical hundred-and-twenty with intact virility and no mental static, but I don't think we're going to find that in our time.

"And I spend a lot of time fighting with insurance companies too. So, for instance, I get this letter back after I write for one of my patients so he can pay for his treatment, and they send me a guideline they got out of a book, and the doctor who sent it — they have doctors doing this now — I talk with him and he says to me, 'I understand your position but these are the guidelines we follow.' So what can I say except that those are not the guidelines *I* follow?"

I tell Phil what Dr. Cabin said about me not being cured, that nobody is ever *cured*, but that I was as close as it gets, and that most of the work he does is like this — it's a major reason he went into cardiology — and that he's aware that it is not like this in other areas of medicine.

"So I look at what you do," I say to Phil, "and I think, if this is what Dr. Cabin gets — what do you get?"

"Well, cardiology is way ahead of us," Phil says again. "But my satisfaction comes from seeing the natural healing take place, and trying to prevent complications. I see myself as a caretaker of the brain, whereas he sees himself as someone who can actively intervene. He can put new blood in you, put a new blood supply through veins. I can't do that yet."

I talk about the theories concerning the infectious causes of heart disease and cancer, and Phil notes that MS, for instance, like other neurological diseases, may be infectious in origin. "Maybe brain tumors are an infectious disease. Maybe it's a virus," he says. "Okay. A lot of people get viruses, but what determines which one will go on to become a brain tumor, and which one will just live in symbiosis with the virus? We don't know that. Maybe, as with Parkinson's, we can inject cells into the brain to grow over it — but we don't know if we can, and we're just beginning. And there are hereditary defects where you don't make enough of a protein, or you make too much, and maybe we can learn to regulate that. Friedreich's ataxia, for instance, is a hereditary genetic disease — it's a balance problem, where you get this unsteady jerking-type gait because of a recessive gene that doesn't make a protein, or maybe an enzyme, that we need.

I ask about a former patient of Phil's who, during the April 20, 1999, massacre at Columbine High School, in Littleton, Colorado (one town over from Greenwood Village), in which two students killed fourteen students and a teacher while wounding twenty-five others — was shot several times. Phil says he happened to see the student this past week — on the day I arrived, in fact, and that the student is going to school and doing well. "He's lucky," Phil says. "His injury was to the left side of his head, and he's left-handed, so he didn't lose use of his dominant hand. He may still have some deficits, though — in walking, and in his speech, I think. He answered all my questions in just monosyllables." Phil smiles. "But I don't know — I mean, how does that make him so different from my son Jared and his teenage friends?"

14 🐚

The Patient's Story

"ON MOST SATURDAYS," Rich says, "my friends and I would hang out in front of Ebbets Field, where the Dodgers played — this was when we were ten or eleven years old — in the hopes that someone would have extra tickets at the last minute and bestow them on us. So we'd stand there and look forlorn, and it worked out for us a surprisingly high percentage of times.

"Well, one day we were there, flipping baseball cards, and up the staircase from the subway came this big black man, and the next thing you know I was blurting out, 'Hey — you're Jackie Robinson!'

"I still remember exactly what he was wearing: tan slacks, brown loafers, and a short-sleeve sport shirt with a white and brown stripe. He was a very dark man, very good-looking, and he said, 'Come here, kid.' And I went over and lo and behold, he takes my hand in his great big huge black hand and walks across the street with me toward the ballpark.

"I mean it was like I was dreaming. And he said, 'You play ball, kid?' and I said, 'Yeah, yeah — and I do everything you do. I do everything just the way you do it!' And I stop right in the middle of the street and assume the Jackie Robinson baseball stance, which was the stance that I had — the bat high over my right shoulder, challenging the pitcher, bent over, and slightly pigeon-toed the way he was — and he cracked up.

"Then he grabs my hand and says, 'Hey — we're gonna get into an accident.' So we walk across to the other side, and he smiles at me and taps me on the hand and says, 'Keep swingin', kid,' and goes into the clubhouse. Well, I did not wash my hand for more than a week, and I was in the ozone layer for a month after that — I told all my friends — and I still get into the ozone layer telling the story fifty years later."

Rich and I are far from Brooklyn, in Palos Verdes, California, on a gorgeous, clear summer day, and while we talk and trade stories, I look out through an open window at the Pacific Ocean, at sailboats drifting gracefully along a horizon speckled in shimmering silvers and golds by a brilliant midday sun. I have swum a mile in the morning, and when we are done taping this part of our conversation, Rich and I will play an hour or two of tennis.

Rich is six feet two inches tall, weighs about 190 pounds, and, in shorts and T-shirt, looks amazingly youthful. He plays tennis several times a week, regularly defeating guys who played varsity tennis in college and are twenty and thirty years younger than he is.

He says that Jackie has always been his great hero, and I tell him Jerry said the same thing when I saw him a few weeks ago. Jackie was my hero too, along with Lou Gehrig (from having read Frank Graham's biography, *Lou Gehrig: A Quiet Hero*), and "Pee Wee" Reese (like Reese, I played shortstop). I tell Rich that the main character in one of my novels marks his life by events in Jackie's life, and we talk for a while about Jackie and the Dodger teams of our youth, and about how and why it is that a bunch of lower-middle-class Jewish kids from Brooklyn so loved, and identified with, this extraordinary black man.

Beyond the fact that we all hoped to play for the Dodgers some day, and the fact that Jackie was the most exciting athlete of his time (in addition to playing baseball for the Dodgers, for the Kansas City Monarchs in the Negro Baseball League, and for his college, UCLA, he was the first four-sport letterman in UCLA history — a baseball player, an All-American in basketball and football, and the NCAA broad jump champion), he was rejected and despised for something — the color of his skin — over which he had no control.

Although, growing up in post–World War II Brooklyn, we did not suffer from anything like the kinds of bigotry, hardship, humiliation, and/or violence most blacks knew — or that our relatives who came from Europe, or did not make it out of Europe, knew — we did know what it felt like to be demeaned for things beyond our control, and what it felt like to have to suck up our rage when injustice prevailed. And we burned with a fierce desire to be accepted — and victorious — in that larger American world that lay beyond our homes and neighborhoods.

Like Jackie, we were determined to do whatever it took to get to the ball, to win a game, to have our moments of glory on the ballfield — and our place in the sun away from the ballfield. We were driven by our parents — to succeed, to excel, to get the best education possible (an education, we were taught, was something nobody could ever take away from us) — and we drove ourselves to get as far away from our parents, and their world, as we could.

We loved playing ball for the sheer joy of playing — the games, the sweat, the camaraderie — and also, I suggest to Rich, because the ballfield and schoolyard were places where life was *fair:* where you were judged not by the heresy of your birth, but according to your merits and deeds — by how hard and well you played, by how you handled winning or losing, adversity or a lucky break.

"There was no arguing a home run or a clutch basket," Rich says. "I mean, being in my home, or at school — which for me was another paramilitary indoctrination situation — there was never any joy in learning. School was strictly a testing ground to see if the home conditioning had succeeded. I knew that early on. After the stultifying environment of my apartment, sports became the great outlet. I lived to play ball, and when I played ball I could let out all the repressed stuff I never expressed at home. Psychologically, sports saved my life.

"I'll tell you a story," he says then. "On the Math Regents one year — the statewide exam we all took — I got a ninety-nine, and I raced home to tell my mother. Characteristically, she was sitting in front of the mirror at her vanity table, putting on her make-up, and preoccupied with that. But I came bursting into her bedroom. 'Mom — guess what?' I exclaimed, and she said 'What?' and I said, 'I got a ninety-nine on the Math Regents!'

"Then my mother, without looking around, and while continuing to put on her make-up, said, 'What happened to that other point?'

"Now, at that moment I knew there was no way I was *ever* going to be able to satisfy her — and right then something changed in me forever. Number one, I knew I would never be good enough — and maybe I wasn't good enough. And number two, I gave up on the idea of looking or hoping for her approval. After that day, I only went through the motions."

I quote a character — a psychiatrist — from one of my novels who posits a revision to Freud's theory about the favorite son of a doting mother going through life with the feeling of being a conqueror. The psychiatrist puts his version this way: that the unloved son of a narcissistic mother goes through life with the feeling that he must *become* a conqueror.

Rich nods, leans toward me. "Playing ball — being in the schoolyard and the rest of it — that was the only place where I could really be me," he says.

We reminisce about Erasmus teams, about games of stickball and three-man basketball in the Holy Cross schoolyard, of football and baseball at the Parade Grounds and in Prospect Park, of dodgeball in the third-floor Erasmus gym when Rich and I were in Boy Scout Troop 369 together, and about our synagogue basketball team. Rich was our team's high scorer, and to his astonishment — I showed it to him when he visited me the previous summer — I still have the scorebook to prove it.

"It was very fortunate I was a good athlete," Rich says. "This was an enormous boon to my battered self-esteem — to my having *any* self-esteem. I was unequivocally good at something, and everyone in that world acknowledged it." Rich worked as hard at being a good tennis player as he later would at becoming a good doctor, and in three years of varsity tennis at Erasmus, he never lost a match.

Several months after my visit to California, when I call and describe a problem I'm having with my (tennis) serve, he immediately diagnoses the problem and gives me a prescription (throw the ball higher, in the same spot each time, and hit it at its peak). When I call back a week or so later to tell him my serve — like my heart? — is working well again, he laughs, and says I called the right guy, because though he doesn't believe he knows much, really, the two things he does feel somewhat confident about are tennis and cardiology.

At Tufts, Rich did not go out for the tennis team, but played freshman basketball and then, though he had not played organized baseball in high school, went out for and made the varsity baseball team as a third baseman. In his senior year, playing in an exhibition game against a minor league team at Braves Field in Boston, he got his team's only two hits, including a home run, against a highly touted bonus baby pitcher.

"After the game, this guy came up to me, and said he was a scout for the Philadelphia Phillies, and we talked for a while, and he made me feel really good," Rich says. "He told me I was a natural and had major league potential, and then he asked what my plans were after graduation, and when I told him I was committed to going to medical school in the fall, he just waved goodbye and walked off."

Rich learned to play tennis during summers spent in Newport, Rhode Island. His father bought a ladies' apparel shop in Newport shortly after World War II, and he worked there five days a week all year long.

"The four of us — my mother and father, and me and my sister Lucy — would get to spend summers together in Newport, and it was a wonderful place for us, and for me," Rich says. "I learned to play tennis there, mostly by sneaking into the country club and watching the older players."

When he was thirteen, Rich entered the city's summer tennis tournament, made it to the finals, and, in a three-set match, won the city's junior championship by defeating Dan Topping, Jr., son of the owner of the New York Yankees.

"He arrived with all his preppie WASP friends —" Rich says, "— the girls in their summer dresses, and the guys in their white bucks, all of them, at least in my memory, very, very blond — and I was behind five-to-two in the third set, but I came back and I beat him, and it felt good, really good.

"I had my first girlfriend that summer," he adds. "Her name was Irene, and she was older than me, and we played tennis together all the time. She was a terrific player — she beat me regularly — and at dusk, when the club members were gone, we would hop the fence and go out onto the courts — the birthplace of tennis in America — and play there until it was too dark to see the ball."

Although Rich entered Tufts intending to become a doctor, his decision had not been based on any great desire to pursue a career in medicine.

"My father was a classic Depression product — worrying endlessly about money," Rich explains. "But we shared a love for baseball, and he was unequivocal in his love for me — he truly thought I was a miracle come to life. He was always gone during the school year, however, and when we were in Newport, I would watch him agonize over his adding machine, trying to make the numbers work, so that the one thing I knew for sure was that I did *not* want to be a businessman like him. But nothing else appealed to me.

"My mother, though, was a fury of ambition for her son, constantly on my case to make up my mind to do something so I could be somebody. She made me take all these aptitude tests, but they only showed that I could probably do well in everything, and they pointed in no specific direction.

"Then one day I come home from school and she informs me she's made an appointment for us to see the wisest and most important person in her life, my pediatrician, Doctor Abram Kanof.

"I was embarrassed because I was fifteen or sixteen years old and even though he was a baby doctor, he was still *my* doctor. I had always loved him when I was a kid — he was a wonderful, sweet man, a very caring man — he made house calls, and he treated me warmly, in a way unlike anything I knew at home — and when he started talking to me about the field of medicine that was his, and that was his wife's also, and told me that both his daughters were going to be physicians, I listened."

I tell Rich that I was friends with Dr. Kanof's younger daughter, Margaret — that we used to play hooky from Hebrew School together after we were let out early from P.S. 246 on Wednesday afternoons for something called "released time for religious instruction," when the Catholic kids would go to their churches, and we were supposed to go to our synagogue.

"But remember," Rich says, "this was a time, in the early fifties, when there were virtually no women doctors. Women were nurses. And when Dr. Kanof talked about his life, and about his feeling for medicine as a kind of holy calling — this came through to me.

"Still, though I was moved by what he said about the wonders of being a physician, this had little to do with my decision. What happened instead was that my mother suddenly cut in and asked what I would have to do in order to become a doctor, and he answered that there was a school in Boston called Tufts, which had an excellent pre-medical program — unlike most other elite New England colleges, it also had less stringent quotas on how many Jews it accepted — and that if I went there it would greatly increase my chances of getting into a good medical school."

Rich says that his mother told Dr. Kanof she had been planning to send him to Brooklyn College, because it was free and because he could live at home, but that if the doctor thought Tufts was the best place for him, she and Rich's father would do whatever it took to send him there.

"And suddenly," Rich says, "I hear — 'Tufts . . . Boston . . . hundreds of miles away from Brooklyn . . . !' — and I immediately agree to becoming a doctor."

I tell Rich about Phil's nightmare, and what Phil has said about his determination to escape Brooklyn and his apartment. Rich nods and, in words identical to those Phil used, declares that he too would have done anything — *anything at all* — to get away.

We talk for a while about convergences in our lives — Rich's grandparents coming to America from places near the villages from which my grandparents came (his mother's mother from Minsk, his mother's father from Pinsk); his mother and father having the same names, Anne and Dave, as my parents; his sister being in junior high and Erasmus with my brother Robert (and Phil's brother Allen); the two of us being trained for our Bar Mitzvahs at Congregation Shaare Torah by Dr. Emanuel H. Baron, and Dr. Baron having trained the two of us (rare event in our synagogue at that time) to chant both the *Haftorah* (a portion from Prophets) and the *Maftir* (a portion from the Torah) — and then I ask if, during his years at Tufts, Rich ever doubted his decision to become a doctor.

"I never thought about it," he replies. "I just knew I had to get certain grades in order to pass muster at home, and to my great joy I found I could get them effortlessly. Two or three days before big exams, I became a demon — I sucked up everything like a sponge, regurgitated it for the exams, got A's, and promptly forgot it all. At Tufts, I didn't think about anything except having a good time. I played on teams — school and fraternity — and I partied, and along the way I also discovered a love for literature, words, philosophy, and for music. These were wonderful years for me, but then the chickens came home to roost.

"I hated every minute of my first two years at Bellevue, you see — they were, and to a large extent in my view, still are, a sort of Marine-like boot camp that has virtually nothing to do with being a physician — and at the end of my second year, I went through a real crisis. I was halfway through to becoming a doctor, and I didn't know anything and I hated all of it. So what was I doing there? I had crammed to pass exams, but it wasn't working anymore — my grades were slipping below acceptable levels, and I began to realize I was going to have to tell my parents that this had all been a gigantic scam.

"And then I saw a miracle take place, where a life was saved right in front of my eyes. What happened was I was working with these two guys, Dan and Jeff — Dan was an intern and Jeff was the resident, and I was assigned to them as part of a three-man team. They were these swashbuckling young doctors right out of M.A.S.H., and we were called down to see a woman in the emergency room, and she was dying, and for the first time Dan and Jeff had no idea of what was going on or of what to do. None at all."

I tell Rich what Arthur has said — how, like me, he grew up believing that doctors knew *everything* — and Rich laughs, says what he has said before about the essence of medicine being fallibility and uncertainty.

"The woman lapsed into a coma, her blood pressure started to drop, froth was coming out of her mouth, and I felt I was in the middle of a nightmare," he continues. "So they telephoned a man, and he came down — he was this little old Czechoslovakian professor Jerry, Phil, and I talk about all the time — Dr. Joseph V. Brumlik — and he has on these pince-nez glasses, and Jeff is waving frantically, and Dan is telling him what little he could figure out about the woman's story — but she had been in a coma, so we knew virtually nothing — and without even seeming to hear these two totally panicked guys, Dr. Brumlik just stood at the foot of the bed with his hands on the soles of the woman's feet, and he studied her, very calmly. Then he looked up, told us the diagnosis — which meant nothing to me — told us what to administer intravenously, and walked out. Jeff and Dan drew the syringe, injected it into her tubing, and within minutes, right there in front of my eyes, the woman woke up.

"It was like a miracle — it *was* a miracle — and I asked Dan, 'Who is that man?' — I mean it was like right out of *Butch Cassidy and the Sundance Kid* — and then — well, the short of it is that Dr. Joseph Brumlik became my mentor, and my life was changed forever.

"Dr. Brumlik had been a professor of cardiology in Prague when the Nazis took over in 1938. He fled for his life, wound up in Mexico City for a while, where he worked as a cardiologist, and then somehow made his way to Bellevue. And from the moment I met him — from that moment in the ER — I became a born-again cardiologist. I mean, when I finished medical school I hardly knew where the liver was, but I had become a sophisticated cardiologist from having sat for two years at Dr. Brumlik's feet.

"He ran a famous clinic at Bellevue called The Thursday Night Cardiac Clinic, and for some reason he invited me in even though my grades for my first two years were atrocious. Then, in my fourth year, he and about a dozen of the leading cardiologists in New York would gather at Bellevue every Saturday morning and look at the most interesting, involved, and difficult cases. Dr. Brumlik was the acknowledged leader of the group, and he and the other doctors would evaluate the patients, and discuss them, and I would sit there and just suck it all up."

I mention having read a book by Bernard Lown, the Nobel Prize–winning cardiologist responsible for the invention of the defibrillator and the development of the cardiac care unit — a man under whom Rich worked in the late sixties when Rich was a research fellow at the National Heart Institute and Peter Bent Brigham Hospital in Boston — and I cite Lown's claim that a doctor who takes a careful history will reach a correct diagnosis 70 percent of the time, and that taking a careful history is far more efficient than relying on all the elaborate tests and technologies currently available. Lown also reports that in his forty-five years of experience with thousands of patients whose presenting complaint was chest pain, he could, through just an unhurried interview, rule out a diagnosis of angina pectoris 90 percent of the time.

"You could quibble about the percentages, but essentially I do not disagree with him," Rich says, and then: "I mean, you are the classic example of that, Jay. I made the diagnosis of what was going on in you from three thousand miles away, on the phone, by listening to you give me your history. I didn't have to examine you, let alone do a fancy test. All the fancy test did — the coronary angiogram — was to confirm what was already clear from talking with you."

He begins to explain how and why he knew this — he talks about what Osler taught still being true: about the patient giving you the diagnosis if you listen carefully enough — and I tell him about Phil answering his patients' questions with a shrug and an "I don't know" — and ask if many doctors would do the same.

"Damned few," Rich says. "Ninety-nine percent of doctors, in my experience, will just make something up. It's remarkable that Phil does that, and quite wonderful from my perspective, you see, because all my life I have taught that the very first step is to admit out loud that we do not know things, and that only by acknowledging this can we really find anything out. If you fool yourself with a lot of biomedical jargon, it can obscure the basic fact — what many doctors cannot acknowledge, and what is too scary for them — and that is the vast sea of ignorance in which we all work."

After we return from playing tennis, we return to our discussion of how it was Rich could diagnose my condition by telephone, and I thank him again, but he only repeats what he said to me a few weeks before: that I should really be thanking my brother Robert and the Redondo Beach Public Library. For if I had not written a book about Robert, and if Rich hadn't come upon a copy of the book in his library, and if the book hadn't moved him to write me, we might not be sitting here today and talking.

"You may not remember this now," Rich says, "but I was pushing you very hard to get the angiogram a.s.a.p. You were sitting on a time bomb, and I knew that one hundred percent."

"Yet you were the only person, in the two months before surgery, who believed this," I say, and I remind him that Phil called a few times to suggest I have an x-ray, that he thought what I was describing — the discomfort between my shoulder blades — might be due to a dissection of the aorta (a condition in which the inner lining of the aorta is sheared off, so that the blood stream "dissects" its way through the lining of the blood vessel, forming a double opening that is life-threatening and, characteristically, causes pain between the shoulder blades).

"But Phil trying to diagnose your situation would be like me trying to diagnose a nuance of where in the hippocampus a stroke was taking place," Rich says. "It's why I agree with him about the drive toward having more family practitioners and fewer specialists being the reverse of the way things should be.

"But that's another subject," he says, and he backtracks to our discussion about what was happening in the weeks preceding surgery, and walks me through the experience again.

"There were two main reasons why I knew your condition was very severe," he says. "First of all, not only did you have a clear-cut angina, even though it was in a somewhat unusual place — between your shoulder blades — but the symptoms were progressive. They were occurring more frequently, and they were occurring with less physical activity — and I learned this from your telling me about what was happening when you went swimming.

"The second critical factor was that along with the discomfort between your shoulder blades, you were also becoming short of breath, and this told me that when you were experiencing the anginal symptoms, a very large area of your heart was becoming dysfunctional."

Rich explains: "What happens to the heart when you get angina is this — you are exercising, so your heart needs more oxygen, but because there's a blockage in an artery in that area of the heart which the artery is supplying, the heart is not receiving the oxygen it needs. So two things occur: One is that the heart says 'Ouch' — which is what you feel in the symptoms — but what also happens to that area of the heart muscle is that it quite literally *stops contracting*. And the reason it does this is because it's making an effort to stay alive — and the way to do that is to minimize the amount of oxygen it's going to use.

"But when a critical area of the heart muscle stops contracting in order to preserve its oxygen sources as well as it can, the blood backs up into your lungs, and you experience this as shortness of breath.

"Thus, a typical patient with angina will get chest discomfort, pressure, heaviness, or a squeezing — and it can be located in many places: the neck, the jaw, between the shoulder blades — but you will *not* get shortness of breath along with that unless there is a very large area of the heart involved."

I ask why he thinks my family doctor diagnosed asthma, and Rich says that for a general doctor to diagnose my condition would be like having a neurologist look at a cardiology problem.

"A family doctor cannot have the depth of perception about the across-the-board panoply of diseases they are called upon to be insightful about," he says. "So when you told me what your doctor said, I told you with exclamation points that this asthma diagnosis was absolute nonsense." Rich adds that it *was* a good thing my doctor eventually realized this (when the inhaler he had prescribed had no effect on my shortness of breath), and that he had ordered a stress test.

But why, I ask, as the weather grew colder, did it get harder and harder for me to walk outdoors?

"Because cold tends to constrict your blood vessels," Rich answers. "They constrict in order to shut down the blood supply to the skin so that you can maintain body heat. But by doing that, the work that the heart has to do is *increased* — so the harder the heart has to work, the more oxygen it needs. But a limitation has now developed on how much oxygen you can get through the blocked arteries — those coronary arteries that are the suppliers of oxygen to the heart muscle."

Rich reminds me that the first time I called, he urged me to go to Boston and see two doctors he knew at Massachusetts General Hospital, and I ask why he was so concerned at the outset, especially since I had few if any risk factors, and virtually no symptoms.

"I've always had an intuitive sense of when a patient is in danger — it's an instinct I've learned to trust," he says. "In your case, even though you lived a healthy lifestyle and the only risk factor you really had was your father's history — his heart attack, but, then too, he was a chain smoker — all that stuff goes out the window. When tell-tale symptoms develop, factors like family history, cigarette smoking, and cholesterol levels no longer matter. The symptoms themselves are all that count, and they register as being significant and urgent or they don't."

I ask what the results of the EKG and the echocardiogram — both of which I had faxed to him — told him.

"Well, the EKG showed an unequivocal abnormality, and an EKG is quite valuable, but only if it's abnormal. Then it can provide clues. But if it isn't, it can often be misleading and miss a lot of things. What the echocardiogram did was to confirm my concern about there being a lot of weakness in the way the heart muscle was contracting. This told me that there was a very extensive area of the heart involved in the process, which suggested that several of your coronary arteries had significant blockages. When added to the increasing frequency and severity of your symptoms, the picture that emerged was that you had widespread, severe coronary artery disease, *and* that the abnormalities had become unstable. One of your major arteries was about to close down and cause a massive, possibly fatal heart attack."

I remind Rich that when I reported the results of the echocardiogram to him, and reported that the cardiologist had said, "I think it's viral," Rich had exploded for the first time, telling me it wasn't viral — "*goddamnit!*" — and that he wanted me in the hospital as soon as possible.

"You know, my level of concern had been high from the outset," Rich says. "Only I did not want you to know because I didn't want you to panic. What I wanted was to get you into a good hospital where they knew what they were doing, and to get this sorted out and fixed."

But if what was happening was so obvious, why had two doctors missed it?

"Look," Rich says. "The EKG and echo simply provided lab evidence that confirmed what your story was telling me loud and clear on the phone from three thousand miles away. And what happened was a microcosm of a central problem with technology — that a lab test can only be used correctly in the context of the patient's symptoms.

"This cardiologist was looking at the fact that the whole heart muscle was not contracting well — something that occurs in people with viral infections of the heart muscle — and he was making a misdiagnosis because he was forgetting that you had told him you were also having symptoms of angina. And people with viral heart disease do not get any symptoms of pressure, tightness, or pain — what you were having between your shoulder blades — they simply develop shortness of breath.

"So he misread the echocardiogram because he forgot the fundamentals — he forgot about you. You start with the patient's story, and the tests you run are only valuable if they add dimension to that story. But they do not let you be seduced away from the story."

Rich talks for a while about what Phil and Jerry have been talking about: the ways technology has lured physicians toward quick-fix procedures, and away from the primary source of diagnostic information, and why, because this is happening, we are often kept from knowing what is really going on. He declares that I would not have been able to benefit from the incredible technological advances we *do* have at our disposal — bypasses, coronary care units, revolutionary medications — if people wedded to technology had had the final say.

"What has happened, it seems to me," Rich says, "is that the diagnostic acumen of the physician at the bedside, on the phone, or in the office has been severely compromised because the mindset now — and this is also the main reason medical costs keep going up — has become, 'Well, the tests will tell me anyway, so I don't have to spend a lot of time listening. I can just run a battery of tests, and the tests will tell me the diagnosis.'

"First the nurse said, 'Why don't we just schedule you for a full exam,' and then you had a diagnosis of asthma, and then you had a diagnosis of 'Well we don't know,' and then you had a diagnosis of a heart attack, and then you had the doctor saying, 'No, there's no heart attack, but we have a viral cardiomyopathy,' and all the while the symptoms are progressing, you're hanging on by a single artery which is itself hanging by a thread, and something catastrophic is about to occur. Let me say it again, Jay. There is no question in my mind that we wouldn't be sitting here today if you hadn't gone to high school with the right guys."

In our talks in Palos Verdes, we return frequently to what we talked about in the days immediately following my surgery: what we do and don't know about heart disease.

"Theories have come and gone," Rich says, "yet we are no closer to a true understanding of the causes of atherosclerosis — of what happened to you — than we were a generation ago. We do, however, know that smokers are several times more likely to develop heart disease than nonsmokers.

"The evidence is unequivocal there. We know that people with really high cholesterol levels are more likely to develop heart disease. The same is true for patients with hypertension, or with diabetes, or for patients who are obese — we have very strong *statistical* correlations in these instances. But if you compare what we know to what happened when medicine first became scientific — when Pasteur made his discovery of the germ theory: that germs cause infectious disease — and when Koch provided the scientific standard for proving cause and effect with respect to these diseases — we come up short. Statistics have almost nothing to do with cause and effect — they only show *associations* — and we cannot yet show cause and effect when it comes to atherosclerosis.

"If you give antibiotics to one hundred people who have pneumococcal pneumonia, all one hundred will be cured. Nothing like that exists regarding atherosclerosis — though we do know the causes of other heart diseases, such as rheumatic valve disease, which is caused by streptococcus."

According to Koch's postulates, an organism must be present in every instance of a particular disease; it must be capable of being isolated in pure form from the disease lesion and possess the capacity to reproduce the disease in a healthy animal through inoculation with a pure culture; and the same organism must then be capable of being retrieved from the inoculated animal — in the lesions of the artificially produced disease — and of being cultured anew.

The assumption, and hope, still with us 120 years after Koch formalized his postulates in 1882 — as we see in the immoderate rhetoric that accompanies much recent genetic and biomedical research and drug company advertising — is that each disease will be shown to have a specific causative agent, and that once this agent has been discovered and isolated, we will be able to control and cure the disease.

But the world of biology and disease is rarely this simple. Even when we *do* find what appear to be single causative genetic abnormalities, as with Huntington's chorea, Friedreich's ataxia, sickle cell anemia, cystic fibrosis, and muscular dystrophy, developing means for controlling such agents (in these instances, defective genes) frequently eludes us.

"Phil was right when he said that except for the possible genetic link with your father, you had at very most only minor risk factors," Rich continues. "Now, for people who have a strong family history of coronary disease, particularly early-age coronary disease — if, say, your father had had a heart attack at age thirty-eight or forty-two — then that would make the genetic link, and the danger, much more likely."

I say that after hearing my stories of how the common early warning signs and symptoms for the illnesses Robert and I had (schizophrenia, coronary artery disease) were largely absent, people have usually responded by saying, "Oh, then it must be genetic." Rich agrees that "It must be genetic" is simply another way of saying "We don't know why these things happen" — and that the use of a scientific term such as *genetic* does somehow reassure people.

It is much the same, I say, with diagnoses. For years, when people would ask what my brother's diagnosis was, and I said "manic-depressive," or "schizophrenic," or schizo-affective" — whatever the most recent diagnosis happened to be — people would nod knowingly, and then move on to another topic of conversation.

I had come to group such responses under the heading of "The Consolation of Diagnosis," and had taken to following up with questions of my own: "So now that I've given you a word — a clinical term — what does it tell you about my brother?" I'd ask. "What do you know about him now that you didn't know before — when you met him, or heard me talk about him, or read about him — ?" I would, that is, use the question as an occasion to talk about Robert as a man with an idiosyncratic personality, a complex history, an unenviable series of breakdowns and hospitalizations, and an identity at least as unique as anyone else's.

In point of fact, it turns out that the genetic basis for coronary artery disease, as for the major mental illnesses, is modest. Twin studies of coronary artery disease show a concordance rate between identical twins of 19 percent, and of 8 percent for nonidentical twins. (Compare this, for example, to a rate of 50 percent for identical twins in insulin-dependent diabetes, and of nearly 100 percent in non-insulin-dependent diabetes.)

I ask what high blood pressure (where the genetic factor is also modest, the concordance rate for identical twins being only 30 percent) does to the arteries that makes it a risk factor.

"You ask the right questions," Rich says. "But again, though theories abound — perhaps it weakens the walls of the arteries, or it induces dysfunctions in the endothelium, which is the innermost layer of blood vessels and is critical in determining the contractile state of the underlying smooth muscle, or it may reduce the activity of nitric oxide, which has anti-atherosclerotic effects — the real answer is that we don't know.

"What we *do* know is that high blood pressure is *statistically* associated with higher rates of heart disease and heart attacks, though *labile* hypertension — the condition you evidenced — so-called white coat syndrome, where your pressure goes up when you're in the doctor's office and see the white lab coat in front of you — is not anything like the risk factor other, more repeatable and predictable patterns are.

"And all of this is why I keep saying that you are living evidence, my friend, of a much larger point."

Which is? I ask.

"That we simply don't know what causes atherosclerosis. But remember — these statistical correlations *do* have great importance from a preventive point of view, because a lot of information shows that people with severe elevations of cholesterol who lower them with diet, drugs, or exercise have lower rates of atherosclerosis. People who take aspirin have fewer coronary events, and if you stop smoking, treat your high blood pressure, your obesity, et cetera, your risk will go down — statistically — and this is important. But it is by no means conclusive.

"Because the average temperature in Palos Verdes on August 21 is sixty-eight degrees, doesn't mean that it will be sixty-eight degrees today. Because it might be sixty-eight degrees in Northampton today doesn't mean that every flower that blooms here can bloom there. Because, let's say, we discover that most cardiologists who own fancy cars also play tennis well doesn't mean that being a cardiologist and owning a fancy car will make you a good tennis player. As I said to you when you were at Yale, when 'n' equals one — when it comes to each individual instance: to the patient we are treating — associations and statistics break down."

Arthur and I have talked about this — yes, an airplane is statistically the safest way to travel, he says, unless you happen to get on the wrong plane — and I quote him to Rich now, Arthur saying that it used to be "Neugie died of a heart attack," but now it's "Neugie died of a heart attack because he ate too many Mallomars . . . or too many eggs, or because he didn't exercise enough."

Rich laughs, and says that what is true for heart disease — that we don't really know why somebody with few if any risk factors dies, and somebody with a multitude of risk factors lives to a ripe old age — is also true for cancer.

"Heart disease and cancer — in our time, these are the two biggies," he says.

The reading I've been doing in evolutionary medicine, or what is sometimes called Darwinian medicine, has, with regard to these two killers, been instructive, I say. What those who work in this discipline, most notably, Paul W. Ewald, with whom I've talked about this (he teaches at Amherst College across town from the University of Massachusetts), believe is that medical research and practice could be significantly enhanced if questions of adaptation and historical causation were routinely taken into account along with questions of more proximate physical and chemical causation.

Evolutionary biologists ask intriguing questions: for example, If evolution by natural selection can shape mechanisms as sophisticated as the eye, heart, and brain, why hasn't it shaped ways to prevent nearsightedness, heart attacks, and Alzheimer's disease? If our immune system can recognize and attack millions of foreign, harmful pathogens and proteins, why do we still get sick?

Since we know that smoking and excessive exposure to the sun are implicated in causing lung and skin cancer, why hasn't natural selection eliminated the genes (if genes they are) that make us crave cigarettes and sunshine? And why can't our bodies repair clogged arteries, sun-damaged skin, and brain lesions the way they repair bruises and skin abrasions, and nerve and muscle damage?

When placing present infirmities within evolutionary contexts — taking a long historical view — researchers such as Ewald begin with a fundamental observation: that the bodies and immune systems we now possess have come into being over the course of millions of years, most of which — perhaps 90 percent of the years since we became recognizable as the species we are today — we spent as hunter-gatherers living in small groups on the plains of Africa. Natural selection, therefore, has not in many instances had the time, or the biological wherewithal, to enable us to accommodate to more recent conditions of environment and history.

The gene that causes sickle cell anemia, for example, also prevents malaria — useful on the plains of Africa, but not on the streets of New York. Most of the genes we believe may predispose us to heart disease were harmless until certain other events occurred — the availability of fats, sweets, and tobacco, the migration to densely populated cities, and the public health measures and medical innovations that enable us to have markedly longer average life spans than we did only a hundred years ago.

This is so because natural selection does not select for health, but only for reproductive success. It has no plan, no intent, no direction; survival, that is, increases fitness only insofar as it increases later reproductive capabilities, and fitness leads to survival only when it has aided reproductive success.

Since the gene for Huntington's chorea, for example, causes little harm before the age of forty, and so cannot decrease the number of children born to someone who *later* develops this disease, natural selection does not eliminate the gene. In a similar way, it would seem, since cancer and heart disease commonly occur after the age of reproduction, natural selection has not eliminated those genes that may predispose us to cancer or heart disease.

From an evolutionary point of view, we age and we die in the ways that we do, then, not because we have done something *wrong* (eaten too many Mallomars), but because the diseases that, in our time, generally do us in are those that occur *after* the age of reproduction. What evolution seems to care about — the pathetic fallacy writ large in the example I offer to Rich — is not Rich or Neugie, but simply being able to produce another Rich or Neugie.

Seen from this perspective, we are only, as Richard Dawkins suggests, vessels created by genes for the replication of genes, and thus may be discarded when the genes are through with us.

In addition, as Ewald points out, from an evolutionary perspective it makes no sense that our immune systems would suddenly, early in the twentieth century, begin malfunctioning on their own in a higher and higher proportion of people.

Conversely, after thousands of years of exposure to disease agents such as smallpox and tuberculosis, one would expect natural selection to have produced a population of individuals *all* of whom were resistant to these diseases. But this has not happened, Ewald explains, because "natural selection obtains its power from the differences in the survival and reproduction of competitors within a species, which in turn determine differences in the passing on of the genetic instructions that individuals house." That is where one must look if one wishes to understand why infectious diseases are the way they are and what we can do to control them, because that is where the strategies of pathogens are being shaped.

What evolutionary biologists thus recommend to researchers as holding promise for significant progress in the understanding and treatment of disease is, first of all, the investment of greater resources in investigating those selective processes that favor increased or decreased virulence of viral strains.

The race, they submit, is between what Ewald calls "the biological weaponry" our bodily defenses impose on pathogens, and the pathogens' resistance to them. And, as we know from the increasing resistance to antibiotics, or the decreasing potency of many antiretrovirals — most pathogens evolve much more swiftly, and ingeniously, than we can create medications capable of eliminating, suppressing, or moderating their effects.

Consider, for example, streptococcus. Here is a bacterium that has evolved along with us for millions of years. When we create antibodies that attack strep, these antibodies, which are capable of imitating the codes of our cells, are prone to attack our own tissues too, and while we produce a new generation of Neugies and Riches every twenty years or so, strep evolves and produces a new generation of pathogens every hour or so. Until now, antibiotics have generally proven capable of dealing with these newly evolved variants. But as we know from the alarming rise in the presence and lethal power both of new infectious diseases (AIDS, ebola, legionnaires' disease) and of reemerging diseases (tuberculosis, malaria, streptococcal pneumonia), this may be only a temporary blessing. By the late 1970s, Laurie Garrett informs us in *The Coming Plague,* "strep B was the most serious life-threatening disease in neonatal units all over the industrialized world, and 75 percent of all infections in babies under two months of age were fatal, despite aggressive antibiotic treatment." And by the year 2000, the *New York Times* reports, fourteen thousand people were dying each year from drug-resistant infections contracted in hospitals.

Researchers first began studying the inflammatory process in atherosclerosis in the 1820s, first proposed infectious causation of atherosclerosis in the 1870s, and found evidence that chlamydia was implicated in arterial disease in the 1940s. Evolutionary biologists now contend that atherosclerosis is most probably an inflammatory disease of infectious origin, and the arguments and evidence they present in support of this view are persuasive. Until very recently, they maintain, it was mostly in order to develop a consensus that other medical researchers and cardiologists shied away from statements of causation in favor of a much less informative concept, that of risk factors — high cholesterol, high blood pressure, smoking, obesity, lack of exercise, genetics, et cetera.

None of the risk factors for atherosclerosis, though, appears to be a *primary* risk factor — for each risk factor, that is, many of us are found who do not have it, yet still have atherosclerosis. In fact, as we have known for some time, and as Ewald reminds us, if you add up *all* the known noninfectious risk factors, they still explain only about half the risk of acquiring atherosclerosis, a finding corroborated by Dr. Joseph B. Muhlestein, director of research at the cardiac catherization laboratory, and a professor of medicine at the University of Utah Medical School. "Although much is known about the pathologic process whereby atherosclerotic plaque develops," Dr. Muhlestein writes, "in many cases, the underlying cause remains unclear. Certain risk factors associated with the development of atherosclerosis are well defined, including diabetes mellitus, hypertension, hyperlipidemia, tobacco abuse, and a positive family history. These risk factors, however, combine to account for only about 50% of the observed incidence of atherosclerosis. Additionally, these risk factors generally are only associations, and the exact mechanism by which they may contribute to the development of atherosclerosis is not known."

Moreover, as Lewis Thomas observed more than thirty years ago, and as Ewald argues now, most major achievements in medicine have resulted from principles of *primary* causation: this holds for large theoretical discoveries such as the germ theory of disease, as well as for practical interventions such as surgery, antimicrobial drugs, vaccines, and improved nutrition and hygiene.

Rich agrees. The efficacy — and genius — of vaccines is due not so much to the medications themselves, but more to our ability to make use of what we know about the human immune system. As to risk factors for atherosclerosis, Rich compares each new risk factor put forth as *the* key risk factor to the old flavor-of-the month posted at our local ice cream parlors; and with regard to each such risk factor heralded as "the ultimate bad guy," he likes to tell the story of the cop who comes upon a drunk crawling around on his hands and knees under a lamppost. The cop asks him what he's doing, and the drunk says he's looking for his wallet. "Where did you lose it?" the cop asks. "Oh, I lost it inside the bar," the drunk says. "Then why are you looking for it under the lamppost?" the cop asks. "Because," the drunk replies, "the light's better here."

Still, Rich says, the prevailing theory among cardiologists these days does corroborate Ewald's hypothesis. In fact, he goes on, he and his team at the University of California at Irvine contributed to the discussion of the possible inflammatory origins of atherosclerosis with work they did in the mid-nineties.

"The entire process of atheroma formation is complex and difficult to pin down because, among other things, *lots* of elements seem to play a role," he says. "But what I have believed for years, as you know, is that it is not the atheroma itself — the fatty deposits in the walls of the arteries — that kills people, but the *rupture* of the atheroma, and if we could identify what causes the rupture, and find ways to prevent it, we would make a huge impact on the prevention of heart attacks.

"We have a lot of indirect and experimental evidence to explain the process that leads to coronary disease, and from coronary disease to heart attacks," Rich explains, "and it all seems to indicate that something happens to the inner layer — the endothelium — of the coronary blood vessel. An abnormality develops, which in turn allows cells carrying the bad cholesterol — the LDL — to seep through and get caught up in the artery's wall. When that process matures, cholesterol deposits leak out of the cells and, essentially, form masses, and these masses protrude back into the opening of the artery — the lumen — causing a partial obstruction.

"Sometimes nothing happens — even severe blockages cause at most only three out of every ten heart attacks — and sometimes the obstruction reaches a point where it interferes with the amount of blood flowing through the passageway of the artery. And when the heart is under stress because the oxygen it needs exceeds the ability of the blocked coronary artery to supply it — you're exerting yourself more than usual: swimming, walking fast, playing tennis — this imbalance causes the symptoms of angina pectoris. But the most dangerous thing that can occur is for the atheroma to rupture into the blood vessel itself, causing a clot to form.

"This is the same kind of clot you get when your skin is cut — it's nature's way of healing us — and when these atheroma rupture, their surfaces are very sticky, and platelets bind to them. But the clot closes off the artery and the coronary artery becomes occluded. Suddenly, an area of heart muscle is starved of oxygen, and if this is not relieved quickly enough, that area of the heart dies — in other words, a heart attack occurs. If the area is large enough, you don't survive it."

Rich talks about the experiment he and his research team performed, in collaboration with the local coroner's office and pathology researchers, in which they studied the hearts and arteries of people who had died in automobile accidents, and compared them with the hearts and arteries of people who had died of heart attacks.

"What we found," he says, "was that the people who died of heart attacks had huge collections of macrophages — white blood cells — in their atheroma. More importantly, these macrophages secreted substances with the fancy term of *matrix metalloproteinases,* which are enzymes that digest proteins.

"What these enyzmes were doing was digesting away tissue that contained the fatty deposits, thus weakening the walls of the arteries, and making them susceptible to rupture. And we found something else that was fascinating — and totally unexpected. When we looked at other arteries in the patients whose atheroma had ruptured — at the arteries that had *not* ruptured — we found the same collection of lesions containing macrophages and metalloproteinases.

"Yet this was not the case in those people with atheroma where *no* rupture had occurred. This strongly suggests that the process is systemic — in other words, that the inflammatory process is not taking place only in the one susceptible atheroma.

"Add to this recent studies that have shown that people with elevated levels of C-reactive protein — which are nonspecific markers of inflammation circulating in the blood — are much more susceptible to heart attacks, and that high levels of C-reactive protein, even in the absence of high cholesterol, are fairly reliable indicators of heart disease and of potential heart attacks, and you can see why infectious and inflammatory disease explanations make sense. In addition, it now seems that aspirin and the statins, which we thought were effective against coronary heart disease because they reduced clotting and/or lowered cholesterol, may owe a large part of their effectiveness to the fact that they reduce inflammation.

"All of which suggests that there is some kind of total body inflammatory process involved in triggering heart attacks, and that this process is triggered for reasons no one understands."

My researches confirm much of what Rich tells me. Ewald's hypotheses about the infectious causes of heart disease, along with evidence that he and other evolutionary biologists present — that there are significant associations between atherosclerosis and both *Chlamydia pneumoniae* and gingivitis *(Porphyromonas gingivalis);* that treatment of bypass patients with antibiotics improves their recovery; and that an inflammatory hypothesis makes sense since it does not specify whether the atherosclerotic damage is caused directly by the infectious organism or indirectly through the organism's *stimulation of* an inflammatory response — these arguments are reiterated, reinforced, and expanded upon in an abundance of medical journal articles.

Here, for example, is the simple declarative sentence with which Dr. Russell Ross begins a January 1999 article in the *New England Journal of Medicine:* "Atherosclerosis is an inflammatory disease."

After taking us through a substantial body of evidence to support this proposition, Ross concludes that "atherosclerosis is clearly an inflammatory disease, and does not result simply from the accumulation of lipids.

"If we can selectively modify the harmful components of inflammation in the arteries and leave the protective aspects intact," he adds, "we may create new avenues for the diagnosis and management of disease in the 50 percent of patients with cardiovascular disease who do not have hypercholesterolemia."

"From a clinical standpoint, chronic inflammation, as evidenced by elevated levels of C-reactive protein, has been shown to be directly associated with the development as well as progression of coronary artery disease," Dr. Joseph Muhlestein writes in an article published a year later, in January 2000.

After reviewing research from a sizable number of studies linking various infectious diseases to coronary artery disease, Muhlestein concludes that "the infectious agents with the most evidence to support a causative role in atherosclerosis" include *Chlamydia pneumoniae,* cytomegalovirus (a member of the herpesvirus genus), *Helicobacter pylori* (implicated in causing peptic ulcer disease), and several bacterial agents (including *Porphyromonas gingivalis*) associated with periodontal disease.

Although we may, thanks to the research that lends these propositions their plausibility, be getting closer to understanding the underlying cause or causes of atherosclerosis, what we do *not* know, Rich maintains, is still infinitely greater than what we do know.

He remains highly skeptical of anyone who claims to know, definitively, what can either cause or cure coronary heart disease, and outraged by the ways those claiming such knowledge go directly to the consumer with sales pitches for their products, as in the extensive campaigns to sell us cholesterol-lowering medications.

"I mean, why don't they just put the stuff in the well water and be done with it?" he asks at one point, and here again, everything I read lends credence to his skepticism.

Is Zocor really going to help me "live a longer healthier life"? Has Pravachol really been "proven to help prevent heart attacks in people with high cholesterol or heart disease"? Should I, like Dan Reeves, make taking Zocor "an important part of my game plan" — and will it not only lower my cholesterol by 29 to 45 percent, but enable me to "stay beautiful on the inside"?

In an article in *Science* (March 30, 2001), Gary Taubes, a three-time winner of the Science-in-Society Award from the National Association of Science Writers, reassesses much of what we know about the relation of a diet high in fat to cholesterol and heart disease, and demonstrates that "by the 1970s, each individual step of this chain from fat to cholesterol to heart disease had been demonstrated beyond reasonable doubt, but the veracity of the chain *as a whole* had never been proven" (italics in original).

Nor has it been proven since. In 1991, a study funded by the U.S. Surgeon General's Office determined that cutting fat consumption in the United States would delay forty-two thousand deaths each year. The key word, however, as Taubes points out, is *delay*.

"To be precise," he explains, "a woman who might otherwise die at 65 could expect to live two extra weeks after a lifetime of avoiding saturated fat. If she lived to be 90, she could expect 10 additional weeks."

The proposition that reducing fat consumption, whether by diet or drugs, prevents heart disease and leads to longer, healthier lives is, at best, inconclusive, and at worst, as many medical experts maintain, the result of an enormous, often greed-inspired hoax. Rich talks frequently (and is writing about) what he considers unethical collusion between doctors, hospitals, and pharmaceutical firms. (Corroborating what he has witnessed firsthand, an article in the January 2, 2002, issue of the *Journal of the American Medical Association* reports that nearly nine out of ten medical experts who write guidelines for treating conditions such as heart disease, depression, and diabetes have financial ties to the pharmaceutical industry, and that these ties are rarely if ever disclosed; moreover, approximately six out of every ten medical experts have financial ties to companies whose medications they either considered or recommended in the guidelines they wrote.)

Although more than 80 percent of the money spent on the promotion of prescription drugs is still directed to health-care professionals, annual spending on direct-to-consumer advertising for prescription drugs tripled between 1996 and 2000, when it went from 791 million dollars (9 percent of annual spending), to just under 2.5 billion dollars (16 percent).

Taubes reviews not only the research concerning the relation of dietary fat to heart disease, but the history of the ways in which the general public, encouraged by drug companies, politicians, and the media, has come to accept as axiomatic what has never been proven.

Despite the existence of many trials that "showed no evidence that men who ate less fat lived longer or had fewer heart attacks," Taubes cites *Time* magazine, for example, declaring, in its headline to a feature story (on the magazine's cover, below a plate of bacon

and eggs arranged so as to resemble a doleful face, "CHOLES-
TEROL: AND NOW THE BAD NEWS") — "Sorry, It's True. Cholesterol Really Is a Killer."

"Snatching victory from the jaws of defeat of the verdict of the
[cholesterol] trials," James LeFanu, a London physician and author
(a regular columnist for the London *Times,* and *Daily* and *Sunday
Telegraph*), writes in an examination of the subject in his book, *The
Rise and Fall of Modern Medicine,* "dozens of expert committee reports had persuaded most people that 'Western food is the chief reason for our modern epidemic of heart disease.' This in turn had
been the Trojan Horse by which millions had been prescribed cholesterol-lowering drugs."

LeFanu subjects the claims of the pharmaceutical industry to
close analysis — in one instance, when they assert that according to a
"landmark study" there is "conclusive proof" that taking the drug
cholestyramine reduces the chances of dying from a heart attack by
25 percent, he sorts through the data of a seven-year study used in
support of such a claim.

"After seven years . . . thirty out of the 1,900 taking cholestyramine had had a fatal heart attack compared to thirty-eight of the
similar number in the control group," he informs us. "This indeed
can be interpreted as 'reducing the chances of dying from a heart attack by 25 percent . . .' But put another way, almost 2,000 men took
cholestyramine for seven years to increase their chances of not having a heart attack by less than half of 1 percent. This seems a modest
enough achievement, except that overall cholestyramine made no
difference at all, as the total number of deaths in the 'intervention'
and 'control' groups were exactly the same, with the modest reduction in heart disease mortality in those taking cholestyramine being
balanced by an increased risk of death 'from other causes.'"

"It is much easier to promote a drug on the grounds that it reduces the 'risk of a heart attack by 25 percent,'" LeFanu observes,
"than by pointing out that ruining one's meals with cholestyramine
for seven years increases one's chances of not having a heart attack
by 0.5 percent, at the price of chronic bowel symptoms, depression
and increased risk of death from other causes."

The enormous number of studies on the relation of dietary fat to heart disease validate Rich's assertion: that while reducing cholesterol levels, especially LDL (the so-called bad cholesterol), for individuals who have already had heart disease, or are considered to be at high risk for heart disease, is probably wise, there is a distinct absence of evidence to persuade one that otherwise healthy individuals with normal or borderline cholesterol levels need to take what will, in most instances, become lifetime medications.

"The ideal way to treat atherosclerosis," Rich says, "would be to give patients a pill that would be a medical roto-rooter and ream out the blocked arteries. But we don't have that pill, and we won't have it, if ever, for a good while. In the meantime, we have millions of people taking these medications because Dan Reeves or their doctors tell them to — and taking these meds is not like taking an antibiotic for an infection.

"You take an antibiotic for ten days to two weeks and the bug is killed and that's the end of it," Rich goes on. "Yes, when you need these cholesterol meds, of course you should take them. But these are lifetime medications, remember, and every pill that has ever been manufactured by humankind has its own side effects, and nobody really knows what the effects of these medications will be in your body over the course of a lifetime."

While Rich is exceptionally knowledgeable about the many useful technologies available for the treatment of heart disease (and is himself responsible for the early and ongoing development of several of these technologies, including nuclear cardiology, cardiac electrophysiology, angioplasty, and the use of calcium channel-blocker drugs to treat coronary artery spasm and hypertension), in recent years he has become more attuned to, and passionate about, the role that *non* technological elements play in the healing process.

Increasingly, his life, and his work, have become informed by a range of activities — daily meditation, reading and study of Eastern thought and philosophy (especially, as with Arthur, the writings of the Dalai Lama), and his own writing — that explore experiences that cannot be fully understood or explained rationally.

In one of the books he is working on, he tells the stories of patients whose experiences of, and recoveries from, heart disease can-

not be accounted for by conventional scientific reasoning or observation.

"After a lifetime of caring for sick people, there is no question in
my mind that belief is a powerful force for those good, bad, or indif-
ferent things that happen to people, whether in what we call ordinary life, or in things pertaining specifically to health," he says. "And
I think an awful lot of what happens has to do with what has come
to be called the mind/body connection."

When I recount some of what I've been reading about placebos,
and the placebo effect, Rich shakes his head sideways, and laments
the fact that the word *placebo* has become synonymous with worthless.

"The placebo effect is enormously powerful, and enormously
healing," he says, "and should be mobilized to the max, in addition
to whatever else we may bring to bear on a specific condition. But
the placebo effect is only valuable to the extent that a patient believes it's valuable."

What I wonder about, I say, is this: If the doctor-patient relationship continues to be seriously weakened and devalued — if, increasingly, we and our doctors become strangers to one another — what
happens to all those conditions that have no apparent organic cause,
yet are ameliorated by the simple act of going to a doctor one knows
and trusts?

"Well, we know very little about the causes of illnesses that would
appear to have obvious chemical, biological, genetic, or environmental origins," Rich says. "And we know even less about the mysterious interactions between the mind and the body — and these interactions are crucial in enabling the body to heal itself, and to
modify the course of illness. Thus the great danger if we lose sight of
the doctor's ability to make use of the body's natural power to heal
itself.

"But let me be more specific, and talk about something I call
paragenetics," he continues. "Now we know that genes per se are
rarely the sole or even decisive cause of most common diseases, but
if your father died of a heart attack at age fifty-nine, that festers in
your mind, and through the mind/body connection, in your body as

well. You're forty-eight, and then fifty, and then you reach fifty-nine and something starts to happen.

"Now we know that genetics usually confer a propensity — a potential vulnerability. But will the heart attack that got your dad land on the same part of the time clock for you? Of course not. Still, your mind is programming your body in some way to believe that it will, and what I think about more and more is the power of the patient-doctor relationship to *reset* the mind/body clock — something that has largely been lost in the hoopla of technology all around us.

"And there's also this: in the absence of a healthy doctor-patient relationship — when somebody gets an impersonal lab coat doing all the stuff instead of a caring doctor like Phil or Jerry, or gets a different doctor for each visit — then fear kicks in, and becomes an element that itself inhibits the mind/body's ability to heal itself. And we should never underestimate the role fear and apprehension play in a patient's ability to deal with illness, and to recover from illness.

"So what we're really talking about here, I think, are questions of medical responsibility," he continues. "What I've been teaching for years, for example, is that if you have a patient who is not taking medications, it's *your* responsibility to see that he does. It is because you have not sat down and adequately explained the urgency, or if there are side effects, because you have not given your patient the space — the comfort, the confidence, the necessary trust — to talk with you so that you can look for a suitable alternative. People don't want to talk about the cost of drugs or side effects with a doctor, often, because they're embarrassed, or they're ashamed, and so, here and in myriad other ways, I find that there is tremendous power in the doctor-patient relationship to help in the healing process — but only if we value it, encourage it, and understand its potential both for ill and for good.

"Excellence matters too, of course. Whether it's managing a hotel or a cardiology program, there has to be a commitment to excellence and to care, and that starts at the top, with leadership. In the case of Massachusetts General Hospital, for example, ever since Paul Dudley White, who was Eisenhower's personal physician, was in charge, there has been a standard of excellence there in cardiology and cardiac care that has been passed down from one generation to the next.

"The way I see it, there is content and there is context. The content is the expertise — how good technically are the surgeons and the angiographers, and how up-to-date are they, and so forth. But then there's the context. And the context is: Does the care work? Because the context, you see, is the caring, the wisdom, and the judgment about employing the knowledge and power we do have — this vast array of medications, treatments, and technologies — to best serve individual patients in the way that we were able to serve you, my friend."

15

Natural Selection

How curious, and how wonderful, I think, that these four friends I have known across a lifetime did not start out wanting to become, or knowing they would become, doctors. I think of various small moments that led them to their choices: Rich hearing about a college named Tufts that was far from Brooklyn; Arthur, disillusioned with law school, remembering a sophomore psychology course he had taken; Jerry discovering that becoming a sociologist was not equivalent to becoming a social activist; Phil, believing (at twelve) that he would never be good enough to play for the Brooklyn Dodgers, deciding (at twenty) that he wasn't smart enough to be a research scientist either — and I think, too, of how other such moments in their lives, as in mine, have made all the difference: Rich deciding to go to the Redondo Beach Library on a day when one of my books happened to be displayed; Jerry, about to examine a woman whose sexual partner was infected with HIV, putting his hands on the woman's neck and feeling huge lymph nodes; and my deciding, just before getting off the phone with Rich, almost as an afterthought, to mention my shortness of breath.

In our conversations, then, I remark on the fact that their delayed discoveries of their vocations, so seemingly serendipitous — yet, looking back, so apparently inevitable: can they imagine *not* having become doctors? — have their parallels in the ways many of the most beneficial medical innovations of the past century have occurred.

The discoveries of penicillin and the fuller range of antibiotics that can destroy bacteria that cause infectious diseases (of streptomycin, for example, which provides an effective treatment for tuberculosis); of cortisone (steroids), which enhances the body's ability to heal itself; of antipsychotic medications such as chlorpromazine and lithium, which alleviate severe symptoms of some mental illnesses; of the bacterium (*Helicobacter pylori*) that is a cause of peptic ulcers — these discoveries, along with a host of others, have come about *not* because researchers were specifically working to find the causes and remedies they happened upon (cortisone was originally developed for rheumatoid arthritis; chlorpromazine for its analgesic effects in surgery; lithium as a salt substitute for heart disease) — but through chance, accident, and serendipity.

The stories of such discoveries provide a welcome corrective to the generally perceived notion that science proceeds from ignorance to discovery in a logical and linear way. Such a notion — reinforced in my own childhood by the worshipful attitudes that attended the advent of vaccines and cures for polio, smallpox, pneumonia, and other diseases, and encouraged later on by the optimism attending fund-raising campaigns dedicated to finding cures for cancer, muscular dystrophy, multiple sclerosis, cystic fibrosis, diabetes, leukemia, Parkinson's disease, AIDS, and other diseases for which cures continue to remain nonexistent no matter the amounts of money, time, and research expended on them — dies hard.

Witness, this past year, a Christmas letter in my mail from the actor Christopher Reeve, a letter reminiscent of the appeals I was hearing nearly forty years ago when Jerry Lewis, in his annual telethons, began soliciting donations of money to be used to find *the* cure for muscular dystrophy.

"May I introduce myself?" Reeve writes. "My name is Christopher Reeve. Perhaps you remember when I portrayed Superman.

"But after a riding accident in 1995, I've been paralyzed from the neck down, so I'm dictating this letter to you.

"Still I'm alive, and full of enthusiasm, because I believe that a cure for paralysis will be found before long!

"It can happen!

"I believe it because I head up the Christopher Reeve Paralysis Foundation, and I've talked to some of the world's leading specialists in spinal cord injuries.

"Please believe me, they are zeroing in on a cure," he reports, and in a postscript he asks us to "remember that research costs money and your holiday gift is going to help get people like me up and out of our wheelchairs." (In a TV ad for his foundation, Reeve is shown getting up and out of his wheelchair and, like Superman, once again flying up and away into the skies.)

How wonderful it would be if the multitude of diseases and ailments that continue to afflict us would be as amenable to reason, research, and the scientific method as, in the first half of the twentieth century, many infectious diseases were. How wonderful it would be if all we needed to find cures for disease would be to identify the problem, raise money, and set researchers to work. Our lack of success in finding cures for diseases we have expended great resources on, however — whether spinal cord injury or muscular dystrophy, breast cancer or influenza — hardly encourages such a hope.

Still, like my friends' discoveries of their vocations, or my discovery of my occluded arteries, the history of medical science and of scientific discovery reassures, and it does so because it turns out to be made up of what any interesting life, or story, is made of: the unpredictable and the unexpected — those small, unanticipated moments that turn out to have large and surprising issue.

And there is this too: because we know so little about the causes of most diseases, how much more wondrous are our triumphs when we *do* discover the cause or causes of a disease, and *do* find treatments that alleviate illness and suffering. That we are able to do so — to have available to us an extraordinary range of medications and treatments which, like antibiotics and bypass surgery, were undreamt of a few generations ago — and that we often discover these marvelous technologies *before* we possess any true understanding of why they are effective (for example, our use of lithium and chlorpromazine for bipolar disorder and schizophrenia before we understood the workings of neurotransmitters) — this heartens because it reminds us that medical science is not separate *from* life, but is part *of* life, and so it too is informed by mystery, wonder, and chance.

"The main discovery during this [twentieth] century of research and science," François Jacob, Nobel Prize winner in medicine in 1965 for his work in genetics, writes, "has probably been the depth of our ignorance of nature."

Thus Selman Waksman, a soil microbiologist who received the Nobel Prize in 1952 for his discovery of streptomycin and its uses in the treatment of tuberculosis, came to revise his initial understanding of the nature of antibiotics. Whereas at the time of his discovery he believed that antibiotics were "chemical weapons" produced by bacteria to maximize their own survival chances against other organisms, he later came to see that because antibiotics were limited to a very few species, they could not play a significant role in the ecology of microbial life generally. Moreover, the ability of microorganisms to produce antibiotics was highly dependent on the quality of the soil in which they lived, and could only be reliably produced in a laboratory. For these and other reasons, Waksman came to the view that antibiotics were "a purely fortuitous phenomenon . . . there is no purposeness behind them . . . [and] the only conclusion that can be drawn from these facts is that these microbiological products are accidental."

But why and how a small group of microorganisms that grow in soil should have the ability to create complex chemicals that can cure infectious diseases — why and how they exist at all! — remains, simply, unknown.

That Alexander Fleming, returning from a holiday in 1928, noticed that a contaminating mold in a Petri dish, one that was sitting in a pile of other Petri dishes and waiting to be washed, had inhibited the growth of a colony of staphylococcal bacteria; that an exceptionally cool nine-day period during his absence had favored the growth of this mold (*Penicillium notatum*), and that a subsequent warmer period had favored the growth of the staphylococcus that the penicillin, due to *its* growth during the nine-day cool period, was now capable of subduing; that Fleming chose not to explore his observation further; that it was not until other scientists (Howard

Florey, an Australian professor of pathology at Oxford, and Ernst Chain, a Jewish refugee biochemist from Nazi Germany), while revisiting Fleming's observations about the ability of lysozymes in tears and nasal mucus to dissolve bacteria, came across Fleming's observations about penicillin, and through a sequence of remarkable and remarkably serendipitous events (at the outset they assumed penicillin would have *no* clinical applications) not only discovered the miraculously beneficial qualities of penicillin (effective against staphylococcus, and also against the pneumococcus, gonococcus, meningococcus, and diphtheria bacillus, along with the bacilli of anthrax, tetanus, and syphilis), but elucidated the principles by which *all* antibiotics were to be discovered — such an unlikely and fortuitous series of events is an unexceptional (if marvelously instructive) example of how scientists have most often arrived at their discoveries and at technologies resulting from their discoveries.

When I reflect on the discoveries and technologies that saved my own life, and in so doing return to the moment, at Yale–New Haven Hospital, when I found myself wondering why it was we knew so little about how and why I had nearly died, I become aware of a paradox, one that, yet again, reminds us of nature's curious and mysterious ways: that those very processes within my body that enabled me to survive my childhood are implicated in the processes that nearly did me in when I was sixty.

In their 1994 book, *Why We Get Sick: The New Science of Darwinian Medicine*, Randolph M. Nesse and George C. Williams (in a chapter titled "Aging as the Fountain of Youth") write that "the whole immune system is age biased [because] it releases damaging chemicals that protect us from infection, but these same chemicals inevitably damage tissues and may ultimately lead to senescence and cancer."

Eight years later, on January 22, 2002, the *New York Times* headlines a feature article about inflammation and disease ("Body's Defender Goes on the Attack") with a similar statement: "Inflammation, a normal response of the body to infection or disease, can also cause problems. Scientists now consider that inflammation may have a major role in many chronic diseases not previously associated with it." Inflammation, the body's "fundamental way of protecting itself," the *Times* notes,

> can harm the very tissues it is meant to heal [and] its destructive side has long been evident in diseases such as rheumatoid arthritis, which cripples the joints, and multiple sclerosis, in which it destroys the insulation surrounding nerve endings.
>
> But now scientists are coming to realize that inflammation may underlie many other common chronic diseases that come with aging, including atherosclerosis, diabetes, Alzheimer's disease and osteoporosis. Inflammation is also implicated in asthma, cirrhosis of the liver, some bowel disorders, psoriasis, meningitis, cystic fibrosis and even cancer.

The article then quotes Dr. Russell Tracy, a professor of pathology and biochemistry at the University of Vermont. "It's beginning to look as if getting old and ultimately wearing down and dying," he says, "are tied inextricably with the defense mechanism that keeps you alive and in good repair when you're younger." The reason this is so "may reach far back into human history to the hunter-gatherers who lived in peril of infections and injuries," the *Times* hypothesizes. "Natural selection would have favored those with a vigorous inflammatory response and few would have lived long enough to suffer the long-term consequences."

The *Times* devotes much of the rest of a lengthy article to what both cardiologists and evolutionary biologists have been paying attention to for several years: the role of inflammation in atherosclerosis.

In an article published in *Nature* nearly three weeks before the *Times* article, a team of American, German, and English researchers reveal that a chance discovery about cellular life in mice has led them to the conclusion that the processes that inhibit the growth of cancers in our early lives, as in mice (whose cells are similar to our own), are probably responsible for hastening senescence and the aging process.

The discovery concerns p53, a protein present in every cell of our body (and in those of every mouse), one which, in reaction to any abnormality, especially one that endangers a cell's DNA, forces the cell either to stop growing or to destroy itself. Extensive studies have convinced scientists that cancer occurs when the p53 system in our bodies is somehow damaged, a belief validated by the knowledge that in 50 percent of all cancers, the DNA of the p53 gene is itself directly damaged and rendered useless; and in tumors where the p53 gene is not damaged, it appears that nearby components in its network are somehow made dysfunctional, thereby inactivating p53 indirectly.

In the course of studying p53, one of the researchers, Dr. Lawrence A. Donehower of the Baylor College of Medicine in Houston, engineered a strain of mice that lacked a working gene for p53. As expected, the mice without p53 died of cancer at an early age. Next, Dr. Donehower attempted to create a strain of mice in which the p53 had only a *single* inactivating change, one commonly found in human cancers.

The experiment did not go as planned, however, and Dr. Donehower and his colleagues were disappointed. "We made the mice and kind of forgot about them for a year," he says. He expected that the mice would, like those without any p53, develop cancer early. They did. "But first we noticed they were not just getting cancer when they should have gotten it," he reports. "We also noted that they looked kind of decrepit; they just looked like old mice."

What seems to have happened is that Dr. Donehower's team had inadvertently created mice that possessed unusually large amounts of p53, and that at the same time that the p53 protein was vigorously suppressing various cancers, including lymphomas, osteosarcomas, soft tissue sarcomas, and carcinomas, it was also aging the mice at a rapid pace — they lost weight and muscle, developed osteoporosis, hunched backs, and brittle bones, had generalized organ atrophy, diminished stress tolerance, sparser hair, and thinner skin, healed poorly from wounds, and died much sooner than mice with normal amounts of p53.

Although it is possible the mice suffered from some subtle pathology that resembles the aging process but is different from it, biologists such as Dr. Scott Lowe, of the Cold Spring Harbor Laboratory, are persuaded that the Baylor experiments "raise the shocking possibility that aging may be a side effect of the natural safeguards that protect us from cancer."

Like the blood and tissues of mice, our blood and tissues — our skin, the linings of our stomach and our other internal organs — suffer continual wear and tear, and are continually being repaired by new cells generated by a group of special cells known as stem cells. While we are young, stem cells are highly productive, and the fact that the p53 mechanism may be destroying lots of cells has little apparent effect on our early development. As we grow older and our stem cells become less prolific, however, more stem cells are forced to self-destruct, and our tissues weaken and stop functioning properly. "The mice [with the excess of p53] eventually reach a point in which the proliferative capacity of stem cells is so reduced," the study reports, "that sufficient numbers of mature cells cannot be provided to maintain organ homeostasis. The resulting phenotypes may include reductions in organ mass, function and tolerance for stress."

"The data presented here support a role for p53 in the regulating of aging and longevity in mice," the researchers conclude. "The association of early aging and tumor resistance in [these] mice is also consistent with the idea that senescence is a mechanism of tumor suppression. We propose that an aging-related reduction in stem cell proliferation may have a more important role in longevity than previously recognized."

What the study suggests, then, is that the process that connects childhood survival to aging with respect to inflammation has a parallel in a process that connects early survival from cancer to processes that cause our body's tissues to break down, deterioriate, and die.

"With the current study we realize the double-edged sword of p53," Dr. Lowe comments. "Without it we'd probably all die of cancer before the age of thirty, which is what happens to Li-Fraumeni patients [a syndrome wherein patients have a defective p53 gene]. With it, only one in three of us gets cancer late in life."

But why does only one in three of us get cancer? And why is it that two out of the two hundred mice with the extra p53 neither got cancer nor grew old prematurely? What enabled these two mice to avoid the cancer-or-aging syndrome — and will the same process that occurs in mice occur in us? Are the mice truly aging, or are they being affected by some pathology that *mimics* aging — and are there ways of cheating the p53 system genetically somehow by, say, creating a molecular pathway around it that will encourage its cancer-inhibiting qualities while simultaneously inhibiting its tissue-destroying qualities? Is the p53 mechanism merely modulating some more complex and as yet unknown mechanism implicated in the relation between metabolism and aging — and is it possible that the discovery of such a mechanism will enable us to understand more fully why it is, for example, that a mouse lives, on average, for three years, and an elephant for seventy?

And: Will the discovery of such a mechanism, should it exist, help explain why it is that though we have been able to increase our own average life *expectancy* considerably during this past century, the average life *span* of a human being remains fixed and finite?

Nesse and Williams explain: "During the past few hundred years, the *average* length of life (life expectancy) in modern societies has steadily increased, but the *maximum* duration of life (life span) has not. Centuries ago a few people may have lived to 115; today this maximum remains about the same. All the wonders of medicine, all the advances in public health have not demonstrably increased the maximum duration of life. "If aging is a disease," they conclude, "it seems to be incurable."

One way scientists who study the multitude of factors that contribute to the aging process have of understanding what happens, especially as it involves ways our DNA is damaged over time, is to note that the amount of maintenance and repair of our body tissues and DNA seems always to be less than what is required for indefinite survival. Researchers estimate, for example, that in the United States and Europe the complete elimination of mortality before the age of fifty, which now accounts for about 12 percent of all deaths, would result in an increase of only three and a half years to life expectancy.

There seem, then, to be inherent limits to how long we will, on average, be able to live, no matter the wondrous technologies we create to save and prolong our lives. That recent discoveries strongly suggest this is so with particular regard to the two major killers of our time, cancer and heart disease, is sobering news to anyone obsessed with what Phil calls "the Ponce de León thing." Just as heart disease may be the necessary price we pay for suppressing inflammation and infectious disease when we are young, that is, so the aging of our cells — the source of our mortality — may be the price we pay for suppressing cancer in our early years.

What impresses, too, when we consider the implications of studies suggesting such intimate connections between disease and our immune system — between survival and mortality — is that the more we learn about how and why we survive, and how and why we age and die — how what saves us at one point in our lives may do us in at another — the more natural and inevitable these processes seem, and the more our ignorance of nature becomes palpable.

Although we may, in what many consider the major scientific enterprise of our time, succeed in fully decoding the human genome and so map our genetic endowment in comprehensive detail, our immense genetic diversity, along with our evolutionary history, suggests that the more we discover, the more abundant and complex will be the new questions arising from our discoveries.

But how can this not be, given the complexity of any individual human being? Our genes, for example, exist in pairs, one gene coming from each parent, and the mathematical implications of this, as David Weatherall demonstrates, are staggering. "Genes that reside at the same place, or locus, on a pair of chromosomes are called alleles," he writes. "If the genes at these positions are identical we are said to be homozygous, whereas if one of these genes differs from the other we are called heterozygotes. It turns out that on the average we are heterozygous at about 6.7 percent of our gene loci. At first this does not sound like much genetic variability. However, since we have up to 100,000 genes, it follows that 6700 of them have different alleles. That means there are 2^{6700}, or in base ten arithmetic about 10^{2000} potential new combinations of genetic material that we can pass on to our children. This figure is so large that it is impossible to comprehend."

When it comes to the extraordinary medical procedure that saved my life — coronary bypass surgery — once again it turns out that the technology has been made possible in large part by innovations and discoveries that were not initially directed toward solving cardiological problems, much less toward enabling open-heart surgery.

In his study of the scientific origins of modern cardiology, Weatherall details the ways modern cardiology is, in fact, "a highly technical field that relies on the fruits of work in many disciplines, among them electrophysiology, physics, immunology, and pharmacology." When researchers tried to determine how much of the research that has produced benefits in cardiology was "basic," Weatherall informs us — that is, not directed at a particular clinical question — and how much of it "set out with the express objective of tackling a medical problem," they "found that only 60 percent of the seminal work in modern cardiology was clinically directed and that the remainder was in the basic sciences and had not been carried out with any particular end in view."

There would be no coronary bypass surgery (or coronary transplant surgery), for example, without the heart-lung machine — our ability to shut down the heart and continue to oxygenate the body's circulatory system so as to keep us alive during the hours needed for surgeons to repair (or transplant) our hearts. And here, again, the story of how the heart-lung machine came into being, like that of the discovery of penicillin, is wonderful in the ways it is informed by the chance turns of experience — by what we ordinarily call *timing* (as in "timing is everything") — and by the vagaries and quirks of individual human character.

John Gibbon, the man most responsible for the development of the heart-lung machine, did not, like my friends, start out intending to become a doctor. Raised in an atmosphere of privilege — French governess, private schools, Princeton education, country properties, European tours — he wanted to become a poet or painter, but enrolled in medical school to appease his father, who was himself a professor of surgery (the second American to try to suture a wound in the heart). Gibbon's grandfather, great-grandfather, and great-great-grandfather had also been physicians.

Like Rich, Gibbon was bored by the first two years of medical school. He decided to quit, and told his father he would be doing so. Like Rich, however, he finished medical school, and accepted a two-year internship at Pennsylvania Hospital, during which time he assisted in carrying out a hypertension study. This exposure to research excited his imagination, and he next went to Massachusetts General Hospital to continue his studies under the direction of Dr. Edward D. Churchill. It was here that he was assigned to a team that was caring for a woman on the verge of death. As with Rich, what happened next — or rather, in Gibbon's circumstance, what did *not* happen — changed his life, as well as the course of cardiac care.

The woman had had a gall bladder operation and was recovering well until, two weeks after surgery, she developed a pulmonary embolism — a blood clot in her lungs. On October 3, 1930, Gibbon sat by the woman's bedside for seventeen straight hours, checking her pulse rate and monitoring her blood pressure at fifteen-minute intervals. After seventeen hours, the woman lapsed into unconsciousness, and her pulse and breathing stopped. Gibbon called in his mentor, Dr. Edward D. Churchill, who attempted to save the woman's life by surgically removing the clot and closing the artery, which operation he performed in the incredibly swift time of six and a half minutes. Gibbon's mentor, alas, was not as successful as Rich's mentor would be three decades later. Deprived of blood for more than six minutes, the woman's brain died, and then she died too.

The experience so disturbed Gibbon, he later wrote, that while "helplessly watching the patient struggle for life as her blood became darker and her veins more distended," he began considering the possibility that lives such as this woman's could be saved by a machine that would "do part of the work of the patient's heart and lungs outside the body."

After completing his fellowship in Boston, Gibbon returned to the University of Pennsylvania Hospital, where for the next three and a half years he operated in the mornings and worked on a heart-lung machine in the afternoons — and at home, at night, and on weekends.

He assembled his first heart-lung machine — the prototype for the one we use now — from a secondhand air pump he bought for a few dollars, and from one-way valves he produced by cutting flaps on the sides of rubber stoppers with a razor blade and inserting glass tubes through their centers, after which he fitted these stoppers into slightly larger tubes. He worked assiduously and obsessively, and he persisted in this work for thirty-three years.

In 1970, he described some of what he had done in order to bring into existence a machine that has, in the last four decades, enabled several million people to survive previously inoperable, intractable, and often fatal conditions.

"My wife and I carried out . . . slightly bizarre experiments on ourselves and our friends," he wrote. "We were particularly anxious to learn how slight a shift in body temperature would cause vaso-constriction or vasodilation of the extremities. We got a very sensitive mercury thermometer about three feet long, which would measure temperatures to a hundredth of a degree Centigrade. The bulb of this thermometer would be stuck into my rectum or that of a friend, and the subject would then swallow a stomach tube, down which we poured as much ice-cold water as could be tolerated, measuring the effect on skin temperature of the fingers. I also once got my wife to give me an ice-cold intravenous solution for the same purpose."

(When I say to Rich that if more than a half century ago Gibbon and his friends had not stuck three-foot thermometers up their asses while chugging down ice-cold water, I probably wouldn't be alive today, he nods. "You got it," he says.)

In 1952, after practicing open-heart surgery on dogs, Gibbon attempted for the first time to use his heart-lung machine while operating on the hearts of human beings. The results were disastrous. All his patients died, and Gibbon was so discouraged that he never again attempted open-heart surgery. Nor was Gibbon the only one who was discouraged. "Pessimism was rampant," writes Dr. Walter Lillehai, whose experiments with cross-circulation (a procedure wherein blood is passed not through an oxygenator but through a human volunteer) became a crucial element in the eventual success of open-heart surgery, "[and] by early 1954 the surgical world had become thoroughly discouraged and disillusioned of the feasibility of open-heart surgery."

Although Lillehai believed, in 1954, that "the concept of open-heart correction, however attractive, was doomed," his success in that same year, using the technique of cross-circulation in repairing the hearts of children afflicted with Fallot's tetralogy (a birth defect afflicting so-called blue babies, and resulting from defects in the blood vessels and walls of the heart chamber), dispelled the notion that open-heart surgery was impracticable. Encouraged by their successes with children, Lillehai and others began working to see what modifications and improvements they could make on Gibbon's pump.

At the same time that Gibbon was attempting to operate on human beings while using his heart-lung machine, other surgeons, intrigued by studies of hibernating animals reported on by a Canadian surgeon named Wilfred Bigelow, were experimenting with a different method of making heart surgery possible: cooling the heart to reduce the body's need for oxygen, thereby allowing surgeons more time for their work.

Within a decade of Gibbon's failures, improvements in Gibbon's machine brought about, for example, by the invention of plastic and the substitution of plastic tubing for glass tubing, combined with techniques for cooling the body, for chemical cardiac arrest, and for ventilating the lungs, made Gibbon's dream of doing the work of the heart and lungs outside the body — and what we know as modern cardiac surgery — a reality.

16 🐝

The Prepared Heart

LATE IN THE AFTERNOON of December 26, 2001, my son Eli and I meet at Grand Central Station and take a train north to New Haven in order to spend an evening with Jerry and his family. Jerry, who has just returned from a four-month stay in South Africa, picks us up at the New Haven station.

My journal entry the next morning begins:

December 27, 2001

wonderful reunion with Jerry Friedland! He looks marvelous, loves to hug — what an earth mother of a guy! sweeping wavy silver hair, beard, gorgeous smile — so happy to see me and Eli, and talks almost non-stop re his time in South Africa. Home for 10 days, and figures he has, still, 20% retention of the experience. hard to return, esp to the stuff at Yale — hates the administrative stuff, and (he sez) is not good at it. but the South Africa experience: transformative. (Phil to me, earlier in day: this is what he will do for the last third of his life.)

In the car, Jerry talks about how sophisticated and "Western" much of South Africa is, and he reminds us that the first heart transplant was performed there by Christiaan Barnard (who was Dr. Lillehai's surgical assistant at the University of Minneapolis Medical School in the late 1950s). Still, most blacks are poor, most whites are rich, and South Africa also has the greatest gaps he has ever seen between haves and have-nots. "If you could make New York City ninety percent Harlem, and ten percent Upper East Side," he says, "you would have the picture."

Violence in South Africa is rampant; a recent incarnation involves the widespread raping of young girls, often nine and ten years old, largely a result, Jerry explains, of the myth that having sexual relations with a virgin will lend one immunity from AIDS. Most white people have taken to hiring their own private security forces, so that even the police force in Durban, where Jerry and Gail were living (Gail stayed for two of the four months), employed a security firm to protect them.

Jerry's daughters, Elisabeth (recently engaged to be married) and Sarah (on semester break from a study-abroad program in Cuba), are at home, and in addition to me and Eli, there are five other guests — Brigette and her four children, ages three to ten. Brigette, Jerry and Gail's babysitter when they lived in Boston, now lives with her husband and children in Brooklyn, a few blocks from Erasmus. "Does the world go round?" Jerry asks.

Dinner is festive — lots of good food, good wine, good talk, and laughter — and during dinner Jerry is gently ebullient and glowingly optimistic — happier and more energized than he has been in years. He talks with enthusiasm about the projects he has begun in South Africa ("I am a guest there," he says, "and I want to lend my expertise. It is their country, their AIDS problem, and my hope is to be a catalyst — to be able to help them help themselves"), and says he continues to be guided by the saying he took to heart during his previous visit — that the best time to plant a tree is twenty years ago, but that the second best time to plant a tree is now.

The rates of infection are staggering, he tells us, but what he also became aware of soon after his arrival was that a very high percentage of the nursing and hospital staffs are themselves infected, and so he has been working to develop a program in which the first people to be treated when antiretrovirals become available will be hospital staff members. Because the government refuses to acknowledge HIV as the cause of AIDS, and will not pay for antiretrovirals, the program will have to be administered through the private sector, but Jerry has already convinced one hospital to start such a program. He is confident it will do well — "the antiretrovirals *work!*" he exclaims — and his hope is that success in this hospital will encourage others to initiate similar programs.

"It's estimated that 25% of nursing students and 10–15% of medical students are HIV infected. Can you imagine?" he had written me in early October. "But no encouragement for testing and no antiretrovirals."

In that same letter he wrote about another project he hoped to initiate: integrating HIV and TB prevention and treatment. "The HIV infection rate is 50% among hospital admissions," he wrote.

> There's a 25% in-hospital mortality rate and TB is the most common admitting diagnosis and cause of death among those with HIV. There's minimal connection between the TB programs and the rest of health care and the need to integrate HIV and TB treatment and prevention is so clear, but not done. My TB project to attempt to do this is gathering momentum and hopefully will get off the ground before I leave. I have some colleagues interested in working with me on it and there is enthusiasm for the project but the wheels grind slowly.

I ask about the HIV/TB project and he says that it too is off the ground, and going well. In addition, believing that the primary cause of HIV infection is unsafe sex (a subject not talked about openly), and that the cause of unsafe sex is usually alcohol or drugs (as happens everywhere else, people get high and don't take precautions), he has initiated several programs in education and prevention. He has been flying to various parts of the KwaZuluNatal province with the Red Cross and other doctors to get these programs started and, also a first for the province, to give seminars on HIV to local health professionals.

"I talk about the prevention and management of opportunistic infections, the construction of multidisciplinary comprehensive programs, and antiretrovirals," he explained in another letter, "with the hope and expectation that at some time in the not too distant future, they will have them available."

The overall situation, however, remains grim.

"It's 7 AM, and Gail and I are home this morning of Yom Kippur," he wrote two weeks after his arrival. "My work is going too slowly and I am becoming impatient — but will stay focused and do the best I can. I think things are now getting on track. New figures here estimate that over 4.7 million South Africans are now infected (total population 43 million) — the equivalent of at least 40 million Americans infected in the USA. Most will die."

Nevertheless, he talks enthusiastically about the possibility of progress in the new South Africa, and uses the same words now that he used when writing to me. "There is," he says, "both sadness and amazing hopefulness here."

"The thrill of defeating apartheid has passed and the huge and mundane and seemingly intractable problems left in its wake now must be dealt with —" he wrote on Yom Kippur —

> residual economic inequalities that make the US look like a socialist utopia, racial and religious divides, the boundaries of which are sometimes crystal clear and sometimes so subtle that we need to have them pointed out and translated to us, a fearful sense of danger — violent crime against property and person so that much of life goes on beneath walls and behind fences (how can there be safety with such inequalities?). And now — AIDS. Yet, there is a determination as well to try to make this very diverse and disparate country whole.

Given the scale of the problems, he says, one cannot think globally. For his part, he hopes to return to South Africa soon (in early January, he will fly there for a week), and he plans to spend at least three months of every year there. "It's really simple, Neugie," he says quietly. "I could not just watch. I had to go there. I had to do something — to contribute."

After dinner, and after we have cleaned up the dining room and kitchen, Jerry and I sit in the living room, just the two of us, and Jerry says that if he remembers correctly, this is the first time Eli has stayed over since I was operated on three years ago.

I say that Eli mentioned the same thing during our train ride. We talk about Eli and Sarah, who are good friends, and who, from the time they were young children, clearly adored each other, and we joke, as we have before, about how, were we living in a *shtetl* in the Old Country, we would already have had them promised to each other. We talk about Jerry's sister Rita, afflicted with Alzheimer's disease, who continues to deteriorate, and about my brother Robert, who continues to make gains.

Robert has now been out of the state mental hospital for nearly two and a half years — the longest stretch since his first hospitalization forty years ago. He has a life, I say, and he is not locked up: he gets around the city on his own, he goes out of town on excursions, he attends classes (horticulture, photography, poetry), he works part-time, he has friends, and we see each other regularly.

Jerry asks how the book is coming along, and I say that it appears to be in its final descent, and that what I've been learning these past several years about my friends, and about medicine, has been both inspiring and sobering.

Learning more about Jerry's work in Boston, the Bronx, New Haven, and now in South Africa, for example, has brought home something we knew before, but with more urgency — that the great problem in health care, as he contends, is *access* to health care, and that the first priority is finding ways to make access available to all. The gap in access to basic and competent care between the haves and have-nots remains shamefully wide, even in our own nation, while in the world beyond the United States, the availability and accessibility of even minimally competent medical care are often absent.

Jerry says he does not want to diminish the horror of what happened on 9/11 (in the weeks following the World Trade Center tragedy he wrote me that he and Gail almost returned, their grief and concern were so great) — still, given his work, it is hard not to contrast the response to the deaths of some three thousand people in New York with the response to the millions infected and dying from AIDS around the world. We know that in South Africa alone, five to seven million people will die within the next decade — and that an estimated twenty-five million people in sub-Saharan Africa are infected with HIV, about three million of whom will die annually. We have the means to treat and save most of these people, yet the will to do so is frail and lacking in the extreme. ("I've been musing about how we have such difficulty responding to slow crises," Jerry wrote two weeks after 9/11, "and so little to sudden catastrophes. Do you think it's in our genes?")

We know how to cure a case of TB for fifteen dollars, yet we also know that many poor countries cannot afford even that amount for people with TB. We know how to administer childhood vaccines, a blessedly inexpensive measure (twenty-six cents for a vaccination against measles) that would save three million lives a year, yet in many poor nations vaccine coverage is rapidly falling. In the world's sixty poorest nations, the annual average health spending per year is thirteen dollars. In the United States the figure is $4,500.

Nearly eleven million children, according to the United Nations and the World Health Organization, die each year of *preventable* diseases, eight million of them babies, half of whom die in the first month of life. The causes of death are mainly diarrhea, malaria, measles, pneumonia, HIV/AIDS, and malnutrition, and the major cause of these diseases is poverty — lack of access to proper food, water, and sanitation.

The response of our own nation to the worldwide situation, we agree, has been disgraceful. Of the twenty top industrialized nations, the United States devotes the smallest percentage of its gross national product toward efforts to control international epidemics. When the United Nations launched the Global Fund for AIDS, Tuberculosis, and Malaria, for example, and the secretary general proposed that between seven and ten billion dollars per year would be needed, our government promised only five hundred million dollars, this sum to be spread over three years, and, more niggardly still, to be taken largely from funds *already designated* for existing international health programs, including those for maternal and child health in developing countries.

In addition, because most pharmaceutical research is done by drug companies, and because they have little incentive to produce medicines for people who cannot pay for them, the illnesses that constitute 90 percent of the burden of global disease get only 10 percent of research money. Moreover, only a small percentage of pharmaceutical research money is spent on *new* medications for already existing, newly emerging, or reemerging diseases. The rarer a particular disease, that is, or the poorer the group that has it, the less chance — tough luck, right? — a drug company will develop medications to ameliorate its effects.

Mostly, I say, I've stopped arguing with people about the necessity and responsibility to do what we can, at home and abroad, for those without adequate medical care. One either believes one is, in this, one's brother's keeper — that we are obligated to see that as many people as possible receive at least minimally adequate health care — or one does not. How persuade another of this view if that person believes it is his or her inalienable right to be a free agent acting in a free market where whoever has enough money gets the best possible care, and the hell with everyone else?

As George J. Annas, chairman of the Health Law Department at the Boston University School of Public Health, has observed, because Americans place a high value on liberty and autonomy, especially as these inform market values, they feel they always have a choice, and "choice rhetoric has assumed such prominence in public discourse that merely labeling something as a 'choice' has a tendency to arrest conversation and prevent more than superficial analysis of the nature of the choice in question."

If you "couple the power of choice with the language of rights," Annas adds, "the combined force is all but irresistible." But "market language," he continues, "with its emphasis on choice, tends to marginalize the sick and treat the practice of medicine as just another occupation, and medical care itself as just another commodity, like breakfast cereal."

The notion that choice is always good and government interference with individual choice always bad is, Annas explains, "socially destructive and leads to a law of the jungle with those in power feeding off those for whom choice is always an illusion."

Whatever our beliefs about "market values," or about which system or systems of health care would be most humane and effective, what seems clear, as Annas states, is that "the use of choice as an incantation prevents us from looking more deeply into the causes of real problems, and therefore from trying to solve them."

In his book *Some Choice*, he elaborates on this view of "choice" with reference to a wide range of medical, legal, and ethical issues, and, as with the common instance of teenage sex and pregnancy, he makes the obvious and salient point: "Choice and coercion language simply serves to stop discussion of the much deeper problem of teenage pregnancy and sex, instead of providing an opportunity for deeper reflection and social commitment to try to solve it."

But being generous toward others — or, at the least, when considering one's own health needs, taking into account the basic needs of people and communities beyond our individual selves, families, and nation — while seeming a good thing in itself, would, with respect to health care — like honesty? — also seem to be the best *policy*. As the AIDS epidemic has shown, *all of us* are in danger if, in the global village we now inhabit, we deny the ways in which what happens to a human being in Durban — and to a microbe that infects someone there — has an effect on a human beings in New York or Northampton, Tokyo or Guilford.

The success of bypass surgery, for example — of *all* surgery — is dependent upon our ability to prevent infection. But what happens when antibiotics are so abused and overused that they bring into being a host of pathogens that prove antibiotic-resistant and make us *more* vulnerable to infection? What happens when medical teams have the knowledge and technology to transplant kidneys, eyes, hands, livers, and hearts, but are prevented from doing so because the risks of lethal infection have once again, as in the nineteenth century (when surgeons did not wash their hands), become overwhelming?

Like my friends, I am prepared to put forth specific policy suggestions with respect to a wide range of issues and problems — cholesterol and PSA screening, international vaccination programs, AIDS education programs, the education of medical students, the integration in medical training of public health with clinical care, the regulation of antibiotic use, the financing of care for people with chronic, disabling illnesses, et cetera.

Still, I say to Jerry, our conversations and my researches persuade me that what is more important than new policies — though these are always welcome, and let's not hesitate to advocate for programs we believe will make real and meaningful differences — are the *attitudes and assumptions that underlie and drive policy*, and that therefore determine how resources are allocated.

When it comes to attitudes and assumptions, however, much of what I've been learning hardly seems new, or news. What, through the years, Jerry and I have believed would be helpful and necessary with respect to the prevention, diagnosis, and treatment of people with AIDS and with mental illness would also seem to apply to most diseases, and to most matters medical.

It would be helpful and good, for example, to think — and to act — more in terms of care than of cure, and to think long-range rather than short-term; to think more in terms of early intervention and prevention — of encouraging and expanding public health measures, and investing in basic research — than in terms of end-of-life patch-up technologies; to think in terms of implementing policies that encourage continuity of care, and doctor-patient relationships that are ongoing, so that we thereby encourage the trust essential to so much of good medical care; to think of balancing the often excess amount of screenings and testings (much of it inspired by the fear of malpractice suits) with the need to give doctors and patients more time with each other.

And, for starters, Jerry and I agree, it would be helpful and good — essential — to enact some form of universal health care, because it is in *all* our interests that health care, like the services we receive from police departments and fire departments, be available to everyone and be distributed equitably.

But to do such things, of course, we need to have a coherent approach to health care, and to be able to set viable priorities — to have what, virtually alone among industrialized nations, we do not have: a national health-care policy. How impose regulations, or even sensible guidelines, on a system that is strictly voluntary? How, for example, plan in any practical, long-range way for the enormous and ever-increasing numbers of people who, suffering from chronic conditions, will need the kind of care that is already in unacceptably short supply?

"The demand for autonomy and choice, as well as for high-quality care," Daniel Callahan explains, "represents values that can be scaled back considerably without loss in actual health." It is important, therefore, he submits, "to decide what we are after most: better health, greater choice, or some wonderful combination of both."

Callahan notes the obvious — that "we probably cannot have

both in equal degrees," without, in the name of the public good, being willing "to exempt some health care policies and decisions from the market ideology." Because "whether we like modifying our basic values or not, it seems impossible to achieve equity and efficiency without doing so."

"The demand for priorities," he points out, "arises when we try to live with both decent minimal care and limits to care. At that point we must decide what it is about health care that advances us most as a society and as individuals. We have bet that we could have it all. That bet is not paying off. There remains no reason, however, that we cannot have a great deal."

Valuing freedom of choice over constraints, and individual freedom over government regulation in the specific ways Americans do, we seem a long way from knowing how and when, if ever, we will be able, if in inevitably imperfect ways, to set reasonable and effective national health-care policies.

The reasons are many and complex, the questions numerous, the answers various and debatable: Who will be empowered to deal with the difficult decisions that setting national health guidelines will entail? And who will empower, and watch over, those empowered? Who should get (enormously expensive) organ transplants or implanted defibrillators, for example, and who should pay for them, and how, and should there be age criteria, and how rigid or flexible should such policies be, and who will enact, monitor, and regulate them? Should we, as a nation, continue to invest heavily in so-called lifestyle technologies and in end-of-life technologies, or find ways, consistent with free enterprise (no small task) to redirect resources toward child and infant care, for example, or toward providing higher salaries and better training for health-care workers who tend to people with chronic diseases? Should we allow drug companies to advertise prescription drugs directly to consumers — and what about conflicts-of-interest between drug companies and doctors, insurance companies and hospitals? And just how, in the face of economic restraints, do we balance the claims of better health (for all? for some?) against the claims of individual choice, and are there practicable ways of arriving at good if imperfect combinations of the two? (If your own child, spouse, or parent is seriously ill, don't *you* want to be able to obtain the very best care possible, and the costs — and fairness and equity for others in similar situations — be damned?) Do we have any obligation to curb the aggressive marketing practices of American tobacco companies abroad (for example, having pretty young women give out free cigarette samples) in a world where, according to the Centers for Disease Control and Prevention, tobacco will, within the next twenty years, cause more deaths in developing nations than AIDS, malaria, TB, automobile crashes, homicides, and suicides combined? And how provide and pay for antiretrovirals for all those infected with HIV, here or elsewhere, in a world where greed is often rampant and poverty itself, as Jerry insists, is a disease?

In short, that is, what do we do to make it more possible today than it was yesterday to bring about a situation where increasing numbers of people have access to doctors like my friends, and to the kind of care, and kindness, that they gave me, that they directed me to and monitored, and that I was fortunate enough to receive?

The basics seem fairly clear: Listen to the patient. Make use of the marvelous technologies now available for virtually every disease and condition, but don't be beguiled by them. Be humble before our ignorance of nature. Encourage any and all policies and programs that encourage and enable trust, and that provide for greater access for greater numbers of people to good health care.

The paradox, though, is this: The more complex, useful, and abundant our technologies are, the *more* essential, in employing the technologies and in interpreting their information, a doctor's judgment about each individual patient becomes. Yet the more a doctor knows, from reading, research, and clinical experience, the more, like the Socratic wise man Jerry and I learned about in our freshman courses at Columbia, he becomes aware of how little he knows. It is this humility, however — this ability to say "I don't know" — that allows doctors to be open to those possibilities that make all the difference: in their minds and imaginations, in their researches, and in the particular cases before them.

A hundred years ago, William Osler, reflecting on what he called "the uncertainties of medicine," spoke of "this everlasting *perhaps* with which we have to preface so much connected with the practice of our art."

"Surely," Sherwin Nuland comments, "many would say, things are different in the current era of molecular biology. Paradoxically, the opposite is true. The remarkable advances of ultramodern biotechnology have brought with them complexities of such magnitude that medicine sometimes seems in danger of being overwhelmed by forces of increasing intricacy and incomprehension . . . What conclusions are to be drawn from a hard-to-interpret test of liver function? In what situation is it better to recommend angioplasty rather than coronary bypass? Which of three possible antibiotics is best for a particular resistant bacterium?"

The problem — and, thus, the challenge — is how best to enable the education of knowledgeable and humane doctors, to provide the environments and conditions in which the judgment and skills of such doctors can thrive, and — no small order — to enable increasing access for others to these doctors. Clearly, to judge from my researches, and from conversations with friends and family — with doctors *and* patients — a managed-care system in a health-poor world, no matter its apparent or acknowledged inadequacies, will for many reasons, not least among them inertia and self-interest, tend to resist reform, change, and transformation.

Yet change it will — and has — in response not only to market pressures and internal review and self-criticism, but to pressure from doctors, patients, and advocacy groups who represent doctors and patients. Managed care is a system that began with the promise of reducing the growth of health-care expenditures and initiating accountability from doctors and hospitals with regard to where those insured were cared for, what services were provided, and at what cost, and to do so through various strategies — gatekeeping, restoring the role of primary-care physicians, improving health maintenance and preventive services, reducing administrative costs, providing a more organized structure for thoughtful peer review, instituting practice standards and incentives for achieving these standards, et cetera. As David Mechanic has noted, managed care represented "a shift from relatively invisible fee rationing to more obvious rationing of supply through either implicit processes (capitation) or explicit controls (utilization management)."

But whatever managed care's achievements, medically and/or economically, they have been eclipsed in the public mind, Mechanic notes, "by excessive profit seeking and marginally useful organizational strategies that challenge public trust and patient confidence."

Managed care is not, however, some evil, monolithic beast, but merely the name we often give to those parts of the health-care system that we find — and that too often are! — lamentable, infuriating, and wanting, and that we perceive as originating in certain new modes of organization and practice that came into being in the late 1980s. Before that time, when what we know as fee-for-service prevailed, doctors and hospitals had few restrictions on how they conducted their activities — on what services and procedures they performed, on what referrals they made, on what medications they prescribed, or on what they charged.

But managed care — dominated by large corporations in which people with little background in medicine make major decisions about medical care; claim greater accountability and responsibility while often being accountable and responsible, primarily, to shareholders; and encourage efficiency and reduced expenditures with incentives that reward doctors for withholding care (thus placing doctors' and patients' interests in direct conflict) — has simply become the term that designates a wide variety of health-care plans. It is a synonym for the system that, in its heterogeneity, now prevails and that provides medical care — good, bad, and mediocre — for most of us.

Sitting in Jerry's living room on a midwinter night, and talking about the kinds of things Jerry and I usually talk about, a familiar feeling rises in me — an optimism, doubtless naive, that says: As long as we have doctors like Jerry in the world, all will yet be well. We were boys together, and now we are men, I think, and then another thought, one that has been with me frequently since my surgery, also returns, and it does so in the form of a wish: that everyone should have friends and doctors like my four friends — that everyone should be able to count on friends and doctors they can trust more readily than themselves.

But how to make this happen? We might begin, if only begin, it occurs to me, by thinking in terms of what my friends and I have been talking about — providing those contexts in which greater access to care, continuity of care, long-term care, preventive measures, and public health measures are encouraged and endowed. If, too, we restore the doctor-patient relationship to a central position in medical care, and if we avail ourselves of the marvelous technologies that exist while at the same time remaining skeptical of those technologies that are more expensive than they are curative (and that cause us to neglect more urgent health-care needs), then, I say to Jerry, we have a pretty good shot at making it happen.

If you keep making the right moves, I suggest, eventually the shots go in, though when I repeat the old schoolyard saying, I note that *eventually* is the longest word in the sentence. The technologies and expertise *are*, blessedly, all around us — what we *need*, as with antiretroviral therapies, is the wherewithal that enables us to use them wisely and widely. What we need, as Jerry keeps reminding us, are the attitudes, leadership, and — above all — *the will* that can transform possibilities into probabilities.

A recent study of neonatal intensive care units, a *New England Journal of Medicine* editorial points out, raises "disturbing issues regarding the nation's unquestioning acceptance that more is always better with respect to the supply of specialist physicians and hospital technology." In this national study, researchers found that "regions in the highest quintile of supply had more than four times as many neonatologists and neonatal intensive care beds per 10,000 births as regions in the lowest quintile." Yet this variation in resources had little relationship to the needs of the populations being served, the study discovered, and a greater supply of specialized neonatal services did *not* result in better outcomes for the infants (as measured by the risk of death within the first twenty-seven days of life).

How explain the abundance of neonatalogists and neonatal care

beds, the authors ask, and the fact that "the distribution of these resources bears so little relation to community health needs"?

"One important explanation," they bluntly suggest, "is money,"
since "nenonatal intensive care units are profit-making centers for
hospitals, commanding high payments from private and public insurance plans." The number of specialists in the United States has
tripled in the last forty years, they note, and expensive forms of technology have proliferated. "At least in the case of neonatology," they
conclude, "this uncontrolled growth has less to do with the true
need of communities for effective clinical services rather than with
the financial incentives promoting specialization" and is therefore
"emblematic of how a market-driven health care system with inadequate public planning" can produce "too much of a good thing" and
can come *"at the expense of underinvestment in less glamorous primary care and public health services that avert poor outcomes"* (italics
added).

Recent findings concerning the problematic value of mammograms, and of hormone replacement for women (I am writing this
in July of 2002), make us realize, alas, that the passion for screening
— for early detection and treatment of certain diseases — may, like
the excess of neonatal care units, often be less than valuable. And
what good is a treatment that alleviates one condition yet puts an
individual at greater risk for another, more deadly condition? What
good is it to know you have a disease for which nothing can be done
— or, as with young children tested for the Huntington's disease
(HD) gene, what is gained for the child who learns that he or she
will be afflicted with a late-onset disease that cannot be prevented
("who will be labeled as already 'sick,'" George Annas notes, "and
lose his or her right to decide whether to be tested for the H gene")?

Listen to the patient — of course — but we shouldn't forget that
we, the patients, should also listen to those doctors who listen to us.
Despite our ability to fix what was wrong with me (though we might
not have been able to do so had I not, as Rich says, gone to high
school with the right guys), my researches, my experience, and —
most of all — my talks with my friends make me increasingly certain that in medicine we do best when we begin by understanding

what they have taught me — that, as Osler wrote, "medicine is a science of uncertainty and an art of probability."

"Is radical mastectomy the best treatment for breast cancer?" Sherwin Nuland asks. "Is drinking coffee associated with an increased risk of pancreatic malignancy? Should every ruptured spleen be removed? Is a low-fiber diet the best treatment for chronic diverticulitis? Is acid production by the stomach the key factor in peptic ulcer? Should every man, or nearly all men, with prostate cancer, have surgery? Are most cases of impotence psychosomatic? The answer to every one of these questions was once 'Yes' and is now 'No.'"

After dinner, at breakfast the next morning, and on the way to the New Haven train station (after we arrive at Grand Central Station, Sarah and Eli will head off to the Museum of Modern Art, and spend the day together), Jerry and I fill each other in on what our friends are doing. Isn't it wonderful, he remarks, that in our early sixties — at an age we used to think of when we were growing up as really *old*: as an age when one retires and becomes less active — we are each setting out for new territory.

Jerry is planning, for the first time since he started out as a public health doctor in Nigeria nearly forty years ago, to fulfill a dream deferred: to devote increasing amounts of time and energy to international work in the developing world.

Rich, continuing to teach at the University of California at Irvine medical school and to do private consulting work in cardiology, has completed drafts of several new books, drafts he sends to me for my comments — and he has even, his most recent venture, begun writing a novel: a thriller about a terrorist network that infiltrates our nation's Department of Health.

Phil, reversing the conventional pattern, has left his home in a Denver suburb and moved into the downtown area. (But what to do about his office? A possible solution, I suggest, is to donate it, intact, to the Smithsonian, so that centuries from now children can look in through a glass wall, the way we looked in at reconstructed rooms of colonial homes in the Brooklyn Museum when we were boys, and see what a typical doctor's twentieth-century study was like.)

Phil continues to work long hours as a practicing neurologist, and the idea of retirement is incomprehensible to him. "I think you should be a player," he says. "As long as you're alive and have most of your marbles and can make a contribution, you should try to be a player in the world. I don't think I would be content just to walk around a golf course figuring out what to do next — where the big issue of the day is where to go for supper, or on your next vacation. I want to be a player, you know? To do more sculpting, to learn to sketch better, maybe to discover something — with respect to spinal-cord injury or brain injury, or with MS — that would be helpful to people. I think it keeps you from becoming demented."

He laughs. "Not that you can't get demented if you're a player. But I think two things kill. One is isolation — what I worried about in your case, when you had the surgery. And the other is feeling that you're of no use to anybody else in the world.

"I mean, the idea of retirement where the entire day revolves around what you're going to eat at your next meal is obscene. It's a meaningless existence. So in terms of my own work, I'm more excited than I've ever been. I think about MS a lot, and about other diseases we don't have answers for, and — as with Friedreich's ataxia, where we know the recessive gene — I think about how, if we could just figure out how to get that gene transplanted into the cells and working, we could maybe cure an incurable disease."

Arthur has sold his two-bedroom apartment in New York and moved into a condominium apartment outside Princeton, New Jersey, one built on land that was formerly an arboretum. He has also bought a smaller, one-bedroom apartment in New York City. He has given up his private practice completely ("If I survived Vietnam," he says, "I can survive retirement"), and he and his wife Paulette, who has retired from her law firm, intend to divide their time between the Princeton area — they are already enrolled in courses at the university there — and New York City.

Arthur continues to provide therapy and consultation for former patients — and, several hours a day, for family and friends by the dozens — and he also now puts in one day a week at Gilda's Club in Manhattan, where he works with individuals diagnosed with cancer, and with those close to them. In the wake of 9/11, and given his extensive experience with trauma victims and people suffering from post–traumatic stress disorders, he has offered his services to various organizations in and around New York City, including the police and the Red Cross.

But he is not rushing into his new life. "If people make a quick change or transition in situations like this, they usually revert to what's familiar," he says on the day movers come to take away his office furniture (he laughs when he tells me that their next stop, after his office, is Woody Allen's apartment). "That's why, if somebody is dumped in a relationship, the first person they usually try to connect with is a previous boyfriend or girlfriend — they want to connect with somebody who had once accepted them.

"But I'd rather stumble and bumble for a while before I move into a new life," he explains. "I want to do something new, something different. I've been talking with a lot of people — in the police department, at the UN, in Princeton, in different charities — some people are urging me to write a book — but I'm in no rush.

"What I'd like to do, you see, is not be so frightened of the unknown. And most of the world is unknown to me, from astronomy to exotic travel, and I've never poked around in them and if I don't poke around now I'll die without having done so. So I'm interested in bio-ethics, for example, and, when I fantasize, in contributing to dialogue in and around the operation of a media enterprise — TV, newspapers — but I don't know if I'm going to be strong enough to do it — to process the world in new ways, to have the life I have while generating a new and different life for myself.

"I've gone through life seeing most things through psychological eyes and in terms of interpersonal relationships, and I don't want to see the world this way for the rest of my life — through a single prism. Life's just too various and interesting."

In June 2001, I left my position at the University of Massachusetts, rented my Northampton house to a family with two children, and moved back to New York City, where I now live and write full-time.

Shortly before we head upstairs for sleep, Jerry and I talk again about the time before and after my surgery, and he asks if he ever told me about how my children reacted when I came out of the operating room.

I say that he didn't.

"Well, I brought them to the recovery room," Jerry says, "and they asked if they could see you, so I think I pulled a little string — I don't remember exactly — but we got permission to go in and see you. Apparently, however, Aaron is very queazy about these things."

I say that ever since he was a small child, Aaron has had a needle phobia — that he has fainted several times in doctors' offices when he had to receive injections, and that he even fainted once when, for a routine test, a nurse merely pricked his finger to get a few drops of blood.

"Well, I didn't know that," Jerry says, "but he described the same thing, and it wasn't clear whether he'd be able to do it or not, so I went in and saw you first, and you were completely out of it. But you looked clean and nice. Still, you had tubes coming out here and there, and drains, and this and that.

"Actually, you looked like hell," he says, "but very *clean* — like someone in a casket made to look nice — and quite peaceful, because you were unconscious. So I came out and said, 'You know, I'm not sure you're going to be able to do this, Aaron, because your Dad is fine, but he doesn't look so great. It's very high-tech stuff, and he's attached to all these things,' but Aaron said, 'I want to go.'

"So the four of us — actually five, with Seth — all walked in and just stood around your bed, and everybody looked at Dad, and Aaron was a little pale, but he toughed it out. And I think they were reassured because although you were tied into everything like a space cadet, you looked nice and clean, if a little bit dead, and I think they were relieved to see that you were still alive and had made it through the surgery.

"We walked out of the recovery room and down to the waiting room, and everyone was very complimentary and congratulatory to Aaron, who had really steeled himself for it and pulled together every ounce of his *koiyach* — his strength — to do it. And I think he felt good about himself.

"We went home then, and came back the next day, and you were walking already, and advertising your huge incisions, and after that you had a completely remarkable recovery and at every point you kept saying how fortunate you were.

"Gail and I were grateful — that you were alive, and that we were able to provide a place for your kids. It was very satisfying for us to see them all assembled — to see how important you are in their lives."

I nod, but, as on the evening before surgery two years before, find that I can't speak.

"And I guess I'm also remembering now that Fred Sachs came to see you."

"Yes," I say. "He stopped by to visit me at least once a day, and on the second day, I think it was, he brought me a book about Brooklyn — it had lots of photos, including some of Erasmus and of other places we remembered."

Fred Sachs was associate chief of medicine at Yale, and he had gone to Erasmus with us. At the time of my surgery, Jerry says, Fred was dying from prostate cancer, but he kept the news quiet and never told anybody.

"Do you remember that he had intended to come to the talk you gave a few weeks before your surgery, for the program in Humanities and Medicine, but he called at the last minute and apologized?" Jerry asks. "So that was the reason he couldn't come — because he was very sick with the prostate cancer."

"When Fred visited with me," I say, "we talked easily — as if we'd last seen each other a few weeks ago, instead of forty years ago, and he had the sweetest smile and the kindest manner. He was a brilliant and very unassuming guy."

"Yes he was," Jerry says. "Everybody at Yale loved him. He was very smart, very gentle, very modest. He was a good doctor."

"When we were growing up, Fred lived around the corner from me, on Linden Boulevard, and we used to walk to and from school together sometimes," I say. "I sent him a copy of *Transforming Madness* when it came out a few months after surgery, with a letter in which I said I hoped we'd be able to get together the next time I came down — the three of us — but by the time the letter got to him, he was gone."

Jerry makes sure the fire in the fireplace is out, and then we head upstairs to go to sleep. He gives me a hug goodnight, and I find myself thinking that yes, those qualities that lie at the heart of friendship — that allow us to see and appreciate one another for who we are and thereby to more truly know one another — that inspire trust, constancy, kindness, and generosity — these also lie at the heart of what we hope for in our doctors. I comment again on what I've been thinking about in recent weeks — the parallels between our lives and the ways in which doctors and scientists have often come upon their insights, diagnoses, and discoveries — and on the contingencies of chance, accident, and sheer good luck that conspired to return my life to me — and I quote Pasteur's remark, that "where observation is concerned, chance favors only the prepared mind."

Jerry smiles. "What I think, Neugie," he says, "is that in your case, chance favored the prepared heart."

Acknowledgments

I have benefited enormously from the good sense, expertise, and judgment of friends and colleagues. For early conversations and ongoing encouragement, I am especially grateful to Madeleine Blais, Bob Brick, Jerome Charyn, George Cuomo, Joseph Epstein, Robert Goldstein, Phil Graubart, Sam Tsemberis, and Douglas Whynott. In the course of my research and writing I have had the good fortune to be able to call upon several physicians for information, clarification, and explanations, and am pleased to be able to thank them here. Thanks, then, to Doctors Oscar Garfein, Michael Posner, Sam Rofman, Olav Thorsen, and Gerd-Ragna Bloch Thorsen. For their skills and generosity — for helping to return my life to me — I remain forever in the debts of Doctors Henry Cabin and Sabet Hashim. I am in debt, too, to their staffs, and to the personnel of Yale–New Haven Hospital.

For helping me check out, and enhance, my understanding of specific matters, I am grateful to Paul Ewald, Henry Harpending, Kim Hill, Magdalena Hurtado, Kenneth Ludmerer, David Mechanic, Renee Pennington, Louise Russell, and Allan Silver. Elise Feeley, reference librarian at the Forbes Library in Northampton, Massachusetts, has been a constant friend and resource. Greg Tulonen, in the early months of research, and James Zarnowiecki, in the final months, have provided excellent bibliographical assistance. Jane Rosenberg, of Eva Productions, has searched out much data for me and brightened many a cloudy day.

I owe an especial debt to Gerald Grob, who talked with me all through the writing of this book, from its inception to its completion. Along the way, he referred me to sources, corrected errors, read the entire manuscript, and offered numerous and useful suggestions. His generosity and friendship heartened me and sustained me. Doctors Martin Baskin and Rita Charon also read the entire manuscript and provided helpful reactions and comments.

For invaluable technical assistance, I am grateful to Kim Florek and Merek Press. I am grateful, too, to Susan Zorn, who performed a masterful job of copyediting.

My children, Miriam, Aaron, and Eli, have been wonderfully generous in talking with me and bearing with me throughout the writing of this book. Their love, palpable and deep, is an endless source of joy. My brother Robert's good heart and good will remain an inspiration.

I am blessed in having Richard Parks for an agent and friend. He has shepherded this book, and this author, through many hills, forests, and valleys. I cherish his friendship, his great good sense, and his indefatigable attention to detail.

From our earliest discussions, when I did not know whether or not I could or should write this book, my editor, Susan Canavan, has been a dear friend to me and to my writing. Her skills, and her intuitions, are exceptional, and I have depended upon them mightily.

What to say about Jerry Friedland, Rich Helfant, Arthur Rudy, and Phil Yarnell? They helped save my life, and then they continued, as before, to grace it with their friendship. We were boys together, and now we are men, and to know them, as men, as doctors, and as friends, is, literally — and more and more with the years — to love them. They gave of themselves unconditionally: in hours and hours of conversation, in exchanges of letters, in the reading of drafts of the entire book, and in that ongoing dialogue that is truly life-giving. They did so frankly, warmly, with endless optimism, realism, and good cheer, and without giving any hint, ever, that I was burdening them. The deficiencies of this book are mine. Whatever value it possesses is due largely to them. I trust that *Open Heart* does honor to them.

Notes

1. How Little We Know

4 *He tells me:* The medications Dr. Cabin puts me on are Tenormin, a beta-blocker (slows the heart rate and the force of heart contractions, and lowers blood pressure); Vasotec, an ACE (angiotensin-converting enzyme) inhibitor (helps lower blood pressure and makes the heart beat stronger by preventing particular enzymes from narrowing blood vessels); Lescol (lowers cholesterol levels and reduces inflammation); and aspirin (thins the blood, prevents clotting, and also reduces inflammation).

5 *Hundreds of thousands:* For a delightful, informative account of bypass surgery, see Joseph Epstein's "Taking the Bypass: A Healthy Man's Nightmare," *New Yorker* (April 12, 1999), pages 57–63. In 1999, according to the 2002 Heart and Stroke Statistical Update, published by the American Heart Association, 571,000 coronary artery bypass surgical procedures were performed on 355,000 patients in the United States.

9 *Although he describes:* Jerome Groopman's essay "Heart Surgery, Unplugged: Making the Coronary Bypass Safer, Cheaper, and Easier" (*New Yorker* [January 11, 1999], pages 43–51) is an excellent primer on bypass surgery and its attendant risks. "By now," Groopman writes, "heart surgeons have mastered the techniques of grafting and suturing, and for those patients who qualify for the operation success rates are excellent — greater than ninety-five percent."

Groopman reiterates what Rich has told me — that the majority of serious side effects and fatalities

result not from surgery itself but from the heart-lung machine. The problems begin as the cooled blood flows over the machine's porous membranes: when oxygen bubbles into the blood, it "roughs up" the blood cells. The white cells, which serve to protect against infection, become less effective, and the rate of postoperative infection is relatively high. The roughed-up cells also release inflammatory substances, which irritate the lungs. The blood platelets are damaged by the artificial oxygenation, too, and the patient becomes prone to bleeding. More damage is caused by small clots — composed of blood fats, proteins, platelets, and clumped red blood cells — that form around the oxygen bubbles. When these clots are infused back into the patient, they may block capillaries in sensitive tissues, like those of the brain, the retina, and the lung. Patients on the heart-lung machine have a two-to-four-percent risk of stroke and a twenty-five-percent risk of transitory retinal damage. And from thirty to fifty percent of patients will experience a syndrome [called] "pump head," in which they suffer significant cognitive deficits: memory loss, inability to concentrate, difficulties in recognizing patterns, and an inability to perform basic calculations. Although the cognitive deficits usually subside over a period of weeks or months, they may delay recovery, and some physicians suspect that they contribute to the clinical depression that often afflicts patients after heart surgery. In addition, patients retain about twenty pounds of fluid as a result of the dilution of their blood in the machine and the trauma of surgery, and this excess fluid puts a further strain on the heart and the lungs. In fact, the very sick or the elderly have been considered ineligible for bypass surgery simply because they are too fragile to withstand the rigors of the heart-lung machine.

11 *And this was ten months:* The figure of ninety-eight thousand deaths via medical errors appeared in the *New York Times,* November 30, 1999 ("Group Asking U.S. for New Vigilance in Patient Safety," by Robert Pear), and is based on a study done by the National Academy of Science's Institute of Medicine. Readers should also see "Policing Health Care," by Lawrence K. Altman, and "Preventing Fatal Medical Errors," both in the *New York Times,* December 1, 1999. A follow-up article on deaths due to medical errors, "Getting to the Core of Medical Mistakes," by Lawrence K. Altman, appeared in the *New York Times,* February 29, 2000. Beginning in its June 4, 2002, issue (I am writing this in June 2002), the *Annals of Internal Medicine* is running a series of eight articles that report on medical errors.

My friends' insistence that I go to a major hospital is also borne out in a recent study, "Hospital Volume and Surgical Mortality in the United States," published in the April 11, 2002, issue of the *New England Journal of Medicine (NEJM),* pages 1128–1137. The study, based on data from 2.5 million procedures — cardiovascular procedures and cancer resections — concluded that "in the absence of other information about the quality of surgery at the hospitals near them, Medicare patients undergoing selected cardiovascular or cancer procedures can significantly reduce their risk of operative death by selecting a high-volume hospital." See also the accompanying editorial, "Volume and Outcome — It Is Time to Move Ahead," in the same issue (pages 1161–1163).

13 *When Rich calls:* Here is Dr. Hashim's description of the surgery, from the "Discharge Summary":

> On 2/12/99, coronary artery bypass graft surgery times five was performed using left internal mammary artery to the left anterior descending artery, free right internal mammary artery to the ramus intermedius artery, radial artery to the right posterior descending artery, saphenous vein graft to the diagonal artery, saphenous vein graft to the obtuse marginal artery. Total pump time was one hour and 55 minutes. Total crossclamp time was one hour and 11 minutes.
>
> An intraoperative transesophageal echocardiogram revealed preserved global function with an [*sic*] left ventricular ejection fraction of 50%, no regional wall motion abnormalities, mild mitral regurgitation, no aortic insufficiency, no tricuspid regurgitation, no shunting, normal pulmonary vein and transmitral flows, no thrombus, no effusion, poorly visualized aortic distal arch. Post pump there were no changes except the ejection fraction was improved to 60%.
>
> The patient tolerated the procedure well and was weaned from cardiopulmonary bypass without the use of intropic support and transferred to the Cardiothoracic Intensive Care Unit in stable condition where he awoke from anesthesia with no neurological deficits.

And here is Dr. Cabin's description of what the cardiac catheterization revealed: "Severe triple vessel coronary disease with an ejection fraction of 30–35%. His right coronary artery and left circumflex coronary arteries were totally occluded and filled via collaterals and he had a 95% stenosis of the proximal LAD [left anterior descending artery]."

But note that Dr. Hashim's description of cardiac catheterization is slightly different — a reminder that these numerical figures are not absolute "scientific" realities, but estimates: The patient "underwent cardiac catheterization on 2/11/99. This revealed normal left main. The left anterior descending had 80% stenosis. The circumflex had 95–100%. The right was 100%, left ventricular end-diastolic pressure was 16–20, left ventricular ejection fraction was 30–35%."

When Rich returns the postoperative reports to me, he adds a note: "FYI. Looks great — you're going to outlive all your EHHS buddies! Love, Rich."

3. The Consolation of Diagnosis

25 *Celebrating:* Compare the chimera of total body transplants to this —
sixty-five years ago — from "Lindbergh, Carrel & Pump: They Are
Looking for the Fountain of Age," in the June 13, 1938, issue of *Time:*

> From this moment [we are] opening to experimental investigation a for-
> bidden field: the living human body [Dr. Carrel says] . . . Organs re-
> moved from the human body, in the course of an operation or soon after
> death, could be revived in the [Charles] Lindbergh pump, and made to
> function again when perfused with an artificial fluid . . . When larger ap-
> paratus are built, entire human organs, such as pancreas, suprarenal,
> thyroid, and other glands . . . would manufacture *in vitro* the substances
> supplied today to patients by horses or rabbits.

"In effect," *Time* declares, "Dr. Carrel, with the Lindbergh pump, is
looking for the fountain of abundant, replaceable age."

"It makes an arresting picture," *Time* concludes, "one that French,
Roman Catholic Dr. Carrel is romantic and mystic enough to appreciate — two men, one an ageless seer, the other a young and devoted inventor, sitting on two rocks in the middle of a sea, talking, planning
ways to prolong the life and end the ills of mankind."

Compare also (this time, thirty-eight years ago) a September 24,
1965, *Life* magazine feature, *"Control of Life: Part 3, Manmade and
Transplanted Organs Usher In an Era of Rebuilt People,"* in which we find
the following statement: "So confident are medical researchers in the
feasibility of heart replacement that the U.S. government has launched
a crash program to subsidize the development by industry of an im-
plantable heart that could be put into human patients within five
years."

For a sane, fascinating history of the hopes and disasters that accompanied the attempt to build and implant these artificial hearts, see
Renée C. Fox and Judith P. Swazey, *Spare Parts: Organ Replacement
in American Society.* More often than not, sad to say, the people in
whom these experimental machines were placed seemed to be kept
alive mainly to keep the machines going.

For an excellent overview of the ethical issues involved, see Stanley J.
Reiser's essay, "The Machine as Means and End: The Clinical Introduction of the Artificial Heart," in *After Barney Clark: Reflections on the
Utah Artificial Heart Program,* pages 169–175. "Machines," Reiser writes,
"also can become key agents of a view developed through the Scientific Revolution that nature should be mastered, not lived with. What
greater act of domination could we as humans devise than to substitute
a machine for the most conspicuous agent of life, the heart?" Reiser
alerts us to the dangers of our infatuation with technology: "The ideal

of a value-free science and a compelling desire to apply rapidly what we can produce make for a powerful combination in a modern world in which the capacity to produce innovations may outstrip our capability to wisely integrate them into the fabric of personal life and societal objectives. The creating of technologic means simply comes easier to us than the development of rational and humane ends to apply them" (pages 174–175).

26 *Consider, though:* The data concerning drug-resistant organisms in hospitals are from Laurie Garrett's *Betrayal of Trust: The Collapse of Global Public Trust,* page 278. Jane E. Brody, in a *New York Times* article, "A World of Food Choices, and a World of Infectious Organisms" (January 30, 2001), states that "the potential for widespread disaster has definitely expanded." She cites a study from the Centers for Disease Control and Prevention, which found that "food-borne illness accounts for a staggering 76 million illnesses, 323,914 hospitalizations and 5,194 deaths each year in the United States." In addition, "The disease-control centers estimate that E. coli O157:H7, which was unknown as a cause of food poisoning before 1980, now infects as many as 20,000 Americans a year and kills up to 500."

In our time: The quotation regarding the downgrading of the interaction between patient and doctor is from James LeFanu, *The Rise and Fall of Modern Medicine,* page 223.

27 *Or consider:* The 15 to 75 percent figure regarding the disparity between television resuscitations and actual resuscitations comes from Dr. Richard Horton, "In the Danger Zone," *New York Review of Books* (August 10, 2000), pages 30–34 [30].

28 *And though nearly 40 percent:* The figures regarding the percentage of women who fear dying from breast cancer come from "Fearing One Fate, Women Ignore a Killer," by Benjamin J. Ansell (*New York Times,* January 9, 2001). Readers should also see "Lessons of the Heart: A Devastating Lack of Awareness," by Denise Grady (*New York Times,* June 24, 2001).

Despite our sophisticated testing: For the difficulty of diagnosing heart disease, see especially Chapter 11 of Richard H. Helfant's *The Women's Guide to Fighting Heart Disease.*

The American Heart Association reports: AHA 2002 Heart and Stroke Statistical Update, page 11.

29 *But we now learn:* Stephen Klaidman discusses the absence of ruptured plaque in people who experience heart attacks in *Saving the Heart: The Battle to Conquer Coronary Disease,* page 214.

In addition, studies: For basics concerning statins and their relation to heart disease, see the *New York Times,* January 24, 2001, "Heart Study Affirms Value of Statin Drugs." See also "U.S. Panel Backs Broader Steps to Reduce Risk of Heart Attacks," May 16, 2001, by Gina Kolata; and "Cholesterol Fighters Lower Heart Attack Risk, Study Finds," November 14, 2001, by Lawrence K. Altman. See also "Early Statin Treatment Following Acute Myocardial Infarction and 1-Year Survival," by Ulf Stenestrand and Lars Wallentin, in the *Journal of the American Medical Association (JAMA)* 285:4 (January 24–31, 2001), pages 430–436; and "Executive Summary of the Third Report of the National Cholesterol Education Program (NCEP) Expert Panel on Detection, Evaluation, and Treatment of High Blood Cholesterol in Adults (Adult Treatment Panel III)," in *JAMA* 285:19 (May 16, 2001), pages 2486–2497.

Concerning statins as the best-selling drugs, *IMS Health*'s "Drug Monitor" states, "Top 5 best selling drugs for the 12 months ending March 2002 was [*sic*] again Lipitor, Losec, Zocor, Ogastro, and Norvasc. *Lipitor* continued to show the highest growth in the top five at 29% at constant exchange" (emphasis theirs).

But the paradoxical finding: Louise Russell discusses the correlation (and lack of same) between cholesterol and heart disease in *Educated Guesses: Making Policy About Medical Screening Tests*, pages 45–74.

30 *Furthermore, these risk factors:* For an analysis of the "alternative explanation," see Joseph B. Muhlestein, "Chronic Infection and Coronary Artery Disease," in *Medical Clinics of North America* 84:1 (January 2000), pages 123–148. Readers should also consult P. W. Wilson et al., "Prediction of Coronary Heart Disease Using Risk Factor Categories," *Circulation* 97 (1998), pages 1837–1847.

In an article entitled "C-Reactive Protein, Inflammation, and Coronary Risk," we find the following: "Despite progress in the prevention of cardiovascular disease, a significant proportion of first cardiovascular events occurs among individuals without traditional risk factors" (David A. Morrow and Paul M. Ridker, *Medical Clinics of North America* 84:1 [January 2000]). See also Paul W. Ewald, *Plague Time: How Stealth Infections Cause Cancers, Heart Disease, and Other Deadly Ailments* (page 117): "If all the noninfectious risk factors are combined, they explain only about half the risk of acquiring atherosclerosis. In other words, about half of the people with atherosclerosis acquire it even though they do not have elevated risk factors for the disease. Something big is missing from the picture."

In addition, some researchers: David Weatherall discusses the correlation between low birth weight and the risk of heart disease in *Science and the Quiet Art: The Role of Medical Research in Health Care*, pages 173–174. See also a study by D. J. P. Barker et al., "Fetal Nutrition and Cardiovascular Disease in Adult Life," *Lancet* 341 (1993), pages 938–941.

"in both healthy subjects": Information regarding the predictive power

of established risk factors versus exercise capacity comes from Jonathan Myers and Manish Prakash et al., "Exercise Capacity and Mortality Among Men Referred for Exercise Testing," *NEJM* 346:11 (March 13, 2002), pages 793–801.

31   *But they are:* Klaidman discusses the unreliability of using diagnostic tests such as angiography as treatment guides: "In recent years, however, it has become clear that angiography is not good enough. It does not spot all blockages in the coronary arteries, and more importantly, many of the ones it misses, either because they are relatively small or not in the biggest arterial channels, are more likely to cause heart attacks than most of the ones it identifies" (page 206).

"Put a patient": When, in the spring of 2002, my doctors in New York City — my general practitioner and cardiologist — suggest I go on a low dose of beta-blockers, since statistical studies indicate that they prevent heart attacks in people who have already suffered from heart disease, Rich disagrees. My resting heartbeat is now about 48 to 50 (my blood pressure steady at about 115/75; my cholesterol 148; HDL 43; LDL 75), and the beta-blockers would lower my heart rate even further. Rich sees no need for it: the possible gains are not worth what he sees as the probable risks associated with the long-term use and side effects of any medication. When I call Martin Baskin, my family doctor (an internist), and tell him what Rich has said, he laughs. "Well," he says, "that's why medicine is an art, and not a science."

Compare the clinical judgment of a doctor, and its relation to a doctor's training and clinical experience, to the following, from an interview with Lincoln Quappe, a firefighter who died in the World Trade Center on 9/11:

When you're in a fire, things are running through your brain a million times a minute, and you're just trying to do your job. In those situations you look back at your experience. You think, I got burnt the last time I stayed around in this situation. I won't let that happen to me again. You go by all the telltale signs and from what other firemen have told you. Guys say, Listen, we saw this happen. We talk about fires all the time. We're constantly learning, learning every day, and even in a mundane fire you learn something, and you're like, Oh, man, I didn't know that. Or I forgot about that, but now it's reinforced in my mind. I've been burnt before so I have an idea of how much heat I can take . . .

It's hard to say which fires are most dangerous. Each is completely different. Some fires that seem small can be the most horrific with firemen dying. Even a silly little fire can get a guy killed. It all comes down to fate. But there are signs that you can pick up on at a fire when it's getting bad. I don't have all the answers but I have an idea when it's time to go. I use other guys in my company as barometers. I'll be in contact with my guys. I know what they look like as far as body features. I hear them on the radio. If Bobby says it's time to get out, I'm going. I use him as my guardian angel, because I know he's seen a lot of things in the past. The captain too. If the captain says, We're getting out of here, I'm going. I don't want to die here.

(*New York Times,* "A Voice from the Rubble," interview by Tom Downey, September 23, 2001)

31 *"In fact":* See Russell, for example, pages 58–60, for a discussion of the variability and unreliability of laboratory test results.

Lab tests for cholesterol are not alone in being unreliable. When a federal environmental initiative designed to cut down on the use of mercury, which can pollute air and water if not disposed of properly, led hospitals and doctors to switch from mercury-based blood pressure cuffs to electronic cuffs, leading medical experts, joined by the American Heart Association and the National Heart, Lung, and Blood Institute, questioned the reliability of the electronic blood pressure cuffs. Many critics claimed they are often dangerously flawed and give readings that can be in error by 30, 40, or even 50 points. See the front page article by Gina Kolata, "Risk Seen in Move to Replace Gauge of Blood Pressure," *New York Times,* June 16, 2002.

32 *By contrast:* LeFanu discusses this paradox ("the more tests a doctor performs . . ."), and Medawar's views on the "art and science" of medicine, on page 222.

"would go further": Sherwin Nuland, "Whoops!"(a review of Atul Gawande's *Complications: A Surgeon's Notes on an Imperfect Science),* *New York Review of Books* (July 18, 2002), pages 10–13 [11].

. *Thus, for example:* Both LeFanu (page 222) and Russell (pages 10–11) provide clear, informative discussions of the significance of false positives and unnecessary treatments.

33 *Even if one receives:* Klaidman, page 173, cites the low effectiveness of so-called optimal treatments.

"Clinical judgment": Ibid., page 174.

34 *"The cardiologists":* Ibid., pages 173–174.

"The great secret": Lewis Thomas, *The Lives of a Cell: Notes of a Biology Watcher,* page 100.

What happens: "Contrary to expectations," David Mechanic writes in *NEJM* 344:3 (January 18, 2001), page 198, "the growth of managed health care has not been associated with a reduction in the length of office visits. The observed trends cannot be explained by increases in physicians' availability, shifts in the distribution of physicians according to sex, or changes in the complexity of the case mix . . . The average duration of office visits in 1989 was 16.3 minutes according to the NAMCS and 20.4 minutes according to the SMS survey. According to both sets of data, the average duration of visits increased by between one and two minutes between 1989 and 1998." Still, partly because, as Mechanic notes, "physicians are expected to do more now than they were in the past during each visit with a patient" (page 202), both patients and physicians — everyone *I* talk with — continue to believe that office visits are, or seem to be, shorter.

35 *These studies also show:* Concerning gatekeeping and patient trust, Mechanic writes, "Aware that their physicians are uncomfortable with some issues, patients must either directly broach the issue, which may undermine their close relationship, or keep their problems to themselves and thus forgo treatment that would be covered by their insurance. Either way, trust in the physician is strained." *JAMA* 275:21 (June 5, 1996), page 1695.

 "the perpetually increasing": John Kirklin's comment is from Klaidman, page 173.

 "While directors": Salvatore Mangione and Linda Z. Nieman, "Cardiac Auscultatory Skills of Internal Medicine and Family Practice Trainees: A Comparison of Diagnostic Proficiency," *JAMA* 278:9 (September 3, 1997), pages 717–722.

36 *"if they did not":* Osler's adjuration to his medical students is from Michael Bliss's marvelous biography, *William Osler: A Life in Medicine,* page 270. In addition to being an excellent biography of Osler, Bliss's book gives us a rich, fascinating, well-informed history of medicine and medical practice during the years of Osler's life, 1849 to 1919.

37 *"50 percent":* On the basis of an interview with Stephen Oesterle, Klaidman (page 192) cites the figure of 50 percent for unnecessary angioplasty. See also "Study Finds Inefficiency in Health Care; Employers Are Said to Pay $390 Billion a Year in Unneeded Costs," by Milt Freudenheim, *New York Times,* June 11, 2002.

 In addition, many cardiologists: Klaidman calls our attention to such conflicts of interest on page 192ff; readers should also see a series of articles entitled "Medicine's Middlemen," in the *New York Times:* "Medicine's Middlemen: Questions Raised of Conflicts at 2 Hospital Buying Groups" (March 4, 2002), by Walt Bogdanich; "When a Buyer for Hospitals Has a Stake in Drugs It Buys" (March 26, 2002), by Mary Williams Walsh; and "Hospital Group's Link to Company Is Criticized" (April 27, 2002), also by Walsh. (Other articles in this series appeared on April 23, April 30, and June 7, 2002.) See also Melody Petersen, "Methods Used for Marketing Arthritis Drug Are Under Fire" (April 11, 2002) and "Suit Says Company Promoted Drug in Exam Rooms" (May 15, 2002), both in the *New York Times*. For a recent view of what might be done to prevent or manage conflicts of interest, see "Managing Conflicts of Interest in the Conduct of Clinical Trials," *JAMA* 287:1 (January 2, 2002).

38 *"All they know"*: Klaidman, page 223.

"The time invested": Bernard Lown, *The Lost Art of Healing*, page 16.

"The good physician": Francis Peabody's speech, "The Care of the Patient," is reprinted in *The Caring Physician: The Life of Dr. Francis W. Peabody*, by Paul Oglesby, pages 155–174.

39 *In all significant categories:* A. K. Jha, M. G. Shlikpak, W. Hosmer, C. D. Frances, and W. S. Browner, "Racial Differences in Mortality Among Men Hospitalized in the Veterans Affairs Health Care System," *JAMA* 285:3 (January 17, 2001), pages 297–303. For information on the gap in health care for blacks, see Sheryl Gay Stolberg, "Race Gap Seen in Health Care of Equally Insured Patients," *New York Times*, March 21, 2002.

40 *"some patients":* The quotations from Hippocrates and Plato are from Stanley Jackson's *Care of the Psyche: A History of Psychological Healing*, page 40.

For the two million people: Concerning the condition of people living in poor nations, Helen Epstein and Lincoln Chen write,

> Indignation over the high cost of AIDS drugs has helped focus international attention on the global AIDS epidemic and by the end of 2001, an antiretroviral drug cocktail could be obtained in some developing countries for $300 to $500 per year, many times less than the price in the West. However, for a variety of reasons, including the sluggishness of government bureaucracies, the stinginess of drug companies, and the fact that even at these low prices the drugs are still too expensive and difficult to distribute, few AIDS patients in developing countries are actually receiving these drugs or, for that matter, any modern medications at all beyond the cheapest antibiotics. ("Can AIDS Be Stopped?" *New York Review of Books* (March 14, 2002), pages 29–31 [30])

Readers should also see "How Sick Is Modern Medicine?" by Richard Horton, *New York Review of Books* (November 2, 2002), pages 46–50 (especially page 50).

41 *And the key element:* Jerry has published a number of papers on adherence and antiretroviral therapy, papers demonstrating that adherence is central to successful suppression of HIV, and that trust — the doctor-patient relationship — is central to successful adherence. He has also, in these and many other papers, suggested strategies that make trust — and success — more likely. See, for example: A. Williams and G. H. Friedland, "Adherence, Compliance, and HAART," *AIDS Clinical Care* 9:7 (1997), pages 51–54, 58; F. L. Altice and G. H. Friedland, "The Era of Adherence in Antiretroviral Therapy," *Annals of Internal Medicine* 129

(1998), pages 503–505; G. H. Friedland and A. B. Williams, "The Future: Attaining Higher Goals in HIV Treatment: The Central Importance of Adherence," *AIDS* 13, Suppl 1 (1999), pages S61–S72; B. Soloway and G. H. Friedland, "Antiretroviral Failure: A Biopsychosocial Approach," *AIDS Clinical Care* 12:3 (2000), pages 23–25, 30; and F. Altice, F. Mostashari, and G. H. Friedland, "Trust and the Acceptance of and Adherence to Antiretroviral Therapy," *Journal of Acquired Immune Deficiency Syndromes* (2001), pages 47–58.

43 *Nor, in two-thirds:* Klaidman, page 222, argues that "invasive treatments such as surgery and angioplasty are being used without good evidence that they provide any survival benefit over drugs. Where a benefit is provided, it is in pain relief and exercise tolerance." See also pages 180–181.

Rates of restenosis — a return of blockages after angioplasty, stenting, or bypass — vary widely. A study in *Circulation* (November 2001) reports as many as 40 percent of patients having a return of blockages and requiring additional treatment; after six months, 607 out of 2,690 patients (reported on in this study) had blockages of 50 percent or more in the arteries where angioplasty had been performed. Early studies of stents coated with an immunosuppressive drug are promising and show restenosis rates below 5 percent. See "Comparison of Angioplasty with Stenting, with or Without Abciximab, in Acute Myocardial Infarction," by Gregg W. Stone et al., in *NEJM* 346:13 (March 28, 2002), pages 957–966; and also "A Randomized Comparison of a Sirolimus-Eluting Stent with a Standard Stent for Coronary Revascularization," by Marie-Claude Morice et al., in *NEJM* 346:23 (June 6, 2002), pages 1773–1780.

When I ask Rich about this, he writes back: "Restenosis: without stent — 30–50% after 3–6 months; with stent — 20–30% after 3–6 months; with drug coated stent — < 5%. But this is based on VERY preliminary experimentation, and history shows that early enthusiastic reports do NOT hold up. Should be helpful, but how much (in my mind) is an open question."

44 *"a significant mental decline":* As to postsurgical depression, according to the *New York Times,* "there are no conclusive statistics about the incidence of depression after surgery. Estimates vary widely, from fewer than a third of patients to more than three-quarters" (Randi Hutter Epstein, "Facing Up to Depression After a Bypass," *New York Times,* November 27, 2001). The quotation regarding mental functioning after bypasses is from "Mental Decline Is Linked to Heart Bypass Surgery," by Denise Grady, *New York Times,* February 8, 2001. See also, for example, *Circulation* 105:1176 (2002).

45 *"the kinds of things":* Thomas, pages 35–42.

4. It's Not Viral, Goddamnit!

49 *My journal entry:* I have transcribed my journal entries as in the original, complete with abbreviations, spelling errors, grammatical errors, and gross lapses of judgment.

64 *"V worried":* When Rich reads this journal entry, he writes that he is struck by two things: First — your deep premonition and recognition that you had a life-threatening illness, despite what your doctors were telling you. I've long believed that on some level, patients *know* how sick they really are, and how close they are to death, but for whatever reason (overwhelming fear, admission of vulnerability), need to keep it a deep, dark secret within. Second is that the pain was . . . often too in chest . . . shit!" You certainly NEVER told me about that, and I doubt you told your docs. I've long suspected that patients often keep crucial tell-tale symptoms from "the doctor," know that the diagnosis they dread will probably then be made . . .

65 *"The Berlin-born":* Nuland, *How We Die: Reflections on Life's Final Chapter,* page 33.

66 *I have dinner:* When I call my friend John O'Sullivan, a physical therapist, and describe my symptoms for him and tell him that Doug thinks the problem is muscular but that I've been worried it might be my heart, he says it doesn't sound like a muscular or rotator cuff problem, and advises me to see a cardiologist. (I call him after I arrive home from Yale–New Haven. "You were right," I say, and tell him the story.)

70 *This property of aspirin:* For the story of Dr. Craven and aspirin, see Weatherall, pages 103–104; and LeFanu, pages 311–312. For more recent views of aspirin's uses, see Weatherall, pages 103–104; LeFanu, pages 311–312; Michael S. Lauer, "Aspirin for Primary Prevention of Coronary Events," *NEJM* 346:19 (May 9, 2002), pages 1468–1474; and both "Aspirin: Superhero or Problem Pill?" and "How Aspirin Works Its Magic," by Abigail Zuger, *New York Times,* April 18, 2000. See also an October 24, 2002, article in *NEJM* by Dennis T. Mangano and others, "Aspirin and Mortality from Coronary Bypass Surgery," which concludes that "early use of aspirin after coronary bypass surgery is safe and is associated with a reduced risk of death and ischemic complications involving the heart, brain, kidneys, and gastrointestinal tract" (vol. 347, pages 1309–1317).

5. Coronary Artery Bypass Graft Times Five

77 *I think of:* Susan Sontag, *Illness as Metaphor,* page 31.

6. The Ponce de Leon Thing

86   *"Indeed"*: Gerald Grob, *The Deadly Truth: A History of Disease in America*, page 1.

87   *"Our lack of success"*: Weatherall, page 88.

    "Our ability": Ibid., page 92.

90   *"it was time"*: When Gerald Grob and Dan Fox, director of the Milbank Memorial Fund, tried to trace the origin of the surgeon general's statement, it turned out that he had never made it. "What probably happened was that he was misquoted," Gerald Grob says, "and the misquote was passed down from author to author" [personal communication].

    "developments in research": William B. Schwartz, *Life Without Disease: The Pursuit of Medical Utopia*, pages 149, 153.

    "The virtual disappearance": Weatherall, page 18.

91   *In 1900:* When considering the 1900 figures, note that in 1900 only eight states and the District of Columbia were regularly reporting causes of death; coverage would expand gradually, but complete national coverage would not occur until 1933. In addition, in the years prior to 1933 urban areas were overrepresented, and rural areas underrepresented. The differentials between white and nonwhite populations, thus, were somewhat overstated, though urban blacks probably had higher death rates than blacks from the rural South, the region where most blacks then lived. See "Trends in Infectious Disease Mortality in the United States During the 20th Century," by Gregory L. Armstrong, Laura A. Conn, and Robert W. Pinner, *JAMA* 281 (January 6, 1999), pages 61–66; and Grob, page 316, footnote 32.

    I've taken statistics on mortality from the National Center for Health Statistics (NCHS) and the U.S. Census Bureau. See especially NCHS, *Health, United States, 2000, with Adolescent Health Chartbook*, Hyattsville, MD, 2000.

    From 1911 through 1935: Figures on mortality are from Grob, Chapter 9, "The Discovery of Chronic Illness," pages 217–242.

    "Of the fifteen leading causes": The statistics are taken from Grob (pages 200 ff and 248) and John B. and Sonja M. McKinlay, "The Questionable Contribution of Medical Measures to the Decline of Mortality in the United States in the Twentieth Century," *Milbank Memorial Fund Quarterly: Health and Society* 55:3 (Summer 1977), pages 405–428.

92   *"Unsurprisingly"*: Herrick's remark is quoted in Klaidman, page 19.

    Although Herrick's theory: See Klaidman, pages 15–19, for more about Marcus DeWood's confirmation of Herrick's theory.

93   *In 1900:* See Grob, page 192.

94 *The mortality rates:* The death rates for those under one year of age was 162.4 per thousand, while the comparable figure for the one-through-four-year-old group was 19.8 per thousand. (The death rate represents the percentage of deaths in any given year relative to total population; the mortality rate represents the percentage of a specific age group dying by a certain age — for example, infant mortality represents the number of live-born babies dying within the first year of life.) Grob, pages 192–193.

However, by 1940: The infant mortality rate in 1940 was 47 per thousand. For this and the figures concerning the falling mortality rates of infants and toddlers, see Grob, pages 200–201.

Moreover, infectious disease: For the decline of measles, whooping cough, and scarlet fever as causes of death, see Grob, page 205.

"nearly 85%": This and other statistics on infant and child mortality are from "Annual Summary of Vital Statistics: Trends in the Health of Americans During the 20th Century," by Bernard Guyer, Mary Anne Freedman, Donna M. Strobino, and Edward J. Sondik, in *Pediatrics 2000,* vol. 106, pages 1307–1317.

For the poor record of the United States, see Garrett, page 550.

95 *The belief:* "The military metaphor has historically had the most pervasive influence over both the practice and financing of medicine in the United States," George J. Annas writes in *Some Choice: Law, Medicine, and the Market,* page 45. "Examples are legion," he continues. "Medicine is a battle against death. Diseases attack the body, uniformed physicians intervene. We are almost constantly engaged in wars on various diseases, such as cancer and AIDS . . ."

96 *The U.S. remains:* See a *New York Times* interview with Dr. Sandra Adamson Fryhofer and Dr. Richard Dolinar, conducted by Gale Scott, August 21, 2001, "Facing Off: Prescription Pitches — Are Direct-to-Consumer Pharmaceutical Advertisements Confusing to Patients?"

In widely dispersed: I quote from a Dan Reeves ad in the *New York Times,* December 19, 2000.

Columbia Presbyterian: The Columbia/Cornell ad appeared in the *New York Times* on June 18, 2000. The America's Pharmaceutical Companies ad is from the *New Yorker* (June 5, 2000).

97 *Phil is blunt:* Consider, with respect to direct-to-consumer advertising, a sixteen-page brochure promoting Bayer aspirin — "Become a Heart-Strong Woman" — in which Bayer invites women to "Get Smart About Cardiovascular Disease." ("Did You Know . . . ," the headline on the front page reads, "Heart Disease Is the Number 1 Killer of Women in the United States?")

"Women — take charge of your health," the brochure advises, and after listing the common symptoms of heart attacks and stroke (and advising: "Consider Aspirin to Prevent a Stroke"), it asks women to assess their risk factors. To do this, women are given a Heart/Stroke Quiz ("Factors You Can Control"). There are eleven questions. A woman receives 3 points for every "a" answer (increases risk), 1 point for every "b" answer (lowers risk), and 2 points for every "c" answer ("don't know"). If a woman answers "b" for all eleven questions — that is, if a woman does not smoke, has a cholesterol level below 200, does not have high blood pressure, is not overweight, exercises often, is not frequently tense, angry, or irritable, follows the USA-recommended daily diet, does not have a family history of heart disease or stroke, is not African American, is not going through menopause or postmenopausal, and does not have diabetes, her score will be 11. "Now, add up your points," the brochure says, and if your score is between 11 [*sic*] and 17 points, the brochure announces, "you have *some* risk factors for heart attack and stroke" (italics added).

"I call it": For an excellent summary concerning the sham and scam of anti-aging remedies, see "No Truth to the Fountain of Youth," by S. Jay Olshansky, Leonard Hayflick, and Bruce A. Carnes, in *Scientific American* (June 2002), pages 92–95, and the accompanying website: *www.sciam.com/explorations/2002/051302/aging/*. The article's lead headline reads: "Fifty-one scientists who study aging have issued a warning to the public: no anti-aging remedy on the market today has been proved effective. Here's why they are speaking up." Not only do none of the remedies slow, stop, or reverse aging, but some, the scientists warn, "can be downright dangerous."

"The belief that disease": The quotations regarding the unknown etiologies of many modern diseases are from Grob, pages 2–5.

Then, too: "Certainly," LeFanu writes concerning the genetic causes of disease, "the imagery of DNA as the 'master molecule, the blueprint from which everything flows' is vivid enough, but genes by themselves can do nothing without interacting with other genes operating within the context of the whole cell within which they are located" (page 278). And based on a study of 44,788 "pairs of twins listed in the Swedish, Danish, and Finnish twin registries," conducted "to assess the risks of cancer at 28 anatomical sites for the twins of persons with cancer," the authors of a study in *NEJM* conclude, *"Inherited genetic factors make a minor contribution to susceptibility to most types of neoplasms.* This finding indicates that the environment has the principal role in causing sporadic cancer" (italics added). Paul Lichtenstein, Niels V. Holm, et al., *NEJM:* 343:2 (July 13, 2000), pages 78–85.

For a comprehensive listing of single-gene diseases, of which there are over four thousand, see Victor A. McKusick, *Mendelian Inheritance in Man: A Catalog of Human Genes and Genetic Disorders.*

98 *Writing in:* Daniel Callahan, "Death and the Research Imperative," *NEJM* 342:9 (March 2, 2000), pages 654–656.

"Since we are": William Haseltine, quoted by Nicholas Wade, "Apostle of Regenerative Medicine Foresees Longer Health and Life," *New York Times,* December 18, 2001.

7. Listen to the Patient

103 *According to figures:* The figure on infant mortality is from 1996 and is in *Health, United States, 2000,* published by the NCHS, page 157.

106 *Thus, in one recent:* Meir J. Stampfer et al., "Primary Prevention of Coronary Heart Disease in Women Through Diet and Lifestyle," *NEJM* 343:1 (July 6, 2000), pages 16–22.

107 *So dramatic:* The study about type 2 diabetes, "Prevention of Type 2 Diabetes Mellitus by Changes in Lifestyle Among Subjects with Impaired Glucose Tolerance," is from *NEJM* (May 3, 2001), pages 1343–1350, and is reported in the *New York Times* ("Diet and Exercise Are Found to Cut Diabetes by over Half," by Kenneth Chang), August 9, 2001.

Most of us: In 1935, for example, 6.5 million Americans — 5 percent of the population — were over age sixty-five; in 2001, 13 percent of the population — more than 35 million Americans — were in this age group. These statistics are from Jane E. Brody, "Ways to Make Retirement Work for You," *New York Times,* July 24, 2001, page 225.

The distinction between "life span" and "life expectancy" is from Steven Harrell's letter to the editors, *New York Review of Books* (December 16, 1999).

108 *Consider the following:* Grob, page 61. Malaria was also present in New England; though of lesser significance than in the Chesapeake area and southern colonies, it did not disappear from New England until the end of the eighteenth century (Grob, page 60). For information on mortality and disease in early American colonies, see Grob, especially Chapter 3, "Colonies of Sickness," pages 48–69.

In the United States: For the decline of infant mortality in the United States, decade by decade, see S. Jay Olshansky and A. Brian Ault, "The Fourth Stage of the Epidemiologic Transition: The Age of Delayed Degenerative Diseases," *Milbank Quarterly* 64:3 (1986), page 375.

There is little evidence of infectious disease being important at any age in hunter-gatherer societies. Instead, as Kim Hill explains, "trauma, accident, violence, parasites, etc. are much more common in hunter-gatherers (indeed, theoretical work in epidemiology would lead one to doubt whether small human residential groups could be effective reservoirs for most modern infectious diseases). Human hunter-gatherers are like most other mammals. Mortality rates of the young are very high, but not from infectious diseases usually" [personal communication].

Approximately 55 percent of foraging hunter-gatherer (!Kung, Hadz, Agta, and Cuiva) children survive to age fifteen. About 65 percent of Ache and Kutchin children survive to fifteen. But "it is clear," writes Renée Pennington, "that adults living under the worst conditions (such as the Agta) have a good chance of surviving the reproductive span." Given the high proportion of survivors during the adult years — among Ache living on reservations since 1970, 40 percent of those who live to twenty live to seventy; among !Kung Bushmen, those who live to fifteen probably live past seventy — it is apparent," Pennington notes, "that most 15-year-olds have a better chance of surviving the next 35 years than they did getting through the first 15." The quotation is from "Hunter-Gatherer Demography," in *Hunter-Gatherers: An Interdisciplinary Perspective*, page 194.

Given how utterly wretched the living conditions are for these hunter-gatherers, these findings tell us much about the history of our species' mortality. I am indebted to Kim Hill, Henry Harpending, Renee Pennington, and Magdalena Hurtado for a brief glimpse into this fascinating world, and refer readers to Hill and Hurtado's *Ache Life History* and Nancy Howell's *Demography of the Dobe !Kung*.

109 *The introduction of antibiotic:* See *Pediatrics, 2000*, for information on child and infant mortality.
"*that the introduction*": McKinlay and McKinlay, page 406.
"*after which*": Ibid., pages 414 and 408. See also Thomas McKeown et al., "An Interpretation of the Decline of Mortality in England and Wales During the Twentieth Century," *Population Studies* 29, pages 391–422 [422].

110 *Dr. Thomas McKeown:* "The main influences on the decline in mortality," McKeown states, "were improved nutrition on air-borne infections" and "reduced exposure (from better hygiene) on water- and food-borne diseases," and he suggests that "the advancement in nutrition was the major influence" on the decline of mortality.
"*epidemiological transition*": Grob, page 201.
"*from infectious diseases*": Ibid., page 205.

111 *We live healthier:* On why we live longer, see Grob, page 182 ff, as well as Garrett, pages 9–13, and Horton ("In the Danger Zone"), page 47.
And there is this: In 1930, the annual rate of cancer mortality was 143 per hundred thousand; in 1990, adjusted for the rising age of the population, it was 190 per hundred thousand. See Robert Weinberg, *One Renegade Cell: How Cancer Begins*, as quoted in Daniel J. Kevles, "Cancer: What Do They Know," *New York Review of Books* (September 23,

1999), page 18. And, as with heart disease, mortality from cancer is directly and consistently related to age; the older we are, that is, the more likely it becomes that we will suffer from one or the other of these two diseases.

On the incidence of cancer, see Grob, pages 255–258. In "The Political Scientist" (*New Yorker* [June 7, 1999], page 68), James Fallows notes that "after three decades [since Nixon's "war on cancer"] and an investment of more than thirty-five billion dollars in cancer research, annual cancer deaths have increased." For an informative summary of what has happened since 1971, when President Nixon declared war on cancer, see Jerome Groopman's essay, "The Thirty Years' War," in the *New Yorker* (June 4, 2001), pages 52–63. "In the course of a lifetime, one of every three American women will develop a potentially fatal malignancy," Groopman writes, and he goes on to make much the same point about the use of militaristic language that Sontag, Annas, and others have made: "All the same, the triumphalist rhetoric that animated the war on cancer still shapes public opinion: many people believe that cancer is, in essence, a single foe, that a single cure can destroy it, and that the government is both responsible for and capable of spearheading the campaign" (page 54).

112 *More surprising:* The mortality rates of cancer from 1950 through 1998 are from Grob, page 255; see also *Health, United States, 2000,* page 191.

The reasons: Here is Gerald Grob's description of age-adjusted mortality:

> Let us assume that there are two population groups of 100 each. Assume further that 10 people in each group die in a given year. But there is one difference. The average age of one group is 30 and the average age of the second group is 50. If you simply took the raw death rates, the two groups would be equal. But obviously we would expect a much higher death rate in the group with an average age of 50. Hence you must correct the raw data for age distribution. That is what is meant by age-corrected rates. You have to be certain that you are not comparing apples and oranges.

"Too many statistics are presented without appropriate corrections," he adds, "and hence give a misleading picture. As age advances, we expect higher death rates — hence correction for age distribution is vital" [personal communication].

In a study: Vincent De Vita's 1981 prediction is quoted on page 389 of Laurie Garrett's *Betrayal of Trust.* See John C. Bailar and Heather L. Gornik, "Cancer Undefeated," *NEJM* 336:22 (May 29, 1997), page 1573. (The 1986 article on cancer mortality is by John C. and Elaine M. Smith, "Progress Against Cancer?" *NEJM* 314:19 [May 8, 1986], pages 1226–1232.) "In our view, the best single measure of progress against cancer is change in the age-adjusted mortality rate associated with all cancers combined in the total population," Bailar and Gornik conclude. "According to this measure, we are losing the war against cancer, notwithstanding progress against several uncommon forms of the disease, improvements in palliation, and extension of the productive years of life" (Bailar and Gornik, page 1226).

115 *"the major issue"*: Horton, "How Sick Is Modern Medicine?" page 50.

"we are learning": The quotations from President Clinton and Frances S. Collins are from a front page article by Nicholas Wade: "A Shared Success: 2 Rivals' Announcement Marks New Medical Era, Risks and All," *New York Times,* June 27, 2000. The quotation from *Time* is from an article by Frederic Golden and Michael D. Lemonick, "The Race is Over," *Time* 156:1 (July 3, 2000), page 19.

For a refreshingly clear introduction to understanding the significance of mapping the human genome, see Richard Lewontin's essay in the *New York Review of Books,* "After the Genome, What Then?" (July 19, 2001), pages 36–37. "And what is significant in the human genome sequence?" he asks.

> The major irony of the sequencing of the human genome is that the result turns out not to provide the answer to the chief question that motivated the project. Now that we have the complete sequence of the human genome we do not, alas, know anything more than we did before about what it is to be human. At the time of the completion of the human genome sequence, scientists already knew the complete DNA sequences of thirty-nine species of bacteria, a yeast, a nematode worm, the fruit fly, *Drosophila,* and the mustard weed, Arabidopsis.

"So knowing all the genes of a human being doesn't really tell us what we want to know," he explains. And, later in the essay:

> As interest shifts from genes to proteins, so the promises of cures for all of our ills will shift from genome fixes to protein fixes. The special Human Genome issues of *Science* and *Nature* already prefigure this change. Amid the many articles of the standard sort like "Toward Behavioral Genomics" and "Cancer and Genomics" is one called "Proteomics in Genomeland," and one, "Dissecting Human Disease in the Post-Genomic Era," which describes the shift from genomics to proteomics as one of the "Paradigm Shifts in Biomedical Research." As yet the promise that the study of DNA sequences will lead to cures for illness has remained unfulfilled for any human disease, although some gene-based drugs are undergoing clinical trials.

For a more extended elaboration of the significance (and insignificance) of mapping the genome, see his book, *It Ain't Necessarily So: The Dream of the Human Genome and Other Illusions.*

"research tends": Horton, "How Sick Is Modern Medicine?" page 48.

116 *"the prospects":* Weinberg is quoted in Daniel J. Kevles, *New York Review of Books* (September 23, 1999), page 20.
"the effort to link": Grob, page 96.

117 *"a preventable illness":* The Harvard Center for Cancer Prevention's study is called "Volume I: Human Causes of Cancer" in *Cancer Causes and Control 7,* Suppl 1 (November 1996).
"that the etiology": Grob, page 260.

119 *Age-adjusted mortality figures: Health, United States, 2000,* page 163. See also Gina Kalata, "Gains on Heart Disease Leave More Survivors, and Questions," *New York Times,* January 19, 2003.
"over the past 30 years": Daniel Levy and Thomas J. Thom, "Death Rates from Coronary Disease — Progress and a Puzzling Paradox," *NEJM* 339:13 (September 24, 1998), pages 915–916.

8. They Saved My Life But . . .

133 *On August 26:* The deaths from Baycol are caused by a disorder called rhabdomyolysis, in which muscle cells break down and overwhelm the kidneys with cellular waste — a known side effect of statins. Some experts, the *New York Times* reports, claim that the estimates of injuries and deaths attributable to statins have been "very conservative." "Because doctors and hospitals are not required to report adverse reactions [to drugs]," the *Times* notes, "academic, industry and governmental statisticians have calculated that there were probably about 10 cases of side effects for each case reported to the F.D.A." Regarding the recall of Baycol, see "Anticholesterol Drug Pulled After Link with 31 Deaths," by Gina Kolata and Edmund L. Andrews, in the *New York Times,* August 9, 2001. On the repercussions in Europe of the recall, see "Drug's Removal Exposes Holes in Europe's Net," by Edmund L. Andrews, in the *New York Times,* August 22, 2001.

9. One Year Later

148 *Yet at least:* Two wonderfully lucid, moving, and unsentimental books about living with chronic, disabling conditions are Andrew Potok's *A Matter of Dignity: Changing the World of the Disabled,* and Andrew Solomon's *The Noonday Demon: An Atlas of Depression.* Consider this, for example, from the preface to Andrew Potok's book (page 12):
> In those early years of my advancing blindness, I did take care of myself by learning new skills but, while in the middle of a doctoral program, I also bolted the rational world to pursue an insane "cure" offered by a woman in London who claimed she could cure retinitis pigmentosa with bee stings. My attempt to obliterate my unacceptable limitations

cured me of ever looking for "cures" again. Finally, I have come to realize that many of life's essential problems aren't soluble. Misery doesn't always lend itself to remedy. As a matter of fact, this kind of attitude, I have come to believe, misunderstands what makes life interesting. Being cured of one's disability, one's peculiar psychology, one's angst, though sought avidly, runs the risk of leaving a residue of dullness and uniformity. All of this must seem silly to a society intent on ease, comfort, normalcy, a desire not to stand out in nonconformist ways, as crazy, poor, disabled, loud, different. But just as tragedy is not due merely to error, every question is not answerable, every ill is not always curable, everything does not always come out well in the end. "Everyone who is born holds dual citizenship in the kingdom of the well and the kingdom of the sick," Susan Sontag wrote. We are all a little bit ablebodied and a little bit disabled. The degree to which we are the one or the other shifts throughout life.

150 *We know:* For data concerning people who are at increased risk for heart attacks when isolated or living alone, see "Emotional Support and Survival After Myocardial Infarction: A Prospective, Population-Based Study of the Elderly," by Lisa F. Berkman, Linda Leo-Summers, and Ralph I. Horwitz, in *Annals of Internal Medicine* 117:12 (1992), pages 1003–1009.

Figures concerning increased mortality rates of widows and widowers are from Jaakko Kaprio, Markku Doskenvuo, and Heli Rita, "Mortality After Bereavement: A Prospective Study of 95,647 Widowed Persons," *American Journal of Public Health* 77:3 (March 1987), pages 283–287. See also C. Murray Parkes, B. Benjamin, and R. G. Fitzgerald, "Broken Heart: A Statistical Study of Increased Mortality Among Widowers," *British Medical Journal,* issue 1, pages 740–743.

151 *"I feel this":* Montaigne, "Of Friendship," *The Complete Essays of Montaigne,* pages 186–197.

153 *We know that mental:* Martin Stone, "Shellshock and the Psychologists," in W. F. Bynum, Roy Porter, and Michael Shepherd (eds.), *The Anatomy of Madness: Essays in the History of Psychiatry,* vol. 2, pages 250–251, quoted in Jackson, page 132.

154 *In one survey:* "The Importance of Placebo Effects in Pain Treatment and Research," by J. A. Turner et al., in *JAMA* 271 (1994), pages 1609–1614, cited in Anne Harrington (ed.), *The Placebo Effect: An Interdisciplinary Exploration,* page 22.

In the relief of depression: F. J. Evans, "Expectancy, Therapeutic Instructions, and the Placebo Response," in L. White, B. Tursky, and G. E. Schwartz (eds.), *Placebo: Theory, Research, and Mechanisms,* cited by Harrington, page 21.

In a 1999 study: Irving Kirsch and Guy Sapirstein, "Listening to Prozac but Hearing Placebo: A Meta-Analysis of Antidepressant Medications," in Irving Kirsch (ed.), *How Expectancies Shape Experience.*

154 *"the presence of major depression":* "Task Force 3. Spectrum of Risk Factors for Coronary Heart Disease," by Richard C. Pasternak et al., in *Journal of American College of Cardiology* 27:5 (April 1996), pages 964–1047 [984].

In another study: "Adherence to Treatment and Health Outcomes," by R. I. and S. M. Horwitz, in *Archives of Internal Medicine* 153 (1993), pages 1863–1868, cited in Harrington, page 42.

155 *On the cover:* "A popular operation for arthritis of the knee worked no better than a sham procedure in which patients were sedated while surgeons pretended to operate," the *New York Times* reports on July 11, 2002 ("Arthritis Surgery in Ailing Knees Is Cited as Sham," by Gina Kolata). Each operation, "more than 650,000" of which "are performed each year," according to the article in the July 11, 2002, issue of *NEJM* (J. Bruce Moseley et al., "A Controlled Trial of Arthroscopic Surgery for Osteoarthritis of the Knee," 347:2, pages 81–88), costs roughly $5,000. The study's conclusion: "In this controlled trial involving patients with osteoarthritis of the knee, the outcomes after arthroscopic lavage or arthroscopic debridement were no better than those after a placebo procedure." See also the accompanying editorial in *NEJM*, pages 132–133.

"that the placebo effect": Talbot, *New York Times Magazine,* January 9, 2000, pages 34–39, 44, 58–60.

156 *"It may seem strange":* Leston Havens, *A Safe Place: Laying the Groundwork of Psychotherapy,* page 88.

In talking: In "Disease and Illness" (*Culture, Medicine and Psychiatry,* vol. 1 [1977], page 11), Leon Eisenberg explains the difference this way: "illnesses are *experiences* of disvalued changes in states of being and in social function; diseases, in the scientific paradigm of modern medicine, are *abnormalities* in the *structure* and *function* of body organs and systems."

"the history of medical treatment": Arthur Shapiro, "The Placebo Effect in the History of Medical Treatment (Implications for Psychiatry)," *American Journal of Psychiatry* 116 (1953), pages 298–304, cited in Jackson, page 281.

Some researchers: Regarding skepticism about the placebo effect, see Gina Kolata, "Placebo Effect Is More Myth Than Science, Study Says," *New York Times,* May 25, 2001; and Richard A. Friedman, "Can the Placebo Treat Depression? That Depends," *New York Times,* June 25, 2002.

"no evidence": Howard Spiro, "Clinical Reflections on the Placebo Phenomenon," cited in Harrington, pages 37–55 [49, 50, 51, 53]. Spiro distinguishes between placebo *response* ("behavioral change in the person receiving the pill") and placebo *effect* ("change attributable to the symbolic effect of the medication") (page 49).

10. In Friends We Trust

158 *"the astonishing total"*: Shapiro, "The Placebo: Is It Much Ado About Nothing?" in Harrington, page 13. The quotations from Galen are also on page 13.

159 *"these issues"*: Jackson, page 31.

For the doctor: Regarding *philanthropia* and *philotechnia,* see Pedro Laín Entralgo, *Doctor and Patient,* trans. Frances Partridge, pages 21–22. Citing Entralgo's text (page 40), Jackson says that Entralgo "has argued that friendship (*philia*) was the cornerstone of the doctor-patient relationship in the ancient world (pages 17–29); and he goes on to reason that, in one form or another, it continued to be a crucial element in the art of healing during subsequent centuries."

Jackson also emphasizes what my friends emphasize: the importance of attentive listening. The kind of attentiveness to the patient that inspired confidence and healing several thousand years ago, Jackson argues, does the same in our time, and not only, or primarily, because such attentiveness can bring comfort and relieve pain, but for clinically pragmatic reasons.

"Turning to the context of a general physician's consultation room," he writes,

> we find proof that attentive, interested listening can turn an inchoate litany of complaints into a gradually coherent story of distress and discomfort. The patient has been the better for having told the doctor, whether it has been a confessing, a confiding, a catharsis, or a revealing of physical symptoms that would have otherwise gone undetected; and the doctor has been the better for having been *with* the patient in a healing endeavor rather than having rapidly gotten rid of him or her with the aid of a prescription pad. Often enough, the physician's listening has allowed the emergence of more private concerns and symptoms which have been the issues that were more crucially in need of therapeutic attention. (page 92)

Like my friends, Jackson does not want anyone to get "the mistaken idea" that "healing is nothing but a matter of employing psychological factors to influence sufferers toward better health." He does, however, "wish to emphasize that these factors will frequently not be sufficient, but that they will very frequently be necessary" (page 391).

In a series: David Mechanic's work on trust is summarized in "The Importance of Trust in Medical Care: Papers and Publications by David Mechanic, Ph.D.; Executive Summary," in the Robert Wood Johnson Foundation's *Author Series* 1:12 (April 2000).

160 *"Frustrations"*: Jerome P. Kassirer, "Doctor Discontent," *NEJM* 339:21, pages 1543–1545 [1543]. "It is difficult, however," Mechanic comments,

"to assess how much this chorus of complaints reflects physicians' anxieties about control over their professional lives and future incomes and how much it reflects deficiencies of current medical care." This quotation is in "The Managed Care Backlash: Perceptions and Rhetoric in Health Care Policy and the Potential for Health Care Reform," *Milbank Quarterly* 79:1 (2001), pages 35–54 [40].

160 *"The public has"*: Mechanic, "The Managed Care Backlash," pages 37, 38, 47.

161 *"It is not merely"*: Leon Eisenberg, "The Search for Care," *Daedalus* (1977), pages 235–246 [236–237]. Neither cost nor access "explains away the paradox that although we know the 'old family doctor' had almost no decisive remedies to offer for serious disease," Eisenberg writes, "we nevertheless lament his disappearance."

"The potency of the witch-doctor's pharmacopoeia may not have matched ours," he continues, but "he gave a name to what had been mysterious, he offered an explanation for its cause, he prescribed a ritual for its exorcism, and he legitimized dying. At the least, the patient felt less alone; at best he was restored to his former health."

163 *"swung back and forth"*: Jackson, page 391. Part of the reason for the priority given to medical biotechnology is economic. John Lantos, a pediatrician who was a member of President Clinton's Health Care Reform Task Force, comments: "From the perspective of hospital budgets, the best treatments have been those that require long and intense hospitalizations: heart surgery, transplantation, cancer chemotherapy, neonatal intensive care. In these cases, one needs lots of technology, lots of people, and lots of money, and it all goes toward intervention in a crisis for an identifiable patient."

"Subtle, preventive treatments don't capture our imaginations," he goes on, "don't commandeer the same resources, and those who provide such treatments are thus much more peripheral to this modern medical enterprise." These remarks are from his eminently sensible book, *Do We Still Need Doctors?* pages 79–80.

End-of-life care: See Horton, "In the Danger Zone," page 34; Robert J. Blendon and John M. Benson, "Americans' Views on Health Policy: A Fifty-Year Historical Perspective; Because Americans' views conflict, policymakers must be cautious about interpreting the public's mood based on isolated public opinion questions," in *Health Affairs*, March–April 2001; Christopher Hogan et al., "Medicare Beneficiaries' Costs of Care in the Last Year of Life," *Health Affairs*, July–August 2001; Anne A. Scitovsky, "'The High Cost of Dying' Revisited," *Milbank Quarterly* 72:4 (1994); and James D. Lubitz and Gerald F. Riley, "Trends in Medicare Payments in the Last Year of Life," a Special Article in *NEJM* 328:15 (April 15, 1993), pages 1092–1096.

Rich says: Rich, who has taught at several medical schools, would eliminate most of the basic science courses that dominate the first two years of training, starting with the dissection of cadavers. "Pathology, psychology, biochemistry — these courses are fairly worthless, since you learn what you need to know about them as you go into the various specialties of clinical medicine," he says, "and then you learn them in a much more pragmatic way."

164 *"these innovations":* The reasons Mechanic advances for the importance of effective communication merit repeating: "Effective communication allows the physician to understand the patient's expectations and concerns; to obtain accurate information, thereby facilitating diagnosis; to plan and manage the course of treatment; and to gain the patient's understanding, cooperation, and adherence to treatment." See "Public Trust and Initiatives for New Health Care Partnerships," *Milbank Quarterly* 76:2 (1998), pages 281–302 [281]. Quotes in text from pages 298, 281, 282.

166 *Jerry pauses:* Regarding the debts incurred by medical students, see "Removing Career Obstacles for Young Physician-Scientists — Loan-Repayment Programs," by Timothy J. Ley and Leon E. Rosenberg, in the "Sounding Board" section of *NEJM* 346:5 (January 31, 2002), pages 368–371. According to the article, "The late bloomers are most likely to incur debt during medical school. Only 17 percent of all medical students graduate free of debt. For the class of 2001 overall, the average debt was more than $99,000. Among students in private medical schools, the average debt was nearly $119,000, and one third of this group had debts that exceeded $150,000" (page 369).

167 *"sick-man":* Nicholas Jewson, "The Disappearance of the Sick-Man from Medical Cosmology," *Sociology* 10 (1976), pages 225–240 [229], cited by Jackson, page 61.
     "began to take shape": Jackson, page 61.

168 *Such changes:* Kevin Patterson, "What Doctors Don't Know (Almost Everything)," *New York Times Magazine,* May 5, 2002, pages 74, 76–77.
     "As the scientific mode": Jackson, page 62.
     "In effect": Weatherall, page 57.
     In Time to Heal: For Kenneth M. Ludmerer's account of the rise of a "separation of functions" between "clinician-teachers" and "physician-scientists," see *Time to Heal: American Medical Education from the Turn of the Century to the Era of Managed Care,* pages 288–295.

169 *"carried negative implications":* Ibid., page 361.
     "to revert": Ibid., pages 381, 383, 389.

170 *"Is this the best":* Weatherall, page 328.

171 *"The contemporary disarray":* Daniel M. Fox, *Power and Illness: The Failure and Future of American Health Policy,* pages 1, 323. "As Daniel M.

Fox has discussed," Ludmerer writes, "in the era of chronic diseases, the system of health care financing and delivery remained based on an acute disease model. Thus, third party payers would often pay for renal dialysis but not for the outpatient treatment of high blood pressure that could have prevented the kidneys from failing in the first place" (page 286).

172 *We currently spend: Crossing the Quality Chasm: A New Health System for the 21st Century,* Institute of Medicine (Washington, DC: National Academy Press, 2001). The figures on chronic care are from *Chronic Care in America: A 21st Century Challenge* (August 1996), prepared by the Institute for Health and Aging, University of California, San Francisco, for the Robert Wood Johnson Foundation, Princeton, New Jersey.

173 *"The resistance":* Fox, page 88.

174 *Sometimes, it seems:* "In the second half of [the nineteenth] century, the growing perception that the threat of infection was receding coincided with the ascendancy of new theories for understanding disease and intervening to prevent and treat it," Daniel Fox writes. "Most important, the great advances in bacteriology in these years led to the concept, in the words of a classic study of human disease, that 'each human ailment must have a singular and specific cause.'" Fox's quotation is on page 23; the quotation about each human ailment having a singular and specific cause is from M. S. R. Hutt and D. P. Burkitt, *The Geography of Non-Infectious Disease,* page 1.

"It is the sheer": Weatherall, page 322.

"it is not information": Nuland, "The Proper Dosage of Judgment," *New York Times,* July 10, 2000.

175 *More:* See, for example, "Geographical Mobility: Population Characteristics," March 1999 to March 2000, or "Why People Move: Exploring the March 2000 Current Population Survey (Special Studies)," March 1999 to March 2000.

at this writing: Figures for the exact number of uninsured Americans vary, but generally are estimated at being between 39 and 45 million. A *New York Times* article claims that, according to government figures, "the number of uninsured Americans remains at 39 million" ("Paralysis in Health Care," May 29, 2002), though two years earlier, the government, using a different method of calculating this figure, stated that the number of uninsured was 44.3 million ("Still Uninsured, and Still a Campaign Issue," by Robert Pear, *New York Times,* June 25, 2000). On September 30, 2002, the Census Bureau stated that the number of uninsured was 41.2 million, or 14.6 percent of the population. *New York Times,* September 30, 2002, "After Decline, the Number of Uninsured Rose in 2001," by Robert Pear.

A Robert Wood Johnson Foundation forecast is hardly sanguine —

"The most likely scenario puts the number of uninsured at 47 million in the year 2010, while the worst-case scenario estimates there will be 65 million in 2010" (from "Health and Health Care 2010: The Forecast, the Challenge," a special supplement to *Advances*, issue 1, 2000).

In an article entitled "Uninsured America: Truth and Consequences" (December 19, 2001, distributed by the National Academy of the Sciences), Arthur L. Kellermann claims that 40 million Americans are without health insurance. And according to a White Paper put out by the American Society of Internal Medicine in 2000 ("No Health Insurance? It's Enough to Make You Sick"), uninsured Americans, compared with those insured, are "1.5 times more likely to report only fair or good health; up to 3.6 times more likely to delay seeking care; up to 2.8 times more likely to be hospitalized for diabetes; up to 2.4 times more likely to be hospitalized for hypertension; and up to 1.6 times more likely to be hospitalized for a bleeding ulcer."

"Clinical research": Horton, "How Sick Is Modern Medicine?" page 49.

11. So Why Did I Become a Doctor?

182 *"Many of the Peace Corps"*: G. H. Friedland, C. Ellis, and S. Long, "The Prevalance of *S. Hematobium* in the Okene Area of Nigeria," *West African Medical Journal* 17 (1968), pages 21–24. For a recent and comprehensive review article on schistosomiasis, see Bartley Ross et al., "Schistosomiasis," *NEJM* 346:16 (April 18, 2002), pages 1212–1220.

186 *In 1982:* Jerry talks about his realization that AIDS was transmitted heterosexually in *AIDS Doctors: Voices from the Epidemic,* by Ronald Bayer and Gerald M. Oppenheimer, pages 26–27.

Jerry was also: Jerry's two seminal articles about the transmission of HIV are "Lack of Transmission of HTLV-III/LAV Infection to Household Contacts of Patients with AIDS or AIDS-Related Complex with Oral Candidiasis," *NEJM* 314 (February 6, 1986), pages 344–349; and "Medical Progress: Transmission of the Human Immunodeficiency Virus," *NEJM* 317 (October 29, 1987), pages 1125–1135.

187 *"Although we are confronted":* Friedland, "Medical Progress: Transmission of the Human Immunodeficiency Virus," page 1133.

Just as, for Jerry: When students, interns, and residents presented papers or reviewed individual cases — reporting, at the start of each day, on admissions from the night before — Jerry stayed very much in the background, and if and when he spoke it was always in the most equable way — with great specificity and gentle humor.

I was surprised, then, after a student presentation one morning, to have Jerry ask me what I thought (I was impressed), and to have him say, matter-of-factly, "I would have given her a C+." His kindness and sympathetic manner, that is, did not compromise his medical judgment.

188 *"Then go there"*: "You don't know what a good doctor he is," Gail said once when I was telling her about people I'd met at the clinic, and of watching Jerry interact with them. "He is so good with *people* — that's his great gift — so very good." (Gail and Jerry met on the acute chest disease ward at Bellevue — "lots of TB and emphysema," Jerry says — where Gail was a head nurse and Jerry was a resident.) And she said this even though she sometimes became frustrated because of Jerry's lack of availability, the long hours he put in at work, and how often he was away from home.

I knew firsthand of Jerry's devotion to Gail and his children (and to his sister Rita, who was in a nursing home in Brooklyn, afflicted with Alzheimer's), and when we were together, whether in one of our homes or at the hospital, we talked mostly about our families — about my brother and his sister, and about our children. On this visit, Jerry talked at length about an apartment one of his daughters had just rented in a dangerous neighborhood of New York, and of the talks he and Gail were having about what to do: they didn't want to control her life — but they felt she was being naive in some ways, and putting herself at undue risk.

189 *He worked in Roxbury:* There Jerry was, among other things, medical director of the Mary Eliza Mahoney Family Life Center and of Adult Services at the Dimock Community Health Center.

191 *Jerry has written:* "Breaking the Silence" is an editorial in *AIDS Clinical Care* 12:8 (August 2000). In it, Jerry lists some preliminary elements of what he calls "the prescription many of us took home from Durban" — the imperative for rich governments to provide debt relief (how battle AIDS when Africa must pay $15 billion in interest to the developed world each year?); the necessity for increasing prevention efforts with resources in the billions, not millions; the need for the pharmaceutical industry to lower drug prices, and for governments to encourage policies such as parallel importing and compulsory pricing; the need for governments and international organizations to build infrastructure and to provide education that makes antiretroviral use possible and effective; the need for an uncompromising battle against stigma and discrimination; and the imperative for political leaders in the developed and developing worlds to act courageously.

"Political will and courageous leadership *do* make a difference," Jerry says. "Look at what's happened in Uganda and Senegal, where they have had successful HIV prevention campaigns. In Senegal the rates remain low and stable and they've reversed the epidemic, while in Uganda the rates have continued to go down — yet Uganda was one of the most heavily impacted countries initially."

See Peter Piot's op-ed piece, "In Poor Nations, a New Will to Fight AIDS," *New York Times,* July 3, 2002. Piot notes that AIDS "will kill 68 million people in the 45 most affected countries over the next 20 years."

"This need not happen," he states. "HIV prevention campaigns work, and there is overwhelming evidence that the AIDS epidemic can be controlled — but only when governments make fighting AIDS a priority."

After reviewing basics about prevention and treatment campaigns that have worked, and the money that will be needed for global success, he concludes: "Uganda, Zambia, Cambodia, Brazil and other developing nations have demonstrated that AIDS is a problem with a solution. Now the world must match this leadership and commitment with the resources needed to get on with the job. Otherwise, the new spirit of hope and vigor in the AIDS fight will be dashed. The costs of that are too devastating to contemplate."

The United Nations (UNAIDS), in July 2002, reported that of the forty million HIV-infected people worldwide, only 700,000, or 1.75 percent, were receiving antiretroviral drugs at the end of 2001. "The overwhelming majority of these, 500,000," the *New York Times* wrote, "live in high-income countries where combinations of anti-HIV drugs have prolonged the lives of many people. In these [high-income] countries, in 2001, fewer than 30,000 of the 28.5 million infected people were receiving anti-HIV treatment at the end of 2001" ("Report, Reversing Estimates, Forecasts Big Increase in AIDS Death Toll," *New York Times,* July 3, 2002).

194   *It is this understanding:* In the summer of 1986, *Newsweek* ran a twelve-page story about Jerry. On the cover was a photo of Jerry, with the caption: "THE **AIDS** DOCTOR." And accompanying the photo, this: "Gerald Friedland has treated nearly 300 men and women with AIDS. More than 200 are dead. The rest are dying. This is the story of his caring and his struggle." *Newsweek* 108:3 (July 21, 1986), pages 38–50.

196   *"Our family started":* Jerry discovered the fact of his father's hospitalization at Hillside when, after their parents' death, his sister came across a bundle of letters in their mother's dresser — letters his father had written from Hillside Psychiatric Hospital.

12. A Safe Place

203   *"What a man knows":* Adlai E. Stevenson, *What I Think,* page 174.
204   *Arthur and I talk:* In the course of this conversation, Arthur also notes

ways in which psychoanalytically oriented therapy has been found to be inefficient. "I love psychoanalysts, because they are very, very respectful of the dignity of each person," he says. "They are thoughtful. They listen. They listen *carefully,* and the person they work with is always treated with great regard. I have always resented colleagues who talk down and trash their patients. But it takes analysts years to accomplish some of the things you can now accomplish in six weeks with medications, and some discrete conditions like obsessive-compulsive disorder, panic attacks, and depression respond very well to medications."

204 *In a World Health Organization study:* "The Global Burden of Disease: A Comprehensive Assessment of Mortality and Disability from Diseases, Injuries, and Risk Factors in 1990 and Projected to 2020," by Christopher J. L. Murray and Alan D. Lopez (eds.), published by the Harvard School of Public Health on behalf of the World Health Organization and the World Bank, pages 2–4 and 18–21.

207 *I say:* "He is the most amazing diagnostician," Phil says of Arthur.
You tell him a story — what's going on with one of your children, what you're worried about for yourself — and he sees right through to the heart, and he tells you what is and isn't possible, and he's totally direct, and he always makes sense.
And even though you come to him with problems you're upset about, he makes you feel that you're important, that what you say has value — and you feel good because you're *his* friend. I remember in high school, how he would go into a group of guys for the first time and immediately be able to make friends — to say the right things and listen in a way that made people gravitate to him and like him — that he had this uncanny ability to relate to people.

212 *"No quality":* The first passage from David Hume is from *A Treatise of Human Nature,* page 316. The second passage is on page 593. Hume describes "the nature and force of *sympathy*" as follows:
The minds of all men are similar in their feelings and operations, nor can any one be actuated by any affection, of which all others are not, in some degree, susceptible. As in strings equally wound up, the motion of one communicates itself to the rest; so all the affections readily pass from one person to another, and beget correspondent movements in every human creature. When I see the *effects* of passion in the voice and gesture of any person, my mind immediately passes from these effects to their causes, and forms such a lively idea of the passion, as is presently converted into the passion itself. In like manner, when I perceive the *causes* of any emotion, my mind is convey'd to the effects, and is actuated with a like emotion. (pages 575–576)

214 *"By the way":* Rereading Arthur's letters, and being reminded of how

the quality of human sympathy in him (as in Hume's description of it, which includes what we understand as "empathy") has been at the heart of our friendship, as well as of his friendships with others (and his work as a psychotherapist), I find — with reference to the quality of mercy — the familiar passage from *The Merchant of Venice* sweetly appropriate:

> "The quality of mercy is not strain'd,
> It droppeth as the gentle rain from heaven
> Upon the place beneath. It is twice blest:
> It blesseth him that gives and him that takes . . ."
> (Act IV, Scene I)

13. It's Not the Disease

215 *"I'm just"*: Most of the conversations with Phil in this chapter take place on the last evening of a week-long visit during which Phil's house has been a busy place. Barbara, who works in Phil's office one day a week doing nerve conduction velocity studies and electromyography (a diagnostic procedure that measures electrical impulses passing through muscles, and going from the nerves to the muscles), has been taking intensive summer courses toward her certification as a homeopathist. (Barbara started out as a physical therapist; she and Phil met when he was the only man in an employee fitness program she ran at the Spalding Rehabilitation Center, where Phil was director of medical education.) Phil and Barbara's son Jared, about to enter his freshman year at Montana State University, has arrived home from an archaeological dig in Israel, and their daughter Katie, a high school junior, has left for a training center to prepare for a year of study in Israel. (Phil spent extended periods of time, in 1977 and 1983, as visiting professor of neurology at the Hebrew University Medical School of Hadassah Hospital in Jerusalem.) And Phil's brother Allen, who went to junior high school and Erasmus with my brother Robert, where they were friends, has been visiting for several days with his wife and two young children.

216 *"No one really"*: Concerning the brain's ability to heal itself, researchers working with stem cells now report experiments that provide some hope that we may ultimately happen upon ways to repair the brain. "Transplanted cells," the *New York Times* reports, "which are types of stem cells, migrate to the site of damage and release factors that ameliorate or may even replace dead tissues." Although there have been some laboratory successes, "scientists say that they still do not understand the basic biology of this process, and that huge hurdles still remain. For example, it is not clear if stem cells are making the right connections inside the brain or if they will even survive over the long term. Moreover,

the field is threatened by religious and political arguments about abortion" ("In Early Experiments, Cells Repair Damaged Brains," by Sandra Blakeslee, *New York Times,* November 11, 2000).

Similarly, stem cells may aid the heart's ability to repair itself. In an article in the *New England Journal of Medicine,* "Chimerism of the Transplanted Heart," by Federico Quaini et al., 346:1 (January 3, 2002), pages 7–15, researchers report "a high level of cardiac chimerism caused by the migration of primitive cells from the recipient to the grafted heart. Putative stem cells and progenitor cells were identified in control myocardium and in increased numbers in transplanted hearts." Although "our knowledge of these events is less than scanty," the *NEJM* reports, these new findings "raise the hope that, counter to traditional beliefs, the heart can repair itself. If it can, we will have opportunities to enhance the process that regenerates damaged myocardium" (page 5).

217 *"We don't have a splint":* Although Phil is a man who can understand the most subtle complexities of science — whether physics, biology, chemistry, anatomy, geology, or neuroscience — when it comes to the practice of medicine, and to dealing with his patients, he remains uncomplicated in the best, most sensible ways, so that often, when I become aware of my own tendency to worry a situation too much, I will stop and say to myself: Whoa, Neugie — what would Phil see here, and what would he say? How would he cut through to the heart of this — to the basics?

218 *Phil has written:* Phil's article, "Bifrontal Brain Trauma and 'Good Outcome' Personality Changes: Phineas P. Gage Syndrome Updated," was published in the *Journal of Neurological Rehabilitation* 4 (1990), pages 9–16.

Since my arrival: "He's genuinely shy," Phil's wife Barbara says when I talk with her about how hard it is to get Phil to agree to tape a conversation. "And he doesn't always make eye contact either, so sometimes people aren't sure if he's listening. But he is. He's the best listener I know, and he never treats anything — *any* patient — routinely. In the middle of the night I often find he's gotten out of bed and is in his office, poring through his medical books and trying to figure something out about one of his patients."

226 *"perceptions of a career":* Jack Hadley et al., "Young Physicians Most and Least Likely to Have Second Thoughts About a Career in Medicine," *Academic Medicine* 67:3 (March 1992), pages 180–190 [180].

227 *"The psychic toll":* Michael D. Burdi and Laurence C. Baker, "Physicians' Perceptions of Autonomy and Satisfaction in California," *Health Affairs* 18:4 (July–August 1999), pages 134–145 [142–143]. See also "Effects of HMO Market Penetration on Physicians' Work Effort and Satisfaction," by Jack Hadley and Jean M. Mitchell, *Health Affairs* 16:6 (November–

December 1997), pages 99–111; "Physician Behavior: Perceived Financial Incentives, HMO Market Penetration, and Physicians' Practice Styles and Satisfaction," by Jack Hadley et al., *Health Services Research* 34:1 (April 1999, Part II), pages 307–321; and "How Satisfying Is the Practice of Internal Medicine?" by C. E. Lewis et al., *Annals of Internal Medicine* 114 (1991), pages 1–5.

14. The Patient's Story

237   *"There was no arguing":* On another occasion, after recounting some of Arthur's speculations about our friendships, and about the role of sports in our early lives, I offer a literary comparison: that the schoolyard was for us what the Mississippi was for Mark Twain, and the sea for Melville. I talk about an essay originally published in 1948 by Leslie Fiedler, "Come Back to the Raft Ag'in, Huck Honey!" in which, writing about *Huckleberry Finn* and *Moby Dick* (and other books — all "boy's books," Fiedler notes) Fiedler proposes that what they have in common is a kind of passionless passion — a homoerotic love between men, at once gross and delicate, and possessing an innocence above suspicion. And this love, and these friendships — the feeling and affection of Huck for Jim, of Ishmael for Queequeg — exist in an American male's version of paradise: a world where men, and only men, work and play together — where they struggle against the elements, rejoice in their camaraderie, and exist in an idyllic, preindustrial American pastoral. "Come Back to the Raft Ag'in, Huck Honey!" in *Adventures of Huckleberry Finn: A Case Study in Critical Controversy.*

243   *Then he looked up:* The intravenous solution ordered by Dr. Brumlik was digitalis.

I mention: Lown, pages xiv and xv.

249   *According to Koch's postulates:* For a description of these and how he arrived at them, see Roy Porter's *The Greatest Benefit to Mankind: A Medical History of Humanity,* page 436 ff.

250   *The assumption:* For a discussion of single causative agents in disease — their rarity, and our success rates in finding treatments for them — see Weatherall, page 256 ff, and Victor McKusick, cited in note xx, chapter x.

251   *Twin studies:* The statistics on concordance rates are from Weatherall, pages 280–281. For an excellent explanation of the relation of genetics to heritability — twin studies, family studies, linkage studies, concordance rates, et cetera — see "Genetic Research on Mental Disorders," by Stephen O. Moldin, in *Genetics and Criminality,* ed. Botkin, McMahon, and Francis, pages 115–149.

253   *Evolutionary biologists:* The kinds of questions evolutionary biologists

ask — along with some answers and hypotheses concerning the relationship of disease (cancer and heart disease, in particular) to natural selection — are set forth clearly in Randolph M. Nesse and George C. Williams, *Why We Get Sick: The New Science of Darwinian Medicine,* especially pages 3–6, 96–97, and 134–135.

254 *In a similar way:* For a discussion of the relation of genetics, disease, heritability, and reproductive age, see Nesse and Williams, pages 96–97.
Seen from this perspective: Richard Dawkins's remark is from Nesse and Williams, page 15.
"natural selection": Ewald, page 12.

255 *"strep B was":* Laurie Garrett, *The Coming Plague,* page 415. The report on fourteen thousand people dying each year from drug-resistant infections is from an editorial in the *New York Times,* "Losing Ground Against Microbes," June 18, 2000.
There is a large body of literature concerning the increase in drug-resistant infections — for example, an article in the *Archives of Family Medicine* 8:1 (January–February 1999), by Jon S. Abramson and Laurence B. Givner ("Bacterial Resistance Due to Antimicrobial Drug Addiction Among Physicians") noting that

> until 1974, all pneumococci reported in the United States were susceptible to penicillins and cephalosporins. Resistance levels increased slowly thereafter until the 1990s, when the rates increased substantially. The US Pediatric Multicenter Pneumococcal Surveillance Study Group prospectively studied almost 1300 systemic infections caused by pneumococci at 8 children's hospitals. They found that from 1993 to 1996, the overall percentage of pneumococci that were penicillin nonsusceptible increased from 14% to 21%. The resistance rate for ceftriaxone tripled, from 3.1% to 9.3%.

Until 1992, the Centers for Disease Control spent only $55,000 a year on antibiotic-resistance surveillance — yet by 1992, as an article in *Science* noted in that year ("On the Track of 'Killer' TB," by Rich Weiss),

> years of poor compliance among TB patients unwilling to take their medicine for the full 6 to 18 months needed to kill the bugs has led to the gradual development of strains that are now resistant to as many as 9 of the 11 most commonly tested drugs. And although a trend toward drug resistance has been obvious for some time, the severity of the crisis went largely unrecognized in recent years, in part because the federal surveillance programs designed to track TB drug-resistance were eliminated in 1986 for budgetary reasons. (*Science* 255:5041 [January 1992], pages 148–150)

Nesse and Williams, pages 1–49 and 246, provide a good introduction to the subject. See also Ewald, pages 1–30. Laurie Garrett's *The Coming Plague* is full of stories and data on drug-resistant diseases.

Richard Preston's writings, especially *The Hot Zone,* and "Annals of Warfare: The Bioweaponeers" (*New Yorker* [March 9, 1998], pages 52–65), provide a primer on the possible uses and effects of lethal drug-resistant viruses.

256 *None of the risk factors:* For a fascinating discussion of inflammation and its relation to the immune system and heart disease, see Ewald, especially pages 107–116. Joseph B. Muhlestein's quotation is from "Chronic Infection and Coronary Artery Disease," in Killian Robinson (ed.), *Medical Clinics of North America: Risk Modification for Cardiac Disease* 84:1 (January 2000), pages 123–148 [123].

Moreover, as Lewis Thomas: For Ewald's discussion of principles of primary causation and their relation to heart disease, see pages 116–121 in *Plague Time.*

257 *"The entire process":* For other discussions of the processes that lead from the buildup of atheroma to its rupture, see Dr. Peter Libby, "Atherosclerosis: The New View," *Scientific American* (May 2002), pages 47–53. See also Klaidman, pages 204–205, 199–200, 211–215; and Weatherall, pages 94, 280–285.

Dr. Libby, chief of cardiovascular medicine at Brigham and Women's Hospital in Boston, provides a good summary of recent research on the relation of inflammation to cardiovascular disease. The most interesting finding, he suggests, is that "the long held conception of how the disease develops [fat-laden gunk gradually building up on artery walls and closing them off] turns out to be wrong."

"Most heart attacks and many strokes," Libby writes, "stem instead from less obtrusive plaques that rupture suddenly, triggering the emergence of a blood clot, or thrombus, that blocks blood flow." Sometimes, of course, plaque does grow so large that it halts blood flow to an artery, thereby generating a heart attack or stroke, Libby explains. "Yet only about 15 percent of heart attacks happen in this way."

This "new view" of atherosclerosis helps "explain why many heart attacks seem to come from out of the blue: the plaques that rupture do not necessarily protrude very far into the blood channel and so may not cause angina or appear prominently on images of the channel." Some plaques, that is, are more prone to rupturing than others, and we really don't know why.

For more detailed discussions of the relation of inflammation to coronary artery disease, see "Inflammation, Aspirin, and the Risk of Cardiovascular Disease in Apparently Healthy Men," by Paul M. Ridker et al., *NEJM* 336:14 (April 3, 1997), pages 973–979; "Measurement of C-Reactive Protein for the Targeting of Statin Therapy in the Primary Prevention of Acute Coronary Events," by Paul M. Ridker et al., *NEJM* 344:26 (June 28, 2001), pages 1959–1965; and also Weatherall, page 186.

Although the evidence for inflammatory causation is persuasive, the process that produces the ruptures in the atheroma that lead to heart attacks, as Rich often reminds me, remains mysterious. Thus the following, from an editorial article, "The Value of Inflammation for Predicting Unstable Angina," *NEJM* 347:1 (July 4, 2002), pages 55–57: "Although the link between inflammation and clinical cardiovascular events is strong, there remain important gaps in our knowledge. For example, although chronic systemic infection may accelerate the clinical course of atherosclerosis, the relative contribution of this 'extralesional' inflammation to events within the arterial wall remains to be determined. Similarly, the precise mechanism by which atherosclerosis initiates an inflammatory response is not known" (pages 56–57).

258 *"Add to this"*: For information on C-reactive protein and its relation to the detection and prevention of atherosclerosis and to statin therapy, see Paul M. Ridker et al., "Measurement of C-Reactive Protein for the Targeting of Statin Therapy in the Primary Prevention of Acute Coronary Events"; and Paul M. Ridker, "Evaluating Novel Cardiovascular Risk Factors: Can We Better Predict Heart Attacks?" in *Annals of Internal Medicine* 130:11 (June 1, 1999), pages 933–937. For an understanding of the concept of risk factors, see four excellent articles in the March 2001 issue of the *American Journal of Public Health* 91:3: "Risky Concepts: Methods in Cancer Research," by Alfredo Morabia, pages 355–57; "Cancer Culture: Epidemics, Human Behavior, and the Dubious Search for New Risk Factors," by Graham A. Colditz, pages 357–359; "The Search for Cancer Risk Factors: When Can We Stop Looking?" by Colin B. Begg, pages 360–364; and "The Privatization of Risk," by Beverly Rockhill, pages 365–368.

Beverly Rockhill's conclusions are cogent: "It is likely," she writes, "that the ability to predict the futures of individuals will always remain out of reach, despite ever-increasing knowledge about alleged independent factors or genes that may elevate disease risk in exposed groups."

The dangers in "designating the individual the *sole* locus of 'risk' and thus the locus of responsibility for 'risk reduction,'" are twofold. First is "the amplification of existing socioeconomic health inequities, as individuals in lower socioeconomic strata are less likely to have regular contact with the health care system, to comprehend the arithmetic behind risk information, and to have the psychologic, social, and economic resources needed to voluntarily alter the factors contributing to their 'personal' risk."

Second, Rockhill writes,
the labeling of these risk factors as the "causes" of individual cases of dis-

case, and the implication that responsible individuals who avoid such risk factors will prevent their own case of disease, represent strong denials of the inability of statistics and medical science to predict the future of individuals. Further, the equating of risk factors with the causes of individual cases fosters an indifference to the social determinants of risk factor distribution and thus contributes to ineffectual disease prevention policies at the population level. (pages 367–368)

259 *Here, for example:* Russell Ross, "Atherosclerosis — An Inflammatory Disease," *NEJM* 340:2 (January 14, 1999), pages 115–126.

"From a clinical standpoint": Muhlestein, "Chronic Infection and Coronary Artery Disease," page 125.

261 *"To be precise":* Taubes, "The Soft Science of Dietary Fat," *Science* 291:5513 (March 30, 2001), pages 2536–2545. See also his companion piece on dietary fat, "What If It's All Been a Big Fat Lie?" *New York Times Magazine,* July 7, 2002, page 22 ff.

Rich talks frequently: Regarding the unethical collusions between doctors, hospitals, and drug companies, see, for starters, the articles cited in note xx, chapter x. See also "When Physicians Double as Entrepreneurs," by Kurt Eichenwald and Gina Kolata, *New York Times,* November 30, 1999; "Study Says Clinical Guides Often Hide Ties of Doctors," by Sheryl Gay Stolberg, *New York Times,* February 6, 2002; "Drug Companies Profit from Research Supported by Taxpayers," by Jeff Gerth and Sheryl Gay Stolberg, *New York Times,* April 23, 2000; "Drug Companies and the Third World: A Case Study in Neglect," by Donald G. McNeil, Jr., *New York Times,* May 21, 2000; and "How Companies Stall Generics and Keep Themselves Healthy," by Sheryl Gay Stolberg and Jeff Gerth, *New York Times,* July 23, 2000.

Although more than 80: The statistics on direct-to-consumer promotion are from "Promotion of Prescription Drugs to Consumers," by Meredith B. Rosenthal et al., in *NEJM* 346:7, pages 498–505. Regarding the pharmaceutical industry's relation to consumers — and to research — consider this too: two-thirds of prescription medications approved by the FDA from 1989 to 2000 were either modified versions of existing drugs or drugs identical to those already on the market. According to the National Institute for Health Care Management Foundation (which receives 40 percent of its financing from Blue Cross/Blue Shield), medicines "with new chemical ingredients that offer significant improvements over existing drugs" made up only 15 percent of drugs approved during this period ("New Medicines Seldom Contain Anything New, Study Finds," by Melody Petersen, *New York Times,* May 29, 2002).

For a look at drug companies' promotional techniques, including direct-to-consumer advertising, see "What's Black and White and Sells

Medicine?" by Melody Petersen, *New York Times*, August 27, 2000; and "High-Tech Stealth Being Used to Sway Doctor Prescriptions," by Sheryl Gay Stolberg and Jeff Gerth, *New York Times*, November 16, 2000.

261 *"showed no evidence":* Both LeFanu, page 308, and Taubes, page 2541 of "The Soft Science of Dietary Fat," make reference to this *Time* magazine article.

262 *"Snatching victory":* LeFanu, pages 289–317 [310].
"After seven years": Ibid., page 308.

15. Natural Selection

270 *"The main discovery":* Jacob, *Of Flies, Mice, and Men,* page 152.
"chemical weapons": The quotation from Waksman, along with the story of his discovery of streptomycin and his evolving views about antibiotics, is drawn, in part, from LeFanu, pages 14–15.
That Alexander Fleming: Like Waksman's story, the story of Fleming's discovery of penicillin has been told often. See, for example, LeFanu, pages 6–14, and Porter, pages 454–458.

271 *"the whole immune system":* Nesse and Williams, page 116.
"Inflammation": Mary Duenwald, "Body's Defender Goes on the Attack," *New York Times,* January 22, 2002.

272 *In an article:* "p53 Mutant Mice That Display Early Ageing-Associated Phenotypes," by Stuart D. Tyner et al., *Nature* 415 (January 3, 2002), pages 45–53.

274 *"With the current study":* Reactions to the *Nature* article on p53 are from the *New York Times:* "In Search of an Extra-Long Life," January 7, 2002 (editorial); and "Cancer Fighter Exacts a Price: Cellular Aging," by Nicholas Wade, January 8, 2002.

275 *"During the past":* Nesse and Williams, page 108.
One way: For a discussion of the effects of aging on DNA and life expectancy, see Weatherall, pages 217–219.

276 *"Genes that reside":* Ibid., page 190. The estimate of the number of genes in the human genome has changed since Weatherall's book was published in 1995, and continues to change. The generally accepted number is now somewhere between 30,000 and 40,000. See, for example, Nicholas Wade's article in the *New York Times,* "Human Genome Appears More Complicated," August 24, 2001, and Andrew Pollack's article in the *Times,* "Citing RNA, Studies Suggest a Much Deeper Gene Pool," May 4, 2002.

277 *"a highly technical":* Weatherall, page 107.
John Gibbon: Gibbon told his story many times. His accounts are consistent, but he elaborated on the experience a bit differently in each new

telling. Basic accounts are given in Klaidman and LeFanu. I am quoting from Gibbon's 1978 essay, "The Development of the Heart-Lung Apparatus," *American Journal of Surgery* 135 (May 1978), pages 608–619.

279 *"Pessimism":* Walter Lillehai, "A Personalized History of Extra Corporeal Circulation," *Transactions of the American Society for Artificial Organs* 28 (1982), pages 5–16.

16. The Prepared Heart

285 *We know how:* The information on curing a case of TB, on vaccinations against measles, and on annual average health spending in the U.S. and elsewhere is from an editorial, "Health Aid for Poor Countries," *New York Times*, January 4, 2002. Note, also, that the prevalence of TB in the United States has declined to its lowest level ever, a drop of 39 percent from 1992 to 2000, with the rate of multidrug TB resistance down by 70 percent ("Tuberculosis — The Global View," *NEJM* 346:19 [May 9, 2002], pages 1434–1435).

Data on TB, vaccines, average health spending, and death from preventable diseases are from the *New York Times*, "U.N. Says Millions of Children, Caught in Poverty, Die Needlessly," by Elizabeth Olson, March 14, 2002.

286 *The response:* For a sense of the national response concerning global disease and poverty, see Natalie Angier, "Case Study: Globalization; Location: Everywhere; Together in Sickness and in Health," *New York Times Magazine*, May 6, 2001; and Helen Epstein, *New York Review of Books* (March 14, 2002).

When the United Nations: But note President Bush's proposal, in his 2003 State of the Union message, to triple spending for AIDS relief in Africa and the Caribbean.

In addition, because: That the illnesses that make up 90 percent of the global burden of disease receive only 10 percent of research money is from a *New York Times* editorial, "The Plagues of Poverty," March 19, 2002.

287 *"choice rhetoric":* Annas, pages x–xv. Annas (page xiv) quotes Jedediah Perdy on the notion that individual choice is always good: "Boundless individualism in which law, community, and every activity are radically voluntary, is an adolescent doctrine, a fantasy shopping trip without end" ("The God of the Digerati," *American Prospect*, March–April 1998, pages 86–90).

"Choice and coercion": "Introduction," *Some Choice*, page xv. Annas elaborates:

It has become commonplace for communitarians to argue that liberty or choice has become the only American value and has overwhelmed our sense of community and of obligations to our fellow citizens. There is something to this, but I think (and argue in this book) that the choices that are honored by our contemporary society very often turn out to be "some choice" in both senses of the words: They do provide another option and with it the illusion of control, but the choice is usually not a particularly good one, and is virtually irresistible because of more powerful factors such as poverty, illness (both mental and physical), and social status.

Three examples presented by two thoughtful commentators who have urged us to curb our "culture of autonomy" are illustrative: 1) a mentally ill street person who is in need of medical care, but is left on the street to die because he tells emergency medical technicians that he refuses treatment; 2) the right of a pregnant woman to refuse to be screened for HIV infection, even though the risks to her future child of contracting AIDS could be significantly reduced if she is infected and takes zibovudine during the pregnancy and childbirth; and 3) the demise of a program to pay teenagers a dollar a day to avoid pregnancy on the basis that this is coercive and thus a denial of their autonomy. (xiv)

289 *"The demand for autonomy":* Callahan, "Rationing Medical Progress — The Way to Affordable Health Care," *NEJM* 322:25 (June 21, 1990), pages 1810–1813. For a full elaboration of these ideas, see his book, *What Kind of Life: The Limits of Medical Progress.*

291 *Do we have any:* The figure on future deaths from tobacco is from Bob Herbert's column, "Death in the Ashes," *New York Times,* July 26, 2001. According to the World Health Organization, by 2030, tobacco-related deaths will reach 10 million annually ("W.H.O. Treaty Would Ban Cigarette Ads Worldwide," by Elizabeth Olson, *New York Times,* July 22, 2002).

292 *"Surely":* Nuland, "Whoops!" page 11.

293 *"by excessive":* Mechanic, "Managed Care as a Target of Distrust," *JAMA* 277:22 (June 11, 1997), pages 1810–1811. Mechanic has written widely and wisely on the subject. See, for example, "Managed Care, Rationing, and Trust in Medical Care," *Journal of Urban Health: Bulletin of the New York Academy of Medicine* 75:1 (March 1998), pages 118–122; and "Responses of HMO Medical Directors to Trust Building in Managed Care," *Milbank Quarterly* 77:3 (1999), pages 283–303. (See also "The Managed Care Backlash: Perceptions and Rhetoric in Health Care Policy and the Potential for Health Care Reform," *Milbank Quarterly* 79:1 [2001], pages 35–54.)

The literature on managed care is enormous. Here, for starters, is a summary description of "The Growth of Managed Care," from an article by H. T. O. Davies and Thomas G. Randall, "Managing Patient Trust in Managed Care," *Milbank Quarterly* 78:4 (2000), pages 609–624:

> Since the late 1980s, a new health care environment has emerged in many parts of the United States. Previously, indemnity insurance and fee-for-service reimbursement prevailed. Independent physicians, hospitals, and other caregivers provided medical services and billed the charges to the patient's insurance company, or government paid with little regard to the appropriateness of services delivered. Physicians had few, if any, constraints on their authority to order tests, perform procedures, make referrals, and prescribe medications. In general, patients perceived that such unbridled authority for physicians to expend resources on their behalf aligned the physicians' interests (autonomy and personal financial gain) with their own (access to all interventions regardless of cost).
>
> In the new health care environment, private employers and the federal and state governments have changed from passive payers to aggressive purchasers of health care. As such, they demand more accountability from health plans with respect to where their insured employees are cared for, what types of services are provided, and how much they will pay. In turn, health insurance companies have devised a variety of managed care plans (e.g., group and network model health maintenance organizations) that shift some of the risk of controlling health care costs to the care providers. When at financial risk for the cost of the services they provide, physicians and hospitals have a strong incentive to manage carefully the entire continuum of care for their enrolled patient population. Hence the origins of the term managed care. (pages 610–611)

294 *"disturbing issues"*: "Neonatalogists earn more than general pediatricians," the editorial on neonatal technology informs us. "One of the few investor-owned physician groups to remain financially successful in recent years is Pediatrix. Pediatrix employs nearly 600 neonatologists and fetal-maternal medicine specialists in 185 neonatal intensive care units across the United States and earned more than $30 million in net profits for investors in 2001." These and the other quotes about neonatal technology are from the editorial "Specialists, Technology, and Newborns — Too Much of a Good Thing," by Kevin Grumbach, *NEJM* 346:20 (May 16, 2002), pages 1574–1575. The study Grumbach is commenting on is "The Relation Between the Availability of Neonatal Intensive Care and Neonatal Mortality," by D. C. Goodman et al., *NEJM* 346 (2002), pages 1538–1544.

295 *"who will be labeled"*: Annas, page 108. With regard to the imbalance of supply and demand in medical care — an imbalance in which supply often drives demand — see a *New York Times* front-page article, "More

May Not Mean Better in Health Care, Studies Find," by Gina Kolata, July 21, 2002.

296 *"Is radical mastectomy"*: Nuland, "Whoops!" page 11.

301 *"where observation is concerned"*: Until I returned to the original — in Sherwin Nuland's *Doctors: The Biography of Medicine* — I had always thought that what Pasteur said was that "chance favored the prepared mind." What he actually said was that "chance favors *only* the prepared mind." Here, in French, are his words (quoted in *Doctors* on page 363), spoken on December 7, 1854, at the inaugural assembly of the Lille Faculty of Science, in France: "Dans les champs de l'observation, le hasard ne favorise que les esprits preparés."

Bibliography

Annas, George J. *Some Choice: Law, Medicine, and the Market.* New York: Oxford University Press, 1998.

———. *Standard of Care.* New York: Oxford University Press, 1993.

Bayer, Ronald, and Gerald M. Oppenheimer. *AIDS Doctors: Voices from the Epidemic.* Oxford: Oxford University Press, 2000.

Bliss, Michael. *William Osler: A Life in Medicine.* New York: Oxford University Press, 1999.

Botkin, Jeffrey R., William M. McMahon, and Leslie Francis, eds. *Genetics and Criminality: The Potential Misuse of Scientific Information in Court.* Washington, D.C.: American Psychological Association, 1999.

Bynum, William F., Roy Porter, and Michael Shepherd, eds. *The Anatomy of Madness: Essays in the History of Psychiatry.* 2 vols. London: Tavistock.

Callahan, Daniel. *What Kind of Life: The Limits of Medical Progress.* New York: Simon & Schuster, 1990.

Cassedy, James H. *Medicine in America: A Short History.* Baltimore: Johns Hopkins University Press, 1991.

Chronic Care in America: A 21st Century Challenge. August 1996. Prepared by the Institute for Health & Aging, University of California, San Francisco, for the Robert Wood Johnson Foundation, Princeton, New Jersey.

Cornwell, John, ed. *Nature's Imagination: The Frontiers of Scientific Vision.* Oxford: Oxford University Press, 1995.

Cousins, Norman. *The Healing Heart: Antidotes to Panic and Helplessness.* New York: W. W. Norton, 1983.

———. *Anatomy of an Illness as Perceived by the Patient: Reflections on Healing and Regeneration.* Toronto: Bantam Books, 1981.

Dubos, René. *A God Within.* New York: Scribner's, 1972.

———, *Mirage of Health: Utopias, Progress, and Biological Change.* New Brunswick, N.J.: Rutgers University Press, 1987.

Entralgo, Pedro Laín. *Doctor and Patient.* Trans. Frances Partridge. London: World University Library/Weidenfeld and Nicholson, 1969.

Ewald, Paul W. *Plague Time: How Stealth Infections Cause Cancers, Heart Disease, and Other Deadly Ailments.* New York: Free Press, 2000.

Fox, Daniel M. *Power and Illness: The Failure and Future of American Health Policy.* Berkeley: University of California Press, 1993.

Fox, Renée C., and Judith P. Swazey. *Spare Parts: Organ Replacement in American Society.* New York: Oxford University Press, 1992.

Frame, Donald M., trans. *The Complete Essays of Montaigne.* New York: Anchor Books, 1960.

Garrett, Laurie. *Betrayal of Trust: The Collapse of Global Public Trust.* New York: Hyperion, 2000.

———. *The Coming Plague.* New York: Penguin, 1995.

Goldstein, Martin, and Inge F. Goldstein. *How We Know: An Exploration of the Scientific Process.* New York: Plenum Press, 1978.

Graff, Gerald, and James Phelan, eds. *Adventures of Huckleberry Finn: A Case Study in Critical Controversy.* Bedford, Mass.: St. Martin's Press, 1995.

Grob, Gerald N. *The Deadly Truth: A History of Disease in America.* Cambridge, Mass.: Harvard University Press, 2002.

Harrington, Anne, ed. *The Placebo Effect: An Interdisciplinary Exploration.* Cambridge, Mass.: Harvard University Press, 1997.

Havens, Leston. *A Safe Place: Laying the Groundwork of Psychotherapy.* Cambridge, Mass.: Harvard University Press, 1989.

Helfant, Richard H. *The Women's Guide to Fighting Heart Disease.* New York: Perigee, 1993.

Hill, Kim, and Magdalena Hurtado. *Ache Life History.* New York: Aldine de Gryter, 1996.

Howell, Nancy. *Demography of the Dobe !Kung.* New York: Academic Press, 1979.

Hume, David. *A Treatise of Human Nature* (1739). Ed. L. A. Selby-Bigge. Oxford: Clarendon Press, 1964.

Hutt, Michael S. R., and Denis P. Burkitt. *The Geography of Non-Infectious Disease.* Oxford: Oxford University Press, 1986.

Jackson, Stanley W. *Care of the Psyche: A History of Psychological Healing.* New Haven: Yale University Press.

Jacob, François. *Of Flies, Mice, and Men.* Trans. Giselle Weiss. Cambridge, Mass.: Harvard University Press, 1998.

Kirsch, Irving, ed. *How Expectancies Shape Experience.* Washington, D.C.: American Psychological Association, 1999.

Klaidman, Stephen. *Saving the Heart: The Battle to Conquer Coronary Disease.* New York: Oxford University Press, 2000.

Lantos, John. *Do We Still Need Doctors?* New York: Routledge, 1997.

LeFanu, James. *The Rise and Fall of Modern Medicine.* New York: Carroll & Graf, 1999.

Lerner, Barron H. *The Breast Cancer Wars: Hope, Fear, and the Pursuit of a Cure in Twentieth-Century America.* Oxford: Oxford University Press, 2001.

Lewontin, Richard. *It Ain't Necessarily So: The Dream of the Human Genome and Other Illusions.* New York: New York Review of Books, 2000.

Lown, Bernard. *The Lost Art of Healing.* Boston: Houghton Mifflin, 1996.

Ludmerer, Kenneth M. *Time to Heal: American Medical Education from the Turn of the Century to the Era of Managed Care.* Oxford: Oxford University Press, 1999.

McKusick, Victor A. *Mendelian Inheritance in Man: A Catalog of Human Genes and Genetic Disorders.* 12th ed., 3 vols. Baltimore: Johns Hopkins University Press, 1994.

McNeill, William H. *Plagues and Peoples.* Garden City, N.Y.: Anchor Books, 1976.

Medawar, P. B., and J. S. Medawar. *The Life Science: Current Ideas of Biology.* New York: Harper & Row, 1977.

National Center for Health Statistics. *Health, United States, 2000, with Adolescent Health Chartbook.* Hyattsville, Md., 2000.

Nesse, Randolph M., and George C. Williams. *Why We Get Sick: The New Science of Darwinian Medicine.* New York: Vintage Books, 1996.

Nuland, Sherwin. *Doctors: The Biography of Medicine.* New York: Knopf, 1988.

———. *How We Die: Reflections on Life's Final Chapter.* New York: Knopf, 1994.

———. *How We Live* [originally published as *The Wisdom of the Body*]. New York: Vintage Books, 1997.

Oglesby, Paul. *The Caring Physician: The Life of Dr. Francis W. Peabody.* Cambridge, Mass.: Harvard University Press, 1991.

Panter-Brick, Catherine, Robert H. Layton, and Peter Rowley-Conway, eds. *Hunter-gatherers: An Interdisciplinary Perspective.* Cambridge: Cambridge University Press, 2001.

Porter, Roy. *The Greatest Benefit to Mankind: A Medical History of Humanity.* New York: HarperCollins, 1998.

Potok, Andrew. *A Matter of Dignity: Changing the World of the Disabled.* New York: Bantam, 2002.

Preston, Richard. *The Hot Zone.* New York: Random House, 1994.

Rosenberg, Charles E., and Janet Golden, eds. *Framing Disease: Studies in Cultural History.* New Brunswick, N.J.: Rutgers University Press, 1997.

Russell, Louise. *Educated Guesses: Making Policy About Medical Screening Tests.* Berkeley: University of California Press, 1994.

Schwartz, William B. *Life Without Disease: The Pursuit of Medical Utopia.* Berkeley: University of California Press, 1998.

Shaw, Margery W., ed. *After Barney Clark: Reflections on the Utah Artificial Heart Program.* Austin: University of Texas Press, 1984.

Solomon, Andrew. *The Noonday Demon: An Atlas of Depression.* New York: Scribner's, 2001.

Sontag, Susan. *Illness as Metaphor.* New York: Doubleday, 1990.

Stevenson, Adlai. *What I Think.* New York: Harper and Brothers, 1956.

Thomas, Lewis. *The Lives of a Cell: Notes of a Biology Watcher.* New York: Bantam, 1975.

Verghese, Abraham. *My Own Country: A Doctor's Story.* New York: Vintage Books, 1995.

Weatherall, David. *Science and the Quiet Art: The Role of Medical Research in Health Care.* New York: Norton, 1996.

Weinberg, Robert. *One Renegade Cell: How Cancer Begins.* New York: Basic Books, 1998.

White, Leonard, Bernard Tursky, and Gary E. Schwartz, eds. *Placebo: Theory, Research, and Mechanisms.* New York: Guilford Press, 1985.

Index

technology (*cont.*)
  as a modern miracle, 85, 88
  need for proper training, 37–38, 133
  needless and costly overuse, 37, 101,
    146, 162–63, 294
  short timeframe for obsolescence,
    37–38
  trends in, 25–26, 94–95
  vs. listening to the patient, 38, 167–
    68, 202–3, 243–44, 248, 291
  vs. "science," 85, 88, 95
Thomas, Lewis, 256
Thorsen, Dr. Gerd-Ragna Bloch, 177,
  178
Thursday Night Cardiac Clinic, 243
thyroid scan, 77
thyroxine, 86
*Time Special Issue: The Frontiers of
  Medicine,* 27
Time to Heal (Ludmerer), 168–69
tobacco. *See* smoking
Transforming Madness (Neugeboren),
  53, 66, 82, 300
trauma, 153. *See also* post-traumatic
  stress disorder
traumatic injury to the brain, 105,
  220–23
trust
  adherence to medications and, 41,
    153–54, 180
  lack of continuity and time to de-
    velop. *See* managed care
  mind-body relationship and, 154,
    265
  qualities that engender, 146–47, 153.
    See also listening to the patient
  role in psychotherapy, 202
  role in recovery, 153–54
tuberculosis
  economic aspects of vaccinations,
    285–86
  integration with HIV prevention
    and treatment, 283

  as major cause of death, 1800s–
    early 1900s, 91
  mortality rate decline, late 1900s, 109
  reemergence, 102
  streptomycin treatment, 268, 270
  treatment curriculum developed by
    Friedland, 192
  United Nations program, 286
typhoid, 109

United Nations, 286
United States
  average health spending annually,
    286
  dismal response to international
    epidemics, 286
  health-care system. *See* managed
    care
  Medicare, 163
  mortality rates. *See* mortality
universal health care, 166, 175, 289
University of Massachusetts
  basketball games, 13–14, 17, 80, 120
  teaching position (as professor and
    writer in residence), 13, 57, 82

vaccinations
  economic aspects, 285–86
  effects on mortality rate, 109–10
  immune system and, 256
  for polio, 88–89
vasodilators, 70
Vasotec, 70
ventricular assist devices, 94–95
Viagra, 97, 99, 137, 150
viral infection. *See also* HIV
  antiretroviral treatment, 40–41, 255,
    282–83
  diagnosis of possible, 8, 70, 71, 247
  ebola, 255
  heart disease symptoms, 248
  natural selection and, 255
vitamin E, 138, 140, 143, 145